4/23/10

PRISONERS IN WAR

The Changing Character of War Programme is an inter-disciplinary research group located at the University of Oxford, and funded by the Leverhulme Trust.

Prisoners in War

Edited by
SIBYLLE SCHEIPERS

OXFORD
UNIVERSITY PRESS

OXFORD
UNIVERSITY PRESS

Great Clarendon Street, Oxford OX2 6DP

Oxford University Press is a department of the University of Oxford.
It furthers the University's objective of excellence in research, scholarship,
and education by publishing worldwide in

Oxford New York

Auckland Cape Town Dar es Salaam Hong Kong Karachi
Kuala Lumpur Madrid Melbourne Mexico City Nairobi
New Delhi Shanghai Taipei Toronto

With offices in

Argentina Austria Brazil Chile Czech Republic France Greece
Guatemala Hungary Italy Japan Poland Portugal Singapore
South Korea Switzerland Thailand Turkey Ukraine Vietnam

Oxford is a registered trade mark of Oxford University Press
in the UK and in certain other countries

Published in the United States
by Oxford University Press Inc., New York

British Library Cataloguing in Publication Data

Data available

Library of Congress Cataloging in Publication Data

Library of Congress Control Number: 2009938806

Typeset by SPI Publisher Services, Pondicherry, India
Printed in Great Britain
on acid-free paper by
the MPG Books Group,
Bodmin and King's Lynn

ISBN 978–0–19–957757–6

1 3 5 7 9 10 8 6 4 2

Contents

PART III DETAINEES IN IRREGULAR CONFLICTS

PART IV CONTEMPORARY PROBLEMS AND CHALLENGES

Acknowledgements

This book is the result of a conference on 'Prisoners in War' conducted by the Leverhulme Programme on the Changing Character of War in December 2007 at Oxford University. It is also the outcome of the work of the Changing Character of War Programme and its team in a more general sense. It was the research framework provided by the Programme that ultimately brought together practitioners and scholars from a variety of disciplinary backgrounds to discuss the historical, political, moral, and legal aspects and implications of prisoners and detainees in war. Particular thanks are due to the Changing Character of War Programme's Director Hew Strachan and the Progamme's Director of Studies (2004–7) Audrey Kurth Cronin for their invaluable input at all stages of the project.

Thanks are also due to Andrea Baumann and Martin Bayly for their diligent and careful proofreading and copy-editing. Very special thanks to Andrea Baumann, whose assistance was indispensable during the later stages of preparing the manuscript and the index.

Both the conference and the subsequent work on this book would not have been possible without the generous funding by the Leverhulme Trust and Nuffield College, Oxford to which we are very grateful for their support.

List of Abbreviations

ALN	National Libération Army
ARBs	Administrative Review Boards
CDR	Centre for re-education
CMI	Centres Militaires d'Internés
CPT	Committee for the Prevention of Torture
CRC	Convention on the Rights of the Child
CRRB	Combined Review and Release Board
CTT	Centres de tri et de transit
DPW	Directorate of Prisoners of War
FARRA	Foreign Affairs Reform and Restructuring Act of 1998
FFI	French Forces of the Interior
FLN	Front de Libération Nationale
FSS	Federal Security Service
GC	Geneva Convention
GC III	Third Geneva Convention
GOC	General Officer Commanding
GPRA	Provisional Government for the Algerian Republic
ICCPR	International Covenant on Civil and Political Rights
ICRC	International Committee of the Red Cross
IDP	internally displaced persons
IHL	International Humanitarian Law
ILA	International Law Association
IPOWC	Imperial Prisoner of War Committee
IRA	Irish Republican Army
ISAF	International Security Assistance Force
JIC	Joint Intelligence Committee
JSIW	Joint Services Interrogation Wing
LRCS	League of Red Cross Societies
MCA	Military Commissions Act
NCO	non-commissioned officers
NGO	non-governmental organization
OKW	*Oberkommado der Wehrmacht*
OSCE	Organization for Security and Co-operation in Europe
PAMs	Pris les armes à la main

PCIJ	Permanent Court of International Justice
PMC	private military companies
POW	prisoner of war
PWD	Prisoners of War Department
RSFSR	Russian Soviet Federated Socialist Republic
RUC	Royal Ulster Constabulary
SEP	surrendered enemy personnel
SO	Special Organization
TVPA	Torture Victim Protection Act
UAV	unmanned aerial vehicle
VCGS	Vice-Chief of the General Staff

List of Contributors

John B. Bellinger III was Legal Adviser to the Secretary of State, US Department of State, 2005–9.

Dr Huw Bennett is Lecturer in Defence Studies at the Joint Services Command and Staff College, Shrivenham/King's College War Studies Department.

Dr Raphaëlle Branche is Senior Lecturer of Modern and Contemporary History, University of Paris-1-Panthéon-Sorbonne.

Dr Alia Brahimi is Global Security Fellow at the Center for Global Governance, London School of Economics.

Professor David D. Cole is Professor of Law, Georgetown University Law Center.

Dr Matthew Happold is Professor in International Public Law, University of Luxembourg.

Professor Isabel V. Hull is John Stambaugh Professor of History, Department of History, Cornell University.

Professor Alan R. Kramer is Professor of European History at the Department of History, Trinity College Dublin.

Chia Lehnardt is Doctoral student at Humboldt University Berlin.

Professor Frédéric Mégret is Assistant Professor of Law, Law Faculty, McGill University, Canada Research Chair on the Law of Human Rights and Legal Pluralism, and Director of the McGill Clinic for the Sierra Leone Special Court.

Professor Bob Moore is Professor of Twentieth Century European History, Department of History, University of Sheffield.

Dr Stephen C. Neff is Reader in Public International Law, School of Law, University of Edinburgh.

Dr Rüdiger Overmans is Researcher (ret.) at the Military History Research Institute, Potsdam.

Dr Bettina Renz is Lecturer in International Security, School of Politics and International Relations, Nottingham University.

Professor Sir Adam Roberts is Senior Research Fellow of the Centre for International Studies, Department of Politics and International Relations, Oxford University, and Emeritus Fellow of Balliol College.

Dr Sibylle Scheipers is Director of Studies of the Changing Character of War Programme, Oxford University.

Dr Philip Towle is Reader in International Relations, Centre of International Studies, Cambridge University.

Professor Peter H. Wilson is Grant Professor of History, Department of History, University of Hull.

Professor Neville Wylie is Associate Professor in Politics, School of Politics and International Relations, Nottingham University.

1

Introduction: Prisoners in War

Sibylle Scheipers

At first glance, prisoners and detainees may appear as a mere by-product of war. Arguably captivity was for a long time a state of transition for a surrendering soldier (or, for that matter, a civilian unfortunate enough to be in the vicinity of the battlefield or inside a besieged town), followed by execution, enslavement, or release for ransom, on parole, or in exchange for prisoners taken by the opponent. However, the number of prisoners taken on the battlefield and the length of captivity increased substantially with the emergence of mass armies and the nationalization of war following the French Revolution. This development culminated in the Second World War, in which the average soldier spent more time in captivity than on the battlefield.[1] In addition to this quantitative increase, the twentieth century also witnessed a qualitative shift towards greater political relevance and even politicization of prisoners and detainees. According to Geoffrey Best, 'POWs [prisoners of war] have been at the centre of a series of IHL [international humanitarian law] rows since 1950.... Parties to armed conflicts have repeatedly exploited the weaknesses of the POW regime and the vulnerability of its objects in order to serve their own political interests.'[2] The current debates surrounding the issue of detention in the so-called war on terror indicate that this trend will most likely continue into the twenty-first century.

Apart from its increased relevance in quantitative as well as qualitative terms, the issue of prisoners and detainees is in many ways a prism through which more general research problems related to war become visible. First, the treatment of prisoners and detainees seems to be a litmus test for compliance with cultural, legal, and moral norms aimed at mitigating the effects of war. According to a statistical survey on compliance with the law of armed conflict, the treatment of POWs has one of the lowest compliance rates compared to other issue areas.[3] This is partly attributable to the large scope for individual non-compliance in the treatment of prisoners and detainees as opposed to issues such as the use of biological or chemical weapons, where the state or the military leadership has a greater degree of direct control.[4] Individual non-compliance with legal rules pertaining to POWs and detainees can serve as an indicator for training, discipline, and the success of enforcement measures within the armed forces or armed groups more generally. Non-compliance emanating from the state or leadership level, in contrast, often reflects the specific characteristics of the military culture of a state or armed group. If violations of the law occur as a response to previous non-compliance on the part of the opponent, the treatment of prisoners and detainees can become the focus of efforts to adjust reciprocity between the adversaries. The fact that POWs were frequently the main object of reprisals is a case in point.

Secondly, the issue of prisoners in war tells us something about the success and progress of the humanitarian project as such. It is one of the issue areas that saw the greatest efforts at legal codification and regulation over the last one-and-a-half centuries. After both world wars the legal provisions in this field were revised. Yet the treatment of detainees is far from being a sweeping success story. True, with the 1949 Geneva Conventions (hereafter GCs) it seemed as if POWs had become 'the most favoured war victim',[5] and the Third Geneva Convention (hereafter GC III) is the most comprehensive and detailed of all four conventions. But it only offers detailed protections for those individuals that clearly fall within the boundaries of its applicability; that is, first and foremost members of regular armed forces. A large array of other individuals involved in armed conflict either sit uneasily 'between the Conventions', most notably between the prisoner convention and the civilian convention (GCs III and IV), or can only claim minimum protections under Common Article 3 of the GCs and customary international law. Arguably, the 1977 Additional Protocol I to the GCs attempted to widen the group of individuals qualifying for the protections of POW status, but it has not been as widely ratified as the GCs, and the provisions on national liberation movements remain one of its most contested parts.[6] According to Stefan Oeter, 'the real problem are those situations and groups of individuals that were deliberately excluded from the protections provided by the traditional law of armed conflict pertaining to POWs'.[7] The trajectory of the legal protections pertaining to prisoners in war is thus indicative of a more general problem: the codification of the law of armed conflict often comes at the expense of exclusionary measures towards certain groups and practices. It offers protections, but at the same time it tends to exclude those who do not fit a certain template of warfare.

Thirdly, while it is commonly assumed that the treatment of prisoners depends on the nature of the war in question, this equation sometimes also works the other way round. In wars of decolonization and insurgencies the question of whether captured insurgents or members of the national liberation movement qualify for POW status is frequently the centrepiece of the broader debate over the political legitimacy of the parties to the conflict. In the Algerian war, for instance, the Front de Libération Nationale (FLN) demanded that the French treat captured FLN fighters as POWs, or at least apply Common Article 3 of the GCs. The FLN itself claimed to grant captured French soldiers POW status. The FLN's insistence on POW status for its captured members reflects only to a small degree its concerns about their well-being (although they had every reason to be worried given the widespread use of torture by the French armed forces). It is mainly an expression of the FLN's claim to belligerent status, and, by extension, to the political legitimacy of its cause and its recognition as an international actor.[8] The French government, in contrast, aiming at denying the Algerian liberation movement, precisely this recognition, 'resolutely refused to consider the conflict as anything other than an internal one, in which domestic law and order provisions were applicable'.[9] The issue of prisoners and detainees thus frequently forms the focal point of much broader conflicts at the interface of politics, law, and strategy.

HISTORICAL OVERVIEW

For a long time in the history of war, captivity was merely a transitory period between the moment of surrender or capture and the prisoner's final fate: execution, enslavement, or release. Wars in archaic and early classical Greece were constrained by a set of cultural rules that also regulated the treatment of prisoners: prisoners had to be offered for ransom to the opponent after the battle.[10] However, it is difficult to say to what extent this rule was observed. Enslavement was a common alternative fate of prisoners.[11] Massacres of prisoners did happen, but there is some debate on the circumstances in which they took place. Josiah Ober argues that massacres were typical for wars between Greeks and barbarians such as the Persian Wars (490–478 BC) and for the period of the breakdown of the early classical system of cultural constraints on warfare during the Peloponnesian War (431–404 BC).[12] In contrast, Raoul Lonis holds that the pattern of atrocities was less clear-cut and often depended on the specific political purposes of the victorious party.[13] Ancient Roman warfare offered a similar picture, although the significance of enslavement was possibly greater. From the Roman perspective, prisoners were sometimes the main purpose of war rather than a mere by-product.[14] Often the inhabitants of whole towns and settlements were captured and enslaved. Mass enslavement was the result of a convergence of strategic and economic objectives. Strategically, it facilitated enforcing claims to conquered territory. Economically, enslavement was a source of additional income for the armed forces, in particular for the ordinary soldier.[15] Mass enslavement made no distinction between combatants and civilians.

War in medieval Europe was characterized by an evolving quasi-legal code of conduct restraining violence in warfare. This development was tied to the emergence of a warrior elite. Ransoming and executing prisoners continued to be common practices, whereas religious norms prohibiting the enslavement of Christian adversaries had emerged. Ordinary soldiers had thus largely lost their economic value, since ransom could only be expected for members of the nobility.[16] The inequality in the economic value of prisoners and the confinement of the chivalric code of conduct to the nobility were mutually reinforcing. For common men fighting in war, chances of surviving capture were low: 'Armed peasants and townsmen . . . could be massacred at will.'[17] Inhabitants of a besieged town refusing to surrender would often meet the same fate if the besieger succeeded in taking it.[18] Apart from war fought within the constraints of the chivalric code of conduct (*bellum hostile*) and siege warfare,[19] however, there was a third category of war in the Middle Ages called *bellum Romanum* or *guerre mortelle*, which covered first and foremost (though not exclusively) armed conflicts between Christians and non-Christians, such as the Crusades. While *bellum Romanum* is often depicted as the lawless and unrestrained antithesis of the rule-bound *bellum hostile* supposedly resembling a fair and honourable contest among equals, such dichotomies should be treated with caution. As Frédéric Mégret outlines in Chapter 2, although indiscriminate massacres, torture, and enslavement of prisoners were common practices, there were also examples of restraint and even generosity towards captured opponents. Moreover, the treatment of non-Christian prisoners in the Crusades bore many similarities to the treatment of peasants and townsmen in *bellum hostile*, except for enslavement, which did not occur in medieval wars among Christians.

The end of the Middle Ages saw the decline of the warrior elite and, by extension, a decrease in the economic value of prisoners belonging to this elite. Whilst in medieval wars ransoming was confined to the nobility, ordinary soldiers largely belonging to mercenary armies were now integrated into the ransoming system.[20] The role and the fate of prisoners in war in early modern Europe slowly changed. According to Geoffrey Parker, the sixteenth and seventeenth centuries mark the beginning of a development that led to greater restraint in warfare and to increased efforts to enforce the laws of war.[21] The gradual emergence of a states system in Europe, in which the armed forces became a regulated part of the state apparatus, and the deconfessionalization of war created the conditions for a transition towards greater restraint, although its trajectory was non-linear and characterized by numerous setbacks. As Peter Wilson outlines in Chapter 3, this transition saw a variety of practices including execution, exchange, imprisonment, enslavement, release, and pressment into the captor's forces. The practice of pressing soldiers was often attractive to both captors and captives, since it provided the former with additional manpower and gave the latter access to food and shelter. However, as Wilson argues, whilst early modern European armies consisted largely of mercenaries, they were not necessarily indifferent as to what side they fought on. Therefore, pressment often substantially increased the chances of desertion.

The prevalence of siege warfare in the sixteenth and seventeenth centuries also meant that massacres were a widespread fate of prisoners.[22] Yet from the beginning of the seventeenth century exchanging prisoners with the opponent slowly became a common practice that considerably enhanced the captives' chances of survival.[23]

The system of prisoner exchange through bilaterally negotiated cartels continued throughout the seventeenth and eighteenth centuries. Prisoner exchange was a rational solution, since soldiers held captive were of no use to either side. Prisoners were either exchanged man-for-man or for ransom. Although this worked in favour of the rank-and-file soldiers, their value was still far lower than that of officers. Considerable efforts were made to specify accurate 'exchange rates' for different military ranks.[24] An alternative to exchange was release on parole. Officers were allowed to return to their home country or to reside on their own in certain designated 'parole towns' under the condition that they gave their word of honour to refrain from returning to the ongoing conflict.[25] Ordinary soldiers were more likely to be induced to switch sides and join the adversary's armed forces.[26] The unequal treatment of officers and rank-and-file prisoners in all three practices—exchange, parole, and pressment into the opponent's armed forces—reflected and reproduced the inequality in their status that had already emerged in medieval warfare, albeit with less deadly consequences for the lower ranks.

The Revolutionary and Napoleonic Wars of 1792–1815 marked once again the beginning of a period of transition in the treatment of prisoners characterized by the typically muddled picture of the partial persistence of old practices, the emergence of new ones, and the occasional breakdown of all constraints. Exchange cartels continued to exist, although the prisoner cartel between Britain and France broke down repeatedly. This was not due to nationalistic fervour among the armed forces commonly associated with these wars. According to Gunther Rothenberg, despite some revolutionary rhetoric, the French army had maintained a high degree of professionalism and aimed at upholding established norms on the treatment of detainees. The breakdown of the cartel was based on a political decision on the part of the French and the British leadership rather than on the military's desire to do away with constraints.[27] The military, on the contrary, often attempted to negotiate better treatment for their prisoners bilaterally.[28] Atrocities towards prisoners occurred as well, depending on the circumstances of their capture, most notably in siege warfare, in campaigns against guerrilla forces and resistance movements, during the invasion of Russia, and in situations in which prisoners became a burden for their captors.[29]

The need for new regulations on the treatment of prisoners became once again evident during American Civil War of 1861–5. Exchange cartels broke down again, this time over the question of whether black troops qualified as exchangeable POWs.[30] As a result, prisoners had to be held in large numbers. As Stephen Neff argues in Chapter 4, this led to increased efforts to codify legal standards for their treatment. The Lieber Code of 1863 contained provisions to this effect. While the Lieber Code and the 1874 Brussels *projet* were the work of legal experts (although the former was promulgated by the US government), the Hague Conferences in 1899 and 1907 marked the beginning of a process of the codification of legal constraints on the treatment of prisoners in war as a state-led endeavour. However, these early efforts partly adopted a conservative perspective, inasmuch as they drew upon traditional customs and practices in the treatment of prisoners, despite the fact that some of them were already about to be abandoned. For instance, the Lieber Code regulated the exchange of prisoners in cartels, and Articles 10–12 of the Hague Convention IV (Annex) contained rules on the release of prisoners on parole.[31] In other parts, however, the Hague Conventions ventured into new terrain, for instance in setting out standards for prisoner labour (Article 6).

These regulations proved to be crucial during the First World War, although they also quickly turned out to be insufficient. The unprecedented level of socio-economic mobilization during the First World War soon led to the 'discovery' of prisoners as an exploitable workforce (see Chapter 5). The 1907 Hague Rules on the Laws and Customs of War on Land contained no provisions on the specific conditions of prisoner labour other than 'the task shall not be excessive and shall have no connection with the operations of the war'.[32] The second provision was frequently violated, as a large number of Allied prisoners held by Germany were forced to work in the operations zone. Prisoners inside Germany often suffered from harsh working conditions and poor provision of food and shelter. This started a downward spiral of Allied reprisals against prisoners from the Central Powers. Although extensive prisoner labour was a new aspect, there were continuities in the treatment of prisoners during the First World War. According to Kramer, regarding the conditions of captivity 'the most significant distinction was not that between nationalities, but between officers and ranks'—a clear continuity from previous centuries. A second continuity was that the protection of civilians from the consequences of war—which had been a concern for a long time, first of the Church in the Middle Ages[33] and later of the Enlightenment legal thinkers,[34] but had frequently not been achieved—was once again ignored with respect to captivity: large numbers of enemy civilians were deported or interned due to suspicion and security fears.

The exploitation of prisoner workforce continued to be a defining feature of captivity during the Second World War. The 1929 Geneva Prisoners Convention was an attempt at regulating the treatment of prisoners in more detail; specifically, it contained extended provisions on prisoner labour and aimed at strengthening supervision of the application of the legal rules. Yet many prisoners in the Second World War faced a worse fate than during the First World War. As Neville Wylie explains in Chapter 6, this was not due to the weakness of the Convention. Rather, it was due to the unwillingness of certain states to apply the Convention unambiguously. The Convention was generally followed on the Western front, where prisoners were, by and large, treated well (see Chapter 7). Here it was the mutual threat of retribution that largely ensured the lawful treatment of POWs. The treatment of prisoners on the Eastern front and in the Pacific theatre was rather different. Two factors account for this: (*a*) racial and ethnic stereotyping and (*b*) military culture. Racial and ethnic stereotyping played a certain role on the Western front as well, where, according to Moore, non-white troops from the French and British colonies were subject to maltreatment by the Germans; but it was more important on the Eastern front. Rüdiger Overmans shows in Chapter 8 how the stereotypical ascription of 'Asian cruelty' to Soviet soldiers tied in with certain features of military culture on both sides: from the German perspective, surrender was seen as an irrational act of self-abandonment into the hands of an exceptionally cruel opponent, whereas Stalin branded surrender as a traitorous act of cowardice. In the Pacific theatre, it was arguably certain features of Japanese military culture that led to widespread maltreatment of POWs. First, notwithstanding the fact that Japan had signed the 1929 GC, it regarded this GC as an example of 'the alien Western system of values which [it] hoped would disappear from Asia' (Philip Towle, Chapter 9, this volume). Secondly, imperial Japanese military culture was at odds with the idea of restraint in warfare in general and viewed surrender as an unheroic and thus inconceivable act in particular. Both in the Pacific theatre and on the Eastern front prisoner labour still served economic purposes, but there was only a fine line between the ruthless overexploitation of POWs on the one hand (such as the construction of the Burma railway and the work of German prisoners in Soviet coal mines) and the deliberate annihilation of prisoners in work camps on the other—a line that the German treatment of Soviet prisoners had crossed.

Despite the importance of the economic use and value of prisoner labour in both world wars, the political aspects of POWs in the first half of the twentieth century should not be underestimated. In the aftermath of both world wars, the legal conventions on prisoners were revised and updated. According to Geoffrey Best, this was not owing to the fact that POWs had suffered more atrocities than other protected groups. Rather, it reflected the extent to which POWs had become the focus of popular national sentiment and emotion—a smokescreen onto which both claims about one's own humanity and *ressentiments* towards the enemy could be projected.[35] Although it briefly looked as if prisoners were to become the best-protected category of the law of armed conflict after 1949, the detailed rules on their treatment never resulted in a vast improvement of their actual protection. Two trends were particularly important in this respect: first, in later conflicts, states such as Korea and Vietnam refused to apply the legal protections to US and British prisoners, arguing instead that they were war criminals who were to be tried before Korean and North Vietnamese domestic courts.[36] This argument essentially breaks down the separation between *ius ad bellum* and *ius in bello* that had allowed for a more humane treatment of prisoners in war in the first place: the idea that individual soldiers were not to be held accountable for their governments' decision to go to war.[37] It is an indicator for the continuing, or even increased, politicization of the issue of prisoners in war in the second half of the twentieth century. The second trend is the contested limits of applicability of the law of armed conflict pertaining to prisoners. This trend towards politicizing the law also has its roots in the late nineteenth and early twentieth centuries. As Isabel Hull shows in Chapter 10, the legal reasoning at that time was that the law of armed conflict did not apply in colonial warfare. The question of the applicability of the law became even more important in the wars of decolonization in the second half of the twentieth century, since, as mentioned above, granting POW status to prisoners in those wars was often perceived as acknowledging the political legitimacy of their cause.

USES OF PRISONERS IN WAR

Taking prisoners has a number of military advantages, the most obvious of which is the tactical benefit gained by depriving the opponent of manpower and increasing one's own advantage in terms of the ratio of troop numbers. This advantage can even be increased by inducing captives to join one's own armed forces. Furthermore, taking prisoners affects the adversary's morale as well as the morale of one's own troops. Not least, prisoners are a potential source of military intelligence. Yet none of the military reasons for *taking* prisoners suggests that *holding* prisoners captive is equally useful. On the contrary, prisoners tend to be a burden. They need to be guarded and fed, which can be particularly challenging in difficult tactical situations or when logistical support is weak. Killing prisoners in such situations was often claimed to be a solution warranted by military necessity.[38] Releasing prisoners, exchanging them, or enslaving them are alternative ways of avoiding the difficulties of holding them captive. In fact, the extensive organizational requirements and costs of holding large numbers of prisoners for a long time are probably the main reason why POW camps only emerged after the establishment of large state bureaucracies in the nineteenth century. Once prisoners were held in camps for the duration of the war, however, they became important potential targets for reprisals intended to ensure the adversary's compliance with legal norms in warfare in general and in their treatment of prisoners in particular. At the same time, this development also provided new opportunities for the use of prisoners in political and economic contexts.

The use of prisoners for political purposes has occurred at all times in the history of war. Parading prisoners through capitals as a proof of military success with the aim of boosting civilian morale and as a symbol of victory has been an almost universal practice.[39] During the twentieth century, prisoners became an increasingly important aspect of war propaganda. Emphasizing one's own humane treatment of prisoners and condemning the opponent's treatment of prisoners was often intended to enhance the international reputation of a state. For instance, according to Uta Hinz, German propaganda about POW camps during the First World War painted a picture of moral and cultural superiority allegedly reflected in the humane treatment of prisoners in German camps while at the same time denouncing the Allied Powers' practices as barbarian.[40] This trend continued in the second half of the twentieth century. During the Korean War (1950–3) North Korea coerced captured US and British troops to confess war crimes publicly and make allegations of 'germ warfare' against the United States. Similar 'confessions' occurred in the Vietnam War.[41] North Vietnam also attempted to use the repatriation of US prisoners during the war as a propaganda tool.[42] Conversely, the Nixon administration utilized US prisoners held by North Vietnam to rally domestic support for its war effort.[43] Moreover, prisoners have been used as a political asset in peace negotiations and in the implementation of peace agreements. India refused to release several thousand Pakistani POWs after the armistice in 1971 and made their repatriation dependent on the fulfilment of its demands in the peace negotiations. Prisoners were also used as a bargaining chip by all conflict parties after the Yom Kippur War of 1973.[44] Finally, the repatriation of US POWs after the 1973 Vietnam peace agreement was 'programmed to coincide with the departure of American forces in South Vietnam'.[45]

Prisoners in war have always been used for economic purposes but the patterns of this use have shifted since the emergence of POW camps. Until the nineteenth century, economic uses of prisoners were largely confined to ransoming or enslavement, with enslavement becoming increasingly unacceptable in wars among solely Christians or Muslims in the Middle Ages. Ransoming has continued to occur at all times, though it is today far less widespread. In contemporary wars, releasing prisoners for ransom is mostly practised by irregular armed groups such as the insurgents in Chechnya (see Chapter 13). Ransoming is attractive for these groups, firstly because it is profitable, and secondly because they rarely possess the infrastructure and resources for detaining prisoners for a long time. In conventional wars during the twentieth century, however, POW camps became the prevailing feature of captivity. With their emergence, and in particular with the increased economic requirements created by the comprehensive socio-economic mobilization during both world wars, prisoner labour developed into the most important use of prisoners. Economic purposes, however, were sometimes at odds with other objectives. According to Overmans, extermination was an objective that often conflicted with economic exploitation in the German treatment of Soviet POWs during the Second World War.[46] Similar arguments hold with respect to the treatment of Herero prisoners in Southwest Africa (see Chapter 10). The Germans saw prisoner labour in the colonies mainly as a disciplinary and punitive measure and were thus not concerned about its exterminatory consequences. The difference between this attitude and a purely economic approach to prisoner labour becomes evident in the substantially lower death rates of prisoners working in the private sector in the German colony.

TIMELINE OF CAPTIVITY

As outlined above, surviving captivity was by no means certain for prisoners in war. Before the nineteenth century, the fate of prisoners was decided soon after their capture, with options ranging from killing to release. Even after the emergence of POW camps, the first phase of captivity continued to be the most critical: 'The greatest risk of being killed as a POW occurs from the time the soldier attempts to surrender to the time the soldier enters a holding area behind enemy lines.'[47] Factors contributing to the killing of surrendering troops on the Western front in the Second World War were, according to Bob Moore, legal uncertainty as to when precisely the legal protections for POWs set in, the desire for instant retaliation, and reports about the adversary's fight-to-the-finish mentality. As Kramer explains, the first phase of detention was also often crucial for prisoners' long-term chances of survival, since the captor determined in this phase in which conditions (clothing and shelter) prisoners would be held.

During the phase of captivity itself, the question of whether prisoners are of use to their captors can be decisive regarding their fate. If prisoners are of political or economic use to their captors, their chances of survival might be slightly better, although the numbers of prisoners who died due to harsh labour conditions or under torture are not very encouraging. Their chances of survival are best under certain conditions of reciprocity; that is, when their home country cares about their treatment and is able to retaliate against prisoners of the captor state (see also the section 'Reciprocity' later in this chapter). Not least, prisoners have at many times been the most favoured target for reprisals.

In addition, prisoners' chances of survival and their treatment in captivity depended on their social class and/or their rank. From the Middle Ages to the world wars, this seems to be the most striking continuity: medieval knights were less likely to be massacred than peasant fighters, from early modern times to the eighteenth century only officers were released on parole and not rank and file, and during the world wars officers were more likely to be held in better conditions than soldiers.

If prisoners were used as a bargaining chip for peace negotiations, their release and repatriation were frequently delayed after the termination of hostilities. But such delays also occurred due to economic reasons. As Kramer mentions in Chapter 5, the British and French governments withheld almost half a million German POWs after the end of the First World War claiming that the extended exploitation of their workforce should be seen as legitimate 'reparation labour'. The last German POWs in the Soviet Union were repatriated as late as 1956. In the first years after the Second World War, their workforce was a vital part of Stalin's first five-year plan, whereas in the 1950s their value as a political bargaining chip with Germany was more important.[48] Moreover, there were also instances in which prisoners refused repatriation after the termination of hostilities, such as 23,000 Korean POWs after the end of the Korean War. This figure was not quite matched by the twenty-one American POWs who decided to stay in North Korea.[49] Finally, sometimes repatriation did not improve the lot of prisoners, as was the case with Soviet POWs returning to the Soviet Union after the Second World War. In line with Stalin's edict that they were 'traitors', a substantial number of them were sentenced to forced labour or vanished in the Gulag system.[50]

PRISONERS IN 'THE OTHER WAR' OR PRISONERS IN WAR AS THE 'OTHER'?

There is a widespread perception that the distinction between regular and irregular wars is a dividing line accounting for massive differences in the treatment of prisoners and detainees. In fact, the four chapters on irregular wars in this book (German South-west Africa, Algeria, Northern Ireland, and Chechnya) seem to confirm a tendency to keep detainees in irregular wars outside the normative and legal framework and to treat them worse than their counterparts in regular wars. Extrajudicial killings, disappearances, detention without trial, torture, ill-treatment, and collective punishment appear to be characteristic practices in these wars. At first glance, it seems plausible to ascribe this to the nature of irregular wars, in particular the difficulty in distinguishing between combatants and non-combatants, the increased need for intelligence, and the temptation to adopt a deterrent and punitive approach to insurgencies. Moreover, differences concerning the legal status and the codification of legal rules may appear to be an additional factor accounting for the variation between regular and irregular armed conflicts. The question of whether a particular war counts as an international armed conflict (in which the GCs and, subject to ratification by the conflict parties, also Additional Protocol I apply) is often contested. If the conflict is perceived as non-international, fewer legal provisions apply (Common Article 3, Additional Protocol II, customary international law, and, to a certain extent, human rights law), meaning that the legal situation of detainees in such conflicts is less clearly defined. It may seem reasonable to assume that fewer legal protections result in more instances of maltreatment of detainees.

Yet there are several observations that should caution against such a simple dichotomous reading. First, gross instances of ill-treatment of prisoners bordering on exterminatory practices occurred in irregular as well in regular warfare despite the fact that the legal provisions for the treatment of prisoners in regular wars are more clearly defined. The German treatment of Soviet POWs during the Second World War is the prime example in this respect. Moreover, there was a remarkable continuity in the German treatment of prisoners in colonial wars and in the First World War owing to the fact that these practices belonged to the standard repertoire of German military culture in the late nineteenth and the first half of the twentieth century. According to Isabel Hull, in particular the suppression of the civilian population in the occupied territories in Belgium, northern France, and Eastern Europe followed a military cultural template of occupation that had already been practised in German colonial wars.[51] Military culture, in particular if its specific characteristics include a focus on combat and decisive victory and if it is almost unconstrained by political guidance and scrutiny (as was the case with Germany in the late nineteenth and early twentieth centuries),[52] can thus be a crucial structural–organizational reason for the systematic ill-treatment of prisoners in war. It affects regular and irregular wars alike.

Secondly, the assumption that prisoners in irregular conflicts are treated worse because they enjoy fewer legal protections is based on a naturalized reading of the law that grossly underestimates the strategic and political dimensions of this phenomenon. The lack of clarity of the law is itself first and foremost a product of political and diplomatic negotiations and decisions by states. The contemporary law of armed conflict is biased towards regular inter-state wars.[53] This development arguably began before the emergence of legally codified constraints on warfare. In fact, constraints on warfare featured at all times an exclusionary tendency in that they tended to apply only in conflicts between actors belonging to a recognized group of 'civilized' polities, whereas unlimited warfare was admissible in conflicts with 'savage' outsiders.[54] This exclusionary mechanism could coincide with geographical boundaries, for example intra-Hellenic wars versus the Persian Wars, medieval intra-European wars versus the Crusades, but it could also apply to deviant categories of armed groups within 'civilized' polities. In the sixteenth century, for instance, Baltasar Ayala argued that rebels did not constitute *iustus hostis*. They were thus to be denied the right to make war and could not enjoy the protections of the laws of war if captured.[55] In the nineteenth and early twentieth centuries the bias of the constraints on warfare was reflected in the Eurocentrism of the 'standard of civilization',[56] according to which customary international law and the Hague Conventions did not apply in armed conflicts between Europeans and non-Europeans in the colonies.

After the Second World War, the Eurocentrism of the law of armed conflict turned into state-centrism. In 1949 attempts at extending the applicability of the GCs to non-international armed conflicts failed, according to Geoffrey Best, due to 'two big and serious arguments: one rooted in political philosophy, and relating to the rights and duties of States and subjects; the other entangled with the ideological argument about the rights and wrongs of empires and colonialism'.[57] The 1977 Additional Protocols made an attempt at mitigating the state bias of the law of armed conflict, but they have not reached universal ratification yet.[58] As a consequence, the contemporary law of armed conflict, especially when subjected to a certain reading, reaffirms the hierarchical distinction between two different types of opponents: 'regular' troops fighting on behalf of a recognized state authority and 'irregulars'. Whilst the 'regular' opponent, despite fighting on the other side of the conflict, is recognized as belonging to the same kind of entity—the armed forces of a state, militias, and volunteer corps—the 'irregular' represents a different kind of entity with entirely different cultural and organizational features, motivations, and habits of fighting. In short, the irregular opponent is not only the enemy; he is the 'other'.[59] The attribution of this label is a politically powerful tool, since it denies the opponent legitimacy. While denying legitimacy to terrorists and guerrilla fighters is often intended, this exclusionary dynamic targets *all sorts* of irregular fighters, even though some of them may actually need special protections. Matthew Happold outlines in Chapter 15 how the particularly vulnerable category of child soldiers falls into this trap. To a certain extent, this dynamic also applies to members of private military companies (PMCs), as Chia Lehnardt describes in Chapter 14.

There is a second political dynamic at play in the distinction between 'civilized' and 'uncivilized', 'regular' and 'irregular' opponents—a dynamic concerning the application of these categories to empirical conflict parties. The label 'savage', 'barbarian', or 'irregular' is often attributed not on the basis of the actual characteristics of certain conflict parties, but rather on the basis of political aims. The above-mentioned case of FLN fighters in Algeria is a prime example, but this tendency precedes the formal codification of the law of armed conflict. There is evidence that the treatment of the 'barbarian' outsiders by both the Greeks and medieval European troops was often restrained by political considerations.[60] During the Second World War, the British government recognized Tito's partisans in Yugoslavia as belligerents because it fitted its political agenda.[61] The American command in Vietnam tacitly recognized Viet Cong combatant status in order to avoid further killings of US POWs by the Viet Cong, which could have turned US public opinion against the war effort.[62] Conversely, sometimes civilians or regular troops were labelled 'irregulars' in order to justify their harsh treatment. During the Second World War, the Germans regarded non-white soldiers of the British imperial forces as 'irregular' troops and treated them worse than their 'regular' white fellow soldiers—a politically motivated exclusion underpinned by racism (see Chapter 7). In the first few months of the First World War, several thousand Belgian and French civilians were taken captive by the Germans and summarily executed as *francs-tireurs* (civilians who had taken up arms illegally). However, these civilians had never engaged in armed resistance efforts against the German occupation. The '*francs-tireurs* myth' served as a political narrative justifying German atrocities in the occupied territories.[63] This example shows how deterrence and collective punishment practices emerging from military culture and the political dynamics of exclusion can be mutually reinforcing.[64]

Finally, in many of those conflicts that could be considered as non-international, such as the Algerian war, the British counter-insurgency campaign in Kenya, and the two Chechnya campaigns, the colonial or counter-insurgent/counter-terrorist power disputed the applicability of any law of armed conflict provisions, arguing instead that those conflicts were 'riots', 'emergencies', or 'troubles' (in the case of Northern Ireland) that could be dealt with within the framework of domestic law. While this at first sight seems to promise the applicability of domestic constitutional rights and protections to the insurgents or 'rebels', in most cases a range of those rights were suspended through the introduction of emergency measures. Chapters 11–13 are instructive in this respect. As Oren Gross and Fionnuala Ní Aoláin explain, emergency powers tend to be exclusionary in the sense that they draw boundaries between the 'safe' homeland and the 'dangerous' areas in which rebels and insurgents operate (as was the case in Algeria, Kenya, and Northern Ireland).[65] Alternatively, they may target the 'other' within a political community, the most prominent example being counter-terrorism measures based on racial and ethnic profiling.[66] Yet despite their inherent characteristic to demarcate the realm of the exception from the realm of normalcy and safety, emergency measures have a tendency to spill over into areas of domestic law and to corrupt its standards. In the early 1960s the French police came to apply the same measures against captured suspects from the Algerian community within France that the French armed forces used in Algeria against the FLN.[67] Similarly, emergency measures included in the 1974 Prevention of Terrorism Act and in the system of Diplock Courts had a corrosive effect on British civil law.[68] Finally, the notorious five techniques used in the interrogation of terrorist suspects in Northern Ireland had been 'imported' from earlier British colonial campaigns, defying the idea that the use of these measures could be restricted to colonial territory.[69]

The tendency of emergency measures and detention practices such as torture and ill-treatment to spill over into the domestic legal system or into other conflicts also cautions against the idea that the treatment of prisoners in irregular wars simply follows the logic of unrestrained military necessity.

True, military necessity or, rather, the sense that the situation cannot be controlled within the established legal limits is often the initial motivation for the creation of zones with lowered legal standards: 'It was less a case of the law dictating the war than of the war dictating the law', as Branche remarks with respect to the war in Algeria.[70] However, such a dynamic tends to take on its own life. It has often led to a downward spiral of atrocities on both sides as well as the breakdown of even the most minimal constraints in the treatment of prisoners and detainees. Once a particular category of prisoners or detainees have been defined as 'outlaws', it also becomes difficult to bring them back into the remit of the law, which would be a necessary step in the transition to a post-war, post-insurgency political order. According to Peter Paret, in the Algerian war 'recourse to atrocities made re-education in a non-totalitarian sense impossible'.[71] Over time, these practices may be integrated in the organizational memory of the armed forces and can thus become a part of their military culture. In short, the dynamics of legal exclusion reaffirm the dehumanized status of the prisoner, thereby making further atrocities more likely, and tend to have unintended consequences that are difficult to control, especially when the political and strategic situation changes.

RECIPROCITY

Since its inception, the legally codified POW regime has been a decentralized one, meaning that there is no central enforcement mechanism. Governments are expected to train their armed forces to comply with the legal standards on the treatment of prisoners in war and to punish occurrences of non-compliance, with the possibility of retaliation against POWs held by the opponent being their main incentive for doing so.[72] Protecting powers (in the first half of the twentieth century) and the International Committee of the Red Cross (ICRC) help monitor compliance in order to prevent the escalation of reprisals due to inaccurate information, but they do not themselves enforce these rules. International courts and tribunals have sometimes dealt with cases concerning the ill-treatment of prisoners and detainees (most notably the Nuremberg trials, but see also Chapter 6 for details on the inter-war Leipzig trials and Chapter 12 on the ruling of the European Court of Human Rights in the case of *Ireland v. United Kingdom*). The establishment of the International Criminal Court promises to confer continuity on these efforts. However, the main enforcement mechanism for the lawful treatment of detainees and therefore the greatest, theoretical, source of immediate protection for POWs is reciprocity.

There are two basic problems with reciprocity that tend to work to the disadvantage of prisoners in war. One is related to reprisals and one to the failure of reciprocity itself. As Overmans explains, reciprocity is a double-edged sword.[73] It is the principal source of protection for POWs, but at the same time it makes them a preferred target for reprisals. Whilst reprisals are intended to keep the conduct of hostilities within the confines of the law of armed conflict,[74] they can create a downward spiral of uncontrolled tit-for-tat retaliation that 'replaces international law with the naked reciprocity of violence' (Kramer, Chapter 5, this volume). An example for such a dynamic is the treatment of POWs during the First World War. As a result of this experience, the 1929 GC explicitly prohibited reprisals against POWs—a provision, however, that was frequently ignored during the Second World War (see Chapter 6). A further problem in this context is that reciprocity presupposes an interest on the part of the addressee in the well-being of the POWs held by the adversary. Both world wars provide examples that this was not necessarily the case. If the home governments of POWs regarded surrender as cowardice, as the Italian government did in the First World War (Kramer, Chapter 5, this volume) and the Soviet government in the Second World War (Overmans, Chapter 8, this volume), POWs were more likely to suffer in captivity, since their governments neither threatened reprisals for harsh treatment and labour conditions, nor were willing to change their own behaviour as a result of the opponent's reprisals. Yet there were instances in which reciprocity worked to the advantage of POWs and prevented their treatment from sliding into lawlessness. A prime example is the 'shackling crisis' in the Second World War between Britain and Germany (see Chapter 7).

A second problem concerns situations in which reciprocity does not emerge or, rather, its emergence is suppressed by the dehumanization of the opponent. This pertains in particular to conflicts in which the opponent is not regarded as the enemy, but rather as the 'other' (see the section 'Prisoners in "the other war" or prisoners in war as the "other"?'). The exterminatory treatment of Soviet POWs by the Germans during the Second World War was underpinned by the notion of the racial inferiority of these prisoners (and exacerbated by the fact that the Soviet government did not care about the fate of their POWs in German captivity). The problem in this respect is that reciprocity does *not* automatically develop over time out of mere self-interest, contrary to what Geoffrey Parker argues.[75] The initial lack of reciprocity is frequently cited as one of the main reasons for excluding the opponent from the legal protections for prisoners in war. The German military, for instance, justified the treatment of Herero prisoners in South-west Africa by pointing out that the Hereros' conduct in war was unconstrained by moral or legal norms and excessively cruel: 'However, since in this war the enemy himself expects no leniency, even the wounded defend themselves as long as they are able.'[76] Cruel behaviour on the part of the opponent (or accusations thereof) reinforces the notion that the opponent belongs to a subhuman, dissimilar category of adversary. Ensuing atrocities may be framed as reprisals, but they are not intended to bring the adversary back on legal tracks. Instead, they are collective punishments or 'acts of terror'.[77] The denial of reciprocity and the exclusion and dehumanization of the opponent thus form a vicious circle in which every atrocity committed by the opponent serves at the same time as a reaffirmation of their subhuman status and as a justification for further terror against them.[78] Reciprocity presupposes a basic sense of identification with the opponent; that is, the perception of the opponent as the enemy or *iustus hostis* rather than the 'other'.[79]

If this precondition is not fulfilled, reciprocity is unlikely to emerge. Moreover, reciprocity is sometimes consciously rejected on the basis of legal and strategic arguments. Some lawyers hold that the denial of POW status and protections to irregular fighters provides an incentive for the latter to comply with the law of armed conflict.[80] Yet there is no evidence that this incentive has ever worked. It is more likely to start off a race to the bottom in which the adversary gains support from harassment or atrocities committed against him, as Alia Brahimi explains in Chapter 19 on al-Qaeda's reaction to the Western detention regime in the 'war on terror'.

STRUCTURE OF THE BOOK

Part I of the book covers the historical transition from the chivalric code on the treatment of prisoners to the emergence of codified treaties and conventions in this field. It explores the boundaries of medieval constraints on warfare during the crusades and traces the evolution of new rules and standards during the emergence of the European states system up to the legal codification of the POW regime in the late nineteenth century. The First World War was the first major 'practice test' for this regime. Although it exposed its flaws, the inter-war period and the adoption of the 1929 GC on POWs reflect a certain sense of optimism that these shortcomings could be remedied by legal means.

As evidenced in Part II, this hope was to be disappointed during the Second World War. Whereas the 1929 GC was largely upheld on the Western front, the Eastern front and the Pacific theatre present a different picture. The three chapters on the Second World War show that clear and binding legal rules cannot prevail against cultural factors such as contempt for surrender or exterminatory practices motivated by racism and the dehumanization of the opponent.

Part III is devoted to the treatment of detainees in irregular conflicts. Although the distinction between regular and irregular conflicts should not be overstated, the four chapters show striking similarities concerning the treatment of prisoners in these conflicts. Despite the differences in their contexts—two of the chapters deal with colonial conflicts and two with domestic rebellions and terrorism campaigns—the suspension of legal standards, indiscriminate detention and harsh treatment of prisoners, and sometimes even exterminatory detention policies emerge as common practices.

Part IV deals with contemporary challenges to the treatment of prisoners in war. One of the most important and most widely debated problems in this respect is detention in the 'war on terror'. Chapters 16 to 19 provide a multifaceted perspective on the complex challenges in this area. They reflect the debates within the West, and also trace the dynamics between Western detention policies and the narratives and tactics of terrorist networks such as al-Qaeda. Yet this focus should not obscure other contemporary challenges to the legal regime on prisoners in war, which receive less public attention but are nevertheless crucial: PMCs and child soldiers (Chapters 14 and 15, respectively). Finally, the conclusion discusses whether and how the prisoners in war regime can or should be further developed.

NOTES

1. Rüdiger Overmans, ' "In der Hand des Feindes" Geschichtsschreibung zur Kriegsgefangenschaft von der Antike bis zum Zweiten Weltkrieg', in Rüdiger Overmans (ed.), *In der Hand des Feindes: Kriegsgefangenschaft von der Antike bis zum Zweiten Weltkrieg* (Köln: Böhlau Verlag, 1999), 20.
2. Geoffrey Best, *War and law since 1945* (Oxford: Oxford University Press, 1994), 350.
3. James D. Morrow, 'When do states follow the laws of war?', *American Political Science Review*, 101/3 (2007), 569.
4. Ibid.
5. Best, *War and law since 1945*, 135.
6. Additional Protocol I lowers the requirements an individual has to fulfil in order to retain combatant status and thus to qualify for POW status. According to Article 44, he has to carry arms openly '(a) during each military engagement, and (2) during such a time as he is visible to the adversary while he is engaged in a military deployment preceding the launching of an attack in which he is to participate' (printed in Adam Roberts and Richard Guelff (eds.), *Documents on the laws of war* (Oxford: Oxford University Press, 2000), 445). In contrast, Article 4 of the Third Geneva Convention [hereafter GC III] stipulates that in order to qualify for POW status, members of militias and volunteer corps have to 'fulfil the following conditions: (a) that of being commanded by a person responsible for his subordinates; (b) that of having a fixed distinctive sign recognizable at a distance; (c) that of carrying arms openly; (d) that of conducting their operations in accordance with the laws and customs of war' (ibid., 246).
7. Stefan Oeter, 'Die Entwicklung des Kriegsgefangenenrechts: Die Sichtweise eines Völkerrechtlers', in Rüdiger Overmans (ed.), *In der Hand des Feindes*, 58 [original in German].
8. See George J. Andreopoulos, 'The age of national liberation movements', in Michael Howard, George J. Andreopoulos, and Mark R. Shulman (eds.), *The laws of war: Constraints on warfare in the Western world* (New Haven, CT: Yale University Press, 1994), 204.
9. Ibid., 202.
10. Josiah Ober, 'Classical Greek times', in Howard, Andreopoulos, and Shulman (eds.), *The laws of war*, 13.
11. Pierre Ducrey, 'Kriegsfangene im antiken Griechenland: Forschungsdiskussion 1968–1998', in Overmans (ed.), *In der Hand des Feindes*, 78.
12. Ober, 'Classical Greek times', 18.
13. Raoul Lonis, 'La guerre en Grèce: Quinze années de recherché, 1968–1983', *Revue des Etudes Grecques*, 98/2 (1985), 366f.
14. Jörg Rüpke, 'Kriegsgefangene in der römischen Antike: Eine Problemskizze', in Overmans (ed.), *In der Hand des Feindes*, 83.
15. Ibid., 91f.
16. Overmans, ' "In der Hand des Feindes" Geschichtsschreibung zur Kriegsgefangenschaft', 10.

17. Robert C. Stacey, 'The age of chivalry', in Howard, Andreopoulos, and Shulman (eds.), *The laws of war*, 30.
18. Ibid., 38.
19. Michael Howard subsumes siege warfare under *guerre mortelle*; Michael Howard, *War in European history* (Oxford: Oxford University Press, 1976), 6. In contrast, Robert Stacey explains that from a legal point of view siege warfare was a 'special case', following the rules of neither *bellum hostile* nor *guerre mortelle*: 'Strictly speaking, . . . [a] siege was not an act of war but the enforcement of a judicial sentence against traitors who had disobeyed their prince's lawful command' (Stacey, 'The age of Chivalry', 38).
20. Michael Glover, *The velvet glove: The decline and fall of moderation in war* (London: Hodder and Stoughton, 1982), 159.
21. Geoffrey Parker, *Success is never final: Empire, war, and faith in early modern Europe* (New York: Basic Books, 2002).
22. Ibid., 154.
23. Ibid., 161.
24. Daniel Hohrath, '"In Cartellen wird der Werth eines Gefangenen bestimmet" Kriegs-gefangenschaft als Teil der Kriegspraxis des Ancien Régime', in Overmans (ed.), *In der Hand des Feindes*, 165.
25. Francis Abell, *Prisoners of war in Britain 1756 to 1815* (Oxford: Oxford University Press, 1914), 284.
26. Glover, *The velvet glove*, 162f.
27. Gunther Rothenberg, 'The age of Napoleon', in Howard, Andreopoulos, and Shulman (eds.), *The laws of war*, 90f.
28. Ibid.
29. Ibid.
30. Reid Mitchell, '"Our prison system, supposing we had any": The Confederate and Union prison systems', in Stig Förster and Jörg Nagler (eds.), *On the road to total war: The American Civil War and the German wars of unification, 1861–1871* (Cambridge: Cambridge University Press, 1997), 565–85.
31. Oeter, 'Die Entwicklung des Kriegsgefangenenrechts: Die Sichtweise eines Völkerrech-tlers', 50.
32. Printed in Roberts and Guelff (eds.), *Documents on the laws of war*, 74.
33. Stacey, 'The age of chivalry', 29.
34. Geoffrey Best, *Humanity in warfare: The modern history of the international law of armed conflict* (London: Weidenfeld and Nicolson, 1980), 53ff.
35. Uta Hinz, '"Die deutschen 'Barbaren' sind doch die besseren Menschen." Kriegsge-fangenschaft und gefangene "Feinde" in der Darstellung der deutschen Publizistik 1914–1918', in Overmans (ed.), *In der Hand des Feindes*; Best, *War and law since 1945*, 135.
36. Richard A. Falk, 'International law aspects of repatriation of prisoners of war during hostilities', *American Journal of International Law*, 67/4 (1973), 465–78; Donald L. Zillman, 'Political uses of prisoners in war', *Arizona State Law Journal*, 6/2 (1975), 237–74.
37. See Best, *Humanity in warfare*, 53ff.
38. See Rothenberg, 'The age of Napoleon', 90. Even if prisoners are considered a source of intelligence, their chances of survival do not necessarily increase, especially when torture comes into play. As Paul Aussaresses, who served with the French armed forces in the Algerian war, notes succinctly in his memoirs about the interrogation of a

captured FLN fighter: 'It was important that he talk because we had been surprised by this wave of violence.... The man refused to talk and I decided to use violent methods.... But it was useless that day because the man died without talking' (Paul Aussaresses, *The battle of the Casbah: Counter-terrorism and torture* (New York: Enigma Books, 2002), 30).

39. Overmans, '"In der Hand des Feindes" Geschichtsschreibung zur Kriegsgefangenschaft', 30f. Although the 1929 and the 1949 Geneva Conventions explicitly prohibit exposing POWs to public curiosity, parading prisoners continued to be a common practice throughout the twentieth century.
40. Uta Hinz, '"Die deutschen 'Barbaren' sind doch die besseren Menschen." Kriegsgefangenschaft und gefangene "Feinde" in der Darstellung der deutschen Publizistik 1914–1918', 339–62.
41. Zillman, 'Political uses of prisoners in war', 253ff.
42. Falk, 'International law aspects of repatriation', 465–78.
43. Zillman, 'Political uses of prisoners in war', 266.
44. Ibid., 263.
45. Ibid., 261.
46. Overmans, '"In der Hand des Feindes" Geschichtsschreibung zur Kriegsgefangenschaft', 17f.
47. James D. Morrow, 'The institutional features of the prisoners of war treaties', *International Organization*, 55/4 (2001), 976.
48. Stephanie Carvin 'Caught in the cold: International humanitarian law and prisoners of war during the Cold War', *Journal of Conflict and Security Law*, 11/1 (2006), 70.
49. See Eugene Kinkead, *Why they collaborated* (London: Longmans, 1960).
50. Carvin, 'Caught in the cold', 71.
51. Isabel V. Hull, *Absolute destruction: Military culture and the practices of war in Imperial Germany* (Ithaca, NY: Cornell University Press, 2005).
52. Ibid.
53. See Theo Farrell, 'World culture and military power', *Security Studies*, 14/3 (2005), 485.
54. Georg Schwarzenberger, *The dynamics of law* (Abingdon: Professional Books, 1976), 82.
55. Parker, *Success is never final*, 149.
56. Gerrit W. Gong, *The standard of 'civilization' in international society* (Oxford: Clarendon Press, 1984).
57. Best, *War and law since 1945*, 171.
58. Moreover, Additional Protocol I provides protections only for certain irregular fighters—members of national liberation movements—while at the same time excluding others: mercenaries (Best, *War and law since 1945*, 350). This has added to the legal difficulties surrounding the status and treatment of captured members of Private Military Companies (PMCs). Louise Doswald-Beck, 'Private military companies under international humanitarian law', in Simon Chesterman and Chia Lehnardt (eds.), *From mercenaries to market. The rise and regulation of private military companies* (Oxford: Oxford University Press, 2007), 122f.; see also Chapter 14 in this volume.
59. The theoretical distinction between different forms of enmity can be traced back to Carl Schmitt's *Theorie des Partisanen*. However, Schmitt tends to argue that different forms of enmity are determined by different factual forms of war (see Gabriella Slomp, 'The theory of the partisan: Carl Schmitt's neglected legacy', *History of Political Thought*, 26/3 (2005), 518). In contrast, my argument is that the perceived form of

war is a result of a political battle over definitions, which is at the same time a battle for political legitimacy.

60. Ducrey, 'Kriegsfangene im antiken Griechenland', 78; Yacoov Lev, 'Prisoners of war during the Fatimid-Ayyubid wars with the Crusaders', in Michael Gervers and James M. Powell (eds.), *Tolerance and intolerance: Social conflict in the age of the Crusades* (Syracuse, NY: Syracuse University Press, 2001), 23. I am grateful to Frédéric Mégret for pointing out the literature on the Crusades.
61. Andreopoulos, 'The age of national liberation movements', 196.
62. Zillman, 'Political uses of prisoners in war', 249.
63. John Horne and Alan Kramer, *German atrocities, 1914: A history of denial* (New Haven, CT: Yale University Press, 2001).
64. See Hull, *Absolute destruction*, 331.
65. Oren Gross and Fionnuala Ní Aoláin, *Law in times of crisis: Emergency powers in theory and practice* (Cambridge: Cambridge University Press, 2006), 171ff.
66. Ibid.
67. Ibid., 194.
68. Michael Yardley and Dennis Sewell, *A new model army* (London: W H Allen, 1989), 174.
69. Gross and Aoláin, *Law in times of crisis*, 189.
70. Raphaëlle Branche, *La torture et l'armée pendant la guerre d'Algérie, 1954–1962* (Paris: Gallimard, 2001), 199 [original in French].
71. Peter Paret, *French revolutionary warfare from Indochina to Algeria: The analysis of a political and military doctrine* (London: Pall Mall Press, 1964), 76.
72. Morrow, 'The institutional features of the prisoners of war treaties', 982.
73. Overmans, '"In der Hand des Feindes" Geschichtsschreibung zur Kriegsgefangenschaft', 27.
74. 'A reprisal is a measured, purposeful, unlawful act in response to an unlawful act of the enemy's; illegal though the reprisal may be, its justification is that nothing less will serve to stop the other in his lawless tracks' (Best, *War and law since 1945*, 311).
75. 'Cooperation between enemies requires neither rationality (for if it works, it will continue), nor trust (thanks to the penalties of defection), nor mutual communication (because deeds speak louder than words). Only durability is essential: some recognition of adversaries from earlier encounters and some certainty that the two sides will meet again' (Parker, *Success is never final*, 167).
76. General Theodor Leutwein, quoted in Hull, *Absolute destruction*, 15.
77. Best, *War and law since 1945*, 312.
78. A crucial question in this respect is whether a conflict that was initially characterized by reciprocity can spin out of control to such an extent due to reprisals that the opponent is no longer perceived as the enemy, but as the 'other'. Carl Schmitt would have answered this affirmatively: according to him, 'European states entered the First World War as conventional enemies and left it as real enemies [Schmitt's term for the dehumanized "other"]' (Slomp, 'The theory of the partisan', 518).
79. For a similar argument on reciprocity and cooperation in international relations more generally see Alexander Wendt, 'Collective identity formation and the international state', *American Political Science Review*, 88/2 (1994), 384–96.
80. John C. Yoo and James C. Ho, 'The status of terrorists', University of California Berkeley, *Boalt Working Papers in Public Law*, 25 (2003), 14.

Part I

The Emergence of Legal and Ethical Standards Before the Second World War

2

A Cautionary Tale from the Crusades? War and Prisoners in Conditions of Normative Incommensurability

Frédéric Mégret

At a time when mention of 'Crusades' has appeared as a recurrent theme in much talk about international violence (most notoriously and dubiously in the context of the war against terror), it seems pertinent to raise the issue of how the original Crusades dealt with the waging of violence, particularly the issue of treatment of prisoners. Much of what happened in the Crusades is shrouded in mystery and not always well understood, but it seems that many simplifications are often involved, by both those who manipulate the term as a galvanizing call to arms, and those who see the Crusades as an unmitigated source of evil. The Crusades, at least at first glance, offer us a glimpse on the distant past (and the issue of how norms might have existed before the emergence of modern laws of war), at a time when it has become necessary to think seriously about the 'future' of international humanitarian law.

My main hypothesis is that the Crusades are both extremely remote from our current reality and that they also, sometimes in unexpected and lateral ways, raise some issues of undeniable contemporary relevance. Perhaps the foremost of these issues is what happens to prisoners in military confrontations when parties to such confrontations are not bound by some overarching shared normativity? Historically, this has in fact been very much the problem, and one that the laws of war have tried to transcend in a post-Westphalian world. It is often claimed that this effort is increasingly called into question in a world that appears to have become more fragmented into deeply incommensurable beliefs. The idea of common laws of war as a bridge between fighting enemies was always a tenuous link, but (or so the argument goes) it is even more so under present conditions. But was the record of the Crusades in terms of treatment of prisoners really all that bad? Is there not a risk that one will project an image of the progress of restraint in warfare that portrays modernity as necessarily the depositary of the last word on the matter?

This chapter attempts to shed some cursory light on this little-discussed issue. It concentrates on the purely normative aspect of the problem, namely the extent to which rules, whether of a legal or a moral character, have an impact on the treatment of prisoners. The possibility of other, non-normative factors that might have had an impact on respect for restraint in warfare is left for further research. It is true that contemporary scholars of the laws of war have often contrasted the modern, secular war-regulatory project with the Crusades as the very antithesis of what a humane war should be. Whilst it is not denied that the Crusades were indeed very violent, and that this may have been partly because they arose in an age that had not come up with a sophisticated distinct concept of the laws of war, it is also argued that the Crusades deserve better than the caricature that is sometimes made of them. In this respect, I challenge the modernist narrative that proper regulation of warfare necessarily requires the assistance of international law. Indeed, it is contended that the reality of crusading parties' treatment of prisoners was complex and it is precisely because of this complexity, and that the Crusades were so fraught with contradictions, that they are an interesting, if lateral, metaphor for our own, rather complex, world.

The discussion begins with a more descriptive section whose goal is broadly to characterize the Crusades and to give a raw assessment as to what their record was in terms of treating prisoners. This is followed by a section which lays out the broad normative framework of the Crusades to show how it conditioned the nature and quality of restraint in warfare.

THE CRUSADES AND PRISONERS

The term 'Crusades' designates a variety of military enterprises launched by Christendom from the late eleventh to the thirteenth centuries. Motivations, organization, and even the goals of Crusades varied quite substantially, but the common traits seem to outweigh the differences, so that it makes sense to talk of the 'Crusades' as an analytical whole. The Crusades are a very peculiar episode in the history of human violence that bears resemblance to some contemporary forms of conflict, but is also strikingly different in some respects.

The Record

The following is simply a raw image of the 'actual treatment of prisoners' during the Crusades, relatively unencumbered by explanation or characterization. Giving a broad and representative description of the treatment of prisoners throughout the Crusades is of course an almost impossible task, at least short of very significant historical research. This portrayal of that treatment will therefore be very broadly brushed and partly based on anecdotal evidence, emphasizing what seems particularly emblematic.

Overall, there is strong evidence, in accordance with today's dominant perception, that the Crusades were a bloody and not particularly humane affair. Great crimes were committed, including against other Christians (e.g. the sacking of Constantinople in 1205). Killing of those who had surrendered was quite common and was in fact sometimes specifically ordered by commanders. This was even though those surrendering (often the besieged) might have been lured to do so by promises that they would not be executed. Such was the case following the surrender of the Christian garrison of Marash (1150), the fall(s) of Acre (1191 and 1291), and the battle of Nicopolis (1396, with 3,000 taken prisoner).[1] Execution of captives sometimes occurred on the spur of the moment as a form of spite or revenge (a possible explanation for Richard's Acre massacre), but at times was the result of a deliberate policy.[2]

An indication of how relatively acceptable these massacres were, was the fact that they were portrayed with some relish and no obvious sense of shame by some contemporary commentators. For example, Raymond of Aguilers, an eyewitness to the slaughter of Muslims, Jews, and Christians, talked of how 'the land stank with Moorish blood, and the aqueduct was choked with their corpses. It was a delightful sight.'[3] De Mézières thought that the sacking of Alexandria was a '*prise glorieuse*'.[4] There was, in fact, much rejoicing about and recounting of ghastly exploits:

> Two thousand seven hundred, all
> In chains, were led outside the wall,
> Where they were slaughtered every one...
> For this be the Creator blessed![5]

If combatants passed the dangerous aftermath of surrender or battle and were 'fortunate' enough to be made prisoners,[6] they could expect often harsh conditions of detention, such as those that awaited Saladin's captives in the 'dungeons' of Aleppe. Torture was not unheard of and sexual abuse was quite common.[7] Tafurs, for example, were said to be in the habit of raping women during the First Crusade.[8]

It was not unheard of for prisoners to be used as human shields. Bishop Günter of Bamberg, one of the leaders of the great German pilgrimage to the Holy Land (1064–5), 'advised setting their Muslim captives out naked in chains to take the force of enemy missiles'.[9] Occasionally, some hostages were tied to siege engines as a deterrent.[10] Use 'of live Moslems [*sic*] as projectiles'[11] was witnessed, whilst Muslims would occasionally sling individuals over walls during sieges or, like Ilghazi after the battle of Tel-Danith, use Christian prisoners for target practice.

Alternatively, forced labour was a conspicuous feature of many episodes of detention. In fact, in violation of cardinal contemporary laws of war principles, prisoners were often forced to participate in the enemy military effort, typically by contributing to defensive structures. During the First Crusade, after the Hattin defeat, Frank prisoners were forced to build siege machines that were used against Jerusalem;[12] during the Third Crusade, they were forced to dig counter-mines in Acre.[13] Byzantine mines were at times worked by Muslim prisoners of war. Christian prisoners are said to have been employed by Saladin for the construction of fortifications in Cairo, Acre, and Jerusalem.[14] Christians also put Muslim women to work. Prisoners of choice might be paraded as curiosities, as seems to have been the case of King Guy under the custody of Saladin; less noteworthy prisoners were sometimes simply humiliated in public.

In fact, detention was at times a direct path to being sold into slavery or was at any rate virtually indistinguishable from slavery. Saladin is said to have liberated 20,000 Muslim slaves upon recapturing Jerusalem in 1187. In any event, the detained might expect to be held for very significant durations, sometimes years, and in many cases long after the actual conflict, in the course of which they had been captured, had ended. Lengthy detentions had a tendency to become permanent, so much so that significant prisoner populations developed, sometimes in the midst of big cities such as Byzantium. Aspects of these individuals' conditions of detention rather than the possibility of their liberation would, over time, be the focus of lengthy diplomatic and political exchanges. For example, the rulers of Egypt intervened many times so that the freedom of worship of Muslim prisoners in Byzantium be respected and that they be allowed to visit the mosque.

So likely was the chance of execution or so horrendous the prospects of detention that many may have killed themselves rather than be caught. At Ma'arrat, during the First Crusade, many Muslims jumped down wells to their death to avoid torture. Of course, it is hard to say whether the treatment of prisoners was worse than in many modern episodes of warfare, arising in an era marked by the laws of war. By one measure, however, it seems reasonable to say that the Crusades were at least not noticeably better and probably somewhat worse than many of today's conflicts. Being taken prisoner depended on chance rather than any sense of systematic compulsion, and being a prisoner was an unenviable fate.

At the same time, what makes the Crusades so interesting (and puzzling from the point of view of one seeking to understand how conditions propitious to respect for prisoners arise) is that some of these abhorrent practices coexisted alongside a number of gestures that were stunningly generous, at least by today's standards. The record of the Crusades is thus more complex than some contemporary international humanitarian lawyers make it to be. Although the Crusades were the locus of tremendous atrocities, they also witnessed some startling acts of humanity. There was no dearth of gallantry generally. Perhaps one of the best known incidents is when, after Richard Coeur de Lion was dismounted, Saphadin had two horses sent to him across the battle lines. Indeed, both were known to have frequently sent presents to each other, and Coeur de Lion had made Saphadin's son a knight.[15] Whilst prisoners might be very openly tortured to death, they might also be treated royally. Some prisoners at least were treated extraordinarily well, more as guests than as detainees. 'High-ranking Franks were accorded great respect, given fur robes against the cold, fed at banquets, allowed to send for their clothing from their camp and to write letters, before being sent to Damascus under escort on Saladin's horses.'[16] There were many examples of charity: of taking care of the prisoners, carrying the wounded, or exchanging goods.[17] Moreover, evidence documenting unilateral and unconditional releases of prisoners exists. Mahomet had given the example early on. Some prisoners of Saladin were 'freely allowed to return to the Crusader camp',[18] and on one occasion Saladin personally made sure that the detained child of a woman who had come pleading to him was released.[19] Yâqoûb, prince of the Almohades, who defeated Alphonse VII, captured 20,000 prisoners, but freed them all out of chivalry (1195).

One last thought is worth voicing here. Although it is very difficult to generalize on such matters, it is also quite clear that 'parties' to the Crusades did not exactly behave according to the same standards. There is some evidence that suggests that overall the Saracens behaved in a way that was more regulated and constrained at first, whilst the Crusaders often brought to the Orient particularly vicious battle mores. This divergence too will have to be explained, and may hold some of the keys to understanding how in the midst of the same military episodes, extreme opposites of behaviour could coexist.

THE NORMATIVE FRAMEWORK OF THE CRUSADES AND ITS IMPACT ON PRISONERS

The normative framework of the Crusades is not the only factor that might explain treatment of prisoners, but it was certainly a crucial factor. When speaking of the normative framework of the Crusades, this does not refer merely to what might be described as their *regulatory* framework, but truly their *constitutive* normative framework: the rules that made the Crusades what they were, in addition to the rules that decided how the Crusades would be fought. Both, at any rate, are intimately interwoven and it is impossible to understand how the Crusades were supposed to be fought in isolation from an understanding of the sort of conflict in which they unfolded.

The Impact of *Jus Ad Bellum*

Leaving aside for the time being the question of the existence and potency of traditions of restraint in warfare, a particular problem arose as a result of the specificity of the Crusades. The Crusades highlight the difficulty of developing a specific normative sphere for restraint in warfare in a context of otherwise massively legitimized violence. In other words, this was a time when the laws of war had not truly emerged as a body of rules distinct from general rules regarding warfare, and in particular the legitimacy of war. To speak in the contemporary terms that have become familiar to us, even though respect for *jus in bello* might be one way of appreciating whether a war was just in the first place, the converse was more often true: that the fundamental justness of one's cause (at the level of *jus ad bellum*) had the effect of very much moderating one's obligations at the level of *jus in bello*. The risk was that the more just the war, the fewer were the restraints in actual warfare, leading the Crusades inevitably down a path of violence without limitation.

This is clearly a recurring theme in the modern humanitarian literature, in which the 'justness' of wars is many commentators' favourite factor explaining battlefield horrors. According to Jean Pictet, for example:

> It may be said that as long as the conception of the 'just war' was the paramount consideration in Christian thinking on this subject there was not much chance of any Christian control of the actual conduct of the fighting, or reform in the practices of warfare. Indeed, the very premise of the just war concept led logically and necessarily to the lack of restraint in the manner of its performance.[20]

Indeed, the Crusades are presented as the archetype of the just war, with potentially abominable consequences: '[T]he most serious consequence of the idea of a just war...is the use which men on all sides have made of it, to justify the cruelties which abounded in that sanguinary age.... We need cite only one example, the Crusades, which were perhaps the most perfect examples of "just wars." '[21] Or as François Bugnion put it: ' "holy wars", "Crusades", "just wars": history shows that the belligerents who are loudest in proclaiming the sanctity of their cause are often guilty of the worst excesses.'[22]

I am not satisfied, however, that the explanation based solely on the 'justness' of the Crusades goes far enough, or highlights quite what it was about the justness of the Crusades that made them violent in the way they were. Nor do I believe that it sufficiently explores what lay behind the Crusades' particular justness. There is, in fact, a modern tendency to view the Crusades as much more extreme than they were. This is often based on a distinctly modern and retrospective vision of what the Crusades were, rather than on an attempt to understand how contemporaries understood the Crusades.[23]

The important point is that there is no logically strong reason a priori why a war that is 'just' should be waged murderously and outside any restraint. The laws of war should ideally be committed to the idea of just war, in the same way that many visions of the just war have emphasized the need to abide by basic standards of humanity. Saint Augustine, for example, often presented as the Christian origin of ideas of the just war, was appalled by the excesses of war—any war—and considered them blameworthy, building on the ideas of Cicero. Indeed, both concepts coexist relatively well today, even though *jus in bello* often seems under threat in contexts where the justness of one's cause is stressed particularly stridently.[24] The Crusades, in other words, could have been both just *and* humane, and may even not have been just (according to the standard theory) *because* they were not humane.

A first type of explanation for the Crusades' particular roughness might rely on the fact that the Crusades were not simply like an ordinary 'just' war (say, an ordinary war in self-defence), but were a sort of 'super-just' war in that they combined, on both sides, all conceivable elements of justness. The Holy Land was presented as Roman land that rightly belonged to its Christian heirs and which had been occupied by the Saracens. Moreover, the Crusaders also saw themselves at times as coming to the rescue of Oriental Christians by freeing Eastern churches in Jerusalem, and providing protection for Byzantium. There were thus both elements of territorial and personal legitimacy to the entire endeavour.[25] This sense of legitimacy could easily be matched on the Muslim side, where a sense of being attacked and of seeing oneself as acting in self-defence prevailed.

Perhaps more crucially, a second type of explanation might underline that the Crusades were not so much just, as religiously *right*, and in furtherance of the highest religious goals. One often finds a conflation of the concept of the just war and the Crusades (as in the quotes from modern humanitarian lawyers above) that is problematic. Much more than 'just wars', the Crusades were first and foremost 'holy' wars. Even though the debate on the relationship between just and holy war is very much alive, and there are undoubtedly structural analogies between the two,[26] a simple equation is not satisfactory. In some ways, a 'holy war', such as the Crusades, is precisely not a just war, in the sense that the latter is restricted by some authors to violence between temporal powers. In fact, a divine war may be a war that is particularly murderous and violent precisely because papal enthusiasm for providential violence against unbelievers had not been tempered by Augustinian just war restraints.[27]

Contrary to the vision of a secular cause for justness, for example, the Crusades were seen as realizing the will of God. Their legitimacy thus naturally tended to be felt with particular devotional fervour, and they were fought with equal absolutism. This was all the more so given that the Crusades surfed on a wave of religious fervour and fanaticism, leading to a renewal of interest in pilgrimages and relics that had swept Christendom (and was often encouraged by the Church). Institutionally, the Crusades were also very much headed or inspired by the Church and an attempt to enlist the laity in its service, starting with the famous sermon of Pope Urban II at Clermont Ferrand. The more general conception of knights as servants of the Papacy ('Knights of Christ') led to a complex mixing of the Christian and chivalrous ethos (through the militarization of the former and the Christianization of the latter), culminating with the emergence of quasi-religious military orders. On the Saracen side, defending the Holy Land against the Crusades could also be seen as the discharge of a religious obligation, in a context where the Quran imposes a duty to protect one's faith, if need be through the lesser *jihad* of war.

Indeed, it is important to stress that the Crusades did not involve states, like modern wars, or even rival temporal powers, as with medieval wars, but more significantly *religious* efforts. They were fought between armies of believers and headed, at least on the Christian side, by the leaders of the Church themselves. The Rousseau idea that 'la guerre n'est ... point une relation d'homme à homme mais une relation d'Etat à Etat'[28] would have been alien to the Crusaders and the Muslim defenders, who had very often voluntarily embarked on a personal quest for redemption. Crusades were often entered into for penitential reasons and included vows,[29] in exchange for which the Church's protection (e.g. making the property of pilgrims inviolate in their absence) and absolution was granted.[30]

Crusaders, at least by some accounts, aspired to martyrdom.[31] Both victory and defeat would be interpreted as signs of God's will, the latter showing that Christians had turned away from religion and were thus chastised for it. In a context where the shedding of blood—both Christian and Muslim—increasingly came to be seen as intimately linked to the remission of sin and 'against [a] background of war as a proving ground for the people of God', it is not surprising, as John Gilchrist puts it, 'that the popes not only did not condemn the horrors of war but generally accepted them'.[32] Perhaps more perversely, the idea was that, since the Crusaders were fighting a just war fulfilling God's will, those who resisted were necessarily sinning. War was at least partly seen as punitive rather than a more classical political struggle and the defeated could rightly be chastised for having had the impudence to put up a fight.

The Saracens, similarly, found themselves in a position where they could also see their cause as doubly warranted in the religious sense in that they protected their faith from the assaults of Christianity, and that in fighting they were upholding the value of *jihad* which, as a result of the Crusades, came to be increasingly understood in its military, faith-defending dimension. In very theoretical terms, there is still no reason why even a holy war should be fought that differently from temporal wars (ones in which, needless to say, personal passions may be equally aroused). Just war theorists have typically not 'advocated the use of unrestrained violence in the prosecution of religious war', the general tendency being 'toward a single, universalizable standard for military conduct' applicable in both 'political' and 'holy' wars, and 'presumably applicable to both believers and infidels'.[33] In practice, however, the religious zeal of the Crusades did sometimes make a difference and occasionally could be seen to have a direct impact on the likelihood of being made prisoner rather than, say, being executed.

The Crusades were certainly not primarily, or in fact significantly, proselytizing ventures.[34] Saladin, for example, is supposed to have said that 'one never saw a bad Christian become a good Saracen, nor a bad Saracen become a good Christian'[35] and St Thomas had similar reservations about forced conversions. However, the Crusades did involve the occasional, opportunistic efforts by both sides to convert the other. In practice, this meant that the defeated were at times taken prisoner only for so long as it took to offer them the possibility of abandoning their faith. It is hard to know how often this option was chosen, but the consequences either way were quite clear. Those who embraced the other's faith could be seen as simply switching sides and therefore in all likelihood no longer prisoners at all. However, they might then switch faith back if they returned to their camp. In many cases though, and in the conditions of the time, the option to switch faith was probably little more than a ritual prelude to the response that was sure to come in case of refusal: immediate execution.

On the Muslim side, respect for prisoners was at times uniquely tied up with the perceived offence made to Islam. When a raid was launched by the Franks against the Red Sea in 1183, for example, Saladin ordered every last prisoner to be killed because of the affront made to sacred sites (and the need to avoid leaving anyone alive who knew the way to them).[36]

Finally, because of the way the goals of the Crusades were formulated, it should be said that it was in their nature that they could never be fully won without a very permanent defeat of the enemy. The Crusades were not only potentially endless, but potentially absolutist in their drive to conquer once and for all. This was moderated in practice however by significant bouts of coexistence following victory, as in the Latin Kingdom for example.

The Impact of Traditions of Restraint in Warfare

Apart from the context in which they unfolded, traditions of restraint in war on each side also had their own internal weaknesses, and demonstrated what might be described as a communication problem.

First, the usages of war were at very different stages of development even when and where they were held to apply. Violence was endemic in much of Europe. The laws of war in Christendom were still in the early stages of formation and were restricted both functionally—for example, in the use of certain weapons such as the arch bow, certain practices such as siege warfare, or in the division of the spoils of war—and personally, in governing relations within a warrior class rather than standing for some more general concept of humanity. It was widely considered that the victors had a right of life and death upon the captured, so that almost any atrocity was conceivable. Rules such as those applicable in times of siege certainly seem quite gruesome in relation to contemporary norms. As far as the Byzantine Empire is concerned, it is fair to say that there was hardly any tradition that resembled the laws of war, although the Empire did in due course develop practices relating to prisoners, including the idea of their liberation once the conflict was over.[37]

Islam, by contrast, did possess a more sophisticated tradition of what was to be done in warfare in general, and how to treat prisoners in particular, founded on a strong concept of restraint.[38] The Quran explicitly enjoins believers to 'fight in the way of Allah with those who fight with you, and do not exceed the limits'.[39] Instructions had been given by Mohammed's successor Caliph Abu-Bakr (573–634) to the first Syrian expedition that civilians and civilian property should be respected. The 1280 Villiyet was an ambitious attempt at codifying what was, by then, a tradition of restraint in war stretching back a century, which prohibited torture and mutilation of prisoners as well as perfidious and disloyal actions. It also more explicitly decreed that belligerents could 'fight with (enemies) until there is no persecution...but if they desist, then there should be no hostility'.[40] On top of this it also anticipated prisoner exchanges.[41] Indeed, the Quran went as far as to suggest that prisoners could be 'set free as a favour'.[42] Of course, even Islam was occasionally quite ambivalent about its humanitarianism (as are, one might argue, the contemporary laws of war), and could simultaneously justify great licence in the administration of violence. The Prophet himself, after all, had ordered the execution of prisoners evacuated at the battle of Badr,[43] and generally executing prisoners was considered legal under various Muslim traditions. But on the whole, such instances were often disapproved of, and at least a solid theological basis existed for good treatment of prisoners.

In both cases, regardless of their normative development, the issue would have been whether the rules made any difference on the battlefield and beyond—a problem very familiar to contemporary laws of war. Perhaps more importantly, what was at stake was not so much the level of development of norms as their *status*. It is interesting to speculate what difference it made that most relevant norms were *religious* in essence, and as such a far cry from contemporary international law, which has long seen in its purported secularism a significant progress towards making the laws of war applicable to all.[44] Contrary to some modern simplifications, the impact of religious norms on warfare is perhaps best described as ambiguous. On the one hand and with all other things being equal, such norms may be held in higher credit and reverence than those on waging war. As Caroline Evans put it in a remarkable study on the impact of religion on humanitarian law, religion 'can add an important moral or emotional dimension to reasons for compliance with international law'.[45] Indeed, there is evidence that Saladin, a follower of the Chafeite school, frequently consulted with religious advisers on the treatment of Frank prisoners. Contrary to contemporary bases for the laws of war in positive law on inter-state commitments, at least a religious basis binds each individual directly. For the ordinary foot-soldier, it probably made a difference that in violating certain usages he would be committing a sin or that Allah (who 'does not love those who exceed the limits') would 'hear and know',[46] as opposed to violating a commitment undertaken internationally by his state.[47] In some ways, one can see the contemporary laws of war as continuously striving to re-enchant respect for restraint in warfare, in circumstances where the fact that one's state has ratified an international humanitarian law treaty will probably have little mobilizing force.

On the downside, the religious basis of restraints in warfare created a risk that they would be seen as applying primarily if not exclusively within a community of faith. The Christian tradition of restraint in warfare, in particular, existed mostly as an attempt to regulate the relations of distinct secular powers within Christendom. The European laws of war emerged as a way to tame the practice of war by one Christian group against another. As is well known, for instance, the Lateran Council of 1139 made it clear 'that deadly art of the crossbow and longbow, hateful to God, is forbidden'.[48] What is less well known and is in fact often conveniently forgotten is that it was forbidden 'as against Christians and all other Catholics'.[49] It could, in other words, be used quite freely against non-Christians and was in fact used with considerable success against Turcoman and Arabic horsemen. At any rate, what offended God was precisely not that heretics, pagans, or unbelievers might be butchered, but that fellow believers'—'baptized Christians' blood'[50]—would be sacrificed. Institutions such as the 'Peace of God' that are associated with the gradual pacification of war were inherently reserved to war between Christians.

The same thing could not be said about the Islamic tradition of warfare, which, perhaps because it was more rooted in the Quran, was also couched in broader moral terms, which lent themselves to a more universal application. The perception was that in a religious war, sinning would actually make one weaker.[51] However, it is relevant in assessing why courteous treatment was at first extended to Christian captives and then occasionally withdrawn, that Islam did seem to contemplate a requirement of reciprocity ('[s]o as long as they are true to you, be true to them'), which would very often have been frustrated.

In that respect, it is probably not irrelevant that the Christian laws of war were already largely discriminatory 'internally' to the extent that they applied above all between nobles, at the expense of the peasantry. As one author points out, '[T]he discriminatory character of these rules allowed medieval knights to behave with charity toward one another and toward other persons of acceptable status and class. Concurrently, these medieval knights could behave with utter ruthlessness toward non-Christians during the Crusades.'[52] The Crusades were therefore not so abnormally different from the ordinary violent practices of the Middle Ages—but rather simply a particularly brutal case thereof.

Finally, modes of enforcement of these early laws of war were largely circumscribed within a theological framework which could only have any meaning for particular believers (although within that community they would have had a significant impact). For example, the common penalty for violating usages of war was excommunication or even anathema (in the case of use of the crossbow). Anathema, or 'major excommunication', is interesting because it meant a complete exclusion from the Church (rather than simply from attendance at worship), and was thus the punishment most associated with heretics. To have used the crossbow against fellow Christians, therefore, was quite literally to have excluded oneself from the Church, and one can imagine the threat was quite potent.

CONCLUSION: THE FRAGILITY OF RESTRAINT

To conclude, it may be worth pointing out that some of the key factors affecting respect for restraint in warfare operated at the intersection of *jus ad bellum* and *jus in bello*. Certainly, the perceived absolute legitimacy of the Crusades or the response to them at the level of *jus ad bellum*, combined with the absence of a common normative language of *jus in bello*, could in some cases produce a particularly lethal, brutal, and unrestrained result. This is nowhere more clear than on the Christian side in the dubious fusion of both strands of the regulation of war in the so-called *bellum Romanum*. The Crusades borrowed heavily from Roman thought on such issues. Roman thinkers had developed a fairly sophisticated concept of war's justness, but tended to see war as relatively unrestrained otherwise. They had, in particular, conceived of a war against barbarians as particularly limitless. This was the so called *bellum Romanum* or *guerre mortelle* ('war to the death') which was, in theory at least, the most violent of wars, one in which the defeated could be killed or enslaved. Medieval thinkers reinterpreted this idea in light of the Crusades and understood it as legitimizing almost all means against the infidel 'other'. The idea of the non-Roman enemy was reinterpreted as meaning non-Christian, so that Muslims (or heretics) were often described not only as legitimate enemies but as almost absolute ones.[53]

The price to be paid for the increasing regulation of war within Christendom, therefore, seems to have been the absence of any war-constraining rules in the relationship of Christian forces with the Saracens. In the same way, the Crusades can be analysed more generally as a redirecting of internal Christian violence towards Christianity's exterior.[54] The regulation of violence that was starting to gather strength within Christianity was not matched by a corresponding regulation of violence in the relations of Crusaders with non-Christian enemies. In fact, it is almost as if a higher unleashing of violence in the Crusades was precisely the consequence of violence having been increasingly regulated within Christianity.

However, nor was boundless violence inevitable. It seems, in particular, that Islam was better at two things. First, the legitimacy of the war that the Saracens fought to defend themselves during the Crusades did not seem to translate into any idea that they could mistreat prisoners. This may be because the Quran, although not incorporating a strict distinction between *jus ad bellum* and *jus in bello*, did seem to subsume the two under a more general principle of proportionality.[55] Second, Islamic jurisprudence had less of a problem with extending the protection of restraint in war to infidels, something which fitted well with the personal magnanimity of some rulers.

A few lessons can be learnt from these distant episodes. One of them is that vigorous thinking about the justness of one's cause is not incompatible with restraint in warfare, as long as the two are indeed distinguished. Another is that it is not religion per se that is the problem, but the complex articulation of religion with the issue of war. Forms of religious thought that produce exclusion and designate certain individuals as beyond the realm of protection will produce condemnable excesses, but it hardly seems worth pointing out that religion does not have a monopoly on such discriminatory practices. Finally, whilst secular laws of war provide a common bridge between different traditions that may otherwise find it difficult to communicate, they also do so at the cost of uprooting respect for the laws of war from faith, in favour of the need to respect an abstract international legality, which can create problems of its own.

NOTES

Research for this chapter was made possible by the funding of the Canada Research Chair Program. I would like to thank Daria Boyarchuk for her research assistance.

1. Jim Bradbury, *The medieval siege* (Woodbridge: Boydell Press, 1992), 217.
2. In general, many prisoners were only prisoners so long as it took to execute them. See
   G. I. A. D. Draper, M. A. Meyer, and H. McCoubrey (eds.), *Reflections on law and*

armed conflicts: The selected works on the laws of war by the late Professor Colonel G.I.A. D. Draper, OBE (The Hague: Kluwer Law International, 1998), 17.

3. Quoted in Ronald C. Finucane, *Soldiers of the faith: Crusaders and Moslems at war* (New York: St Martin's Press, 1983), 99.
4. Nicolae Iorga, *Philippe de Mézières, 1327–1405, et la croisade au XIVe siècle* (Paris: É. Bouillon, 1896), 473.
5. Ambroise quoted in Finucane, *Soldiers of the faith*, 98.
6. It must be noted that many of the captured were not actually combatants at all, but simply civilians living on the land, whether they were related to warring armies or not. The fate of such non-combatants was quite often that of being sent into slavery.
7. See, for example, the account of Thomas of Marle's behavior by Guibert of Nogent quoted in Jonathan Riley-Smith (ed.), *The Oxford illustrated history of the Crusades* (Oxford: Oxford University Press, 1995), 15.
8. Lewis A. M. Sumberg, 'The "Tafurs" and the First Crusade', *Medieval Studies*, 21 (1959), 224–46.
9. Finucane, *Soldiers of the faith*, 106.
10. Bradbury, *The medieval siege*, 81.
11. Finucane, *Soldiers of the faith*, 106.
12. Ibid., 110–11.
13. Ibid., 111.
14. Lev Yaacov, 'Prisoners of war during the Fatimid-Ayyubid wars with the crusaders', in M. Gervers and J. M. Powell (eds.), *Tolerance and intolerance: Social conflict in the age of Crusades* (Syracuse, NY: Syracuse University Press, 2001), 17.
15. George A. Campbell, *The Crusades* (London: Duckworth, 1935), 326–7.
16. Finucane, *Soldiers of the faith*, 107.
17. Bradbury, *The medieval siege*, 191.
18. Finucane, *Soldiers of the faith*, 110.
19. Stanley Lane-Poole, *Saladin and the fall of the kingdom of Jerusalem* (New York: G.P. Putnam's Sons, 1898), 371–2.
20. Jean Pictet, 'Development and principles of international humanitarian law', course given in July 1982 at the University of Strasbourg as part of the courses organized by the International Institute of Human Rights (Dordrecht: Martinus Nijhoff, 1985), 14.
21. Ibid.
22. François Bugnion, 'Just war, war of aggression and international humanitarian law', *International Review of the Red Cross*, 847/84 (2002), 523–46.
23. LeRoy Walters, 'The just war and the crusade: Antitheses or analogies?', *Monist*, 57 (1973), 593.
24. However, I would tend to view this phenomenon as largely circumstantial in a context where the laws of war are somehow always under threat, rather than an intrinsic feature of any attempt to uphold a strong concept of *jus ad bellum*.
25. '...one aim was the liberation of people, the baptized members of the churches, the other was the liberation of a place.' See Jonathan Riley-Smith, *The First Crusade and the idea of crusading* (Philadelphia, PA: University of Pennsylvania Press, 1986), 18.
26. Ibid.
27. John Gilchrist, 'The Papacy and war against the "Saracens" 795–1216', *International History Review*, X (1988), 174 97.
28. Jean-Jacques Rousseau, *Du contrat social* (Paris: Flammarion, 2001), chs. I, IV.

29. The vows typically involved the wearing of a cross and had the effect of putting crusaders temporarily under the jurisdiction of the Church as ecclesiastics. They also meant that those who had promised to join the Crusades but then failed to do so could be excommunicated.

30. Jonathan Riley-Smith, *What were the Crusades?* (3rd edn.; Basingstoke: Palgrave Macmillan, 2002).

31. '. . . they do not fear to shed their own blood as martyrs, and thus rejoice eventually to end their lives for God alone.' See Julio González, *El reino de castilla en la época de Alfonso VIII*, vol. 2 (Madrid: Consejo Superior de Investigacio Científicas, 1960), 745–7.

32. Gilchrist, 'The Papacy and the war against the "Saracens" ', 192.

33. Walters, 'The just war and the crusade', 591.

34. Benjamin Z. Kedar, *Crusade and mission: European approaches towards the Muslims* (Princeton, NJ: Princeton University Press, 1984), 99. See also Elizabeth Siberry, 'Missionaries and crusaders, 1095–1274: Opponents or allies?', *Church History*, 20 (1983), 103–10. There was strong resistance among the Crusaders to seeking to convert Muslims, based on both religious and pragmatic considerations. See Alan Forey, 'The military orders and the conversion of Muslims in the twelfth and thirteenth centuries', *Journal of Medieval History*, 28/1 (2002), 1–22. As presented in Forey's article, this does not mean that there were not pressures for military orders to take missionary activity more seriously.

35. Jean sire de Joinville and Geoffroi de Villehardouin, *Chronicles of the Crusades*, trans. with an introduction M. R. B. Shaw (Baltimore, MD: Penguin Classics, 1963), 246.

36. Malcolm Cameron Lyons and D. E. P. Jackson, *Saladin: The politics of the Holy War* (Cambridge: CUP, 1984), 186–7.

37. Michel de Taube, 'L'apport de Byzance au développement du droit international occidental', *RCADI*, 67 (1939), 316–28.

38. See for example Ahmed Rechid, 'L'Islam et le droit des gens', *RCADI*, 60/2 (1937), 449–61.

39. The Quran, 2. 190.

40. The Quran, 2. 193.

41. See the Quran 47. 4–5; see also Yaacov, 'Prisoners of war', 19–20.

42. The Quran, 47. 4.

43. Quoted by Yaacov, 'Prisoners of war', 13.

44. James Turner Johnson, *The holy war idea in western and Islamic traditions* (University Park: Pennsylvania State University Press, 1997).

45. Carolyn Evans, 'The double-edged sword: Religious influences on international humanitarian law', *Melbourne Journal of International Law*, 6/1 (2005), 3.

46. The Quran, 2. 190, 244.

47. In fact, at least one branch of contemporary international humanitarian law has arguably been tempted by, on the one hand, attempts to 're-enchant' commitment to them by emphasizing basic canons of morality or honor, and on the other hand, making obedience to the laws of war a matter of personal responsibility (via international criminal law).

48. Quoted in Draper, Meyer, and McCoubrey (eds.), *Reflections on law and armed conflicts*, 15 n. 3.

49. Ibid.

50. Quoted in Tomaž Mastnak, *Crusading peace: Christendom, the Muslim world, and Western political order* (Berkeley: University of California Press, 2002), 334.

51. See Rechid, 'L'Islam et le droit des gens', 452. Rechid quotes Khalife Omar: 'Je te recommande à toi et à tes soldats de craindre Dieu par-dessus toutes choses. La crainte de Dieu est la meilleure munition contre l'ennemi et le meilleure stratège dans la guerre.... Les fautes d'une armée lui nuisent plus que l'ennemi.... Nous leur sommes inférieurs en nombre et en équipement ; si nous leur sommes égaux en désobéissance à Dieu, ils auront la supériorité sur nous ; autrement nous les vaincrons par notre supériorité morale, et non par la force.'

52. Edwin Smith, 'The laws of war and humanitarian law', *Global Governance*, 9/1 (2003), 115.

53. As Finucane put it, 'Religious rivalry, when added to all the other marks by which the "enemy" is identified, only widens the gap: the enemy becomes something not really human; the likelihood of torture, atrocities and—even in a military sense—pointless slaughter increases. In the crusading era there is ample evidence of this zeal, which sometimes exploded into throbbing fanaticism and glee at the destruction of the enemy whether Christian, Moslem or Jew' (Finucane, *Soldiers of the faith*, 90).

54. Some contemporaries were relatively clear about this connection. Urban II is generally credited with the idea that the Crusade against the infidel could act as a sort of outlet for the warring passions of Christendom; see John Barnie, *War in medieval English society: Social values in the Hundred Years War, 1337–99* (Ithaca, NY: Cornell University Press, 1974) 124, 130. As Draper put it, 'the Church had, as a price for clearing Western Europe of turbulent knights in the service of the Cross and imposing vows upon such men, to accept much of their evil way of life and their love of fighting'; see G. I. A. D. Draper, 'The interaction of Christianity and chivalry in the historical development of the law of war', *International Review of the Red Cross*, 46 (1965), 3–23. On Philippe of Mézières' views, see Norman Housley, 'The mercenary companies: The Papacy and the Crusades, 1356–1378', *Traditio*, 38 (1982), 253–80.

55. See the Quran, 2. 190.

3

Prisoners in Early Modern European Warfare

Peter H. Wilson

EARLY MODERN WARFARE

The place of prisoners in early modern European warfare is acknowledged as an under-researched subject.[1] The topic merits a few pages at best in general discussions, with the partial exception of the captivity of British and German soldiers during the American Revolutionary Wars.[2] This brief sketch concentrates on identifying general trends and key questions. It ranges from the late fifteenth into the early nineteenth centuries, with the main focus from roughly 1580 to 1760. Discussion will be restricted to Europe, excluding the European experience elsewhere in the world, but it will include conflicts against the Muslim Ottoman Turks. For reasons of space, it will also exclude naval warfare that, in any case, involved far fewer prisoners than land warfare.[3]

NUMBERS

Any attempt to calculate prisoner numbers encounters problems general to all early modern statistics, but the available data reveals some interesting patterns across time (see Table 3.1). Prisoners remained overwhelmingly a feature of defeat. There were instances during the Thirty Years War (1618–48) when men were captured from the victorious side, but their numbers were rarely recorded and only feature in reports if prominent officers were taken. Prisoners appear more frequent among the victors during the eighteenth century. One list of 117 major battles between 1688 and 1746 includes sixty-six involving prisoners on the defeated side, compared to only ten cases where the victor also lost men this way. All ten occurred after 1718 and represented an average of just over 11 per cent of the victor's total loss. To put these into what was probably the common relationship, the victorious Prussians captured over ten times as many men as the defeated Austrians in the Second Silesian War (1744–5).[4]

Table 3.1 indicates that the proportion lost as prisoners was lower than previously assumed, but still significant.[5] Prisoners also declined, as a proportion

Table 3.1 Prisoners as a proportion of defeated force's losses, 1618–1746

Period of conflict	Battles in sample	Defeated army size (aggregate)	Defeated losses (aggregate)	POWs	POWs as percentage of losses	POWs as percentage of army
1618–48	43	553,806	271,446	103,151	47.4	18.6
1618–34	24	302,499	106,221	44,466	41.9	15.0
1635–48	17	251,307	111,225	58,685	52.8	23.3
1688–1714	43	1,014,500	259,800	100,600	38.7	9.9
1717–46	23	603,700	117,040	40,688	34.8	6.7

Sources: Peter H. Wilson, *Europe's tragedy: The Thirty Years War* (London: Penguin, 2009); David G. Chandler, *The art of war in the age of Marlborough* (2nd edn.; Tunbridge Wells: Spellmount, 1990), 302–7.

both of the defeated party's total losses and of its army. Closer analysis reveals that this was not a uniform trend, as the highest proportion was lost during the later stages of the Thirty Years War. Comparative data for sieges is also available, though this is less complete than for battle losses for the earlier seventeenth century. Of fifty-four major sieges during 1688–1745, eleven were abandoned by the attackers, while another twenty-two ended with the defeated garrison granted free passage or some other negotiated settlement. The remaining twenty-one involved an average of around half the defeated side becoming prisoners, while the remainder were killed or died of disease.[6]

Concentration on bloody battles and sieges obviously only provides an approximate guide to the number of prisoners in relation to those serving during a conflict. Early modern armies suffered proportionally far higher attrition from desertion and disease than those engaged in later wars. One general study concludes two men died of disease for every one killed in action between the seventeenth and early nineteenth centuries.[7] Some campaigns saw far higher losses, especially those in Hungary and the Balkans, which were notorious for malaria and typhus. The Saxon contingent serving in Greece against the Ottomans in 1685–6 lost sixty-two men from disease for every one killed in action.[8] Against this, however, must be set the numerous prisoners taken in the raids and other small engagements making up what contemporaries called 'little war' alongside major battles and sieges. Only one-third of the 45,664 Austrians and Saxons captured by Prussia in the Second Silesian War were taken in the three main battles. Almost as many were taken when the large Austrian garrison surrendered Prague in 1744, while the rest were seized in small actions.[9] Information is more complete for the Seven Years War (1756–63), suggesting prisoners formed a quarter of each combatant's total loss.[10]

CIRCUMSTANCE

The data indicate that we should pay close attention to the circumstances under which soldiers became prisoners. The likelihood of individuals being captured depended greatly on their proximity to the enemy, unlike the risk of disease that could strike home garrisons and other less exposed units. Of the 724 men serving in the Württemberg artillery train during the relatively uneventful 1760 campaign against Prussia in the Seven Years War, only 1 was captured, compared to 59 deserters and 6 deaths.[11] The Hessen-Darmstadt infantry regiment with the imperial army in the War of the Spanish Succession (1701–14) lost 178 men from its initial strength of around 850 during the 1702 campaign, including only 12 prisoners.[12] No prisoners were recorded in its returns for 1709–10, and only 9 compared to 30 dead, 131 deserted, and 2 executed across 1711–12.[13] The 1713 campaign saw more serious fighting as the regiment participated in fruitless operations to save Landau being captured by the French: 118 men were lost from an initial 782, including 12 prisoners and 15 recorded as missing who could well have been captured, or additional to the 13 listed as deserted.[14] None of the 4,521 Württembergers serving the emperor in 1716–21 is recorded as having been captured, despite the unit's loss of 3,039 men.[15] By comparison, 584 prisoners were among the 1,332 men lost by the Würzburg infantry in Austrian service during 1759 because one of the four battalions was caught unsupported and captured by the Prussians.[16]

Beyond general proximity, it is possible to distinguish two broad categories. More men were captured through negotiated surrender than individual capture. The former involved agreements by officers on behalf of their units that retained at least some cohesion, but whose situation appeared hopeless. They might be summoned by the enemy to surrender, or indicate their willingness by lowering their flags and weapons, or having the drummers beat the *chamade*, an internationally accepted signal used into the nineteenth century.[17] Negotiated surrender was most common in sieges when garrisons capitulated once they had run out of supplies or their main defences had been breached. It also occurred in the field where all or part of an army found its retreat blocked by a geographical feature, or was surrounded. Less commonly, troops surrendered en masse when they were no longer in a condition to fight, such as the starving Scots who were too weak to resist Cromwell at Dunbar in 1650.[18]

Individual capture was less organized and generally involved fewer prisoners, though overall numbers could still be significant in the aftermath of serious defeats. It involved individual bargains between captor and a prospective captive who might be cornered, or otherwise unable to escape. Men would cry for 'pardon' or 'quarter', the accepted terms for mercy. This situation generally occurred during the final stages of an action, as one side tried to disengage, or its units began to disintegrate in flight. It was also common in ambushes and other episodes of 'little war'.

Two further factors were significant. The preponderance of infantry among prisoners was a specifically early modern feature, reflecting military organization. Men on foot not only found it harder to escape than those on horseback, but were more vulnerable with the development of mass, disciplined tactics. Early modern handguns and close-order weapons like pikes were only fully effective when used by large, disciplined formations. Once these lost cohesion, individual soldiers

were ill-equipped to defend themselves. This probably explains the higher proportion of prisoners taken in the later stages of the Thirty Years War when the
numbers and, often, the quality of the infantry declined. Whereas cavalry formed
only around a quarter of total strength in the early stages, horsemen represented
half or more by the 1640s. Unlike the early battles where cavalry units were
interspersed with large infantry formations, they were now massed on the flanks.
If these broke, they could generally escape, but not the infantry they abandoned in
the centre. Whereas only a quarter of the 4,800 imperial cavalry were captured at
the second battle of Rheinfelden in 1638, 1,800 of the 2,600 infantry fell into
enemy hands.[19]

Whether a man was already wounded also affected his chances of being
captured. This is one of the factors complicating quantification of prisoners.
The numbers of defeated dead were greatly increased by the abandoned wounded
who were either murdered by the victors or left to die. There are examples of
captured wounded being treated in the sixteenth and seventeenth centuries, but
no systematic recording of the numbers involved or the care provided. Information is better for the eighteenth century.[20]

THE QUESTION OF AUTHORITY

Both negotiated surrender and individual capture raised the question of authority to both request and accept quarter. The early modern period is characterized
by repeated attempts by political authorities to monopolize and regulate all
aspects of warfare. This process was driven partly by monarchs' desire to assert
authority over lesser, intermediary lords and was reflected in the gradual extinc-
tion of the right to claim prisoners as personal property. By the eighteenth
century, all captives along with symbols like flags and other war material had to
be handed over to the state. Regulation was also promoted by the requirements of
the new organized, disciplined mass tactics. Formations were at risk if individuals
broke ranks to seize prisoners or plunder. This probably explains the coincidence
of orders prohibiting the taking of prisoners with the emergence of characteristically early modern tactics. The Swiss, who pioneered the combination of shock
with limited firepower in the pike phalanx, were notorious for giving no quarter.
Contemporaries distinguished between 'good' and 'bad' war whether prisoners
were permitted. The Swiss exploited their reputation as a terror tactic, but
generally allowed prisoners once the enemy had broken.[21] Concern for discipline
and cohesion lay behind the 'no quarter' orders that were still occasionally issued
into the eighteenth century.[22]

The imposition of hierarchical command over formed, disciplined units also
curbed the right of ordinary soldiers to surrender. Surrender and desertion were
clearly often related, since both involved a similar desire to escape unpleasant
situations. Ulrich Bräker, a Swiss peasant duped into joining the Prussian army
just before the Seven Years War, left his regiment during the battle of Lobositz

(1756) only to be captured by the Austrians.[23] The very cohesion that rulers and generals desired could be turned against them by soldiers who forced their officers to surrender. The commanders of the imperial garrison of Duderstadt surrendered because they feared their mutinous troops more than the besiegers in 1632.[24] Just how common this was before 1650 is difficult to determine, because some commanders used it to excuse not resisting longer.

While rulers denied ordinary soldiers the right to negotiate, they were frequently displeased by the arrangements concluded by their officers. All three commanders of the French border fortresses—surrendering quickly in 1636—fled the country or went into hiding to escape their king's wrath.[25] Even if a ruler accepted an officer's decision to capitulate, disputes could arise over which troops could be included in the terms. The Bohemian rebel leader Count Thurn was captured at the second battle of Steinau (1633) while serving the Swedes. He was held by Wallenstein until he agreed to include all the other Swedish garrisons in Silesia in the terms of his surrender. The units in Liegnitz and Glogau accepted this, but those in six other towns refused, arguing Thurn lacked authority over them.[26]

THE ACT OF SURRENDER

Surrender negotiations were fraught with danger. Commanders who capitulated too readily risked dishonour. Thurn was widely criticized for having traded his life for the Swedish garrisons. Yet, prolonged resistance risked losing the chance of good terms. Becoming a prisoner was a frightening and potentially dangerous experience. While the vanquished faced the greatest uncertainty, the position of victor was also not without risk. Soldiers accepting surrender needed to be sure their opponent no longer posed a threat. Yet, this entailed the defeated party giving up their remaining defensive assets, especially fortified positions, weapons, and tactical formations. Both sides needed a means to communicate despite their recent bloodletting. This explains the significance attached to the formal process of parleying, such as beating the *chamade* during surrender negotiations. Generally, the defeated side retained its arms and positions while its representatives conferred with enemy officers. The terms would be written, signed, and copies would be exchanged in an accelerated version of the peace negotiations ending contemporary conflicts. Various deadlines were agreed for this process, allowing time for both sides to adjust mentally to the new situation. Deliberate delays were a particular feature of siege warfare that often involved considerable hardship for both sides, especially if the besiegers also ran out of food. The defeated garrison was often allowed two, even three days to prepare its departure. Various outworks and access points would be relinquished in the meantime to prevent resistance being resumed. These positions were generally handed over to the victor who usually occupied them with units least likely to bear a grudge against the defeated garrison.

These rituals developed during the sixteenth century and were already common in the Thirty Years War. This point needs to be re-emphasized, since it does not fit the standard, yet misleading, chronology of accepted military history that portrays the period 1517–1648 as one of bloody 'religious wars' followed by allegedly more limited 'cabinet wars' in the next 150 years. It also indicates that considerable efforts were already made to curb, if not eliminate, the practice of killing prisoners.

KILLING PRISONERS

The question of killing prisoners, along with massacres generally, remains under-researched.[27] Motive and intent can prove as controversial today as they were for contemporaries. The convention that a man should not be killed once his life had been spared was clearly well established long before its incorporation by Grotius in his famous legal text in 1625. It was part of the general 'laws of war' (*bellum iustrum*) that evolved in medieval Christian Europe. Always important, these assumed new significance with attempts by early modern rulers to monopolize war, since it made questions of proper conduct and just cause central to political legitimacy at a time when the state's authority over matters of religion and regional affairs were still contested by its subjects.

Systematic, deliberate mass murder of captives was relatively rare. Where it did occur, such cold-blooded brutality generally involved some element of religious or ethnic differences between captor and captive.[28] These differences were relative, not fixed. For example, Irish Catholic prisoners were regularly ill-treated by their Protestant English captors during the sixteenth and seventeenth centuries, but do not appear to have been particularly singled out when captured on the continent in Spanish or French service. Russians suffered through hostility towards their Orthodox faith and the widespread belief that they were not fully 'European'.

These differences were still more pronounced in Christian–Muslim conflict in the Balkans and the Mediterranean, since both faiths prohibited the enslavement of believers whilst permitting that of infidels. Any analysis is complicated by the rhetoric generated by this mutual antagonism that created an image of 'the other' as barbarous and treacherous. Massacres of fugitives and captured garrisons continued into the eighteenth century, but it is clear that the differences between intra-Christian and Christian–Muslim conflict were not as great as Habsburg and other propagandists maintained. Rich prisoners were already exchanged for ransom in the sixteenth century, while the surrender and evacuation of garrisons was usually handled after 1683 according to the same rules prevailing elsewhere in Europe. The principal difference was not so much the likelihood of death, but rather that of enslavement. Slavery had long been a major feature of captive-taking in the ancient and medieval world. It continued in the Mediterranean, Balkans, and Eastern Europe throughout the later Middle Ages, though on a reduced scale. The rise of two powerful, universalist empires at either end of the Mediterranean—Spanish Habsburgs in the west and Ottomans to the east— prompted a resurgence around 1500. One estimate places the number of Muslim slaves in sixteenth-century Italy at around 40,000, while the Turks carried off 8 per cent of the Lower Austrian population in their invasion of 1683.[29]

Enslavement declined from the later seventeenth century, thanks partly to demographic growth that decreased captives' economic value, but also to the greater naval power of Christian European states that ended the activities of the Barbary corsairs. The introduction of new warship designs to replace the oared galley in the Mediterranean was a lesser, additional factor since navies no longer needed slaves or criminals to power their vessels.

Prisoner killing in conflicts between Christians rarely appears systematic or coordinated. Wounded soldiers were often murdered after a battle, or simply left to die. Sometimes this was organized, as after Culloden (1746) when wounded Jacobites were deliberately sought out and butchered.[30] More usually it occurred as victorious soldiers, their dependants, and local inhabitants searched the dead and dying for plunder. Peasants frequently murdered stragglers, especially fol- lowing the rout of an army. However, the highest casualties generally occurred in massacres during or after the capture of a town. While the Cromwellian atrocities at Drogheda and Wexford (both 1649) are the best known in British history, the worst incident was the capture of Magdeburg by imperial troops in 1631 when over 20,000 people died, most burnt alive or suffocated as the city was destroyed by fire.

These events were controversial at the time, but conformed to the broadly accepted laws of war that allowed soldiers to plunder towns captured after rejecting offers to accept surrender. These conventions became increasingly sophisticated and standardized in the seventeenth century, relating the gener- osity of the terms offered to the number of times the defenders refused to submit.[31] Those agreeing to an initial summons or after only brief resistance could expect 'free passage', or the right to march out with their weapons, belongings, and non-combatant dependants to join the nearest friendly force. Further refusals to surrender might mean the besiegers would oblige a defeated garrison to lay down its arms before departing, or agree not to fight for six months or more once it had left. The final chance usually came when a breach had been shot in the inner wall and the besiegers were ready to storm the place. Garrisons that surrendered at this point were most likely to end up captives, especially in the eighteenth century. Those continuing to resist were considered fair game if the city was taken. Emotional and practical factors lay behind this. Long resistance increased the besiegers' own casualties and frustration, building up desires for revenge. It was also very difficult to control attacking troops once they broke into a town. There was usually only one officer to every hundred or more men prior to the 1620s and even in the eighteenth century rarely more than one to every fifty. Assaults were often launched at night and once in a town, attackers frequently encountered booby traps or were shot at from buildings.

Such massacres continued after 1800, notably during the Peninsular War (1808–14), but declined gradually from the mid-seventeenth century. Humanitarian considerations may have played a part, but so did improvements in fortifications as major settlements acquired several concentric rings of defences. These demarcated stages in surrender negotiations, as offers would be made as the outer works fell, in contrast to the poorly fortified towns whose walls were swiftly breached and assaulted in the sixteenth and early seventeenth centuries. By the later seventeenth century, it had become less common to place strategic value on defending small or poorly fortified settlements.

Massacres in sixteenth- and seventeenth-century wars are often explained by reference to religious animosities. Confessional differences were certainly cited to excuse atrocities and could influence decisions for deliberate murder. A good example is Louis XIII's decision to break Huguenot resistance by ordering the execution or expulsion of all 3,000 inhabitants of Privas in 1629, the act that finally ended France's long cycle of confessionally coloured 'Wars of Religion'. However, the confessional composition of early modern armies was hardly homogeneous, while there are numerous cases of troops killing fellow believers. Swedish soldiers entering Donauwörth in 1632 killed welcoming Protestant burghers, as well as the surrendering Catholic garrison.[32]

Fear of reprisal generally exercised a moderating effect. The English Parliament suspended its prohibition against taking Irish prisoners in 1644, after Prince Rupert strung up thirteen of its soldiers in revenge for the hanging of a similar number of Irishmen.[33] This lesson often had to be relearned in each successive conflict with an initial period of brutality followed by more moderate treatment. The general trend was nonetheless towards sparing the lives of surrendering soldiers.

POLITICAL IMPLICATIONS

Acceptance of an enemy's entitlement to surrender represented a major step in revising the laws of war inherited from medieval Christendom. Early modern war-making rested on the principle of inequality between belligerents, reflecting the ideals of singular truth and justice. For Christians to be absolved from the sin of killing, a war had to be 'just'. Since justice was not considered as relative, only one side could be right, denying any legitimacy to their opponent's cause. The situation was complicated by the contested nature of state authority, with various social groups, religious minorities, and regions challenging rulers' claims to decide their affairs. In the absence of a monopoly on violence, rulers relied on subject lords, intermediary bodies, and vassal provinces to provide at least part of their forces. The distinctions between 'public' and 'private' were drawn differently, with a wide range of subjects enjoying the right to bear arms or even maintain formed troops.[34] The erosion of such rights and their replacement by a single monopoly of legitimate violence provided a major source of strife throughout the sixteenth and much of the seventeenth centuries. Together with confessional differences between rulers and ruled, these problems were the principal causes of the numerous rebellions and civil wars. A final factor was the changing theory and practice of international relations, with the trend towards the modern system of formally equal interaction based on sovereign states. This process emerged within a framework that remained essentially hierarchical into the nineteenth century. Status within this system remained associated with symbolic and representational factors, like a ruler's formal rank, that only gradually gave way to a hierarchy grounded in material power.

The right of soldiers to surrender and their subsequent treatment was thus profoundly affected by the status of the power they served. Captured rebels were not invariably badly treated. Much depended on their form of military organization, their leaders' status, and the level of their own engagement in the politics of rebellion. Those involved in what historians generally term 'popular' movements often fared worse than the followers of rebellious aristocrats or formal representative bodies. Captured peasant rebels were often summarily executed, partly to deter others following their example. However, the heavy casualties also stemmed from the character of peasant armies that lacked the discipline to withstand artillery or cavalry charges in open battles. This was clearly demonstrated in the German Peasants War (1524–6), when thousands were massacred in the final stages of defeats by mercenaries hired by the princes. These incidents resembled the situation already discussed for the capture of towns: the peasants' lack of cohesion made it difficult for them to retain formation long enough to negotiate surrender once defeat became obvious. Those taken alive enjoyed a fair chance of survival. Of 3,471 Jacobites taken after Culloden, around 120 were executed, but a third of these seem to have been former Hanoverian deserters found in their ranks.[35]

The treatment of high-born rebels depended on the extent of state power and the prevailing political and legal culture. The prolonged series of civil wars plaguing France for nearly a century after 1562 were led by senior aristocrats, often close relations of the monarch. They were rarely executed if caught because the crown could not risk alienating their families. A similar situation prevailed in the Holy Roman Empire during the Thirty Years War, which the ruling Habsburg dynasty considered a rebellion. Like their French counterparts, German aristocrats led professional armies, not popular insurrections. Their soldiers were effectively granted combatant status, even if the crown contested the legitimacy of their cause. For example, the princes captured at Stadtlohn (1623) were handed over to Emperor Ferdinand II, who confiscated most of their land before pardoning them. Soldiers who had previously served the emperor or his Bavarian allies were executed as deserters, but the others were eventually released.[36]

The problem of captured irregulars was encountered well before the controversy surrounding the *francs tireurs* during the Franco-German War of 1870–1. Irregulars suffered from the same problems of legitimacy affecting rebels. Often they operated independently on their own account, though they could receive assistance from the side they inclined towards, or even formal authorization as in the case of privateers' preying on enemy shipping. Spontaneous or independent opposition from armed inhabitants was generally treated harshly. The Swedes faced serious resistance from Catholic peasants across southern and north-western Germany in 1633 that received support from hard-pressed imperial commanders. Up to 6,000 Alsatian peasants were cut down without mercy in just two weeks, while numerous villages were burnt as reprisals.[37] This problem persisted into the Napoleonic Wars, especially in forested or mountainous regions favouring irregular warfare. The Habsburgs and south-west German princes relied on local inhabitants to defend the Black Forest and Tirol against superior numbers of French invaders during the conflicts of 1672–1714, 1733–5, and again in the 1790s. Defence was formalized through militia structures and peasants received arms and usually some items of uniform. Much depended on how the militia behaved and whether they encountered the invaders in formal engagements or guerrilla warfare. The general tendency was towards both regularizing partisan operations and accepting such 'light troops' as full combatants. For example, the French granted combatant status to the pro-Habsburg Miquelet partisans in 1706, three years after fighting broke out in Spain.[38]

NON-COMBATANT PRISONERS

As the earlier discussion indicates, non-combatants were frequently captured in the vicinity of a defeated army or captured town. Many of these were the 'camp followers' accompanying sixteenth- and seventeenth-century armies. Neither they, nor local inhabitants, were fully 'civilian' in the modern sense. Camp followers fell under the 'articles of war' issued with growing regularity from the 1470s. All soldiers were obliged to swear obedience to these upon enlistment in an act that symbolized their new martial status. Alongside other aspects of discipline, the articles specified how soldiers were to treat non-combatants. They did not define a general category of civilians. Instead, soldiers were prohibited from ill-treating children, the elderly, and women, especially virgins.

The situation was further complicated by the ambiguities surrounding the role of camp followers, peasants, and townsfolk in war. First, virtually every European carried some weapon in daily life, even in peacetime. While these were mostly knives or cudgels, it was not uncommon by the seventeenth century for comparatively humble peasants to own firearms. Many also possessed rudimentary military training through the militia. Inhabitants often assisted soldiers defending their settlement. Peasants were conscripted to dig entrenchments and other military engineering. Camp followers already fell under martial law whilst with the army, and were sometimes called to assist operations.

The lack of a clear distinction between soldiers and civilians made proximity to military operations the key factor for non-combatant prisoners. The fate of those found in captured towns or on battlefields was generally determined by the same circumstances governing whether soldiers were killed or spared.

PRISONERS' VALUE

What happened to non-combatants after capture leads us to the question why people were made prisoners. It has been common to attribute monetary or material motives to the early modern period.[39] Ransom or slavery were certainly important incentives in the ancient and medieval world. Both persisted beyond 1500, though their form changed. Ransom was primarily a feature of individual capture, not mass surrender. Captives would trade their lives for money raised by their friends or relatives to obtain their release. This type of individual arrangement was ill-suited to both the needs of disciplined mass tactics and the claims of early modern states to monopolize war. Monarchs and senior officers sought to regulate ransom by the early sixteenth century. Royal instructions for the English expedition to France in 1513 stipulated that ransom demands were to be negotiated by the officers, who would take a cut from whatever was paid to the men who had taken the prisoners.[40]

The growing scale of early modern warfare also made it difficult for the older pattern of ransom to survive, since soldiers who remained in the field all year in wide-ranging operations found it harder to hold their captives. Ransom remained a feature where war more closely resembled banditry, such as in Hungary where the Habsburg and Ottoman border militias raided each others' settlements, carrying off captives for either extortion or slavery prior to 1699. Minor outposts sustained themselves during the Thirty Years War by raiding enemy or neutral territory for prisoners and supplies. However, this was already considered a regrettable expedient, employed because their home government was unable to pay them regularly. The Dutch garrison in Maastricht waylaid travellers and merchant convoys after 1632 because it was cut off from the main army north of the Rhine. The States-General eventually persuaded the commandant to desist, after protests from the other countries at the Westphalian peace congress that the garrison was disregarding the safe conduct agreed for diplomatic couriers.[41]

Ransom became restricted to senior officers who were held by the captor's government, not its soldiers, from the late sixteenth century. Soldiers who took such prisoners were now more likely to receive a small reward from their commander than a share in the actual ransom. The monetary element was already receding, since ransom demands increasingly reflected a captive's military value, rather than his ability to pay. Renowned generals like Torstensson, Horn, Taupadel, or Werth captured during the Thirty Years War were held for considerable periods not through lack of money, but because their monarch had not captured a general of equal reputation.

Ransom was displaced by hostage-taking that was integral to the phenomenon known as 'contributions'.[42] Armies extorted cash and supplies from neutral or enemy territory by threatening to destroy property. As it was rarely possible to raise these demands immediately, soldiers seized community leaders as hostages so that they did not need to detach units to ensure compliance. This practice persisted into the Napoleonic Wars. Material incentives did not disappear entirely, since prisoners were routinely robbed of their valuables at the point of capture or shortly after. This could still contain an element of direct extortion, as wounded men or fugitives offered inducements to victorious soldiers in return for assistance or sparing their lives.

In contrast to the fading monetary value, prisoners' cultural significance remained important. The ability to take a prisoner enhanced personal reputation, but became more restricted as the opportunities for individual capture declined relative to negotiated surrender. Nonetheless, the capture of senior officers remained a matter of prestige. Sixteenth- and seventeenth-century battle reports routinely list enemy dead and ordinary prisoners in rounded numbers in contrast to generals who appear by name and rank.[43]

The significance for ordinary soldiers is harder to judge, but they certainly participated in symbolic acts intended to humiliate a defeated foe. Such rituals would have reinforced collective identity amongst the victorious troops and provided a way of marking, even celebrating, their triumph. One example was to strip captives before releasing them, sometimes giving them shreds of their flags in mockery of their missing uniforms. In the sixteenth century it was common to give defeated garrisons white sticks to carry instead of their weapons as they marched out. Victorious generals could be particularly vindictive towards personal enemies.[44] Such practices appear much less frequently from the late seventeenth century, but it remained an important point of honour whether defeated officers were allowed to keep their swords.

While the cultural significance of prisoners requires further research, their military importance is abundantly clear. One aspect was the information that could be gleaned about the enemy's dispositions, strength, condition, and intentions. Interrogation was haphazard, largely dependent on how individual generals valued reconnaissance and information-gathering. Far more significant was the way in which prisoner-taking weakened the enemy's ability and will to resist. As the preliminary quantitative analysis suggests, the growing scale of warfare greatly increased the potential prisoner numbers and raised the question of what to do with them.

TREATMENT

One solution was to disarm and release the ordinary soldiers, while retaining officers for ransom, exchange, or, in the case of rebels, punishment. This was relatively common in the period 1500–1650. For example, Cromwell released around half the 10,000 Scots taken at Dunbar because they were so weak and emaciated they no longer posed a threat. The danger inherent in this practice was that the men would rejoin the enemy army. This risk was minimized to an extent by the logistical collapse frequently accompanying defeat that reduced the attraction of rejoining former comrades. Nonetheless, it was clearly a problem by the late sixteenth century when it had become customary to wage protracted wars, retaining armies for years at a stretch, rather than disbanding units at the end of the summer campaign and re-raising them the following spring.

Another option was to impose virtual captivity by requiring defeated soldiers to swear not to take up arms again within a specified period. The exact origins of this remain unclear, but it was probably related to late medieval penal practice whereby convicted felons were obliged to promise good behaviour and forswear revenge before being released. It was already fairly common during the Thirty Years War and standard practice by the eighteenth century. It had the additional advantage of relieving the captor of the burden of maintaining prisoners, whilst obliging the other side to continue paying soldiers it could not use. The consequences for the men involved were not always pleasant, especially if they were kept waiting in miserable conditions before redeployment.

A more common fate was to be pressed into the victor's ranks. Analysis of this phenomenon has been distorted by misunderstandings surrounding the mercenary character of early modern armies. The process was certainly not as smooth as often assumed.[45] A significant proportion of early modern soldiers were conscripts, either drafted through the militia or recruited in more comprehensive systems like those used by Sweden and Denmark. All volunteers were essentially mercenaries as they served for a bounty and pay. Most were their ruler's subjects. Though foreigners were numerous, depending on the army, they were not necessarily indifferent to the cause they fought for.

The attraction of pressing prisoners was threefold: it provided an immediate solution to the difficulty of holding large numbers of captives, and it obtained much-needed trained manpower for one army whilst denying it to the enemy. It could also be attractive to the prisoners themselves, often giving them access to food, shelter, and protection against a vengeful local population. Surrender terms often left it open to the defeated soldiers to join the victor. Article 7 of those agreed at the Parliamentarian defeat of Lostwithiel (1644) stated 'there shall be no inviting of Souldiers, but that such as will voluntarily come to His Majesties service shall not be hindered'.[46] It is clear that many Parliamentarians took the opportunity to join the Royalists rather than embark on the uncertain trek eastwards to find their main army. Around 3,000 of the 14,192 French and Bavarians captured at Blenheim joined the victorious allies and many other examples can be cited.

The practice was clearly open to abuse. The Swedes pressed entire imperial garrisons during their conquest of Pomerania and Mecklenburg in 1631, despite promising them free passage. The drawbacks swiftly became clear. Two-fifths of the Donauwörth garrison were forced into the Swedish army in April 1632, 'but being Papists of Bavaria, as soone as they smelt the smell of their Fathers houses in lesse than ten dayes they were all gone.'[47] The most spectacular and counter-productive case occurred at the start of the Seven Years War when Frederick II of Prussia captured virtually the entire Saxon army of 18,000 men. Entire regiments were simply stuck in Prussian uniforms and expected to fight against their former allies. Within five months most had escaped to form a 10,000 strong contingent in the French army.[48]

Frederick's failure may have contributed to the decline in pressing that is otherwise usually explained by the rise of nationalism and the concept of captives as citizens of an enemy state who could not be trusted.[49] Such considerations were certainly an important element of political discourse, but, as noted, doubts over loyalty were already present in the early seventeenth century. Other, more practical reasons were probably more significant. A combination of sustained demographic growth from the 1730s and improved state administration made it easier for governments to recruit their own subjects in sufficient numbers, lessening the need for pressed prisoners.

Captivity became more common as prisoner release and pressment declined. Holding large numbers of prisoners was scarcely an option for most sixteenth- and seventeenth-century governments that could barely feed and pay their own troops adequately. Prisoners of war were generally held in the facilities already used for civil criminals, such as town gaols, fortresses, and hulked ships. The period of captivity was generally fairly brief, except for high-ranking prisoners. The practice of holding larger numbers for longer periods developed in con-junction with prisoner-exchange agreements known as cartels. These trans-formed the practice of one-way ransom into mutual exchange, initially by assigning cash equivalents to different ranks and later calculating the value of senior prisoners in multiples of ordinary soldiers. The Spanish–Dutch cartel of 1599 is generally considered the first, and was followed by at least four more between these two powers by 1638. Spain signed another four with France in the decade after 1639.

Cartels were clearly prompted as the number of prisoners grew in line with the scale of war. The French signed their second agreement with Spain in July 1643, just two months after capturing over 3,800 men at Rocroi. These were exchanged for a similar number of French taken at Honnecourt the year before. Nonetheless, France still held 1,500 Spanish prisoners in 1644.[50] Exchanges became more frequent and substantial in the eighteenth century. Nearly 31,000 Prussians were returned by Austria in 1758–9. However, arrangements could break down if one side held significantly more than another, or had gained a potentially decisive advantage. Austria suspended exchanges after capturing an entire Prus-sian corps at Maxen later in 1759.

For these reasons, belligerents could find themselves holding substantial num-bers by the eighteenth century. There were 41,100 Austrians in Prussian captivity in 1758, equivalent to a full army in a contemporary battle. Accommodating even small numbers could prove difficult, as the minor south-west German territories discovered in 1760, when they were assigned 1,000 Prussians captured by the imperial army.[51]

The common soldiers posed the greatest challenge, since senior or high-risk officers could easily be locked up if necessary. More usually, officers enjoyed relatively comfortable conditions, either in some form of house arrest on enemy territory, or released on parole. Generally richer, they enjoyed better personal credit and could provide their own maintenance. By contrast, the situation was often dire for the rank and file. In line with civil penal practice, captors were not held responsible for their prisoners' material needs. The Peace of the Pyrenees (1659) obliged France and Spain to refund each other's costs incurred maintaining prisoners over the previous twenty-four years of conflict. General Stanhope had to use his own credit to maintain his 3,900 British soldiers captured by the French at Brihuega in 1710 until his government allocated £7,500 a month. It was still common at this point for bankers to offer credit for governments to pay soldiers held on enemy soil.[52] However, the English Parliament allocated 1 *d* a day in 1645 to maintain Royalist prisoners; and by the mid-eighteenth century captors were generally expected to meet their prisoners' basic needs at their own expense.

Allegations of ill-treatment also appeared much earlier than often assumed.[53] Bernhard von Weimar was furious to discover that thirty of his men had died inside Breisach after he captured the town in 1638. Stories that some of the prisoners had been reduced to cannibalism swiftly circulated in anti-imperial propaganda and were widely accepted as true by later writers.[54] The notion that prisoners were no longer active combatants also became established before the nineteenth century. The Swabian authorities protested when Frederick II ordered 400 of the 'best', meaning still healthy, prisoners from the imperial army to be pressed into his own depleted ranks.[55] Captors were now held responsible for their prisoners' welfare. An agreement between the imperial army command and Prussia after the Seven Years War obliged both parties to provide full lists of all men they had held and to issue death certificates for those no longer alive to be repatriated.[56]

CONCLUSIONS

The growing scale and duration of early modern conflicts greatly increased the numbers of prisoners in European warfare. They comprised much of a defeated army's losses. While overall prisoner numbers rose across the period, their proportional significance declined slightly. This trend remains to be explained fully, but is probably due to improved discipline and training that reduced the likelihood of a defeated army collapsing in rout. Treatment varied considerably depending on several factors. One was the circumstance at capture, with collective surrender en masse becoming more significant than individual capture. Negotiated surrender encouraged the trend towards more uniform conventions across Europe. However, perceived religious or ethnic differences still led to some captives more likely to suffer ill-treatment or death. Social status and military rank remained significant throughout, with nobles and senior officers enjoying better conditions than ordinary soldiers, though this could work against them before 1650 when they were more likely to be detained in contrast to common prisoners who were often released. Prisoners were less likely to be held for monetary or material reasons after the early seventeenth century. Rather than being a source of income, they increasingly represented a burden as larger numbers were held in captivity for longer periods. Military factors appear paramount in this, especially the value of trained soldiers, either to deny them to the enemy, or exchange for one's own men. Fear of retaliation further contributed to the spread of common conventions. Above all, these were associated with honour, both personal in the sense that ill-treatment reflected badly on individual captors, but also wider, more impersonal honour related to an army's collective reputation, and that of its government and country.

NOTES

1. For the most recent overview of the literature, see Daniel Hohrath, ' "In Cartellen wird der Werth eines Gefangenen bestimmet": Kriegsgefangenschaft als Teil der Kriegspraxis des Ancien Régime', in Rüdiger Overmans (ed.), *In der Hand des Feindes* (Cologne, Germany: Böhlau, 1999), 141–70.
2. With reference to the wider literature, see Daniel Krebs, 'The making of prisoners of war: Rituals of surrender in the American War of Independence, 1776–1783', *Militärgeschichtliche Mitteilungen*, 64 (2005), 1–29.
3. For this see Olive Anderson, 'The establishment of British supremacy at sea and the exchange of naval prisoners of war', *English Historical Review*, 75 (1960), 77–89.
4. Frederick II 'the Great' of Prussia, *Histoire de mon temps*, in Gustav Berthold Volz (ed.), *Die Werke Friedrichs des Grossen*, 10 vols. (Berlin: R. Hobbing, 1913), ii, 269. See also the sources cited in the table.
5. Frank Tallett, *War and society in early modern Europe, 1495–1715* (London: Routledge, 1992), 106. Tallett suggested defeated armies lost 20 per cent of their strength as prisoners and 30 per cent killed.
6. Calculated from David G. Chandler, *The art of war in the age of Marlborough* (2nd edn.; Tunbridge Wells: Spellmount, 1990), 308–10.
7. Boris Tzesarevich Urlanis, *Bilanz der Kriege: Die Menschenverluste Europas vom 17. Jahrhundert bis zu Gegenwart*, trans. Gerhard Hartmann (Berlin: Deutscher Verlag der Wissenschaften, 1965), 234–5.
8. Calculated from Jürgen Luh, *Ancien Régime warfare and the military revolution* (Groningen: INOS, 2000), 48–51.
9. Calculated from Frederick II, *Werke*, ii, 269.
10. 78,360 out of 303,591 Austrians lost in Europe, 80,000 of 350,000 French in the colonial campaigns, and 1,118 of 4,936 Bavarians for 1757–9. See Urlanis, *Bilanz*, 67, 304; Karl Staudinger, *Geschichte des Kurbayerischen Heeres*, 5 vols. (Munich, 1901–9), iii, 1070.
11. Strength returns, Hauptstaatsarchiv Stuttgart (HSAS), Stuttgart, A202 Bü.2221.
12. Monthly reports for 1702, Staatsarchiv Darmstadt (StAD), Darmstadt, E8 B207/1.

13. StAD, E8 207/3.
14. StAD, E1 C36/4.
15. HSAS, A6 Bü.30. The unit spent around half of its time in operations against the Turks, who still rarely took prisoners at this point.
16. Eduard Hagen, 'Die fürstliche Würzburgische Hausinfanterie vom Jahre 1757 bis zur Einverleibung des Fürstbistums in Bayern 1803', *Darstellungen aus Bayerischen Kriegs- und Heeresgeschichte*, 20 (1911), 23.
17. Bernhard von Poten (ed.), *Handwörterbuch der gesamten Militärwissenschaften*, 9 vols. (Bielefeld, 1877–80), ii 218.
18. Ian Gentles, *The New Model Army in England, Ireland and Scotland, 1645–1653* (Oxford: Blackwell, 1992), 398.
19. Calculated from Edward Leupold (ed.), 'Journal der Armee des Herzogs Bernhard von Sachsen-Weimar aus den Jahren 1637 und 1638', *Basler Zeitschrift für Geschichte und Altertumskunde*, 11 (1912), 308; William P. Guthrie, *The later Thirty Years War* (Westport, CT: Greenwood, 2003), 82–3.
20. Examples in Urlanis, *Bilanz*, 282.
21. Walter Schaufelberger, *Der alte Schweizer und sein Krieg* (3rd edn.; Zürich,1987), 178–9.
22. For example, prior to Culloden in 1746. See Rex Whitworth, *William Augustus Duke of Cumberland* (London: Leo Cooper, 1992), 89–91.
23. Ulrich Bräker, *The life story and real adventures of the poor man of Toggenburg*, trans. with an introduction by Derek Bowman (Edinburgh: Edinburgh University Press, 1970), 102–43. See generally M. Sikora, *Disziplin und Desertion* (Berlin: Duncker und Humblot, 1996), 178–9.
24. Gustav Droysen, 'Der Krieg in Norddeutschland von 1632', *Zeitschrift für Preußische Geschichte und Landeskunde*, 9 (1872), 301–5.
25. Daniel P. O'Connell, *Richelieu* (London: Weidenfeld and Nicolson, 1968), 348–9.
26. Franz Taeglichsbeck, *Das Treffen bei Steinau an der Oder am 11. Oktober 1633* (Berlin, 1889), 29–45.
27. Mark Levene and Penny Roberts (eds.), *The massacre in history* (New York: Berghahn, 1999); Joseph Canning, Hartmut Lehmann, and Jay Winter (eds.), *Power, violence and mass death in pre-modern and modern times* (Aldershot: Ashgate, 2004).
28. Examples in Robert I. Frost, *The northern wars 1558–1721* (Harlow: Longman, 2000), 75–6, 275–6.
29. Robert Davis, 'The geography of slaving in the early modern Mediterranean', *Journal of Medieval and Early Modern Studies*, 37 (2007), 57–74; Paula S. Fichtner, *Terror and toleration: The Habsburg empire confronts Islam, 1526–1850* (London: Reaktion, 2008).
30. Christopher Duffy, *The '45* (London: Cassell, 2003), 523–4.
31. John W. Wright, 'Sieges and customs of war at the opening of the eighteenth century', *American Historical Review*, 39 (1938), 629–44.
32. As admitted by one of their officers, Robert Monro, *Monro: His expedition with the worthy Scots Regiment called Mac-Keys* (1637; Westport, CT: Praeger, 1999), 243–4. Further discussion of this point in Michael Kaiser, 'Cuius exercitus, eius religio? Konfession und Heerwesen im Zeitalter des Dreißigjährigen Krieges', *Archiv für Reformationsgeschichte*, 91 (2000), 316–53.
33. Ian Gentles, 'The civil wars in England', in John Kenyon and Jane Ohlmeyer (eds.), *The civil wars: A military history of England, Scotland, and Ireland 1638–1660* (Oxford: Oxford University Press, 1998), 112.

34. Giorgio Chittolini, 'The "private", the "public", the state', *Journal of Modern History*, 67 supplement (1995), 34–61.

35. Duffy, *The '45*, 129–30, 536–7.

36. Hans E. Flieger, *Die Schlacht bei Stadtlohn am 6. August 1623* (Aachen: Shaker, 1998), 183–92.

37. Walther E. Heydendorff, 'Vorderösterreich im Dreißigjährigen Krieg', *Mitteilungen des Österreichischen Staatsarchivs*, 12 (1959), 135–7.

38. Alan D. Francis, *The first peninsular war 1702–1713* (London: E. Benn, 1975), 212. For the transformation of partisan warfare, see Martin Rink, *Vom 'Partheygänger' zum Partisanen. Die Konzeption des kleinen Krieges in Preußen 1740–1813* (Frankfurt a/M.: Peter Lang, 1999).

39. See generally Fritz Redlich, *De praeda militari: Looting and booty 1500–1800* (Wiesbaden: F. Steiner, 1956).

40. Charles Cruickshank, *Henry VIII and the invasion of France* (2nd edn.; Stroud: Alan Sutton, 1990), 109–15.

41. Wilhelm Fleitmann, 'Postverbindungen für den Westfälischen Friedenskongreß 1643 bis 1648', *Archiv für Deutsche Postgeschichte*, 1 (1972), 12–22.

42. John A. Lynn, 'How war fed war: The tax of violence and contributions during the *Grand Siècle*', *Journal of Modern History*, 65 (1993), 286–310; Peter H. Wilson, *Europe's tragedy: The Thirty Years War* (London: Penguin Press, 2009), 399–409.

43. For example, Torstensson's report of his victory at the second battle of Breitenfeld, 3 Nov. 1642, Haus-, Hof- und Staatsarchiv Vienna, KA 110 (neu).

44. For an example, see Leander von Wetzer, 'Der Feldzug am Ober-Rhein 1638', *Mittheilungen des K.K. Kriegsarchivs*, new series 3 (1889), 133–6.

45. As for example by Matthew Smith Anderson, *War and society in Europe of the Old Regime 1618–1789* (London: Fontana Press, 1988), 65.

46. Quoted in Stephen Ede-Borrett, *Lostwithiel 1644: The campaign and the battles* (Farnham: Pike and Shot Society, 2004), 45.

47. Monro, *Expedition*, 244.

48. Horst Höhne, *Die Einstellung der sächsischen Regimenter in die Preußischen Armee im Jahre 1756* (Halle, 1926).

49. Rüdiger Overmans, 'Introduction', in Overmans (ed.), *In der Hand des Feindes*, 5.

50. For the cartels, see John A. Lynn, *Giant of the grand siècle: The French army 1610–1715* (Cambridge: Cambridge University Press, 1997), 428–9; Hohrath, 'Cartellen', 164–9.

51. HSAS, C14 Bü.180.

52. Lynn, *Giant*, 427–8; Basil Williams, *Stanhope: A study in eighteenth-century war and diplomacy* (Oxford: Clarendon Press, 1932), 106–17.

53. Overmans, 'Introduction', 10–11. Overmans argues it only became a feature of propaganda in the First World War.

54. Fritz Julian, 'Angebliche Menschenfresserei im Dreißigjährigen Kriege', *Mitteilungen des Historischen Vereins der Pfalz*, 45 (1927), 37–92.

55. HSAS, C14 Bü.87a, esp. 19 Nov. 1762. Of 306 men held from Infantry Regiment von Rodt, 19 volunteered, but 218 were compelled.

56. HSAS, C14 Bü.87a, 31 Mar. 1763.

4

Prisoners of War in International Law: The Nineteenth Century

Stephen C. Neff

Our present law and practice regarding prisoners of war is a legacy of the nineteenth century. A look at the picture in, say, the year 1790 would reveal a world very foreign to ours. A similar look in 1900 would yield a picture recognizably like our own, in its essentials if not its finer details. Clearly, very great changes took place during that crucial century.

Prior to the nineteenth century, the dominant policy of dealing with prisoners of war, in European practice, could be described as one of redistribution, rather than of holding or internment. This redistribution took three principal forms. One was the inducing of prisoners to switch sides and serve in the captor's armed forces. This may seem odd from a present-day perspective, but it must be borne in mind that in the seventeenth and eighteenth centuries, the armed forces of the European powers consisted in substantial part of foreign mercenaries (Prussia being a notable exception in this regard). As a consequence, modern ideas of military service as a patriotic duty, marked by personal commitment to lofty causes, were almost entirely absent. The manning of military forces was treated instead, in cold-blooded and rational fashion, as a logistical problem.[1]

A second means of redistributing prisoners of war was by exchange. Here, too, rationalism and calculation were the order of the day. The general practice was to carefully maintain strict equality, so that exchanges were typically agreed between the belligerents during the conflict on what was commonly termed a man-for-man and grade-for-grade basis. These arrangements typically took the form of a written agreement known as a 'cartel'.[2] Equality of benefit in the exchange process was seen as particularly important, since it was accepted that, after exchange, the ex-prisoners would be immediately re-enlisted in their armed forces and redeployed in the war effort. Prisoners that were not exchanged, for whatever reason, were released at the conclusion of the hostilities, generally pursuant to express provisions in peace treaties to this effect.[3]

The third means of redistribution entailed removing the prisoners from the framework of the war altogether through the process known as 'parole'. Prisoners would be released by their captors, without being exchanged, on giving their word of honour (their 'parole') that they would take no further part in the conflict. Typically, the released prisoner would live in the captor's country, but sometimes he was permitted to return to his own.[4] In that case, the soldier's home state was expected to respect the parole arrangement by refraining from conscripting the parolee back into military service. Since parole, in contrast to exchange, barred the parolee from further war activity, there was no concern that the numbers be equal on the two sides. The only limitation on parole, therefore, was the trust that the captors were willing to repose in the parolee's word of honour.

In the nineteenth century, all three of these traditional methods of dealing with prisoners of war fell into disuse in practice, to be replaced by a practice of holding prisoners of war in large numbers for the duration of the conflict. The period also witnessed the corresponding development of a new body of international law to deal with the challenges that this new practice presented. The seminal event in the emergence of a new body of law on prisoners of war was the promulgation of the Lieber Code by the United States in 1863 (named after its drafter, Francis Lieber, a prominent legal scholar and political theorist).[5] This was a set of rules prescribed for the Union forces during the American Civil War, which was then in progress. It had a significant impact on the future codification of the laws of war generally, including rules relating to prisoners of war. Lieber's effort was particularly influential on the Swiss lawyer Kaspar Bluntschli, who later in the same decade devised a treatise on international law generally, in the form of a code or set of articles similar in flavour to those of Lieber. Bluntschli's rules on prisoners of war closely tracked those of Lieber, as will be observed in the discussion below.[6]

The first detailed statement of the laws of war to be drafted by an international body was a set of rules concluded in Brussels in 1874 by a group of technical experts. Since this document was not drafted by governments, it did not constitute a treaty, but was instead given the label of *projet*.[7] Only in 1899 were the laws of war finally put into the form of a legally binding treaty concluded between states. This occurred at the First Hague Peace Conference that year, and accordingly became known as the Hague Rules.[8] The subject of prisoners of war received considerable attention in these Rules, with nearly one-third of the articles devoted to that subject. The Hague Rules remain in force to the present day (although slightly recast at the Second Hague Peace Conference of 1907).[9] The provisions on prisoners of war, however, have been effectively superseded by the later Geneva Conventions of 1929 and 1949.[10]

The following discussion will take a closer look at these trends from the standpoint of international law. First, the passing away of the older system of redistribution of prisoners will be discussed. Then there will be an outline of the development of the principal legal norms on prisoners of war that evolved during the course of the nineteenth century. Finally, there will be a discussion of the means for the enforcement of those rules.

THE PASSING OF OLD WAYS

In regard to the treatment of prisoners of war, the French Revolutionary Wars of 1792–1815 marked the important watershed. It was then that the traditional practices of redistribution were abandoned on a significant scale—with the consequence that, for the first time in European warfare, prisoners of war began to be held in large numbers on an indefinite basis (i.e. for the duration of the conflict at hand). An important effect of this development was significantly to focus attention, for the first time, on questions of treatment of prisoners of war. The suddenness of the change should not, however, be exaggerated. The older ways continued well into the nineteenth century in state practice, and international law continued, to some extent, to make provision for them. By the end of the nineteenth century, though, the disappearance of the older system of redistribution was largely complete.

The Decline of Exchange Arrangements

The practice of exchanging prisoners of war during the various European wars of the seventeenth and eighteenth centuries was closely linked to the character and ethos of war in general during that era. In particular, war in that period was largely lacking in ideological overtones, being more a matter of rational calculation than of patriotic fervour. War was also, in that time and that region, a limited-liability affair. Armies were enormously expensive to maintain, especially in light of the fact that the revenue-raising machinery of governments was primitive in the extreme by modern standards. This meant that governments were perpetually in search of ways of either reducing the costs of war, or alternatively of finding ways of shunting them onto the opposing side.

There were various ways of achieving these goals. One was to quarter one's troops in enemy territory as much as possible. Another was to minimize expenditure on the maintenance of captured enemy soldiers by sending captured enemies back to their home states. This would even take place in the full knowledge that the captured soldiers would be re-enrolled in the enemy's war effort—provided, of course, that the enemy reciprocated, thereby ensuring that neither side achieved a net benefit over the other. The re-enrolment of returned prisoners could be regarded with equanimity so long as it was understood that the conflict was not a war to the death; in other words, that the goal of warfare was to position a belligerent advantageously for peace negotiations rather than to drive the enemy into a state of utter exhaustion.

There was a dramatic departure from this traditional practice of exchange in the French Revolutionary struggles of 1792–1815, when conceptions of patriotism and ideology began to play a significant role in warfare. In the early part of these wars, France pointedly declined to enter into a prisoner-exchange agreement of the usual sort, on the grounds that such arrangement would benefit Britain more. Eventually, it relented and entered into an arrangement with

Britain in 1798.[11] But this proved to be short-lived, as France repudiated it the following year.[12] From then until the conclusion of the Treaty of Amiens in 1802, no arrangement on prisoners was in force between the two sides. In the last phase of the French Revolutionary War struggles from 1803 to 1815, there was once again no exchange cartel between the belligerents.

It should be noted that the practice of exchange did not die an immediate death during the French Revolutionary conflicts: there were two other major instances of it during the nineteenth century. The first was in the Crimean War. A prisoner-exchange agreement was concluded between the belligerents, although not until mid-way through the conflict, in August 1855.[13] This was an arrangement of the traditional kind, an exchange on a man-for-man, grade-for-grade basis. This may have been the last occasion on which such an exchange arrangement occurred in an inter-state conflict.

The other major example of large-scale prisoner exchange was the American Civil War. This should probably be seen as a reflection of the high degree of shared values between the belligerents, notwithstanding the rancour over slavery and other issues behind the outbreak of the hostilities. In 1862, a cartel was agreed between the two sides.[14] The subject of prisoner exchange was also reflected in the detailed attention given to it in the Lieber Code, although it was made clear that exchange was to be regarded as a matter of policy, to be agreed (or not as the case may be) by the belligerents. There was no general rule of law requiring exchanges to take place.[15]

In the event, however, the cartel arrangement broke down, in part over the issue of whether prisoner-of-war status would be accorded by the Confederacy to captured black troops, and in part (perhaps even in major part) over worries on the Union side that the Confederates were gaining more from the arrangement by receiving its troops back in better condition than the Union prisoners. In all events, the break-down of the exchange policy had tragic results, notably in the most notorious of the Confederate prison camps. Union prisoner-of-war camps were far from luxurious,[16] but the most notorious camp was Andersonville in Georgia, where a drastic shortage of resources—supplemented by some calculated brutality on the part of the Confederate administrators—led to appalling detention conditions.

When the Brussels *projet* was drafted in 1874, hardly any attention was paid to the subject of exchange. It was the subject of only one article, which simply stated that any exchange which takes place 'is regulated by a mutual understanding between the belligerent parties'.[17] The Hague Rules did not even have that single provision, as the drafters took the view that it was not possible to devise 'a general rule' on the subject. The drafters did acknowledge, during their discussions, that 'an exchange can of course always result from an agreement between the belligerents'.[18] But it was clear that the practice was now regarded as effectively obsolete.

The Decline of Parole

The practice of parole went similarly out of fashion in the nineteenth century. As in the case of exchange, the demise was not sudden. An example of a typical parole arrangement in the early nineteenth century is afforded by a cartel concluded by the United States and Britain in 1813, during the war which had begun the previous year. This agreement made separate provisions for the liberty of parolees in the detaining state and in the home state, setting out the text of the necessary parole instrument in each case. Furthermore, it was provided that, in case of violation by a parolee resident in his home state—that is, in the event that the parolee should 'become unmindfull of the honourable obligation he lies under'—the home state was obligated to return him to the erstwhile captor country.[19]

The paroling of prisoners of war was practised on a very large scale in the American Civil War. It accordingly received detailed attention in the Lieber Code, which described a parole arrangement as 'an individual but not a private act'.[20] It differed from a purely private contract in that the parole-giver must have the permission of his superior in order to enter into the arrangement.[21] The Lieber Code also carefully specified that release by way of parole was exceptional, and that exchange was the normal method for obtaining liberty.[22] Regarding post-release activity, it was stated that parolees were only precluded from 'active service in the field'.[23] They were therefore not prevented from undertaking various forms of behind-the-scenes assistance to their side, such as paying taxes or performing administrative chores. Paroling en masse, or paroling on the battlefield, was expressly prohibited.[24] Bluntschli's code also dealt with parole, along much the same lines as Lieber's.[25]

The Brussels *projet* and the Hague Rules covered the subject in very similar terms, though much more briefly than did Lieber and Bluntschli.[26] The right to parole was recognized, on the condition that the law of the prisoner's *own* country allowed it. It specified that, in such an event, the prisoner's own government was bound by the agreement reached and was consequently barred from requiring (or even accepting) any kind of service from the ex-prisoner that was 'incompatible with the parole given'.[27] The treatment of parole violation was decidedly draconian, in that a breach of a parole agreement entailed the complete forfeiture of prisoner-of-war status. This is to be contrasted with the position of soldiers who commit 'ordinary' war crimes such as the deliberate targeting of civilians. They are criminally responsible for the particular breach of the laws of war that they commit, and thereby are subject to prosecution and punishment. However, they retain, at all times, their *status* as prisoners of war. In concrete terms, this means that they remain entitled to such privileges as Red Cross inspections of their detention conditions. Parole violators, in contrast, lose *all* the privileges of prisoners of war. They are therefore to be likened to spies rather than to 'ordinary' war criminals.[28]

Parole, though, was now largely obsolete in the practice of armed conflict, with the American Civil War being the last instance of its occurrence on a large scale. It was practised, though only to a very limited extent, in the Russo-Japanese War of 1904–5.[29] During the Second World War, there appear to have been two occasions when parole was practised. The first was by American forces, for the benefit of Italians captured during the invasion of Sicily in 1943. The second was, curiously, a mandatory parole arrangement imposed by the Japanese on troops captured during the conquest of the Philippines. The United States duly honoured the arrangement. But these were quite exceptional situations. In contemporary practice, it is common for armed forces (including, for example, those of the United States, Britain, and France) to prohibit their soldiers from accepting parole offers by enemy forces.[30] Nevertheless, the provisions on parole in the Hague Rules remain technically in force.

THE NEW REGIME: LONG-TERM HOLDING
OF PRISONERS OF WAR

The practice of holding prisoners of war for the duration of the conflict was the direct and immediate result of the decline of the practices of exchange and parole. The decisive period, as noted above, was that of the French Revolutionary Wars. In the absence of agreements on exchange between the principal belligerents, France and Britain, the numbers of prisoners inexorably built up as the wars continued. It has been estimated that by 1814, more than 80,000 French prisoners of war were being held in Britain.

At first, Britain housed its prisoners on ships (the notorious 'hulks'), but eventually the numbers became so large that purpose-built facilities were required. The first such prisoner-of-war camp, in our present sense of that term, was built at Norman Cross in England, near Peterborough, with the first prisoners arriving in April 1797. Additional purpose-built facilities were constructed shortly afterwards in Scotland, at Perth and Valleyfield (south of Edinburgh). Each of these installations held about 7,000 persons. Dartmoor Prison, newly constructed in 1806, was also put to use housing some 6,000 prisoners of war. The administering of these camps appears to have been, in one historian's assessment, 'reasonably efficient and humane'. Mortality was in the range of 1–2 per cent per year (about half what it had been in the hulks).[31] It may be noted that these prisoner-of-war camps were basically for the common soldiers. Officers were typically paroled instead.

In the course of the nineteenth century, various legal issues arising from this new phenomenon of mass, long-term detention were dealt with. The most significant ones will be discussed briefly here.

Maintenance of Prisoners as the Responsibility of the Captor State

Even well before the nineteenth century, it was recognized in the practice of European states that the *possession* of prisoners of war lay with the sovereign of the captor armed force and not with the individual captors.[32] A principal significance of this was that the ransoming of prisoners by individual captors, which was common practice in medieval Europe, was no longer allowed.[33] Distinct from this question of possession of prisoners was the issue of which state was ultimately to be responsible for the costs of holding and maintaining the captives. One of the major developments of the century was the establishment of the principle that the responsibility for maintenance lies with the captor state and not with the home state of the prisoners.

Previously, that had not been the case. Each state was seen to be responsible, at least in principle, for the upkeep of its own forces, even when they were in the hands of the enemy. Sometimes, at least, this expenditure was actually made by the soldiers' home state during the period of captivity. During the Seven Years War of 1756–63, for example, the French king made monthly distributions of a royal bounty from his private purse, for the relief and comfort of French prisoners held by the British, with the actual distribution handled by regularly appointed French agents in Britain. There were difficulties with the distribution process, however, which contributed to the halting of the arrangement in 1759.[34]

It appears that the more common expectation was that the captor state would provide for the upkeep of prisoners that it held, on a provisional basis, with a view to obtaining reimbursement at the conclusion of the hostilities. In practice, though, it was rare for peace treaties actually to provide for this.[35] The probable reason for this lack of attention to the reimbursement question lies in the practice of exchange, as described earlier. The more thoroughgoing the exchange process was, the fewer would be the number of prisoners actually held for extended times—and the less significant would the question of costs be. The result was that, in practice if not in theory, captor states were left, essentially by default, to bear the costs of holding prisoners.

By the later part of the century, the legal rules moved into line with this practice, although it is difficult to trace with exactitude the evolution of thinking on this matter. The Lieber Code, for example, makes no mention of the question. Nor was Bluntschli's code very clear on the point. It stated, somewhat delphically, that '[e]ach State' is required to provide food, maintenance, and health care for prisoners of war.[36] This appears to refer to captor states. And since nothing was said of any right to reimbursement, it would appear that captor states were regarded by Bluntschli as being responsible for the costs of holding prisoners. The matter was finally resolved with clarity, at the level of principle, in the Brussels *projet* of 1874, which explicitly stated that the captor country was to be charged with the maintenance of prisoners.[37] The Hague Rules reiterate this rule.[38]

The Standard of Treatment of Prisoners of War

The idea that prisoners of war are entitled to humane treatment was not an innovation of the nineteenth century. According to Emmerich de Vattel, the Swiss diplomat and international law writer of the mid-eighteenth century, humane treatment of prisoners of war was an established feature of European practice in his time. Vattel's legal rationale for humane treatment, however, would have had little appeal to modern sensitivities. It lay in the principle of military necessity. Once a soldier had surrendered, or fallen into the power of his enemy, he was no longer a functioning member of his armed force—with the immediate logical consequence that no military advantage was to be gained by killing or mistreating him.[39]

The Lieber Code took a somewhat different stance on this question, by stressing the non-penal character of prisoner-of-war status. A prisoner of war, the Code stated, 'is subject to no punishment for being a public enemy' (i.e. for being a member of the opposing armed force).[40] It went on carefully to state, however, that a prisoner of war who committed, or was suspected of having committed, war crimes prior to his capture could be placed on trial for those offences and, if convicted, punished accordingly.[41] But this, of course, referred to punishment for that actual prior misconduct and not for membership in the enemy armed force per se.

The logical consequence of the non-penal character of prisoner-of-war detention was that prisoners were entitled to humane treatment. But the international community was slow to provide specific guidance on this point. The first treaty which regulated the treatment of prisoners (as opposed to arranging for their exchange) appears to have been a bilateral treaty of amity and commerce, between Prussia and the United States, concluded in 1785. The two countries promised that if they should at some future time find themselves at war with one another, they would refrain from sending prisoners away to 'distant and inclement countries' (such as the East Indies, Africa, or Asia) and from confining prisoners in 'close and noxious places'. Specifically, prisoners of war would not be placed in dungeons or prison ships, nor be chained. Instead, officers would be paroled, while the 'common men' would be kept in 'cantonments open and extensive enough for air and exercise' and lodged in 'barracks as roomly and good' as those provided by the detaining power for its own forces. Rations too would be on a par with those given by the detaining state to its own forces. Perhaps most notably, provision was made for the appointment of commissioners from each country to oversee the conditions of prisoners held by the other, and to bring relief supplies to them.[42] It should be noted, however, that the two countries were not at war with one another at the time that this agreement was concluded, nor was there any anticipation on either side that a war between them was the slightest bit likely. So this worthy provision is perhaps best regarded as a general—and harmless—statement of lofty humanitarian ideals, rather than as a set of working rules.

Of rather more importance historically were the rules that were drafted by the British government for the running of the dedicated prisoner-of-war camps which it established (as observed above) during the French Revolutionary Wars. The rules for the administration of the Norman Cross camp were commendably liberal in spirit. Corporal punishment of prisoners of war, for example, was prohibited (at least in the early stages of the camp's history). In addition, the formation of a prisoners' committee was permitted. These rules became a model for the later Geneva Conventions.[43]

Standards of treatment for prisoners of war also featured in the cartel concluded by Britain and the United States in 1813. This was of rather more concrete value than the earlier Prussia–United States Treaty of 1785, since it was concluded by actual belligerents during an ongoing state of war. It provided that there was to be no striking of prisoners with hand, whip, stick, 'or any other weapon whatever'. There were also detailed rules on provisions for prisoners. In the event that a prisoner became 'disorderly', he could be 'closely confined' by his captors and also kept on two-thirds of normal rations for 'a reasonable time not exceeding ten days'. Each government was entitled to supply its troops that had fallen into enemy hands with clothing and with reasonable small allowances. Prisoners' complaints were to be attended to and grievances redressed. Also, each government was given the right to inspect the conditions of detention of its forces in the custody of the other.[44]

The Lieber Code and the various international initiatives that followed it could be regarded as a step backward, in that they did not contain rules that were comparable in detail to those of the 1813 treaty. The Lieber Code simply contained a general requirement that prisoners be 'treated with humanity' and subjected to 'no... intentional suffering or indignity'. More specifically, it forbade the infliction upon prisoners of any 'suffering, or disgrace, by cruel imprisonment, want of food, by mutilation, death, or any other barbarity'. Prisoners of war were to be given 'plain and wholesome food'—though with the somewhat ominous proviso 'whenever practicable'. On the specific point of confinement, the Code provided that prisoners are 'subject to confinement or imprisonment such as may be deemed necessary on account of safety'—referring here, of course, to the safety of the captor side.[45] But the Code did not contain detailed rules on nutritional standards, or any provision as to health care. Nor did it provide any mechanism for the redress of grievances or for inspection of prisoner-of-war camps by either the opposing belligerent or third parties.

The Brussels *projet* and the Hague Rules contained much the same rules as the Lieber Code on the matter of confinement. The Brussels *projet* stated that it is permissible to 'intern' prisoners, in the sense of forbidding them from going beyond 'certain fixed limits'. Prisoners may not, however, be 'placed in confinement' in cells or rooms, for example, except 'as an indispensable measure of safety'.[46] The Hague Rules contain a similar provision, in virtually identical wording.[47]

In several important respects however, the Hague Rules broke new ground on the subject of treatment. For one thing, they specified that, regarding board and lodging, prisoners of war were entitled to equal treatment with the armed forces of the captor power (unless the belligerents agree a special rule to the contrary).[48] Officers (but not common soldiers) were entitled to be paid during their time in captivity, at a rate equal to soldiers of equal rank in the captor's armed force.[49] There was also a provision guaranteeing freedom of religion for prisoners, as well as one for the drawing up of wills.[50]

Punishment for Attempting Escape

Just as it is not a war crime to kill or capture enemy soldiers in battle, so it is not a war crime for a prisoner of war to escape from captivity. The Lieber Code reflected this principle in its explicit provision that no punishment could be inflicted upon a prisoner 'simply for his attempt to escape'. At the same, though, the Code specified that prisoners attempting to escape risked being shot and killed in the attempt, just as they risked being shot and killed in battle by virtue of their status as combatants. It also warned that '[s]tricter means of security' would be justified in the aftermath of an escape attempt. Moreover, punitive measures, including the death penalty, were permissible in two notable situations: in the case of a conspiracy for effecting 'a united or general escape', and also for the plotting of 'rebellion'.[51] If a prisoner successfully escaped, and then was later recaptured in an entirely independent context, then no punishment could be inflicted for the prior escape, although it was permissible for the prisoner now to be 'subjected to stricter confinement' than previously.[52]

This remains the basic law regarding escape, to the present day. It may be noted, though, that, in one respect, the Brussels *projet* and the Hague Rules were rather harsher than the Lieber Code: they permitted the imposing of 'disciplinary punishment' on prisoners who attempt to escape but are apprehended.[53]

Compulsory Labour

It has always been, and continues to be, the case that prisoners of war may be compelled to perform labour. The Lieber Code expressly provided that prisoners could be required to work for the benefit of the captor's government.[54] Bluntschli's code was to much the same effect, although with the proviso that prisoners could not be compelled to take up arms against their home country or give information to their captors that would compromise their home states.[55]

The Brussels *projet* basically followed Lieber and Bluntschli. It stated that prisoners 'may be employed' on 'certain public works which have no direct connection with the operations in the theatre of war'. It also specified that the work could not be 'excessive' or 'humiliating to [the prisoners'] military rank'. Prisoners could also be put to doing private work. They were to be paid wages for their labours—and the cost of their maintenance could be deducted from these wages.[56] All of this was subject to the overriding proviso that prisoners could not be compelled 'to take any part whatever in carrying on the operations of the war'.[57] The Hague Rules are in substantially the same vein. They are somewhat more detailed on the subject of remuneration for work, specifying that payment must be on a par with pay given for similar work to soldiers of the captor army (or, if no troops of the captor force are so employed, then 'at a rate according to the work executed'). The Hague Rules echo the Brussels *projet* in allowing deductions from wages for the maintenance of the prisoners.[58]

Here, too, the modern law is little changed in substance from the Hague Rules, although the detail is much greater. The Geneva Convention of 1949 on Prisoners of War contains elaborate rules as to what categories of work can be involved, as well as on conditions of labour.[59] But prisoners of war remain subject to compulsory labour for their captors.

Reprisals Against Prisoners of War

Belligerent reprisals have a long history as a means of enforcing the laws of war—in other words, as a permissible means of inducing the enemy side to stop committing violations of the laws of war. To the present day, there is no global prohibition against them, although they have become increasingly hedged about with restrictions.[60] Two crucial features of belligerent reprisals are particularly worth highlighting. The first is that a reprisal consists of an act that is *itself* a violation of the laws of war. It is an act that is inherently unlawful, but which is permissible as an emergency measure for the purpose of inducing the other side to halt its *pre-existing* pattern of violations. A belligerent reprisal may therefore be thought of as, in essence, a counter-war crime. It is obvious that a pattern of violations and counter-violations of the laws of war could all too easily spin out of control and degenerate into a series of escalating war crimes. It was with good reason, then, that the Lieber Code bluntly characterized reprisals as 'the sternest feature of war'.[61]

The second key characteristic of reprisals is that, by definition, they are inflicted upon persons *other* than those who actually committed the original offence. The actual culprits are frequently either unknown or are unavailable for personal punishment—typically because they are still serving in the enemy's armed force. In such a case, the alternative is to retaliate against innocent fellow soldiers for the misdeeds. But the very fact that the actual targets of reprisal measures are innocent parties means that reprisals must not be seen, strictly speaking, as punitive measures. Nor are they (in the words of the Lieber Code) acts of 'mere revenge', of merely mechanical repetition of wrongdoing. Rather, they are lawful only to the extent that they function as (again in the language of the Lieber Code) 'a means of protective retribution', as a means of encouraging or promoting adherence to the laws of war and, more specifically, as a means of inducing the opposing belligerent to refrain, in its *future* conduct, from committing further violations of law.[62]

Belligerent reprisals were generally carried out on a strict tit-for-tat basis. Prisoners of war, for obvious reasons, were particularly vulnerable to being used as targets of reprisal actions. The American Civil War provided many instructive examples. In June 1862, for example, the military governor of the largely occupied state of Tennessee informed President Lincoln of reports that some seventy pro-Union prisoners were being mistreated in a Confederate jail. He asked Lincoln's permission to inflict the same treatment on a like number of Confederate captives. Lincoln approved.[63] A more wide-ranging reprisal measure was ordered later in the war by Secretary of War Edwin Stanton in response to reports of inadequate rations for Union prisoners of war in Confederate hands. Stanton ordered that rations to Confederate prisoners held by the Union side be reduced by 20 per cent. There was pressure from the Congress for firmer action, but it was resisted by the Lincoln administration.[64]

It may be noted that this is one important area in which there has been a sharp and clear change in the law since the nineteenth century. The Geneva Convention of 1929, the first multilateral convention concerned specially with prisoners of war, expressly forbade subjecting prisoners to reprisal measures.[65]

ENFORCING THE RULES

Enforcement of international law rules, now as in the nineteenth century, is a major, yet underdeveloped area in international law. In the absence of a world government or standing global police force, enforcement is carried out through a patchwork of methods of varying effectiveness. One such method, as just discussed, is reprisals. Here, there will be a brief survey of three other mechanisms: prisoners' committees and camp inspections; action by the International Committee of the Red Cross; and, most drastically, criminal prosecution.

Prisoners' Committees and Camp Inspections

It was observed above that the treaty of 1785 between Prussia and the United States, as well as the 1813 cartel between the United States and Britain, provided for inspection of prisoner-of-war facilities. There was no such provision, however, in the Lieber or Bluntschli Codes, or in the Brussels *projet*. The Hague Rules, however, made some important innovations in this area. They provided for the establishment of inquiry offices from the outset of the war in the belligerent countries, for the purpose of responding to queries about prisoners of war. To discharge this task, the inquiry offices were to be provided with full information on internments, transfers, releases, escapes, hospitalizations, deaths, and the like. Returns were to be maintained for each prisoner, on an individual basis. Provision was also made for the operation of relief societies, which were to have the right of entry into prisoner facilities for the purpose of distributing relief. Presents and relief supplies for prisoners were to be admitted free of all duties.[66]

The International Committee of the Red Cross

Mention should also be made of the activities of the International Committee of the Red Cross (ICRC), which was founded in 1863, the same year as the promulgation of the Lieber Code in the United States. During the nineteenth century, the ICRC made comparatively little contribution to either the law on or the practices relating to prisoners of war. At the Committee's founding meeting in 1863, the Russian delegate raised the question of prisoners, but the issue was promptly set aside in favour of an aspect of war that was of more immediate concern to the majority of the delegates: the condition of wounded soldiers.[67]

This formed the subject of the first Geneva Convention, concluded the following year, which provided for the immunity of medical personnel and medical installations attending to the wounded.[68]

Despite the Committee's lack of interest, however, the welfare of prisoners of war was a strong personal interest of Henry Dunant himself, the leading figure in the formation of the ICRC. He accordingly embarked on a one-man diplomatic effort to persuade the governments of the world to convene a conference and to draft a treaty on the subject. Success was tantalizingly close as a conference was summoned to meet in Paris in 1874. In the event, however, it never convened, and the matter of prisoners was dealt with instead at the Brussels gathering that same year.[69]

It is worth mentioning, though, that even in the absence of a convention the ICRC took some important steps in ameliorating the treatment of prisoners of war during the Franco-Prussian War of 1870–1. In that conflict—the first one in which the Committee played a part—the ICRC performed various philanthropic and mediating services, thereby acquiring its first substantial reputation in the eyes of the general public. It persuaded both sides to allow wounded (but not, at first, able-bodied) prisoners to write to their families using the Committee as the return address. Soon, the Committee found itself handling about a thousand such letters per day. Prussia, which took prisoners in huge numbers, was persuaded by the Committee to draw up lists of names of wounded prisoners, and then to print the list for distribution throughout France. These arrangements were soon extended to cover all prisoners.[70]

Mistreatment of Prisoners as a War Crime

As long as there were actual legal rules as to the treatment of prisoners of war, it was necessarily the case that a violation of those rules would constitute a war crime and be punishable as such. Only in the nineteenth century, though, did the first clear examples emerge of individual criminal responsibility for the mistreatment of prisoners of war. This took place (as did so much else) in the American Civil War, in connection with Andersonville Prison Camp in Georgia, which received extensive (and sensational) coverage in the northern press.

At the conclusion of the conflict, criminal charges were initially brought, with respect to Andersonville, against several of the Confederate leaders, including General Robert E. Lee and Secretary of War James Seddon. Those charges, however, were dropped, and proceedings were instituted only against the commander of the installation, Henry Wirtz, and one of his subordinate officers. The subordinate was convicted of various acts of misconduct (murder, assault, theft, and withholding of rations from prisoners) and sentenced to fifteen years imprisonment and hard labour.[71]

Two charges were brought against Wirtz. The first was conspiracy to 'impair and injure the health and to destroy the lives' of the prisoners. This charge included, more specifically, subjecting prisoners to 'torture and great suffering', the confining of prisoners in 'unhealthy and unwholesome quarters', and the supplying of impure water as well as insufficient and unwholesome food to his prisoners. The second charge was the murder of thirteen individual prisoners by various means, including shooting, kicking, beating, and tearing by bloodhounds. The trial was held before a military commission, headed by General Lew Wallace (soon to be famous as the author of the bestselling novel *Ben-hur*). Even though it was established in the course of the proceedings that Wirtz had complained to his superiors about food shortages, he was convicted on the first charge, of conspiracy, and was also found guilty of murder for ten of the deaths under the second charge (being acquitted of the other three). He was hanged in November 1865—a dramatic and sobering testimony to the increasing effectiveness of international law in the protection of prisoners of war in the nineteenth century.[72]

CONCLUSION

The nineteenth century marked the crucial transition of the law on the treatment of prisoners of war to substantially modern times. It is true that the Geneva Conventions dedicated to detailed treatment of the subject lay in the future. The first Geneva Convention would be drafted in 1929, and its successor (still in force) would follow in 1949. But the basic principles of humane treatment were established well before those dates.

Only one further point about the law on prisoners of war remains to be made. That is, that perhaps the most important change was not on the material front, in terms of the standard of actual treatment, which was after all far from ideal even by 1914. The most important change, it may be submitted, was a conceptual one, concerning the rationale for the humane treatment of prisoners. In the eighteenth century, as observed above, the justification for humane treatment lay in the law of military necessity. Gradually this changed, in ways that are difficult to pinpoint with any exactitude. But the crucial change was the substitution of a human rights perspective on the subject in place of a military one. Treatment of prisoners of war came gradually to be seen as rooted in the basic inherent human dignity of the individuals concerned, rather than in considerations of military strategy.

In this regard, the law on prisoners of war might be thought of as a sort of juridical miner's canary for the laws of war generally. Where the old law of war, inherited from the Middle Ages and codified in increasing detail beginning in the nineteenth century, concerned itself chiefly with fairness and equity between the contending sides in the struggle, the later law—significantly relabelled 'international humanitarian law'—has as its primary goal the overall minimization of suffering attendant upon the tragedy of armed conflict. International law, in short, has become, and continues to become, more people-centred. And prisoners of war, in the course of the nineteenth century, had the dubious honour of acting as advance scouts in that momentous, and ongoing, process.

NOTES

1. On the changing of sides by prisoners of war in pre-nineteenth century wars, see Michael Glover, *The velvet glove: The decline and fall of moderation in war* (London: Hodder and Stoughton, 1982), 161–3. On the extensive use of foreigners in European armed forces of the seventeenth and eighteenth centuries, see Matthew Smith Anderson, *War and society in Europe of the Old Regime 1618–1789* (London: Fontana Press, 1988), 85–7.

2. For examples of such cartels, see France–Netherlands, Cartel of 26 May 1673, 12 C.T.S. 457; France–Netherlands, Cartel of 21 May 1675, 13 C.T.S. 79; France–Great Britain, Cartel for the Exchange of Prisoners Taken at Sea, 28 Mar. 1780, 47 C.T.S. 287; and France–Russia, Armistice Signed at Tilsit, 22 June 1807, 59 C.T.S. 201, Art 6. The expression 'cartel' also sometimes referred to agreements concluded in peacetime for the mutual rendition of deserters from armed forces. See, for example, Nassau–Netherlands, Cartel Convention, 17 Aug. 1828, 78 C.T.S. 481.

3. See, for example, France–Spain, Treaty of Ryswick, 20 Sep. 1697, 21 C.T.S. 453, Art. 14; France–Netherlands, Treaty of Ryswick, 20 Sep. 1697, 21 C.T.S. 347, Art. 9; France–Great Britain, Treaty of Utrecht, 11 Apr. 1713, 27 C.T.S. 475, Art. 23; France–Great Britain–Netherlands, Treaty of Aix-la-Chapelle, 18 Oct. 1748, 38 C.T.S. 297, Art. 4; France–Great Britain–Spain, Treaty of Paris, 10 Feb. 1763, 42 C.T.S. 279, Art. 3; and Great Britain–United States, Treaty of Paris, 3 Sep. 1783, 48 C.T.S. 487, Art. 7.

4. For a detailed exposition of parole in action in the period 1756–1815, see Francis Abell, *Prisoners of war in Britain 1756 to 1815* (Oxford: Oxford University Press, 1914), 284–356.

5. For the text of the Lieber Code, see Richard Shelly Hartigan (ed.), *Lieber's Code and the law of war* (New York: Legal Classics Library, 1995) [hereafter Lieber Code]. On Lieber's life and career, see Frank Freidel, *Francis Lieber: Nineteenth-century liberal* (Baton Rouge: Louisiana State University Press, 1947).

6. Johann Kaspar Bluntschli, *Droit international codifié*, trans. M. C. Lardy (Paris: Guillaumin, 1870), 313–21.

7. 'Project of an International Declaration Concerning the Laws and Customs of War, 27 August 1874', *American Journal of International Law*, 1 (supplement) (1907), 96 [hereafter Brussels *projet*].

8. Convention Respecting the Laws and Customs of War on Land, 29 July 1899, 187 C.T.S. 429.

9. Convention Respecting the Laws and Customs of War on Land, 18 Oct. 1907, 205 C.T.S. 227 [hereafter Hague Rules].

10. Geneva Convention Relative to the Treatment of Prisoners of War, 29 July 1929, 118 L.N.T.S. 343; and Geneva Convention III Relative to the Treatment of Prisoners of War, 12 Aug. 1949, 75 U.N.T.S. 135.

11. France–Great Britain, Cartel, 13 Sep. 1798, 54 C.T.S. 287.

12. Abell, *Prisoners of war*, 14–18, 30–2.

13. France–Great Britain–Russia, Conditions for the Exchange of Prisoners, 13 Aug. 1855, 113 C.T.S. 307.

14. Cartel for the General Exchange of Prisoners of War, 22 July 1862, in 4 (ser. 2) The War of the Rebellion: A Compilation of the Official Records of the Union and Confederate Armies (Washington: GPO, 1899), 266–8 [hereafter Official Records (US Civil War)].

15. Lieber Code, Art. 109. See also, to the same effect, Bluntschli, *Droit international*, 316–18.
16. See James M. Gillispie, *Andersonvilles of the North: The myths and realities of Northern treatment of civil war Confederate prisoners* (Denton: University of North Texas Press, 2008).
17. Brussels *projet*, Art. 30.
18. Report to the [First Hague] Conference from the Second Commission on the Laws and Customs of War on Land, in James Brown Scott (ed.), *The reports to the Hague conferences of 1899 and 1907* (Oxford: Clarendon Press, 1917), 142.
19. Great Britain–United States, Cartel for the Exchange of Prisoners of War, 12 May 1813, 62 C.T.S. 243, Arts. 4–6.
20. Lieber Code, Art. 121.
21. Ibid. Art. 126.
22. Ibid. Art. 123.
23. Ibid. Art. 130.
24. Ibid. Art. 128. For similar provisions on parole, see Bluntschli, *Droit international*, 318–21.
25. Bluntschli, *Droit international*, 318–21.
26. Brussels *projet*, Arts. 31–3; and Hague Rules, Arts. 10–12.
27. Brussels *projet*, Art. 31; and Hague Rules, Art. 10.
28. For the similar provisions in the Hague Rules, see Hague Rules, Art. 12.
29. Sakuyé Takahashi, *International law applied to the Russo-Japanese war: With the decisions of the Japanese prize courts* (London: Stevens and Sons, 1908), 107.
30. Howard S. Levie, *Prisoners of war in international armed conflict* (Newport, RI: Naval War College Press, 1978), 398–402.
31. N. A. M. Rodger, *The command of the ocean: A naval history of Britain, 1649–1815* (London: Allen Lane, 2004), 501.
32. See William Edward Hall, *A treatise on international law*, 7th edn. by A. Pearce Higgins (Oxford: Clarendon Press, 1917), 433, n. 2.
33. For a detailed and clear exposition of the principal legal issues that arose in this area, see Maurice Keen, *The laws of war in the late Middle Ages* (London: Routledge and Son, 1965), 156–64. See also Bruno S. Frey, 'Prisoners and Property Rights', *Journal of Law and Economics*, 31 (1988), 10–46.
34. Abell, *Prisoners of war*, 4–8.
35. For a rare example of a peace treaty containing such a provision, see France–Great Britain–Spain, Treaty of Paris, 10 Feb. 1763, 42 C.T.S. 279, Art. 3.
36. Bluntschli, *Droit international*, 314.
37. Brussels *projet*, Art. 27.
38. Hague Rules, Art. 7.
39. Emmerich de Vattel, *The Law of Nations; or, the principles of natural law applied to the conduct and to the affairs of nations and sovereigns*, trans. Charles G. Fenwick (1758; Washington, DC: Carnegie Institution, 1916), 280, 284–6.
40. Lieber Code, Art. 56.
41. Ibid. Art. 59. See also, to the same effect, Bluntschli, *Droit international*, 313.
42. Prussia–United States, Treaty of Amity and Commerce, 10 Sep. 1785, 49 C.T.S. 331, Art. 24. These provisions were reiterated in the subsequent agreement of 1799, which replaced the 1785 one. Prussia–United States, Treaty of Amity and Commerce, 11 July 1799, 55 C.T.S. 15, Art. 24.
43. Glover, *The velvet glove*, 177–9.

44. Great Britain–United States, Cartel for the Exchange of Prisoners of War, 12 May 1813, 62 C.T.S. 243, Art. 7.
45. Lieber Code, Arts. 75–6.
46. Brussels *projet,* Art. 24.
47. Hague Rules, Art. 5. See also Bluntschli, *Droit international,* 314.
48. Hague Rules, Art. 7.
49. Ibid. Art. 17.
50. Ibid. Arts. 18–19.
51. Lieber Code, Art. 77.
52. Ibid. Art. 78. For similar provisions, see Bluntschli, *Droit international,* 315–16.
53. Brussels *projet,* Art. 28; and Hague Rules, Art. 8.
54. Lieber Code, Art. 76.
55. Bluntschli, *Droit international,* 315.
56. Brussels *projet,* Art. 25.
57. Ibid. Art. 26.
58. Hague Rules, Art. 6.
59. See Geneva Convention III on Prisoners of War, 12 Aug. 1949, 75 U.N.T.S.135, Arts. 49–57.
60. For a summary of the present law on the subject, see Stefan Oeter, 'Methods and means of combat', in Dieter Fleck (ed.), *The handbook of humanitarian law in armed conflicts* (Oxford: Oxford University Press, 1995), 204–7. For a more detailed study, see Frits Kalshoven, *Belligerent reprisals* (Leyden: Sijthoff, 1971).
61. Lieber Code, Art. 27.
62. Ibid. Art. 28.
63. Mark E. Neely Jr., *The fate of liberty: Abraham Lincoln and civil liberties* (New York: Oxford University Press, 1991), 151–2.
64. Bruce Tap, *Over Lincoln's shoulder: The committee on the conduct of the war* (Lawrence: University Press of Kansas, 1998), 207.
65. Geneva Convention on Prisoners of War, 29 July 1929, 118 L.N.T.S. 343, Art. 2.
66. Hague Rules, Arts. 14–16.
67. Caroline Moorehead, *Dunant's dream: War, Switzerland and the history of the Red Cross* (London: HarperCollins, 1998), 28–9.
68. Convention for the Amelioration of the Condition of the Wounded of Armies in the Field, 22 Aug. 1864, 129 C.T.S. 361.
69. Moorehead, *Dunant's dream,* 126–8.
70. Ibid. 64.
71. General Court-Martial Orders No. 153, 8 June 1866, 8 (ser. 2) Official Records (US Civil War), 926–8. It appears that the convicted person escaped from custody one year into his term of imprisonment.
72. For the report of the Wirtz trial, see General Court-Martial Orders No. 607, 6 Nov. 1865, 8 (ser. 2) Official Records (US Civil War), 784–92.

5

Prisoners in the First World War

Alan R. Kramer

TYPOLOGY OF CAPTIVITY

In the First World War, there were various categories of internment and captivity. The distinction between combatant and non-combatant in relation to prisoners of war appeared to be straightforward. With regular armies fighting other regular armies, it was usually clear that the men they captured were combatants who were accorded due rights as prisoners of war under the Hague Law of Land Warfare. However, there were important categories of non-military prisoners. One group was the Belgian and French civilians accused by the Germans of illegally partici- pating in combat in the first three months of the war. As per the German definition of international law, they were *francs-tireurs*, who had no right to be treated as prisoners of war. Following the execution of some 6,400 Belgian and French men, women, and children as *francs-tireurs*, at least 10,000 French and 13,000 Belgian civilians were deported to Germany. They were interned under harsh conditions in camps, very often together with prisoners of war, and held there during the winter of 1914–15.[1] Similarly, the Austro-Hungarian army deported and interned tens of thousands of Serb civilians, Czechs, Jews, and Ruthenes (i.e. Habsburg Ukrainians), on suspicion of espionage, resistance, or simply being 'Russophile'. A third of the 7,000 Ruthenes interned at Thalerhof camp died of typhus, and 3,000–4,000 Croatians died at Arad camp. In addition, at least 11,400 civilians were executed without even summary trials.[2]

Other civilians were taken captive, especially from 1916, to work as forced labourers in Germany or behind the front (e.g. 120,000 Belgians and 60,000 Lithuanians). Tens of thousands of French civilians were interned in labour camps, including, notoriously, 20,000 women and girls taken from Lille at Easter 1916. Housed in what were known as 'concentration camps', the civilian internees endured poor nutrition, humiliating treatment, beatings, and illness. Around 300,000 immigrant and seasonal workers from Russian Poland who were in Germany at the declaration of war were compelled to stay; and some were interned in what were likewise called 'concentration camps'.[3]

The Russian army evacuated and deported vast numbers of civilians on its eastward retreat before the German advance, with those suspected of national disloyalty, above all 200,000 ethnic Germans and half a million Jews, singled out for harsh treatment, as well as 300,000 Lithuanians, 250,000 Latvians, and 743,000 Poles.[4] Yet despite the intrinsic violence of the expulsions, they were not treated as prisoners.

On all sides, thousands of civilians were interned as enemy aliens.[5] Their history is linked with that of prisoners of war, although they were generally not regarded as combatants. Another category was also easy to distinguish from prisoners of war: the terrorists of 1914. Gavrilo Princip was put on trial and sentenced to a twenty-year gaol term for murder; he died of tuberculosis during the war. To deal with the Bosnian Serb conspirators, normal criminal law was sufficient: there was no need to create fictions about 'illegal combatants'.

INTERNATIONAL LAW AND PRISONERS OF WAR

The forced labour, deportation, internment, and execution of civilians marked the erosion of the standards of legal protection previously afforded to non-combatants. The consensus among historians is that military prisoners, by contrast, were mainly treated in conformity with international law.[6] Conditions in 1914–18 were generally far better than 'the systematic brutality and mass death' in the Second World War, especially in Japanese, German, and Soviet camps.[7]

It is now time to challenge such sanguine views. Between 6.6 and 8.4 million men were taken prisoner in the First World War.[8] That meant that one in eight soldiers fell into captivity, almost the same as the risk of death. More than one in five Russian troops and one in three Austro-Hungarian troops were taken captive.[9] The transformation of the nature of the war from the expected short campaign to near-total mobilization of societies occasioned an historic shift in the treatment of prisoners, military and civilian. Some wartime states attempted the total exploitation of their prisoners as an economic resource, subjecting them to systematic violence.

The trend towards total war collided with the nineteenth-century shift towards the codification of international law in accordance with what we today call humanitarian law. International law made rapid progress in the period after the American Civil War towards ensuring humanitarian treatment of prisoners. The main points of the Hague Convention on Land Warfare of 1899, modified in 1907, were that prisoners were not the captives of individuals, but of the captor state; they were not to be treated as criminals, but as legal, disarmed enemies. Prisoners 'must be humanely treated' and allowed to keep all their private property with the exception of arms. They could be employed in work, so long as it was not related to war operations, nor should it be exhausting or humiliating. The captor nation was responsible for feeding and clothing the prisoners, on the same peace footing as that of its own soldiers.

These principles were valid during the Great War. In addition, during the war, dozens of agreements were reached between the belligerent states, especially relating to the exchange of invalids and the role of neutral inspectors. Some of these restated the need for basic standards of humane treatment. For example, the Stockholm agreements of 13 May and 19 December 1916, between German, Austro-Hungarian, and Russian Red Cross representatives, repeated many of the rules from existing international law. Prisoners were not to be compelled by force or any other methods to impart information about the military situation or their nation (Article I.2). Camp guards were never to be equipped with whips, clubs, or similar implements (Article II. 7). However, there was a deterioration of standards with regard to food: rations were no longer to be equivalent to the captor nation's army rations; they were merely not to fall below the level given to the civilian population. This was potentially life-threatening for prisoners required to work, although those employed in heavy physical labour were supposed to be offered the same degree of extra rations as civilian workers (Article III. 1). Prisoners were also not to be given inferior food, such as potato peelings or cows' heads, except in cases of extreme shortage. Punishment by imprisonment was allowed, but all punishments involving the application of physical pain were banned.[10]

Germany and Britain reached agreements regarding the exchange of seriously ill prisoners at The Hague on 2 July 1917. A new feature was the recognition of a syndrome called 'barbed wire disease' (severe depression). Prisoners suffering from this who had been in captivity for longer than eighteen months could be interned in Switzerland or another neutral country, and if they did not improve within three months could be released to return home. A similar provision was contained in the Franco-German agreement at the Berne conference in December 1917.[11]

Further concessions on the release of men and non-commissioned officers (NCOs) over forty-eight years old were agreed at the Franco-German conferences at Berne in March and April 1918. It was also agreed that prisoners should be removed immediately after capture to camps at least thirty kilometres from the firing line; the ban on war-related work was reiterated, as was the ban on maltreatment of any kind. Men and NCOs had to receive rations to the value of 2,000 calories, plus extra food for those engaged in physical labour; in addition, the German government allowed each prisoner to receive up to two kilograms of bread per week from home. Minimum standards were agreed for the quality and space of accommodation and sanitary facilities in the camps.[12]

REALITIES OF CAPTIVITY AND THE CONFLICT WITH INTERNATIONAL LAW

The legal position thus appeared to be perfectly suited to the humane treatment of prisoners of war. The reality, however, was very different. Conditions were not uniform, as can be seen in the strikingly different death rates which varied from 3 per cent for German prisoners in British captivity, and 3 per cent for French and British prisoners in German captivity (7 per cent on Allied estimates), to 5.39 per cent of Russians and 29 per cent of Romanian prisoners in German captivity. However, the most significant distinction was not that between nationalities, but between officers and other ranks. In those days of rigid class hierarchies, enemy officers were generally, if not always, treated with dignity and given pay according to their rank, provided with comfortable, heated lodgings inside separate areas of camps, sometimes even in hotels, and provided with a manservant. They were able to buy abundant food, and were exempt from the obligation to work.

Conditions for ordinary soldiers were often grim, both inside the camps and outside them. In fact, the great majority of prisoners worked outside the camps. This often involved physically exhausting and even life-threatening labour. For Germany, in the first six months of the war, economic necessity was actually unimportant.[13] Since it was assumed the war would not last long, there was no need for prisoner labour; in any case, until winter 1914–15 there was high unemployment. Nevertheless, as Prussian war ministry instructions put it, prisoners had to be set to work. 'Without continuous and tiring occupation it will be impossible to keep great masses of young men in order.'[14] The point was to impose discipline by means of exhausting labour. Soon, however, the German economy, without the access to colonial labour that Britain and France enjoyed, badly needed prisoner labour. By November 1918, Germany had taken about 2.5 million men captive. In 1916, about 90 per cent of prisoners, or 1,449,000 out of 1,625,000, were at work. Agriculture was the major employer with 735,000, and 331,000 prisoners worked in industry. Prisoners made up over 12 per cent of the workforce in the Ruhr coal mines in 1916, rising to 16 per cent by 1918.[15]

Prisoner labour was so important that the state and employers usually tried to ensure adequate nutrition. By winter 1916–17, however, when Germany was afflicted by a serious food supply crisis, prisoners' rations were also cut: coal miners' rations were cut from 675 grams of meat and salami per week in June 1917 to 375 grams in August. The standard of nutrition was in general worse than that of German civilians, especially for prisoners who did not receive food parcels from home (above all Russians).[16] On the other hand, prisoners living on German farms often ate better than working-class civilians (except for privileged workers in war industries).

Prisoner labour was vital also for the Habsburg economy. Over the course of the war at least 1.3 million, possibly as many as 1,860,516, soldiers fell into Austro-Hungarian captivity.[17] By January 1918, over one million prisoners were working: 490,931 in agriculture, 268,219 in industry and transport, and 309,772 for the army at the front.[18]

The legal problem was not the extent, but the conditions of labour and the degree of coercion. Here national law conflicted with international law: in Germany and Austria-Hungary officers and NCOs were allowed to beat their men, and guards were thus allowed to use violence against prisoners. The director of the prisoner of war department at the British War Office, Lieutenant General Sir Herbert Belfield, noting the infliction of heavy punishments on prisoners in Germany, blamed the German military code.[19] Tying a prisoner to a post—a painful punishment that could lead to fainting and even death—was common in Germany and Austria-Hungary.

While the Prussian war ministry issued instructions to comply with international law, employers and the military administration went their own way. The Ruhr industrialist Paul Reusch, director of the Gutehoffnungshütte in Oberhausen, wrote:

> We are in the position that we do what we consider necessary. Therefore, if a prisoner will not comply, we let him go hungry for two to three days.... This occurs with the silent approval of the military administration. It is naturally a breach of the Hague Agreement. The military administration is, however, delighted when we can enforce a little order onto the men in this way.

The Berlin industrialist Ernst von Borsig reported his satisfaction at the violence inflicted by the guards on British prisoners of war.[20]

Moreover, the attempt to raise production at all costs from 1916 occasioned ever more ruthless policies. According to a representative of the war ministry in a meeting on 27–28 September 1916 to discuss the demand for prisoner labour, in view of Germany's struggle 'to be or not to be', international law should now be ignored. 'Hague Convention must no longer be regarded, it has made us bankrupt. We only mention it when it suits us.'[21] This was no chance remark. The 1916 edition of the commentary on the military penal code stated: 'Commanding power... may explicitly or implicitly declare international law to be a part of its will, but it can also reject it in part or totally. It is therefore basically always our own law, and only our own law, that determines our way of war.'[22] Seldom does one find such a frank admission of dissent from international law. As Heather Jones argues, by 1916, at any rate in some belligerent states, 'the concept of the prisoner of war as a non-combatant... had collapsed'.[23] This fundamentally revises the prevailing consensus.[24]

Harsh measures of coercion, whether in the camps or on labour detachments, were widespread. The evidence given by escaped French and British prisoners almost unanimously confirmed widespread physical punishment and poor quality and quantity of food, as early as 1915. Ex-prisoner Private Frank Byrne reported: 'Men were frequently tied up for two hours to posts and deprived of their dinner. The English were treated worse than the French, but the Russians even worse than the English. The Russians were flogged for instance in a way in which no others were.'[25] That was confirmed by an internal German report: an order issued by the Prussian war ministry on 29 July 1915 revealed that despite orders not to mistreat prisoners, 'Russian prisoners continue to be subjected to beatings by German personnel—often in the most violent manner'.[26]

By contrast, German prisoners in Britain admitted that although conditions in some camps were substandard, their treatment was in general fair. Only in relation to one camp, Leigh, did an incident of serious physical violence leading to death leave a trace in the existing German files.[27] Nutrition was more than adequate throughout the war, amounting to 2,000 calories per day, although British food was not always to the men's taste. Numbers of prisoners remained low until the last year of the war: In November 1917, there were only 2,300 officers and 45,841 German (and a few Austrian) men in camps in the British Isles;

the majority (70,731 men, no officers) was held in France for labour service. By November 1918, the total number of Germans captured amounted to 308,864, and the number held in the British Isles had risen to 89,937 men and officers, plus 1,491 navy personnel.[28] Unlike in France and Germany, prisoners in Britain were not employed in munitions production. By and large, Britain respected international law in the treatment of prisoners of war; the total of 3 per cent deaths over the entire period (on which British and German calculations agreed) was accordingly low.[29]

Likewise, most camps in mainland France gave few grounds for complaints about violence; many prisoners wrote home saying they were being treated well, and the food was good. There were three main exceptions. The first was the harsh treatment of men from Alsace-Lorraine, Schleswig-Holstein, and Prussian Poland, who had refused the offer of privileged treatment and stated their wish to remain German. They were concentrated in two camps known as *camps d'éliminés*, at Gerzat and Clermont-Ferrand, where, according to the International Red Cross, they were badly treated and frequently beaten. The second was the prisoner of war labour companies at Souilly camp in 1916, and in 1918 at St Hilaire, Vadelaincourt, Vervillers, and again Souilly, where the guards openly hit prisoners. The third was the sending of about 10,000 German prisoners to north Africa to work under African supervision. They resented the new racial hierarchy, and almost all contracted malaria, but the death rate was low.[30]

ILLNESS AND ACCESS TO MEDICAL TREATMENT

The way the captor nation dealt with illness also involved international law. In early 1915, typhus broke out at a number of camps across northern Germany. The typhus outbreak at Wittenberg and Kassel-Niederzwehren, with many deaths among French, British, and Russian prisoners in 1915, was held to be a major war crime for which the British and the French attempted to prosecute suspects after the war. Between January and July 1915, typhus spread to thirty camps, mainly in northern Germany, and 44,732 prisoners contracted the disease. At least 4,248 men died in the epidemic, according to a German medical history of the war. French and British witnesses claimed that in some camps the German authorities deliberately withheld medical assistance, and allowed the seriously ill and the dying to remain in miserable conditions.[31]

There was a direct parallel in Russia. In winter 1915–16, a typhus epidemic broke out among German and Austro-Hungarian prisoners in the large camp at Totskoe, in which at least 10,000 men died out of 25,000.[32] There is no doubt the conditions were quite inhuman, and the camp commanders and doctors showed callous disregard for human life. As in Germany, it was not exceptional: typhus broke out in many camps in Asian parts of the Russian empire.[33] However, the intervention of representatives of neutral powers (from Denmark, Sweden, and Switzerland) and the activities of nurses from Austria and Germany put sufficient pressure on the Russian government to change hygiene policy in the camps. As a result of the Totskoe scandal, no further major epidemics occurred in Russian camps between March 1916 and 1918.[34] It is not possible to generalize from these two epidemics about the standard of medical care. Sick and injured prisoners in Germany often received excellent medical treatment and extra rations, especially if they were in established camps; however, persuading the guards to allow access to the medical system was often a problem.[35] Many Italian sources spoke of inadequate medical care in Austro-Hungarian camps, and by late 1917, the empire had a severe shortage of medicines. In France, there were few complaints about access to medical care.[36]

FORCED LABOUR IN THE WAR ZONE AND REPRISALS

The deployment of prisoner labour in the war zone strikingly illustrated the clash between international law and the radicalization of warfare. Both sides engaged in this illegal, often lethal, practice. It was all the more perilous because neutral inspectors had no access to the war zone. The German army began to deploy Russian prisoners in labour battalions to work behind the western front from September 1915; local commanders often ignored war ministry instructions that they were not to be employed on war work, or to work under fire. In several cases in winter 1915–16, prisoners exposed to artillery fire were injured and killed. The wording of war ministry instructions indicates that British, French, and Belgian prisoners had already been working behind the front, when they were replaced as a matter of policy by Russians.[37]

By early 1916, more than 250,000 Allied prisoners were working in the operations zone, often in the fire zone.[38] According to reports by the International Red Cross, conditions were far worse than inside Germany, with extremely exhausting work and frequently brutal treatment by guards. Moreover, the men suffered constant hunger because the rations were even worse than in Germany. Many were injured and killed by artillery fire from the other side. As deliberate reprisal for the alleged French maltreatment of German prisoners in north Africa, 30,000 French and 2,000 British prisoners were sent in April–May 1916 to the eastern front in Courland (today part of Latvia). The men experienced hard labour on starvation diet, beatings, torture, and illness. After negotiations through Spanish mediation, the French returned the German prisoners from north Africa, and all French prisoners in Courland were sent back to Germany in September. Britain's refusal to negotiate kept the British prisoners on the eastern front until autumn 1917.[39] The Russian and Romanian prisoners, especially those involved in the construction of the Hindenburg Line in 1917, endured some of the worst conditions. Even the German military authorities conceded that prisoners returned from the labour detachments were often too ill to work, or even to have been transported.[40]

After the war, the German government admitted that it had broken international law, but claimed that both sides deployed prisoners at the front. The

German argument was not entirely specious: from the start of 1916, the French had begun to force German prisoners to work for military purposes, sometimes at the front, under fire. This was not officially in reprisal, but on the basis of a need for military labour. By July 1916, 50 per cent of the German prisoners in France were working for the French military, both in the war zone and in the interior, although this proportion was reduced to 36 per cent in November 1917.[41] Unknown to the French government, the Second Army forced some 6,000 German prisoners to labour under fire at Verdun on exhausting war-related work, such as construction and bringing army materials up to the front. The men suffered grossly unhygienic conditions and poor rations; many fell ill, and several were killed or injured by German shellfire.[42]

The German army responded with more reprisals, and by March 1917 about 40,000 French and British prisoners were deployed at the front, suffering similarly harsh conditions. Owing to the pressure of public opinion, the British and French governments decided in April 1917 to withdraw all prisoner labour to a line at least thirty kilometres from the front, against the protests of their army commanders. The German army then withdrew the British and French prisoners from the thirty-kilometre zone.[43] The cycle of reprisals was suspended, and for the rest of 1917, British, German, and French prisoners were generally not deployed at the front. However, prisoners still worked for the army in the rear areas, often in poor conditions and on low rations, with high rates of sickness.[44]

Russian prisoners continued to fare worst, and were deployed in the operations zone under fire, until the German–Soviet armistice of December 1917, and the subsequent peace treaty, brought a shift in this relationship. Russian prisoners working in the occupied territories were replaced by British, French, Italian, and Romanian men; they were exposed to the worst and most dangerous conditions at the front for the rest of 1918. Most of the 75,000 British and 15,000 French soldiers captured in the first wave of the German spring offensive of 1918 were immediately set to work, some being forced to carry shells to the front and dig trenches under fire. Brutal violence by the guards became endemic. This was a policy dictated by the German high command, in conscious breach of international law and the bilateral agreements not to deploy prisoners within the thirty-kilometre zone. By November 1918, approximately 400,000 prisoners of war were working in labour battalions for the German army, under conditions which had become disastrous.[45]

The radicalization of warfare thus replaced international law with the naked reciprocity of violence; in this transnational dynamic, the captor nation with the most prisoners had an inherent advantage. German war policy was the most ruthless driving force, but the other belligerents were also willing to subordinate international law to military necessity. Nevertheless, there were gradations in the degree of respect for humanitarian law: although the British army in France was employing 160,065 German prisoners by October 1918, the available evidence suggests that the army treated them well and adhered to the thirty-kilometre rule; there were no complaints about beatings or starvation.[46]

PRISONERS IN RUSSIAN CAPTIVITY

Between 1.6 and 2.2 million Austro-Hungarians and 167,000 Germans were taken prisoner by Russia.[47] The Tsarist government tried to meet its obligations under the Hague Conventions and wartime agreements. While the treatment of men upon capture was generally good, apart from theft, in the hinterland there were frequent violations of international law because of the incompetence of over-burdened camp administrations and regional authorities, especially in the first year of the war. But from 1915 to 1917 the treatment of prisoners was 'humanized in remarkable manner'.[48]

Estimates of the mortality rate vary from an improbably high 40 per cent (Germans and Austro-Hungarians on German figures)[49] to an impossibly low 1.7 per cent of Germans on Russian figures. A figure of 18 per cent of Habsburg prisoners appears to be realistic, and there is a methodologically sound estimate of 15 per cent of Germans.[50] The state was ultimately responsible for causing permanent harm and death of prisoners through neglect, chaos, exploitation, and maltreatment.[51]

In Russia, too, prisoners were put to work, and conditions varied widely. The most notorious case was the construction of the Murmansk railway, during which 25,000 out of the 70,000 prisoners, mostly German and German-Austrians, died. Yet Murmansk, as Nachtigal has shown, was untypical. Conditions else-where could even be quite tolerable.[52] On the other hand, the Russian army's punishment for refusal to work could be draconian, with a policy of executing 'ringleaders', 'decimating' others, and meting out corporal punishment.[53] When 100 prisoners refused to dig trenches near Lublin in summer 1915, one in ten was shot, and the others were severely beaten.[54]

ITALIAN PRISONERS IN HABSBURG CAPTIVITY

Of the 468,000 Italians in Austro-Hungarian captivity at least 92,451, or 19.75 per cent, died.[55] Was the high mortality rate the result of systematic abuses of international law by the Habsburg state? The Italian historian Giovanna Procacci locates responsibility elsewhere:

> Were the enemy governments really guilty of cruelty and deliberate vengeance, which amounted to a policy of mass murder? As can be seen from what follows, the answer must be no. The mass death of the prisoners of war was provoked by the Italian government, even largely desired, above all by the Supreme Army Command. Italy transformed the prisoner of war problem, which confronted all the belligerent states, into a real case of collective extermination.[56]

The Italian state, as Procacci demonstrates, regarded the prisoners as traitors and cowards for having surrendered to the enemy and, unlike France and Britain, refused to send collective deliveries of food. However, the men's families and the Italian Red Cross were allowed to send them food parcels. This was grossly inefficient, and in winter 1917–18 the system broke down completely, with a huge traffic jam of parcels at the Swiss border. Moreover, parcels were often subject to theft on route, by Italians and, above all, hungry Austrians.

Hunger was certainly the most important cause of death, but the circumstances of capture were crucially important for the men's survival. Many Italian soldiers reported that all their valuables were stolen from them, as well as their winter clothing and boots. After several days of forced march and transport in unheated cattle wagons, they thus arrived in the camps penniless, starving, and freezing. Repeated Austrian army orders prohibited theft from captives, but these were ignored.[57]

Those who survived the appalling conditions of transport were forced to do heavy labour such as quarrying, road-building, and digging trenches. Many returned seriously ill from the labour detachments, and some perished before reaching hospital. Food parcels, even if they had been sent, usually did not reach the men on labour detachments. The Italian prisoners were the victims not merely of an incompetent, and failing, Austro-Hungarian state, but also of new policies emerging piecemeal from the demands of a voracious war economy and a sadistic regime of coercion, in which the human body was regarded as expendable.

THE MOMENT OF CAPTURE AND THE FIRST DAYS OF CAPTIVITY

There are two further disturbing aspects to the moment of capture and the first days of captivity. Almost everyone writing on the history of the prisoners of war says that the belligerents were surprised by the large number of prisoners, and therefore unprepared, but we have to rethink this.[58] Poor conditions did not necessarily result from incompetence or lack of preparation; harsh treatment was a matter of policy in Germany, Austria-Hungary, and Turkey. As early as 31 August 1914, an order from the German Eighth Army, on the transport of Russian prisoners from the eastern front, stated that:

> feeding the prisoners is not possible since due to the uncertainty of the eastern army's supply lines, all food to hand must be reserved for the German troops....
> Prisoners must be treated strictly.... They are not to be given water at first; while they are in the vicinity of the battlefield it is good for them to be in a broken physical condition.[59]

There was thus a policy to 'break' prisoners for reasons of military efficiency. The evidence of Italian soldiers suggests the Austro-Hungarian army adopted the same policy.

One of the worst large-scale incidents of prisoner abuse in the first days of captivity was the treatment of the Indian and British soldiers captured by the

Ottoman army at Kut-al-Amara in Mesopotamia. Besieged since December 1915, when the garrison fell in April 1916 the survivors were sent on a forced march via Baghdad northwards to Anatolia. Deprived of water, the captives were beaten and stoned by Turkish and Arab guards, and kept in compounds without shade or sanitation. Indian and British soldiers (though not their officers), starving and thirsty, fell ill and were left to die by the road. Of the 2,592 British prisoners no fewer than 1,750 died, and of the 9,300 Indian soldiers, 2,500 died on this horrific death march or in subsequent harsh captivity.[60]

The second issue in this context is the killing of soldiers who had surrendered. Each army was guilty of committing this crime, which occurred mostly in the heat of combat. Joanna Bourke has argued that the killing of German captives was routine, an 'important part of military expediency', but her evidence is sparse, and amounts to showing that it was the exception rather than the rule.[61]

There were several documented cases. The German Major General Stenger issued orders to kill all captured and wounded French soldiers on the battlefield at Thiaville in August 1914.[62] French witnesses alleged the killing of over 150 wounded prisoners at Goméry, and German evidence confirmed this and other incidents between August and November 1914.[63] Some British officers issued such orders at the battle of the Somme in 1916.[64] The French army had special squads called *nettoyeurs* who followed advancing troops and 'cleaned out' enemy trenches, killing the captured and wounded.[65] Yet although the discourse of the killing of captives was ubiquitous, the actual practice was self-evidently not. The continued capture of thousands of prisoners every month and their survival would otherwise be impossible to explain. Armies routinely interviewed their men for corroboration of such stories of enemy criminality, but evidence was hard to find or inconclusive, and often produced the opposite result, showing that the treatment of captives was considerate.[66] The thesis of Niall Ferguson, that killing prisoners was so widespread that it prolonged the war since it made soldiers reluctant to surrender, thus remains unproven.[67]

AFTER THE WAR

After the war, Germany faced Allied demands for the extradition for prosecution in war crimes trials of fifty-two suspects for the killing of captured soldiers, and 151 suspects for killings and other maltreatment in the camps.[68] In the event, the Allies allowed Germany to conduct its own war crimes trials before the Reich Supreme Court at Leipzig, which turned out to be less than satisfactory. General Stenger, for example, was acquitted, although he did not deny saying that the captured and wounded Frenchmen should be killed.[69] The disappointments of Leipzig notwithstanding, a precedent had been established for the prosecution of those responsible for crimes against prisoners of war, and during the Second World War, Allied planning for the prosecution of Nazi war criminals expressly drew on that experience.

The end of the war did not mean the end of captivity. The French and British governments decided to retain German prisoners of war as forced labour to help restore the devastated regions. From January 1919 to January 1920, between 270,000 and 310,000 German prisoners worked under French command, and some 200,000 under British command, in atrocious conditions, clearing ordnance and debris from fields, trenches, and canals. While formally not breaching international law, this 'reparation labour' was certainly a disproportionate punishment for men who had suffered double misfortune.[70]

Two conclusions emerge from this survey. The Central Powers adopted, from the start of the war, policies which consciously breached the laws of war, and which the Allies to a lesser degree emulated. By 1916, the risk of death for some nationalities (Italians, Serbs, and Romanians; Germans and Austro-Hungarians in Russian hands) was probably almost as great in captivity as it was at the front; this was the result of a violent system of coercion for maximum exploitation of an expendable resource that was easy to victimize, and varying degrees of intentional neglect. Captivity in the First World War was thus far more violent than historians have previously admitted.

Secondly, there were several long-term consequences. On the positive side of the balance sheet, the International Committee of the Red Cross (ICRC) had played a major role in the inspection of camps, the transmission of information about prisoners, and humanitarian relief. The ICRC campaigned for a new code 'to alleviate the condition of prisoners of war', which came about with the Geneva Convention of 1929. On the negative side, the mass incarceration of civilian and military prisoners and their often harsh treatment were signposts on the road to the concentration camps of the later Fascist and Communist regimes. There had been a lively exchange of information between Germany and Austria-Hungary in relation to the construction and design of prisoner camps, during the period 1914–18. News about the treatment of one's own prisoners influenced the treatment of enemy prisoners. There was clearly a 'learning process' on how to administer vast numbers of prisoners and exploit their labour, but how this influenced policy before and during the Second World War remains to be researched.

NOTES

I am grateful to the Irish Research Council for Humanities and Social Sciences, which awarded me a senior research fellowship in 2006–7. I am deeply indebted to Heather Jones for her generous advice, and to Claudia Siebrecht for several important references.

1. Annette Becker, *Oubliés de la Grande Guerre: Humanitaire et culture de guerre, 1914–18* (Paris: Noêsis, 1998), 53–6. On internment together with prisoners of war, see Heather Jones, 'The enemy disarmed: Prisoners of war and the violence of wartime Britain, France and Germany 1914–20', Ph.D. thesis, University of Dublin (2006), 141 [forthcoming CUP]. On the context see John Horne and Alan Kramer,

German atrocities 1914: A history of denial (New Haven, CT: Yale University Press, 2001); on deportations see ch. 2, esp. 72–7, 166.

2. Anton Holzer, *Das Lächeln der Henker: Der unbekannte Krieg gegen die Zivilbevölkerung 1914–18* (Darmstadt: Primus, 2008), 72–7.

3. Ulrich Herbert, *Geschichte der Ausländerbeschäftigung in Deutschland 1880 bis 1980: Saisonarbeiter, Zwangsarbeiter, Gastarbeiter* (Bonn: Dietz Nachf., 1986), 82–3, 101–4.

4. Alan Kramer, *Dynamic of destruction: Culture and mass killing in the First World War* (Oxford: OUP, 2007), 151.

5. Christoph Jahr, 'Zivilisten als Kriegsgefangene: Die Internierung von "Feindstaaten-Ausländern" in Deutschland während des Ersten Weltkriegs am Beispiel des "Engländerlagers" Ruhleben', in Rüdiger Overmans (ed.), *In der Hand des Feindes: Kriegsgefangenschaft von der Antike bis zum Zweiten Weltkrieg* (Cologne: Böhlau, 1999), 297–321; Matthew Stibbe, *British civilian internees in Germany: The Ruhleben camp, 1914–18* (Manchester: Manchester University Press, 2008).

6. Richard Speed subscribed to this comforting view; see Richard B. Speed III, *Prisoners, diplomats and the Great War: A study in the diplomacy of captivity* (London: Greenwood, 1990).

7. Jay Winter, *The experience of World War I* (1988; London: Guild, 1989), 134. Ulrich Herbert argued that conditions in Germany did not differ from those in other belligerent countries: Herbert, *Geschichte der Ausländerbeschäftigung*, 86. Reinhard Nachtigal argues that the German military expressly prohibited maltreatment of captives and that the Central Powers attempted to maintain the health of their captives by providing better rations than for civilians: Reinhard Nachtigal, *Kriegsgefangenschaft an der Ostfront 1914 bis 1918: Ein Literaturbericht* (Frankfurt: Peter Lang, 2005), 26–9, 50.

8. Estimates cited by Uta Hinz, *Gefangen im Großen Krieg: Kriegsgefangenschaft in Deutschland 1914–21* (Essen: Klartext, 2006), 9. Franz Scheidl estimated 4,500,683 prisoners in the hands of the Central Powers and 3,880,650 prisoners in the hands of the Entente. All figures on prisoners of war have to be treated with caution. For example, Scheidl gives a total of 369,600 Italians in Austro-Hungarian captivity, while the true figure was 468,000. See Franz Scheidl, *Die Kriegsgefangenschaft von den ältesten Zeiten bis zur Gegenwart: Eine völkerrechtliche Monographie* (Berlin: Emil Ebering, 1943), 96–7.

9. Jochen Oltmer, 'Einführung', in Jochen Oltmer (ed.), *Kriegsgefangene im Europa des Ersten Weltkriegs* (Paderborn: Schöningh, 2006), 11–13.

10. Scheidl, *Die Kriegsgefangenschaft*, 98–109.

11. Ibid., 112–13.

12. Ibid., 125–34.

13. Jochen Oltmer, 'Zwangsmigration und Zwangsarbeit: Ausländische Arbeitskräfte und bäuerliche Ökonomie im Deutschland des Ersten Weltkriegs', *Tel Aviver Jahrbuch für deutsche Geschichte*, 27, 156.

14. Cited in Jochen Oltmer, 'Unentbehrliche Arbeitskräfte: Kriegsgefangene in Deutschland 1914–18', in Oltmer (ed.), *Kriegsgefangene im Europa*, 74.

15. Kai Rawe, '... wir werden sie schon zur Arbeit bringen!': Ausländerbeschäftigung und Zwangsarbeit im Ruhrkohlenbergbau während des Ersten Weltkrieges* (Essen: Klartext, 2005), 73–9.

16. Ibid., 105, 109.

17. These are the minima and maxima recorded in various sources by Verena Moritz and Hannes Leidinger, *Zwischen Nutzen und Bedrohung: Die russischen Kriegsgefangenen in Österreich 1914–21* (Bonn: Bernard & Graefe, 2005), 329.

18. Österreichisches Staatsarchiv, Kriegsarchiv Vienna, AOK, Karton 600, Op.- Abteilung Evidenzgruppe B, 1917/1918 Kriegsgefangene, Folio 1–21: Div. Zusammenstellungen über Kgf, 1917/18. 16, Nachweisung über den Stand und die Verteilung der Kgf im Hinterlande mit dem 1. Jänner 1918 als Stichtag. Ibid. 18, Übersicht über die Verwendung der Kgf im Hinterlande und bei der Armee im Felde, n.D.

19. Herbert Belfield, 'The treatment of prisoners of war', *Transactions of the Grotius Society*, 9 (1923), 140; cited in Jones, 'The enemy disarmed', 116.

20. Jens Thiel, 'Belgische Arbeitskräfte für die deutsche Kriegswirtschaft: Deportation, Zwangsarbeit und Anwerbung im Ersten Weltkrieg', Ph.D. thesis, Humboldt-Universität zu Berlin, 2003, 80 n. 272; quoted in Jones, 'The enemy disarmed', 116–17. On the widespread beating of British prisoners, see ibid., 211–14.

21. Cited in Hinz, *Gefangen im Großen Krieg*, 270 n. 572.

22. Cited in Gerd Hankel, *Die Leipziger Prozesse: Deutsche Kriegsverbrechen und ihre strafrechtliche Verfolgung nach dem Ersten Weltkrieg* (Hamburg: Hamburger Edition, 2003), 154, 257.

23. Heather Jones, unpublished paper. On the historiography, see Jones, 'The enemy disarmed', 18–21. For a negative view of French prisoners of war in Germany see Becker, *Oubliés de la Grande Guerre*.

24. The author himself subscribed to this consensus. Alan Kramer, 'Kriegsrecht und Kriegsverbrechen', in Gerhard Hirschfeld, Gerd Krumreich, and Irina Renz (eds.), *Enzyklopädie Erster Weltkrieg* (Paderborn: Schöningh, 2003), 282–92.

25. Cited in Jones, 'The enemy disarmed', 118–19.

26. Cited in Jones, 'The enemy disarmed', 160; see also Nachtigal, *Kriegsgefangenschaft an der Ostfront*, 22, 69.

27. Jones, 'The enemy disarmed', 121–2, 275. Panikos Panayi confirms that there are few reports of physical violence against German prisoners. Panikos Panayi, 'Normalität hinter Stacheldraht: Kriegsgefangene in Großbritannien 1914–19', in Oltmer (ed.), *Kriegsgefangene im Europa*, 137.

28. Panayi, 'Normalität hinter Stacheldraht', 131–6, 145. Total number of Germans captured from Jones, 'The enemy disarmed', 17, table 1.2.

29. Jones, 'The enemy disarmed', 274–80. The incidence of violence against German prisoners in British camps in France remains to be researched.

30. Jones, 'The enemy disarmed', 121–5, 291–5, 144–5.

31. Ibid., 126–38.

32. Reinhard Nachtigal, 'Seuchen unter militärischer Aufsicht in Rußland: Das Lager Tockoe als Beispiel für die Behandlung der Kriegsgefangenen 1915/16?', *Jahrbücher für Geschichte Osteuropas*, 48 (2000), 386.

33. Nachtigal, *Kriegsgefangenschaft an der Ostfront*, 72.

34. Nachtigal, 'Seuchen'.

35. Jones, 'The enemy disarmed', 231–4.

36. Ibid., 295.

37. Ibid., 159–61.

38. Hinz, *Gefangen im Großen Krieg*, 296. The figure was similar in 1917.

39. Heather Jones, 'The German spring reprisals of 1917: Prisoners of war and the violence of the western front', *German History* 26/3 (2008), 340–3.

40. Hinz, *Gefangen im Großen Krieg*, 297–301.

41. Bernard Delpal, 'Zwischen Vergeltung und Humanisierung der Lebensverhältnisse: Kriegsgefangene in Frankreich 1914–20', in Oltmer (ed.), *Kriegsgefangene im Europa*, 153.
42. Jones, 'The German spring reprisals', 343–6.
43. Ibid., 347–52.
44. Details in Jones, 'The enemy disarmed', 188–97.
45. Ibid., 197–219; on conditions in the last months of the war see 220–56. See also Heather Jones, 'The final logic of sacrifice? Violence in German prisoner of war labor companies in 1918', *Historian*, 68/4 (2006), 770–91.
46. Jones, 'The enemy disarmed', 281–7.
47. Reinhard Nachtigal, *Russland und seine österreichisch-ungarischen Kriegsgefangenen (1914–18)* (Remshalden: Greiner, 2003), 80–1. In addition there were between 50,000 and 67,000 Turkish prisoners. Rachamimov has a higher estimate of 2.77 million Austro-Hungarians. See Alon Rachamimov, *POWs and the Great War: Captivity on the eastern front* (New York: Berg, 2002).
48. Nachtigal, *Russland*, 91–3, 96.
49. Gerald H. Davis, 'Deutsche Kriegsgefangene im Ersten Weltkrieg in Russland', *Militärgeschichtliche Mitteilungen*, 31 (1982), 37.
50. Georg Wurzer, *Die Kriegsgefangenen der Mittelmächte in Russland im Ersten Weltkrieg* (Göttingen: V&R Unipress, 2005), 106–7.
51. Nachtigal, *Kriegsgefangenschaft an der Ostfront*, 31. Rachamimov has argued that the treatment of prisoners in Russia was inspired more by nineteenth-century traditions of humanitarian law and chivalry than mid-twentieth-century totalitarianism. See Rachamimov, *POWs and the Great War*, passim.
52. Review article by Peter Gatrell, 'Prisoners of war on the eastern front during World War I', *Kritika: Explorations in Russian and Eurasian History*, 6/3 (2005), 557–66.
53. Nachtigal, *Kriegsgefangenschaft an der Ostfront*, 29.
54. Haus-, Hof- und Staatsarchiv Vienna F36, Karton 448, Krieg 1914–18 Dep. 7 Kriegsgefangenen Varia, Z. 49823/7, K.u.k. Ift. Regt. Frh. Pflanzer Baltin, Nr. 93 IV. Feldbataillon.
55. Alan Kramer, 'Italienische Kriegsgefangene im Ersten Weltkrieg', in Hermann J. W. Kuprian and Oswald Überegger (eds.), *Der Erste Weltkrieg im Alpenraum: Erfahrung, Deutung, Erinnerung* (Innsbruck: Universitätsverlag Wagner, 2006), 247–58.
56. Giovanna Procacci, *Soldati e prigionieri italiani nella Grande Guerra. Con una raccolta di lettere inedite* (Rome, 1993; Torino: Bollati Boringhieri, 2000), 174–5.
57. Archivio dello Stato, Rome, Reale Commissione D'Inchiesta sulle Violazioni del Diritto delle Genti, Busta 18, Fasc. 197, K.u.k 11. Armeekommando. Armeekommando-Reservatbefehl Nr. 3. K.u.k. Feldpost 511, 14 January 1918. Ibid., K.u.k 11. Armeekommando. Armeekommandobefehl Nr. 33, k.u.k. Feldpost 511, 19 February 1918.
58. For example, Oltmer, 'Einführung', in Oltmer (ed.), *Kriegsgefangene im Europa*, 17.
59. Bundesarchiv-Militärarchiv Freiburg, PH 5 II 185, 8. Armee, I. AOK, 1,141 g, Erfahrungen des I. Reservekorps auf dem Gebiete des Gefangenenwesens, der Trophäen usw. Kortau, 31.8.14. I am grateful to Heather Jones for this important reference.
60. Martin Gilbert, *First World War* (London: Weidenfeld and Nicolson, 1994), 244–8; Heather Jones, 'Imperial captivities: Colonial prisoners of war in Germany and the Ottoman Empire, 1914 18', in Santanu Das (ed.), *Race, empire and First World War writing* (Cambridge: Cambridge University Press, forthcoming).
61. Joanna Bourke, *An intimate history of killing: Face-to-face killing in twentieth-century warfare* (London: Granta, 1999), 182; for an example of such 'expediency' in 1917, see ibid., 189.

62. Horne and Kramer, *German atrocities 1914*, 348–51.
63. Jones, 'The enemy disarmed', 85–90.
64. Bourke, *An intimate history of killing*, 242.
65. *Hamburger Nachrichten* 25 August 1916, see Annette Becker and Stéphane Audoin-Rouzeau, *14–18: Retrouver la Guerre* (Paris: Gallimard, 2000), 50, 54.
66. Jones, 'The enemy disarmed', 102–3.
67. Niall Ferguson, *The pity of war* (London: Penguin, 1998), 367–97. See also Niall Ferguson, 'Prisoner-taking and prisoner-killing in the age of total war: Towards a political economy of military defeat', *War in History*, 11/2 (2004), 148–92.
68. Horne and Kramer, *German atrocities 1914*, appendix 4, 448–9.
69. Hankel, *Die Leipziger Prozesse*, 123–42; see also Horne and Kramer, *German atrocities 1914*, 348–51.
70. Delpal, 'Zwischen Vergeltung und Humanisierung', 158–63; see also Jones, 'The enemy disarmed', 358–66.

6

The 1929 Prisoner of War Convention and the Building of the Inter-war Prisoner of War Regime

Neville Wylie

The 1929 convention relative to the treatment of prisoners of war (hereafter POW convention) does not hold a particularly esteemed place in the history of international humanitarian law. Most commentators have viewed it as little more than an addendum to the process of legal codification begun eighty years before, and which reached its apogee in the two Hague conferences in 1899 and 1907. The recognition that captured combatants ought to be accorded certain specific privileges is, for instance, traditionally apportioned equally between the Hague regulations of 1907 and the POW convention, twenty-two years later.[1] Geoffrey Best, the most erudite historian to have tackled the subject, tellingly passes over the 1929 conference in silence and describes the convention as merely 'a straight continuation of pre-1914 trends'.[2] Contemporary observers shared these views. The conference's elected *rapporteur*, Georges Werner, summed up the prevailing view when he remarked that the conference's 'point of departure continues to be the Hague regulations'.[3] It was precisely the apparent symmetry between the 1929 convention and its pre-war antecedents that appeared to destine the convention to irrelevance after 1941. The architects of the Third Reich and the East Asian 'co-prosperity sphere' had little time for the convention's lofty ideals, and naturally those responsible for drafting the 1949 conventions were only too happy to distance themselves from the 'failed' experiments of the past.

But was the 1929 convention little more than a quaint, faint echo of the beliefs and values of Europe's *belle époque*, which had tried, in the words of one critic, to transform the experience of captivity in to a 'halcyon time...a kind of inexpensive rest-cure after the wearisome turmoil of fighting'?[4] This chapter argues that the 1929 POW convention, while clearly a product of its time, nevertheless represented a significant step in the evolution of the POW regime. Other contributors to this collection will evaluate the convention's place in the history of the Second World War, but my aim here is to explore the context within which discussions of the world's first dedicated 'POW' convention took place, and to highlight those issues which divided opinion at the time and proved important milestones in the evolution of the international regime governing the treatment of POWs and detainees. We start, however, with some comments on POW captivity during the Great War, for it was this defining experience that inevitably framed post-war discussion on the shape of the new POW convention.

THE EXPERIENCE OF CAPTIVITY, 1914–22

Over the last decade or so historians of the Great War have become increasingly alive to the 'dynamic of destruction' which seemed to grip Europe after 1914 and give rise to cycles of violence that rapidly broke down pre-war cultural norms of 'acceptable behaviour'.[5] The process was especially pronounced in the treatment of civilians and *francs-tireurs*, but also led to governments sanctioning ever-greater levels of violence towards captured enemy personnel and prisoners of war.[6] By the middle years of the war most belligerents were prepared to condone, even encourage, the vindictive treatment of POWs, and legitimate their actions on crude political grounds—as retaliation to a prior wrong—or out of an exaggerated sense of cultural superiority.[7] Much of the hardship experienced by prisoners after 1914 had its roots in the administrative shortcomings of their captors and the economic burden imposed by the need to fight 'total war', which led to the exploitation of POW labour in ways that did not accord with the sentiments embodied in the Hague regulations. But the willingness of governments to resort to punitive measures against prisoners, to impose on them draconian, and frequently dangerous, working conditions was, in terms of its scale and wilfulness, of an order and magnitude that dwarfed earlier European conflicts, even if it fell short of the kind of depravities encountered after 1941.

The 'lessons' of the Great War, in so far as it related to the issue of captivity, continued to be 'learnt' long after the armistice had been signed. The rapid collapse of centralized government authority across much of Europe meant that when the guns fell silent, many former prisoners were forced to fend for themselves and join the throngs of displaced civilians struggling to return to their homes and loved ones. The prisoners' plight was aggravated, though, by the convulsions that gripped European politics after the war and the deliberate withholding of the right of repatriation to thousands of prisoners, lest their return exacerbate tensions in their homelands. Russian POWs captured by the former Central Powers were kept in their camps until mid-1919. Their Ottoman, Austro-Hungarian, and German counterparts, trapped in Siberia by the outbreak of Russian civil war, had their homecoming delayed until the summer 1922, eight years after the war had begun.[8] The 'memory' of wartime captivity—both for those who experienced it and for those who looked on—continued, therefore, to evolve under the pressure of events long after the return of peace in November 1918. Prisoners of war became, in Bob Moore's telling phrase, 'prisoners of peace'. In this, as in so many other ways, the Great War was a characteristically 'modern' conflict.[9]

The issue of repatriation was the principal but by no means only issue to affect attitudes towards captivity over the course of the post-war decade. Although the lot of prisoners varied enormously during the war, there were sufficient instances of wilful cruelty and neglect for populations on both sides of the conflict to develop a genuine and profound sense of grievance and outrage about the way their countrymen had fared in enemy hands. In London, a 'committee on the treatment by the enemy of British prisoners of war' was established under the chairmanship of Lord Robert Younger in late 1915 to 'collect, verify and record' instances of German and Turkish barbarity. The committee's findings soon featured in British propaganda leaflets and provided the evidence required to press claims against German nationals involved in the mistreatment of British POWs after the war had come to an end. Not to be outdone, Germany also set about recording evidence of alleged abuse. Three separate volumes were pub- lished in 1918, listing the names of Frenchmen implicated in the mistreatment of German POWs during the war, and similar lists and reports were produced detailing the behaviour of Germany's other adversaries.[10] In such circumstances, it was all too easy for governments to belittle the criticisms of their enemies as exaggerated or politically inspired, and silence those in their own camp who sought an 'objective' account of what had gone on.[11]

It was, however, the inclusion of Articles 228–30 in the Treaty of Versailles, allowing the Entente to prosecute individuals guilty of war crimes, that ultimately politicized post-war debates over the treatment of prisoners. Of the 1,059 charges formally brought against individuals in Germany, 14 per cent related to crimes purportedly committed against prisoners. Prisoner ill-treatment also featured, to a lesser degree, in claims made against Turkey.[12] The resultant 'war crimes' trials in Leipzig and Istanbul in 1921, though notable for establishing the principle of individual responsibility under international law, only went to underscore the fragility of the humanitarian regime by this date. Two German soldiers were found guilty of ill-treating British prisoners, but it was the leniency of the sentences (between six and ten months), and not the legal precedents set by their convic- tions, that attracted most attention.[13] Indeed, the Leipzig trials are principally remembered for the opportunity they gave the German military to expound its views upon such concepts as 'military necessity' and 'defence of superior orders' which had so frequently justified the violation of pre-war international norms.[14]

London pronounced itself satisfied with the verdicts and promptly suspended further investigations, but the blatantly political nature of the proceedings in Leipzig was too much for the French and Belgians, who abandoned the trials and pledged to pursue matters through their own courts.[15] The unedifying spectacle, played out over the remainder of the decade, of German officers being found guilty, in absentia, in Belgium and France, only to have their behaviour triumph- antly exonerated by the German *Reichsgericht*, merely prolonged and exacerbated the resentment and bitterness felt by all sides. A measure of the sensitivity shown towards the issue of captivity can be seen in the German reaction to the publi- cation in 1929 of the memoir by George Cahen-Salvador, a former *Conseiller d'Etat* who had played a leading role in French POW policy.[16] The sight of

Cahen's book adorning the windows of Geneva's bookstores was almost too much for the German delegation, which came perilously close to raising the matter in the conference chamber and challenging their French counterparts to account for some of the unsavoury aspects of France's own record on captivity and internment.[17]

A final obstacle to securing agreement on the terms of a new convention lay in the general reluctance shown towards revisiting the laws of war, lest any move in this direction jeopardize the ongoing efforts to banish warfare from the lexicon of contemporary statecraft. Lord Robert Cecil, one of the architects of the League of Nations, epitomized the conundrum facing the international community. Despite long involvement with POW matters, Cecil declined to lead Britain's delegation to Geneva—'on the very Cecilian grounds', as one observer put it, 'that, being a man of peace, he could not associate himself with any work that contemplated war'.[18] The two Geneva conventions of 1929—the new 'POW' code and the revised 'Red Cross' code—were the *only* elements of the pre-war *jus in bello* updated after 1918. All the other legal initiatives taken during these years dealt with those aspects of warfare which had been unknown to the pre-war world.[19]

That these various difficulties were eventually overcome is explained not simply by the palpable shortcomings of the Hague regulations, but by the fact that much of the work for a new code had already taken place during the war itself, when the belligerents concluded a series of agreements to amplify and improve the pre-war legislation. The first of these, signed in Stockholm in November 1915, sprung from the endeavours of the German, Austro-Hungarian, and Russian Red Cross societies and was little more than a statement of principles. Later negotiations, however, involved the governments themselves and resulted in binding treaties, the most important of which were Germany's agreements with France (May 1917, supplemented by a second one in April 1918), Britain (July 1917, and again in July 1918), and the United States (November 1918). The Russian, Turkish, Romanian, Bulgarian, and Serbian governments also came to agreements clarifying aspects of the POW regime, or outlining arrangements for the repatriation or hospitalization of ill, old, or wounded POWs.[20] These wartime agreements, forty in all, encapsulated a wealth of state practice. Though they passed over some issues, and left others unresolved, they bequeathed to the post-war legislators a body of knowledge that fed directly into the post-war debates over POWs.

THE 1929 POW CONVENTION

The history we have of the making of the 1929 POW convention is essentially that of the International Committee of the Red Cross (ICRC). It was the ICRC who initially called for a diplomatic conference to be convened to draw up a new POW code. It was they who kept the matter on the Red Cross agenda in the early 1920s, and ultimately provided the draft text for the Geneva conference in July 1929. The

ICRC was not, however, the only body to pursue the issue over the course of the decade, and while the final convention bore the unmistakable hallmark of the ICRC it was nevertheless shaped by a number of other forces that were no less influential. Of the possible 'solutions' thrown up in discussions, that which was sponsored by the US government was perhaps the most extreme.[21] Washington took a minimalist approach to the enterprise. The basic principles embodied in the Hague regulations remained, in American eyes, entirely valid; what was needed was merely a set of guidelines, or regulations, indicating how these principles ought to be applied in practice. A draft code submitted by the US delegation to the Geneva conference in July 1929 was, then, a slim document, which simply replicated the key provisions of the Hague rules and added a copy of the US–German agreement of 11 November 1918, as a 'model' accord to guide future discussions, as and when required.[22]

The benefits of the American approach were its simplicity and its emphasis on the basic standards of treatment required. It was an approach that appealed to the British. In London, discussion on a POW code was, from the outset, firmly anchored in the wartime experience and the two British–German agreements of 1917 and 1918. Although London was happy to adopt the ICRC's draft text as the basis for discussion in 1929, it shared Washington's desire to see a convention shorn of extraneous or overly complex provisions. The differences between the Anglo-American and Genevan approaches, however, went beyond merely a question of form. At one level there was the matter of shelf-life. For the Anglo-Americans, the ICRC's 'desire to translate . . . matter[s] of principle into terms of present day technique' threatened to saddle the convention with provisions that would quickly be outpaced by the march of progress and technology.[23] For the ICRC—and the majority of the delegations assembled in Geneva—the more precisely the convention could outline states' obligations, the less the chance there was of detaining powers shirking their responsibilities. As the ICRC's Paul des Gouttes put it, 'in the monotonous daily life of the prisoners of war, it is the details which matter'.[24] The German government fully adhered to this approach, and conjured up a host of measures to improve the convention, from stipulating the number of taps and showers required for each barrack block and the monthly ration of soap, to legislating on the thicknesses of prisoners' mattresses.

Behind the arguments over the convention's content—whether it should be 'thick' or 'thin'—lay the more fundamental issue of the latitude states should enjoy in applying the convention in practice. The Americans were, again, ahead of the pack. The sparseness of their draft proposals was grounded in the belief that the US military could be trusted to adhere to the underlying principles without the need to follow exhaustive prescriptions agreed upon through common accord. For a time in the early 1920s, the US War Department even tried to block the right of third parties to supervise the convention and insist that it alone be responsible for overseeing the application of the convention within US forces.[25] While its position softened over time, Washington consistently pressed for a convention that remained the exclusive preserve of state authorities, and repeatedly sought to regulate the position of outside parties such as the ICRC. The Anglo-Saxons were also committed to retaining the right to negotiate their own ad hoc arrangements when required. Thus, the British expressed themselves in favour of a convention capable of protecting prisoners from 'elementary neglects and cruelties in matters of first principle' but one which left 'all the working details to suit the peculiarities of each nation's government and financial system ... [to] special negotiations and arrangements on behalf of the belligerents'.[26]

At one level, the Anglo-Americans' confidence in face-to-face talks made sense. After all, as one of the participants in the Anglo-German talks in July 1917 put it, when an issue was 'dealt with as an existing difficulty, of course the belligerents were prepared to come to a far more elaborate arrangement than you could ever have committed them to in advance'.[27] But there was also something rather curious about the Anglo-American enthusiasm for wartime negotiations, not least since these events had proved highly contentious at the time and created uproar in the parliament and press. The record of achievement was likewise far from inspiring. It was precisely Berlin's failure to live up to its obligations under the 1917 agreement that forced British officials to negotiate a fresh deal the following year. The initial sessions of this second conference were so icy that the German delegation came within a whisker of abandoning the talks and returning home.[28] While, then, officials may have genuinely believed in the need to frame regulations with an eye to the circumstances pertaining to a particular situation, it is more than likely that the root of the issue lay in their desire to retain a free hand over the interpretation and practical application of the convention in the future.

Although the POW convention of 1929 contained five times as many articles as the Hague rules it replaced, it was, on balance, more aligned with the wishes of the Anglo-Americans than those of the ICRC and its supporters. Section VIII, dealing with the 'Execution of the Convention', foresaw the conclusion of 'special conventions on all questions relating to prisoners of war' and anticipated the holding of face-to-face meetings 'at the commencement of hostilities' to facilitate this task (Article 83(3)). In terms of detailed provisions the convention was, in some respects, 'work in progress': few of the technical suggestions tabled by the German and other delegations found their way onto the final instrument. The one detailed section, dealing with the question of repatriation and hospitalization of sick and wounded prisoners, was, tellingly, separated from the main body of the text and relegated to an annex. The 'model draft agreement', designed to act as a guide for future discussions, was precisely the kind of instrument envisaged in the draft code tabled by the United States.[29]

REPRISALS

Where the ICRC was uniquely successful was over the question of reprisals. This was a matter of considerable importance, and one in which the ICRC had invested substantial political capital. All previous POW codes and draft regulations had implicitly or explicitly condoned the use of reprisals against prisoners.[30] Although reprisals were traditionally seen as a means of *limiting* the conduct of warfare, the Great War had found prisoners penalized for a whole host of purported wrongdoings by their governments, and not simply alleged infractions of the POW regime.[31] Legal scholars have explained 1929's prohibition against the use of reprisals on the 'brilliant piece of surgery' achieved by the ICRC in decoupling POWs from the law of armed conflict—Hague law—and integrating them into the corpus of international humanitarian law.[32] It is certainly the case that in making POWs the subject of Geneva law, rather than Hague law, the ICRC strengthened the claim for seeing the prisoner as an innocent victim of war, like the sick and wounded of the original Geneva conventions of 1864 and 1906, rather than merely an 'enemy disarmed', as depicted under the Hague rules. The POW code of 1929 was, in this respect, as important for the rights it bestowed on the prisoner as for the context within which these rights were exercised. As the sick and wounded had generally been considered exempt from belligerent reprisals, it was clearly logical to extend the same privilege to POWs.

The scourge of reprisals had not been dodged in the wartime conferences, but with the genie already out of the bottle, negotiators saw little point in trying to put it back. Efforts were directed instead towards preventing reprisals from spiralling out of control. The first British–German agreement, for instance, committed both sides to providing four weeks' notice before imposing retaliatory measures against POWs. Naturally, penalizing innocents was objectionable from a moral point of view, but reprisals were, at base, an integral component of that concept of reciprocity upon which—in the absence of chivalric or normative constraints on state behaviour—the POW regime ultimately relied. A War Office report into Britain's experience with reprisals written in 1920 reluctantly concluded that 'when the circumstances promised good results' the measures had proved their worth. In some cases, it noted, 'the mere threat of reprisals ... produced the desired results', especially in those instances that involved Germany's alleged ill-treatment of POWs.[33]

It was these facts—uncomfortable though they were—that ultimately shaped the majority opinion over the course of the 1920s. While Geneva doggedly held out for an outright ban on reprisals, most draft codes or proposals aired over the post-war decade sought to make a virtue of necessity. The foremost set of recommendations to emerge at the time was the twenty-two article code adopted by the International Law Association (ILA) in the autumn of 1921. Founded in Brussels in 1873, the ILA was the leading association of international lawyers in the world, with membership drawn from across Europe and the Americas. The author of its POW code, Lord Robert Younger, was, of course, no stranger to the subject, and his code naturally reflected both his own wartime experience and the views of Younger's close confidant in the War Office, the adjutant general, Lieutenant General Sir George Macdonogh. The ILA code thus shunned the ICRC's exalted ambitions and instead endorsed the 'official' War Office line. 'No army', Younger insisted, 'could reasonably be expected to renounce in war so effective and powerful a weapon for the redress or cessation of supposed intolerable wrong upon its own nationals.'[34] The tension between humanitarian aspirations and practical politics thus remained unresolved. Prisoners were 'at all times [to] be humanely treated', but collective reprisals were only 'deprecated', and in lieu of a complete ban, the ILA code merely provided a set of procedures to limit the scope and duration of any punitive measures.[35]

The ILA was not alone in taking a 'pragmatic' view towards reprisals. Indeed, the ICRC's principled stand on the issue initially placed it at odds with a good number of the national Red Cross societies.[36] POW veterans were also wary of dispensing with a mechanism which, in the last resort, was designed to protect their interests. As Friedrich Wolle, a member of Germany's Imperial Association of former POWs, *Reichsvereinigung ehemaliger Kriegsgefangener* (*RvK*), remarked, 'reprisals have the objective of bringing about a symmetrical treatment of POWs', and were therefore the bedrock of any 'principle of justice' in POW affairs.[37] A set of recommendations distributed by the *RvK* in advance of the Geneva conference in early 1929 faithfully reflected this attitude and merely urged antagonists to delay any retaliatory measures for six weeks, to allow time for the dispute to be resolved through diplomatic channels.[38]

Given the strength of feeling on the issue of reprisals, the ICRC's success in securing agreement for their total abolition is all the more remarkable. Its draft code, circulated shortly before the conference opened, elicited numerous suggestions for possible amendments but provoked relatively little comment on Article 2's prohibition on the use of reprisals. When the issue came before the conference, 'one delegation after another rose to condemn measures of reprisals...as a step backwards in civilisation'. Britain's suggestion that states be allowed to apply reprisals *in extremis* found little support and the matter was never put to a vote.[39] It is not clear whether those present genuinely believed in the possibility of eradicating reprisals from POW law or not. None of the belligerents felt the slightest bit constrained in resorting to reprisals after 1939, if they believed their prisoners might benefit as a result. It is likely that most supported the ICRC's proposal out of hope that it might, at the very least, stop states from routinely turning on prisoners whenever their adversaries deviated from the laws of armed conflict. If the blanket prohibition of Article 2 resulted in limiting the use of reprisals to violations of the POW convention, it would, perhaps, have served a useful purpose.

PROTECTING POWERS

One of the striking points to emerge from the inter-war debates over POWs was the near universal faith observers placed on the role of neutral third parties in supervising the application of the convention.[40] This was a judgement grounded on the experiences of the Great War. From early 1915, most belligerents had come round to the view that the involvement of neutral organizations was an essential prerequisite for the successful fulfilment of the Hague regulations. A variety of bodies had been called upon in this capacity, from the officially designated protecting powers to independent, or quasi-independent, organizations, such as the ICRC, the YMCA, the Vatican, and national Red Cross societies. Most were involved in the distribution of comforts and relief parcels for POWs, but some were also assigned supervisory duties by the belligerents and accorded specific rights under the various bilateral agreements over POWs concluded in the final years of the war.

If there was unanimity on the principle of third party involvement, there was less agreement on which bodies should be empowered to fulfil these functions, or the level of the control they would wield. The ICRC staked out an early claim over the area, inspecting POW camps, furnishing reports on their findings, and publishing some of their correspondence in the monthly *Revue Internationale de la Croix-Rouge*.[41] The committee's willingness to act as guardian of international law was clearly evident, and found expression after the return of peace in its devotion to securing a protocol banning the use of poison gas and in the imaginative suggestions embodied in its draft 'code for POWs, deportees, evacuees and refugees', presented to the tenth international conference of the Red Cross in mid-1920. Geneva's ambitions went beyond merely providing humanitarian assistance. The 1920 code empowered the committee to investigate alleged violations of the convention and notify the delinquent state of its findings. In the event of non-compliance, the ICRC proposed referring the matter to the League of Nations or the Permanent Court of International Justice (PCIJ). Nine years later, the committee's ambitions were no less ambitious. The final draft code prepared for the 1929 conference assigned the committee a number of discrete and exclusive functions, and internal ICRC correspondence leaves little doubt over the committee's determination to stake a claim over this area of activity.[42]

The committee's tenacious efforts to win recognition for its work on behalf of POWs needs to be seen in light of the crisis within the Red Cross movement created by the emergence of the League of Red Cross Societies (LRCS) in 1919. Efforts to demarcate the competencies of the ICRC and LRCS dragged on throughout the decade, and only came to an end in 1928 when their respective presidents, Max Huber and Paul Draudt, agreed on a set of statutes for the movement which essentially affirmed the primacy of ICRC to coordinate Red Cross activities in time of war, and left the LRCS to develop the movement's peacetime role.[43] With peace finally restored, relations between the two organizations rapidly improved, and the ICRC did what it could to drum up support for its negotiating position in the League, the national Red Cross societies, and from those formerly neutral states which, it was hoped, might empathize with the committee's wish to augment the role of third parties in the convention.[44]

The principal opponents of the ICRC's plans turned out to be the British and American governments. The attitudes of these governments were prompted, in part, by Geneva's clumsy efforts to umpire relations between the belligerents during the war, and its equally ham-fisted attempt to set itself up as the arbiter for all matters legal after the return of peace. In 1921, anxious to put an end to the acrimony over the alleged violation of international law during the war, the committee took the extraordinary step of offering to investigate claims brought to its notice.[45] Berlin's enthusiastic support for Geneva's offer only went to confirm the Entente's doubts over the wisdom of submitting their wartime record to outside scrutiny, and they quickly stepped in to smother the ill-judged initiative.[46] Some of Geneva's suggestions for the new POW convention were equally tactless. Its proposal that the League Council or PCIJ be given the responsibility to act as the final arbitrator for disputes arising out of the convention was scarcely likely to curry favour in Washington. Moreover its repeated 'run-ins' with the powerful American, and to a lesser extent British, Red Cross societies probably inclined these influential institutions to withhold their support for Geneva's various initiatives in discussions with their respective governments. In the end, it took the intercession of the Swiss government to persuade Washington to withdraw its objection to the ICRC's involvement at the conference, and while it ultimately played an important role in shaping the proceedings, neither it, nor the Sovereign Order of Malta—the only other unofficial organ represented at the conference—were accorded voting rights.[47]

At the heart of the apparent disdain shown for the ICRC lay the simple fact that both Washington and London believed that the interests of POWs were best served by relying upon protecting powers—officially sanctioned and empowered by the belligerent states—not well-intentioned philanthropists. The United States had, of course, seen the war from both sides: as a neutral state and protecting power before 1917, and latterly as a belligerent. True, Washington had been noticeably proactive in protecting British interests in Germany, but all states had benefited from the involvement of protecting powers during the war and had written them into the series of agreements dealing with POW matters over the course of the war. As the American jurist, Charles Hyde, noted shortly after the war, 'by no other process can inhumane treatment in any form on the part of a captor be so readily detected or so fairly estimated'.[48] Other agencies might be allowed to inspect POW camps and report their findings, but these were considered supplementary to the 'official' reports provided by the protecting powers.

Before closing on this point, a few words ought to be said about an American proposal for an alternative mechanism to oversee the operation of the POW convention. Although the proposal was never tabled officially, it appears that the US delegation might have, at the very least, canvassed opinions informally before returning it to their briefcase. Instead of relying on a single neutral state as a protecting power, Washington proposed the creation of a 'standing commission', set up in each capital and staffed by representatives of all those states who had ratified the convention. In the event of war, the neutral members of the commission, fortified, when required, by members of the ICRC and Sovereign Order of Malta, would be responsible for fulfilling the functions normally associated with the protecting power—inspecting camps, arranging for the repatriation of POWs, their hospitalization in neutral countries, and so forth. Apart from being, in the words of one US document, 'the active authorized, representatives of world opinion favoring every possible mitigation of the horrors of war', the standing commission had the advantage of being able to mobilize the wishes and, where necessary, the political clout, of the entire neutral lobby, rather than being dependent on the interests and capabilities of a single power.[49] The American proposal was certainly not without its problems: it assumed members of the commission would speak with one voice, and avoid dividing along political, or ideological, lines.[50] But in itself, the proposal reveals the importance attached by state governments to having robust mechanisms in place to ensure the proper functioning of the POW convention.

Primary responsibility for this task thus fell on the shoulders of the protecting powers: neutral governments officially mandated by the belligerents to look after their interests in enemy territory. The protecting powers' authority flowed from their status under the convention, but there is little doubt that the conference believed that prisoners would best be served if their guardians could call upon the full moral and political weight of a sovereign state. Naturally, there was debate over the balance between the rights of the protecting power on the one hand, and the detaining power on the other. Efforts to have the protecting powers, the ICRC, or ad hoc neutral tribunals *arbitrate* disputes arising out of the convention were firmly quashed: the protecting powers could offer their services to resolve disputes, but they had no power to impose solutions on the disputants. Other rights, required for the effective fulfilment of their mission, were only passed by the narrowest of margins and made the subject of reservations by some of the delegations at the signing ceremony. These included the right to inspect prisoners *wherever* they were held, and the right to converse with POW representatives *in private*. The former was vital if the convention was to prevent a repetition of the abuse seen on the western front, when neutral inspectors were denied access to POW labour detachments working behind the firing line. The latter prevented the camp authorities from pulling the wool over neutral eyes, and victimizing individual prisoners who criticized the camp regime.[51] Interestingly, not all concessions to the 'military mind' were dictated by the military exigencies of the great powers. Some of the smaller state delegations were clearly nervous about allowing the protecting powers to intrude too deeply into the military domain, for fear that their duties under the convention might compromise their own relations with the great powers.[52] Notwithstanding these difficulties, the cementing of third parties into the running of the POW convention represented a major advance in the protection of POWs. For the first time, protecting powers and the ICRC had a clear *locus standi* in POW affairs that could not be ignored by any government that aspired to living within internationally agreed norms. For the first time, too, there was a recognizable system of oversight and verification built in to the functioning of the POW regime.

CONCLUSION

The international community could be rightly proud of the advances it had accomplished in promoting humanitarian norms in the treatment of POWs by

1929. That achievement was all the more impressive considering the often brutal, inhumane, and degrading treatment meted out to prisoners during the Great War and the huge resentment aroused by the Leipzig trials and subsequent court proceedings of the 1920s. Those responsible for drafting the 1929 POW convention may be reproached for failing to anticipate the horrors that befell prisoners after 1939, but the experiences that informed their discussions provided an image of captivity that was a far cry from the sentimentalized 'ideal' evoked by some of the pre-1914 writers on the subject. The new convention may, likewise, have remained wedded to the principles set out in The Hague twenty-two years before, but important steps had been taken to build these into a framework that made non-compliance far harder to either achieve or excuse. In the process, the prisoner's status had been enhanced by placing POWs on the same footing as those who had been made *hors de combat* through wounds or injury sustained on the battlefield. Advances were also made in bolstering the supervisory mechanisms, creating oversight measures that were significantly more far-reaching than anything envisaged hitherto.

The conference's *procès-verbaux* reveal a surprising level of unanimity between the former enemies. For all the vitriol created by the ill-treatment of prisoners after 1914, the debates over the POW convention progressed with remarkably little rancour.[53] As the ICRC's draft echoed the compromises agreed in the wartime agreements, differences of opinion tended to revolve around questions of interpretation and nuance, rather than fundamentals. Indeed, the enemies of the Great War quickly found common cause in puncturing some of the misguided ideas peddled by the minor delegations. 'Next to our Allies in the last war', admitted the head of the British delegation, 'our opponents lent specially favourable support to . . . our proposals', and were often 'the first to propose the adoption of the British text or amendment'. Franco-German relations were rather less cordial, but, according to one outsider, 'no serious difference of opinion on any questions of importance' arose to disturb the prevailing spirit of cooperation and harmony.[54] Within five years, over half of the states represented at the Geneva conference had ratified the POW convention, including Adolf Hitler's new government in Germany. A further twelve states would join the convention before war returned to Europe in 1939.[55] The only delegation to give cause for concern at the conference was the Japanese, whose excessively conservative outlook and dogged defence of military prerogatives frequently put it at odds with the prevailing mood. Most commentators, however, mindful of Japan's shining record towards POWs at the start of the century, were confident of Tokyo coming round to the majority view and ratifying the convention in due course.[56] As for the Soviet Union, which absented itself from the conference on political grounds, the obvious interest it had paid to the emerging POW regime over the 1920s offered the not unreasonable hope that the Soviet government would not only approve of the convention, but even introduce some of its provisions into Soviet military regulations.

Of course, many of these assumptions would be shattered by the events of the Second World War. Ideological, racial, and national prejudices quickly corroded the foundations of the POW regime. Traditional national-conservative attitudes may have survived to influence German policy towards POWs, but this was hardly sufficient to secure the health and well-being of those who fell into Germany's hands. There was, as Geoffrey Best rightly notes, 'an irreducible element of humbug in Nazi propaganda's appeals to the laws of war', which no amount of selective observance could disguise.[57] Yet, with hindsight, it could be argued that what ultimately sabotaged humanitarian project after 1939 was not the *weakness* of the POW convention, or even its fundamental norms, so much as the willingness of belligerents to abandon it in its entirety. The problem lay, in short, in states' wholesale rejection of the convention, denying its validity and withholding its provisions from those it was meant to protect. When the POW convention was applied, its success and essential robustness can scarcely be ignored.[58] Even when prisoners were denied their full rights under the convention, alternative arrangements were invariably put in place to ensure that a modicum of protection remained.[59]

The fault of the inter-war POW regime did not lie in its failure to imagine the horrors of a *Vernichtungskrieg*, but in its reluctance to conceive of the 1929 convention as applicable to all conflicts, and not just those fought between members of the recognized international community. At the heart of the convention lay the assumption that its provisions were primarily intended for conflicts between nations of the civilized world. This was, in a sense, entirely in keeping with Western conceptions of the law of armed conflict since antiquity.[60] The laws of war were binding for wars within the European states system but when those same states encountered peoples beyond their world, laws of an altogether different ilk were deemed to apply. By the early twentieth century, European colonialism had given these practices a veneer of legality. Conflicts within the jurisdictions of European empires were deemed 'internal insurrections' and not 'international conflicts', so the paraphernalia of internationally agreed standards did not apply. European norms were not unknown in these cases, as British suppression of the Arab revolt in the late 1930s showed, but the thresholds of 'acceptable' violence were invariably much higher than traditionally admitted in European theatres.[61]

The issue was not overlooked by inter-war commentators, but most tended to assume that in such 'asymmetrical' conflicts, European states would merely seek to capitalize on their superiority and use the promise of good treatment, facilities, and provisions to entice their enemies into premature surrender.[62] At the same time, however, there were clearly doubts over whether the POW code was applicable to all situations. It is surely telling that the article found in the Red Cross convention, obliging member states to abide by the code even when their enemies were not parties to the convention, was omitted from its sister code for POWs.[63] The thinking behind this omission is alluded to in the remarks of a member of the ICRC delegation to the 1929 conference, the veteran delegate Mme Frick-Cramer. When asked, shortly after the close of the conference, whether she would consider writing a *manuel d'agence* on the ICRC's experiences in the Great War, Frick-Cramer replied that she doubted the utility of such an enterprise. '*Les conditions devant changer considérablement selon le théâtre des hostilités. Pour des Arabes ou des nègres il y aurait des principes tout différents à suivre.*'[64] Different peoples followed different principles. Recognition of the existence of two discrete sets of norms for the conduct of war helps explain, at least in part, the committee's hesitation in pressing the Ethiopian government to accede to the POW convention in mid-1935, and its later willingness to take Italian claims of Abyssinian ill-treatment and mutilation of Italian prisoners at face value.[65] This outlook is important since it admitted, in effect, to a quasi-legitimate set of norms applicable to conditions in which the POW convention had no place. In so doing, it acknowledged the possibility of states not so much derogating from individual provisions of the convention as deciding for themselves whether, and in what circumstances, its adversaries were worthy of treatment in accordance with the Geneva principles. It was a dangerous precedent, for it gave the green light to militarists, xenophobes, racists, and ideologues to behave with impunity and deny the benefits of the convention to countless thousands of prisoners of war in the global conflicts of the 1930s and 1940s.

NOTES

1. Richard D. Wiggers, 'The United States and the denial of prisoner of war (POW) status at the end of the Second World War', *Militärgeschichtliche Mitteilungen*, 52 (1993), 92–3.
2. Geoffrey Best, *Humanity in warfare: The modern history of the international law of armed conflicts* (London: Methuen, 1983), 220. For the convention as a part of customary international law, see Geoffrey Best, *Law and war since 1945* (Oxford: Clarendon, 1994), 8–9.
3. 'Report of Monsieur Werner on the work of the Second Commission (Prisoners of War)'. Enclosure 1 to Appendix F, in E. Wadsworth (US delegation to the Diplomatic Conference, Geneva) to Secretary of State, Washington, 1 Aug. 1929, National Archive and Records Administration [hereafter NARA], Washington D.C. 514/2A12/137. Box 5447.
4. J. M. Spaight, *War rights on land* (London: Macmillan, 1911), 58.
5. Alan Kramer, *Dynamic of destruction: Culture and mass killing in the First World War* (New York: Oxford University Press, 2007). On the general theme, see Theo Farrell, *The norms of war: Cultural beliefs and modern conflict* (Boulder, CO: Lynne Rienner, 2005).
6. See John Horne and Alan Kramer, *German atrocities 1914: A history of denial* (New Haven, CT: Yale University Press, 2001).
7. See Heather Jones, 'The final logic of sacrifice? Violence in German prisoner of war labor companies in 1918', *Historian*, 68/4 (2006), 770–91. Peter Pastor's assertion, that the Gulag system was based on the Russian POW camp model—Samuel Williamson and Peter Pastor (eds.), *Essays on World War I: Origins and prisoners of war* (New York: Columbia University Press, 1983), 113–17—is challenged by Alon Rachamimov, *POWs and the Great War: Captivity on the Eastern front* (New York: Berg, 2002), 78–82. See also Annette Becker, *Oubliés de la grande guerre: Humanitaire et culture de guerre, populations occupiées, deportés civils, prisonniers de guerre* (Paris: Hachette, 1998).
8. See inter alia Yücel Yanikdağ, 'Ottoman prisoners of war in Russia, 1914–1922', *Journal of Contemporary History*, 34 (1999), 69–85; Ivan Völgyes, 'Hungarian prisoners of war

in Russia', *Cahiers du Monde Russe et Soviétique*, 14 (1973), 54–84; Rachamimov, *POWs and the Great War*, 191–5.

9. Bob Moore and Barbara Hately-Broad (eds.), *Prisoners of war, prisoners of peace* (Oxford: Berg, 2005).

10. James Morgan Read, *Atrocity propaganda 1914–1919* (1941; repr. New York: Arno, 1972), 135. Alfred de Zayas, *The Wehrmacht War Crimes Bureau, 1939–1945* (Lincoln: University of Nebraska Press, 1989), 5–10.

11. For interventions in the German parliament see Uta Hinz, *Gefangen im Großen Krieg: Kriegsgefangenschaft in Deutschland 1914–1921* (Essen: Klartext, 2006), 354–5; Horne and Kramer, *German atrocities 1914*, 337–40.

12. See Taner Akçam, *Armenien und der Völkerbund: Die Istanbuler Prozesse und die türkische Nationalbewegung* (Hamburg: Hamburger Edition, 1996); David Bloxham, *The great game of genocide: Imperialism, nationalism, and the destruction of the Ottoman Armenians* (Oxford: Oxford University Press, 2005); Alan Kramer, 'The first wave of international war crimes trials: Istanbul and Leipzig', *European Review*, 14/4 (2006), 441–55.

13. See Lord Cave, 'War crimes and their punishment', *Transactions of the Grotius Society*, 8 (1922), xxix.

14. See Gerd Hankel, *Die Leipziger Prozesse: Deutsche Kriegsverbrechen und ihre strafrechtliche Verfolgung nach dem Ersten Weltkrieg* (Hamburg: Hamburger Edition, 2003), 228–59; Horne and Kramer, *German atrocities 1914*, 345–55; Larry Zuckerman, *The rape of Belgium: The untold story of World War I* (New York: New York University Press, 2004).

15. The court dismissed the case brought by Belgium, and produced only one conviction (and a custodial sentence of two years) for the six French cases.

16. George Cohen-Salvador, *Les Prisonniers de guerre, 1914–1919* (Paris, 1929).

17. Lt. Col. A. Fonck (German Defence Ministry) to Sidney H. Brown (ICRC), 19 Nov. 1929, ICRC Archives (AICRC), Geneva, CR177.1.

18. Ronald C. Lindsey (FO) to Sir Horace Rumbold (British embassy, Berlin), 22 June 1929, Bodleian Library, University of Oxford, MS Rumbold dep 37. Cecil had been responsible for POW affairs in the Foreign Office (1915–16) and had helped shape British thinking on POWs over the early 1920s.

19. The use of gas (1925 Geneva protocol) and submarines (1936 London protocol). See Dietrich Schindler and Jiri Toman (eds.), *The laws of armed conflict: A collection of conventions, resolutions and other documents* (4th revised edn.; Leiden: Martinus Nijhoff, 2004).

20. See André Durand, *History of the International Committee of the Red Cross II: From Sarajevo to Hiroshima* (Geneva: Henry Dunant Institute, 1984), 52–62, 75–6.

21. 'Note de M. Huber sur la conférence diplomatique', 29 June 1929, AICRC, Geneva, CR177.1.

22. See Raymond Stone, 'The American-German conference on prisoners of war', *American Journal of International Law*, 13/3 (1919), 406–49.

23. Minute by O. D. Skelton (Department of External Affairs, Ottawa), 7 June 1929, National Archive of Canada, Ottawa, RG25 Series A 2 Vol. 192.

24. Cited in Durand, *From Sarajevo to Hiroshima*, 255.

25. U.S. War Department memo for the Chiefs of Staff, 10 July 1926, p. 7, The National Archives and Records Administration (NARA), College Park, MD, RG59 514.2A12 Box 5445; F. B. Kellogg (Secretary of State) to Secretary of State for War, 2 Nov. 1927, ibid.

26. Minute by Col. Holt Wilson (War Office and delegate to the Geneva conference), 22 Aug. 1929, The National Archives (TNA), United Kingdom, WO32/5337.

27. Comment by Lord Justice Younger, 25 Nov. 1921, International Law Association (ILA), *Report on the Thirtieth Conference, The Hague, 30 August–3 September 1921* (London: Sweet & Maxwell, 1922), 232.

28. See Lt. Gen. Sir H. Belfield (Director of POWs, War Office), 'Diary of Conference at the Hague, June and July 1918', 8 June 1918, Imperial War Museum (IWM), Department of Documents, London/Duxford, 91/44/1 HEB1/3.

29. 'Model draft agreement concerning the direct repatriation or accommodation in a neutral country of prisoners of war for reasons of health.'

30. 'Instructions for the Government of Armies of the United States in the Field' (Lieber Code), 24 Apr. 1863, Article 59/2. The 1874 Brussels declaration and the Fourth Hague Convention were silent on the issue.

31. See Michael Walzer, *Just and unjust wars: A moral argument with historical illustrations* (2nd edn.; London: Basic Books, 1992), 207. For the use of prisoners as 'human shields', see Christian Geinitz, 'The first air war against noncombatants: Strategic bombing of German cities in World War I', in Roger Chickering and Stig Förster (eds.), *Great War, total war: Combat and mobilization on the Western Front, 1914–1917* (Cambridge: Cambridge University Press; Washington, DC: German Historical Institute, 2000), 217.

32. Frits Kalshoven, *Belligerent reprisals* (Leyden: A. W. Sijthoff, 1971), 71–2.

33. Maj. Gen. Sir Herbert E. Belfield, 'Report on Directorate of Prisoners of War', September 1920, TNA, FO369/1450 K15026; Foreign Office memo by G. Warner, 30 May 1918. Hampshire Record Office, Papers of Sir George Warner, 5M79 A7.

34. ILA, *Report on the Thirtieth Conference*, 191.

35. ILA, 'Proposed International regulations for the treatment of Prisoners of War', 25 Nov. 1921, ILA, *Report on the Thirtieth Conference*, 241–2.

36. See remark by Vizconde de Mamblas (Spanish Red Cross Society), ILA, *Report on the Thirtieth Conference*, 215.

37. Friedrich Wolle, *Grundsätzliches und Kritisches zur Reform des Rechtes der Kriegsgefangenen: Material zur Reform des Kriegsgefangenenrechts, Heft 2* (Berlin: Reichsvereinigung ehemaliger Kriegsgefanger, 1929), 10.

38. RvK, 'Vorschläge für ein neues Kriegsgefangenenrecht unterbreitet von der Reichsvereinigung ehemaliger Kriegsgefangener e. V.', April 1929, p. 25, AICRC, C177.3.

39. Sir Horace Rumbold to Sir Arthur Henderson, 31 July 1929, TNA, FO372/2551 T9201.

40. See Gustav Rasmussen, *Code de prisonniers de guerre: Commentaire de la Convention du 27 juillet 1929, relative au traitement des prisonniers de guerre* (Geneva: ICRC, 1931), review by the British delegate, George Warner, *British Yearbook of International Law*, 13 (1932), 213; and the remarks of the ICRC delegate, Mme R. M. Frick-Cramer, Mme. R. M. Frick-Cramer to Sidney H. Brown (ICRC), 30 Nov. 1929, ACICR, B. CR177.1.

41. See Uta Hinz, 'Humanität im Krieg? Internationales Rotes Kreuz und Kriegsgefangenenhilfe im Ersten Weltkrieg', in Jochen Oltmer (ed.), *Kriegsgefangene im Europa des Ersten Weltkriegs* (Paderborn: Schöningh, 2005), 216–36.

42. Paul des Gouttes, 'Notes pour la délibération du C.I.C.R.', April 1929, AICRC, CR177.2; Remark by M. Paul Logoz, Meeting of the I.C.R.C., 2 June 1927, ACICR, A PV Séances du Comité.

43. John F. Hutchinson, *Champions of charity: War and the rise of the Red Cross* (Boulder, CO: Westview, 1996), 314–45; Durand, *From Sarajevo to Hiroshima*, 174–94.

44. See letters by Max Huber to Ake Hammarskjold (PCIJ), 2 May 1929, and P. Draudt (LRCS), 15 June 1929, AICRC, CR177.4.

45. ICRC circular No. 203, 15 Apr. 1921. The suggestion was officially withdrawn in January 1922.

46. To be fair, the idea was originally put to the ICRC by the Australian and Canadian Red Cross societies at the 10th international Red Cross conference.

47. See State Department to US legation, Berne, 13 June 1929, NARA, RG59 514.2A12 1910–1929 Box 5444. The 11th International Red Cross conference in 1923 voted down the ICRC's suggestion that it be given responsibility for ensuring the application of the 1906 Geneva Convention.

48. Charles Cheney Hyde, *International law: Chiefly as interpreted and applied by the United States*, ii (Boston, MA: Little, Brown & Co., 1922), 340.

49. State Department memo. 'Suggested method of dealing with the Code of Prisoners of War'. n.d., included in the dossier for the US delegation to Geneva, July 1929, NARA, RG59 514.2A12 Box 5447.

50. The difficulties experienced by the 'neutral' commissions charged with overseeing the repatriation of POWs at the end of the Korean War was clearly not envisaged by the drafters of the US proposal.

51. The convention, for the first time, allowed prisoners to elect their own representatives.

52. See E. Wadsworth, US delegation, Geneva, to Secretary of State, 1 Aug. 1929, Red Cross and POW Conference, Geneva, Appendix F, NARA, RG59 514.2A12 Box 5447.

53. International Committee the Red Cross, *Actes de la conférence diplomatique de Genève de 1929* (Geneva: Journal de Genève, 1930).

54. Sir Horace Rumbold to Sir Arthur Henderson, 31 July 1929, TNA, FO372/2550 T9201; Rumbold to Henderson, 31 July 1929, TNA, WO32/3653.

55. For the German ratification process, see Overmans, 'Kriegsgefangenenpolitik des Deutschen Reiches', 29–30.

56. Japan was one of nine signatories to fail to ratify the convention: its offer to apply the convention *mutatis mutandis* in 1941 had little practical effect on POW treatment.

57. Geoffrey Best, *Churchill and war* (London: Hambledon, 2005), 289. See also Neville Wylie, 'Captured by the Nazis: Reciprocity and National Conservatism in German policy towards British POWs, 1939–1945; in C.C.W. Szejnmann (ed.), *Rethinking history, dictatorships and war: Essays in honour of Richard Overy* (London: Continuum, 2009), 107–24.

58. See Neville Wylie, Barbed Wire Diplomacy: Britain, Germany and the Politics of Prisoners of War, 1939–1945, (Oxford: Oxford University Press, 2010).

59. Here I have in mind the Scapini mission in Berlin, which acted as an *Ersatz* protecting power for French prisoners from the spring of 1941. See Yves Durand, *La captivité: Histoire de prisonniers de guerre Française, 1939–1945* (Paris: FNCPG, 1982).

60. See Michael Howard, 'Constraints on warfare', in Michael Howard, George J. Andrepoulos, and Mark. R. Shulman (eds.), *The laws of war: Constraints on warfare in the western world* (New Haven, CT: Yale University Press, 1994), 2–5; and Frédéric Mégret, 'From "savages" to "unlawful combatants": A post-colonial look at international humanitarian law's "other" '; in Anne Orford (ed.), *International law and its others* (Cambridge: Cambridge University Press, 2006), 265–317.

61. See Matthew Hughes, 'The banality of brutality: British armed forces and the repression of the Arab revolt in Palestine, 1936–9, *English Historical Review*, 124 (2009), 313–54. The classic case is the German suppression of the Herero between 1904 and 1907, but Spain's behaviour in the Rif war, 1919–26, was equally savage. For the former, see

Isabel Hull's contribution to this volume and her study, *Absolute destruction: Military culture and the practices of war in Imperial Germany* (Ithaca, NY: Cornell University Press, 2005).

62. See for instance Wolle's remarks on the impact of cultural differences in Wolle, *Grundsätzliches und Kritisches zur Reform*, 10; or the optimism shown by the British delegation over the issue of propaganda: Sir Horace Rumbold to Sir Arthur Henderson, 31 July 1929, TNA, FO372/2550 T9201.

63. Art. 25. 'If, in time of war, a belligerent is not a party to the Convention, its provisions shall, nevertheless, be binding as between all the belligerents who are parties thereto.'

64. Remark by Mme. Frick-Cramer, Meeting of the I.C.R.C., 26 Sept. 1929, ACICR, A PV Séances du Comité.

65. Rainer Baudendistel, *Between bombs and good intentions: The Red Cross and the Italo-Ethiopian War, 1935–1936* (New York: Berghahn, 2006), 220–1.

Part II

Prisoners in Regular Conflicts—The Second World War

7

The Treatment of Prisoners of War in the Western European Theatre of War, 1939–45

Bob Moore

The general perception of the treatment of prisoners of war by both the Allied and Axis powers in western Europe is widely regarded as having been carried out in accordance with the rules set out by the Geneva Convention of 1929. The belligerent powers of 1939 certainly assumed that the war would be a conventional war—both in terms of being fought between recognizable national armed forces and as a conflict governed by the rules and conventions pertaining to warfare. Their signatures and ratification of the 1929 Convention were, in large measure, a result of the democratization of warfare during the First World War, when the fate of prisoners in enemy hands became an important domestic political issue. To a large extent, the western European and African theatres of war bore out this expectation, although even in this environment, the workings of the Convention had been tested up to and beyond its limits by the end of hostilities. This chapter examines the handling of prisoners from three different standpoints: within the terms of the Convention, at the margins of the Convention, and outside the Convention.

THE INTRODUCTION AND IMPLEMENTATION OF THE GENEVA CONVENTION

The Convention of 1929 made comprehensive provisions for the treatment of prisoners of war once in captivity and for reciprocal agreements between belligerent powers on issues not directly covered by its terms. Thus, at the commencement of hostilities the British, French, Germans, and Italians all appointed protecting powers to represent their interests with enemy powers. Ostensibly, most pressing practical issues between Britain and Germany were settled quickly as a result of the relative efficiency of the agencies involved. One exception seems to have been the vexed question of merchant seamen, whom the British assumed to be civilians but the Germans regarded as servicemen and therefore subject to the provisions of the Convention.[1] Similar negotiations between Britain and Italy took much longer—ostensibly due to the prevarication of the relevant Italian authorities—and only when large numbers of Italians began to fall into British hands at the end of 1940 was there some greater urgency.[2] As with the Germans, subsequent discussions also included some matters outside the scope of the Convention. However, many issues remained vague and at the end of 1942, the Foreign Office noted that 'so far as [can be] seen, we have had no reply... which is quite in accordance with Italian methods'.[3] Inevitably, the details of the treaty's finer points had to be sorted out through bilateral negotiation although many of these were never fully agreed between London, Berlin, and Rome.

Lines of communication were also an issue within each belligerent power, with reports and protests coming via the protecting powers being transmitted by Foreign Offices to the army, naval, and air force high commands that retained the responsibility for the prisoners in their charge. In the United Kingdom, the Prisoners of War Department (PWD) at the Foreign Office commenced its work as hostilities began, but the War Office did not establish its Directorate of Prisoners of War (DPW) until 25 May 1940.[4] Moreover, the increasingly multi-national nature of British forces deployed against both the Axis and then Japan also saw the establishment in 1941 of an Imperial Prisoner of War Committee (IPOWC).[5] Perhaps not surprisingly, the Germans and the *Oberkommado der Wehrmacht* (OKW) had been better prepared administratively for the prisoners of war created by the conflict against Poland and the Western powers.[6]

The constantly recurring theme in the documentation surrounding the normal workings of the Convention is that of reciprocity. In this early period, it was the legal (treaties) department of the Foreign Office that acted as the government's conscience. Thus, when it was mooted that German POWs might be sent to other parts of the Empire, it was this arm of the bureaucracy that raised the spectre that such a move might provoke German retaliation and that British POWs might be sent to 'unpleasant places in Poland'.[7] For British officials, reciprocity became a mantra to be invoked when the limits of the Convention were reached. In some respects, this was hardly surprising as the treatment of British prisoners in German, Italian, and later Japanese hands was a matter of public debate and no small amount of official embarrassment. As far as the relations between Britain and the Axis powers were concerned, the work of the protecting powers and the representatives of the International Committee of the Red Cross (ICRC) paid major dividends in providing information for both governments and families, and in ensuring the basic terms of the Convention were followed. There were, inevitably, complaints on specific issues such as food and accommodation by all sides but most were mediated or resolved over time. More complex issues took longer, for example in negotiating the exchanges of sick and wounded prisoners. German demands on numerical equality, it was argued by the British, 'caused great disappointment and much hardship to men who should have been sent home long before they actually returned', whereas with the Italians, allowances had to be made for 'the usual attitude of *laissez-faire* and for incompetence'.[8]

The Italian surrender in September 1943 created further problems. Some British prisoners in northern Italy were ordered by their senior officers to remain in their camps—where the arriving Germans seized them[9]—but others who fled the unguarded camps were able to make their escape and either joined the partisans, attempted to reach Switzerland, or disappeared into the countryside.[10] The status of Italian prisoners in Allied hands also became uncertain, as the Convention had no provision for a power effectively changing sides. Designating them as co-belligerents rather than as Allies allowed London and Washington to keep them as prisoners—and thus as a pliable and very useful labour force.[11] As the war progressed, the British and Americans had encountered many of the problems of military success previously experienced by the Germans. The masses of Italians and Germans captured in North Africa and later in north-west Europe had to be fed and housed, a problem exacerbated by local conditions, for example when the stipulated rations for enemy prisoners exceeded the food available to local Allied civilian populations. The answer was found in moving the prisoners. Those from North Africa were moved to South and East Africa, India, and the United States, whilst a lack of guards, food, and accommodation, alongside fears of disease, meant that those captured in France and Belgium in the summer of 1944 were transferred to the United Kingdom. However, even with this remedy British officials admitted that 'winter conditions [would] make adherence to the Geneva Convention difficult'.[12] As with so many other issues, possible German reprisals against Allied prisoners remained the prime determinant of British Imperial and American policy in dealing with enemy prisoners, especially when conditions inside Germany deteriorated and the Gestapo and SS became more involved in POW matters towards the end of the war.[13]

THE MARGINS OF THE CONVENTION

The Convention stipulated that prisoners were not obliged to give their captors anything more than their 'name, rank, and serial number', but all belligerent powers saw the value of captured enemies as a source of battlefield and wider military intelligence. Thus, prisoners could find themselves subjected to interrogation on capture—an interrogation that might include threats and the use of force if the information sought was required immediately. However, this was seldom the end of the matter, as transit camps and even permanent camps could also be employed to extract military or more general information on the enemy. Both the British and Germans generally eschewed techniques of violence, drugs, hypnotism, and solitary confinement, partly because they were not thought to work, but also because they were likely to lead to complaints to the protecting power and potential reprisals.[14] At the same time implied threats seem to have been commonplace.[15] Even the most feared of the British interrogation centres, the London District Cage in Kensington, did not employ methods prohibited by the Convention, a fact reinforced by the testimonies of prisoners held there.[16]

Most British infringements of the Convention owed their origins either to military or political exigencies being seen as more important, or to downright inefficiency.

The best known of these precipitated the so-called shackling crisis of 1942–3 between Britain and Germany. Berlin complained about a number of instances where forces under British command had been shown to have orders permitting the tying of prisoners' hands.[17] The discovery of four Germans found shot but with their hands tied after the British raid on Sark in October led to German reprisals and tit-for-tat responses by the British. This turned into a very public battle of wills between Churchill and Hitler that continued into 1943 before finally petering out.[18] While an excellent example of the power of reciprocity in the treatment of prisoners of war, this particular incident also caused the British authorities to examine their own policies and interpretations of the Geneva Convention.[19]

It is undoubtedly true that the British attitude to the German charges was ambivalent. As General Ernest Gepp, the Director of the DPW, put it in December 1942: 'The War Office defend the right to tie up prisoners, on the grounds of operational necessity or where the alternative is to kill the man concerned.' This he deemed to be 'by comparison humane'.[20] In justifying the need to tie prisoners' hands, the War Office was able to cite no lesser authority than a captured German Afrika Korps General, Ritter von Thoma. In a classic example of the use of clandestinely acquired intelligence from prisoners, General Thoma was quoted talking to a fellow prisoner:

> The tying of prisoners is perfectly permissible on the field of battle. There are only two alternatives if a small patrol comes across a larger body of men in a pill-box. One is to shoot them—as do the Russians—or else to tie them up.[21]

A further defence of British policy cited by Gepp was that the Convention did not attempt 'to regulate what happens in the actual fighting and is confined solely to the treatment of prisoners who have been securely captured and are in the responsible charge of the hostile government.'[22] Thus, the tying of prisoners for operational reasons on the battlefield was not a breach of the Convention, because its articles did not cover combat situations, but the German actions carried out against defenceless prisoners securely in captivity were clear violations of both the letter and the spirit of the Convention.

Many other examples of retaliation by the Germans for real or imagined infractions of the Geneva Convention were the result of poor conditions reported by the prisoners themselves, via either the Red Cross, protecting powers, or interested third parties. This level of information demonstrated that the inspection system did work, but there were examples where mediators and less-than-disinterested representatives of the protecting powers exaggerated the levels and nature of the complaints for political reasons or just to make mischief.[23] A different type of infraction occurred largely through mismanagement when guards aboard the HMT Pasteur mistreated captured Germans during a voyage from Port Said to Durban. The prisoners' belongings were searched and looted by the guards, but it was the treatment meted out to the two (very) senior German officers on board that evoked the greatest criticism. While German protests were short-lived, it was accepted on all sides that certain accepted boundaries had been crossed and that there should be no repetitions.[24]

However, it was in relation to the use of prisoners as a labour force that the greatest tensions were to arise. Soon after the fall of Poland, the Germans began to see the advantages that prisoners might have in compensating for their labour shortages. Aware that Hitler intended to absorb large swathes of western Poland into the Reich, the German planners nevertheless trod carefully in utilizing Polish prisoners and had many tens of thousands demobilized before they were shipped to Germany as agricultural labourers.[25] The same was true of the masses captured or surrendered during the occupation of western Europe in April, May, and June 1940. Huge numbers of French prisoners taken were rapidly shipped to Germany and employed in agriculture. Only later were they used as bargaining chips to extract the even more desirable skilled industrial workers from France through the deals struck with Vichy via the so-called *relève*,[26] and the Nazis also went to great lengths to persuade the French prisoners to give up their status under the Convention and accept labour contracts—ostensibly with better pay and conditions—which would allow their use in a much wider range of occupations.[27] For other western European countries there were different policies. The 225,000 Belgian prisoners of war taken in May 1940 were soon reduced to around 80,000 after the Flemish-speaking elements were released in June the same year for political reasons.[28] However, those who remained were used in a much wider range of industries than those ostensibly permitted by the Convention, including armaments and aircraft factories.[29] In this respect, Dutch servicemen fared much better, as all save a small number were demobilized and sent home in 1940.[30] While political considerations dominated German calculations on the treatment and status of prisoners of war at the beginning of the occupation, these were eventually superseded by economic imperatives. In this they were undoubtedly aided by the fact that the conquered territories had no reciprocal bargaining positions. The Vichy government held no German prisoners and the relatively small numbers of Germans taken by Dutch and Belgian forces in the short campaigns of May 1940 seem to have been transferred to British control soon after their capture.[31]

The application of Nazi ideology to the treatment of prisoners of war also needs to be examined. In general it seems that the German armed forces made no attempts to identify or separate out the Jews among their Western prisoners. This applied even to those from the British armed forces who had Palestinian nationality, ostensibly because the Germans did not want to aggravate relations with London on the issue.[32] This only changed in 1944 when the SS were given greater powers, and there were examples of American Jewish soldiers being segregated after capture at the Battle of the Bulge and then sent to slave labour camps, but even then there was no concerted attempt to include the prisoners of war in the 'final solution'.[33]

Another exceptional case was of the non-white soldiers serving with the Western Allied armies. This included units of the *tirailleurs sénégalais* as well as North Africans who fought in defence of metropolitan France. As David Killingray has shown, the treatment of these men on capture varied enormously. Some were shot out of hand while others were treated much like their white French counterparts, although their treatment in captivity was generally harsher.[34] Only small numbers were taken to Germany, either for medical research or more bizarrely as film stuntmen,[35] and most were kept inside France, working in construction or clearing bomb damage. Starvation and summary executions were commonplace, although perhaps half survived through the years of occupation. Whether this was policy or just neglect on the part of the responsible German authorities it is impossible to determine. Much the same treatment was afforded to non-white soldiers from the British imperial forces, most notably servicemen from the British Indian Army and those from the South African native militias. Both groups suffered maltreatment from Germans after capture in North Africa, being regarded as irregular troops and therefore not covered by the Convention.[36] However, the Italians were little better as captors; the Indians and Africans they captured 'were singled out for especially bad treatment'.[37] It has been suggested that Waffen-SS units carried out all the atrocities against black troops on the battlefield in north-west Europe and in captivity, and at least one SS Commander in Normandy in June 1944 ordered that 'no Negro prisoners were to be taken alive',[38] although it seems that black soldiers and aircrew also fell victim to general reprisal policies carried out by German civilians in the latter stages of the conflict.[39] There were, however, some exceptions to the general story of discrimination, most notably Mathews Letuku, captured at Tobruk and singled out because he had learned German at a mission school, who was adopted as a mess servant by a Luftwaffe squadron and spent the rest of the war with it before being liberated by the Russians in Germany.[40] The general picture that emerges here is of local commanders and individual German and Italian units making up their own minds about how to treat non-white captives against a background of both underlying and, in the case of the Nazis, explicit racial prejudice fuelled by the 'disgrace' of the 'black shame' inflicted on Germany after the First World War.[41] It may also have been the case that the Axis powers and their military commanders in the field calculated, perhaps correctly, that atrocities committed against non-white troops would elicit fewer and milder protests from the Western powers than those inflicted on white men.

Insofar as there is a consensus on the treatment of prisoners in the western European theatre, it is that the terms of the Convention were largely upheld and that breaches and cases of ill-treatment and death among prisoners were the exception rather than the rule—to be raised and investigated as individual incidents. The terms of the Convention were upheld not only as part of the rules within which the war was fought, but also primarily because each side possessed a sufficient number of enemy combatants to ensure reciprocal adherence to its terms. This general principle is evident from the tit-for-tat reprisals carried out by the British and Germans that served to worsen conditions for prisoners—albeit in a controlled way. There were, however, some exceptions to this general rule as the war progressed. Gestapo involvement in the tracking and interrogation of escaping prisoners and evaders after the escape from Stalag Luft III did lead to more serious, and sometimes fatal, sanctions against fugitives. Although Vichy had no leverage with Berlin, the Free French fighting alongside the allies in North Africa were perceived by the Germans not as regular forces protected by the convention, but as *francs-tireurs* (civilians carrying concealed weapons). Thus, they were subject to ill-treatment and possible summary execution if captured, something that inevitably led to French retaliation.[42] When stories of Free French atrocities against captured German and Italian soldiers began to filter back to Berlin, the Germans lost no time in intimating that this would lead to reprisals against any and all Allied troops in their hands. This uncompromising stance by Berlin resulted in London and Washington agreeing to hand over some Axis prisoners captured by their forces to the Free French—essentially as hostages against German behaviour—or 'working capital' as Churchill phrased it.[43] When the French treatment of these men did not meet the standards required by the Convention and protests arrived from Berlin via the Red Cross, London became increasingly worried lest the Germans realize that the prisoners in question had been captured by the British and Americans, and then take retaliatory action against Allied servicemen incarcerated in German camps. Later still, this same problem reappeared in metropolitan France when the *Wehrmacht* encountered units of the French Forces of the Interior (FFI). Although nominally under Free French command, the Germans also insisted on treating them as *francs-tireurs* and thus subject to the same penalties as partisans and 'terrorists'. However, FFI captures of significant numbers of German soldiers led to tit-for-tat killings that threatened to get out of hand as the liberation proceeded.

BEYOND THE CONVENTION

The Geneva Convention insisted that soldiers became prisoners and therefore entitled to its protection from the moment of their capture, although it was accepted in Foreign Office circles that there might be 'abuses in the heat of battle'.[44] However, the most vulnerable situation for the soldier was the period between the moment of surrender and the point where the individual was taken into captivity. This 'grey zone' was neatly summed up by the American writer and photographer Carl Mydans:

> One of [the soldier's] most harrowing experiences...comes...between the time it takes him to raise his arms...and the moment he has completed the trip...rearward and is delivered alive [to] higher authority. This does not guarantee him life. But it guarantees him that much life. For he has just passed [beyond] the point where the law of war makes killing right.[45]

This very neatly encapsulates the scope of this indeterminate period of time between the initial act of surrender by the armed serviceman in laying down his weapons and raising his hands or waving a white flag, and the moment where he is delivered into 'responsible' hands away from the battlefield. There were perceived distinctions between individual, small group, and mass surrenders,[46] but the testimony of survivors gives only indications of the essential arbitrariness of this process.[47]

Even in the relatively regulated Western theatres of war, protection only really began once captives had been conveyed away from the front line and formally registered in a rear depot. This gave scope for acts of revenge in the form of deliberate ill-treatment or even killing before that occurred. The British authorities identified and investigated a number of cases where their servicemen had been killed after surrendering. For example, over 100 men of the Royal Norfolk Regiment had been killed near Le Paradis on 26 May 1940, and various other crimes were recorded during the Normandy campaign in 1944. All were attributed to SS units rather than to the regular German Army.[48] However, it is instructive that the PWD expressed surprise at the limited number of these cases given the 'foul crimes the Germans committed elsewhere'.[49] The report from which this quote was culled made no mention of Allied troops committing similar crimes, and the outcome of the war and the lack of a German authority to follow up such cases meant that they were forgotten and omitted from the military memory of the war.

An examination of the British attitude to the taking of prisoners on the eve of the Second World War suggests that there was little or no discussion of policy by the military authorities, save their commitment to the implementation of the Geneva Convention. Military units were assumed to operate according to the generally accepted principles of warfare as outlined in the Hague Conventions. These included certain prohibitions: treacherously killing or wounding individuals belonging to the hostile nation or army; killing or wounding an enemy who, having laid down arms, or having no longer the means of defence, has surrendered at discretion; or declaring that no quarter will be given. However, the question of when a surrendering enemy soldier actually became a prisoner of war had not really been considered directly by the British or their allies. Article 2 of the Geneva Convention was quite explicit on the subject—a fact that Gepp and others had been keen to exploit in their defence of British policy:

> Prisoners-of-war are in the power of a hostile government, but not of the individual or formation which captured them. They shall at all times be humanely treated and protected, particularly against acts of violence, from insults and from public curiosity.[50]

This seemed to imply that until enemy servicemen were securely in the 'responsible charge' of the hostile government, they were not prisoners of war as defined by the Geneva Convention—thus begging the question of what principles and customs governed the treatment of surrendering enemy personnel on the battlefield?

At the time of the shackling crisis, and the subsequent North African and Italian campaigns, little further enquiry was made into precisely how British military units dealt with surrendering enemy personnel. Attention was concentrated on the treatment afforded to enemy soldiers who had been taken prisoner. At one level, there was a debate on how prisoners should be handled before being interrogated. An instruction by 11 Corps in early 1943 ruled that prisoners were to be given neither food nor cigarettes before interrogation as this served to restore their morale. The French XIX Corps appeared to adopt similar practices. Higher authority later rescinded all these instructions, lest they provide cause for German retaliation. Similar fears were voiced about the conditions suffered by German and Italian prisoners at the hands of Britain's allies, the Free French. One further War Office discovery to come out of this debate was that it had little or no idea of the practices being adopted by its allies although there is no evidence that any such enquiry was ever carried out. Indeed, the issue arose again in May 1944 when Tito's partisans in Yugoslavia were reported to have shot German prisoners when deployed as part of a British-led force.[51] In a war where the Allied cause was being served by so many armed forces—many of them irregular or of dubious legal standing—there was very little chance of imposing any degree of standardization.

The whole issue re-emerged as the Allied assault on north-west Europe began. On 7 June 1944, Colonel Bagley, an American officer, made what the British described as a 'highly indiscreet' address to a press conference. His comments were reported back to the Foreign Office verbatim:

> Paratroopers have a regular system of getting [snipers] ... they have no intention of taking prisoners. They can't be bothered with prisoners. They are apt in going along the road with prisoners and seeing one of their own men killed, to turn around and shoot a prisoner to make up for it.[52]

The official who reported this also commented on the shock which these statements caused to all those in the room. In spite of attempts to impose a news blackout on the story, the Foreign Office had already received reports of the 'bloodcurdling utterances' from Cecil King of the *Daily Mirror* and *Sunday Pictorial*, who, it was implied, intended to do his best to promulgate them as widely as possible.[53]

While it might have been argued that these were battlefield practices and did not involve prisoners within the definition provided by the Geneva Convention, the shackling crisis had demonstrated that this was a 'dangerous situation' as the Germans would not recognize such niceties if some propaganda advantage might be obtained and would undoubtedly retaliate against prisoners in their hands.[54] However, as there was no real means of keeping this information from the Germans, Ernest Gepp at the War Office Directorate for Prisoners of War felt the best course of action to be to admit that 'incidents of this kind are inevitable in bitter fighting and have occurred on both sides' and to remind the Germans of the murders of prisoners which they had perpetrated, both in 1940 and in 1944.[55]

Even as this discussion was proceeding, other reports were coming in of American behaviour in Normandy. The Surgeon General of the United States' First Army Group, General Kenna, was reported as saying that:

> [t]he American troops are not showing any great disposition to take prisoners unless the enemy come over in batches of 20 or more.... [They include] quite a proportion of 'tough guys' who have experienced the normal peace-time life of Chicago, and other great American cities, and who are applying the lessons they learned there. They are making their fellow soldiers tough like themselves.[56]

While this could be balanced against the recently reported German murders of Canadians in Normandy and the massacre at Oradour-sur-Glane in any discussions with the Germans, the reality was that, to some extent, Eisenhower himself had conditioned the behaviour of the American troops. Worried that the US forces might not fight as hard against the Germans in Europe as they had against the Japanese, he encouraged the dissemination of reports about all German atrocities—with predictable results.

Apart from the stories that came to the attention of the politicians and civil servants, contemporary accounts and subsequent memoirs show how surrendering enemies were treated at an operational level. In very general terms, there was an understanding on both sides of the 'rules' which pertained to the taking of prisoners, neatly summed up by one American GI as 'dead prisoners was not policy'.[57] However, there were instances where this did not apply. For example, it was widely understood that the Germans were expected to fight until their ammunition had been exhausted, yet if they carried out this order and then tried to surrender at the last minute, their opposite numbers were likely to take into account their own comrades who had fallen and exact suitable revenge.[58] Likewise, individuals (and especially snipers) thought to have inflicted casualties on the units who captured them were often victims of instant retaliation.[59] Other German behaviour likely to provoke the captors included arrogance, refusals to treat with inferior officers, and use of the Hitler salute.[60] A combination of all these factors also conditioned American and British attitudes to SS soldiers. Whereas the *Wehrmacht* were seen as 'ordinary soldiers', their SS counterparts were perceived as arrogant, unbending fanatics, whose own behaviour towards captured enemies gave no cause for mercy. It is also true that enemy soldiers being conducted away from the front line were not immune from retaliation. There are stories of them being targeted for arbitrary ill-treatment or even killed in retaliation for the discovery of German 'crimes' or the deaths of Allied servicemen at the hands of 'their' comrades still fighting. This provides yet another example of a 'grey area' where it was unclear whether battlefield or Geneva Convention rules applied.

One additional instance where prisoners were ostensibly taken outside the realm of the Convention came at the end of hostilities when large numbers of German prisoners were redesignated as 'disarmed enemy personnel' or 'surrendered enemy personnel' (SEP). The claim that up to a million German soldiers died as a result of deliberate American policy has been discredited by research that has shown the complexity of the situation.[61] Although some deaths were attributable to neglect and mistreatment, the problem for the military authorities was the sheer numbers of men involved, with the Americans alone having custody of 3.4 million German prisoners.[62] One caveat to this reappraisal remains, namely the transfer of 740,000 German prisoners and SEPs to French control.[63] It was stipulated that they should be under the aegis of the French army rather than partisans, but the reality was somewhat different, and mortality rates among these men were unusually high. While the French blamed the Americans for the poor health of men transferred to them from the infamous Rhine Meadow camps, US officers were on record as condemning the appalling treatment meted out by the French.[64] While the redesignation of the prisoners may have been done for the best of pragmatic reasons, it nevertheless highlighted another potential problem with the Convention, namely that it assumed that there would still be two opposing sides at the end of hostilities that could assume responsibility for repatriated prisoners. Where the war had led to the complete destruction of the German regime, this was no longer the case and principles of protection and reciprocity could no longer be applied.

CONCLUSIONS

A general conclusion to assessment of the Geneva Convention as it applied to the western European theatres of war might be that it worked reasonably well and provided a framework that both sides tried hard to work with. Most deviations and avoidances were to meet pressing pragmatic political or economic problems, or a result of defective administration—at least until the final stages of the conflict. Where the Convention was less successful was in providing any real protection for surrendering enemy personnel. Even among the Western Allied powers, there were different military traditions when it came to the handling of *surrendering* enemy personnel. These may have varied between units and been the result of long-standing military traditions. Killing of surrendering enemies was regarded as an inevitable consequence of warfare; a result of 'red mist', perceived treachery on the part of the enemy, a lack of adherence to accepted forms of warfare, the results of losses sustained on the battlefield, or an operational inability to deal with prisoners. By 1944, when British officials began to ask questions about the implementation of the Convention in north-west Europe, expectations of victory meant that there were unlikely to be any long-term consequences, but this did not prevent anxiety about reprisals against prisoners in German hands as a result of the unregulated behaviour of Allies, whose status as belligerents had not been agreed between all the parties. Likewise, there was little direct protection for surrendered enemies once the war ended, with the Allies asserting their rights to transfer prisoners to other detaining powers and to retain them for as long as their labour requirements demanded. Thus, for example, the last Italians were not sent home until 1947 and the last Germans left the United Kingdom only in 1948.

NOTES

1. The limited numbers of Italian seamen captured at the beginning of the war in June 1940 had all been treated as civilians and interned.
2. United States Chargé d'Affairs Herschel V. Johnson to Anthony Eden, 30 Dec. 1940, The National Archives (TNA), United Kingdom, FO916/2598.
3. 'Report on Special arrangements with Germany and Italy on Geneva Convention and Sick and Wounded Convention (draft) initialled by Sir Harold Satow', 16 Dec. 1942, TNA, FO916/271.

4. Sir Harold Satow and Mrs. M.J. Sée, *The work of the Prisoner of War Department during the Second World War* (Foreign Office, 1950), 5. *The Belfield Report*, written to document British POW policy during the First World War, had been forgotten by 1939 and was only rediscovered in March 1940, after new machinery had been created.

5. Satow and Sée, *The work of the Prisoner of War Department*, 6–7. This did not mean that all the Dominion governments were always at one with the line taken by London. On Canadian reactions to the 'shackling crisis', see Jonathan Vance, *Objects of concern: Canadian prisoners of war through the twentieth century* (Vancouver: UBC Press, 1994).

6. Rüdiger Overmans, 'Die Kriegsgefangenenpolitik des Deutsches Reiches 1939 bis 1945' in Jörg Echternkamp (ed.), *Das Deutsche Reich und der Zweite Weltkrieg* (München: DVA, 2005), IX (part II), 738–42. Vasilis Vourkoutiotis, *Prisoners of war and the German High Command: The British and American experience* (Basingstoke: Palgrave, 2003).

7. Bob Moore, 'Axis prisoners in Britain during the Second World War: A comparative survey', in Bob Moore and Kent Fedorowich (eds.), *Prisoners of war and their captors in World War II* (Oxford: Berg, 1996), 25 n. 21.

8. Satow and Sée, *The work of the Prisoner of War Department*, 17, 47.

9. Roger Absalom, *Strange alliance: Aspects of escape and survival in Italy 1943–1945* (Florence: Olschki, 1991), ch. 1.

10. See, for example, Roger Absalom, ' "Another Crack at Jerry?" Australian prisoners of war in Italy, 1941–1945', *Journal of the Australian War Memorial*, 14 (1989), 24–32.

11. Bob Moore and Kent Fedorowich, 'Allied negotiations on Italian co-belligerency and the prisoner-of-war question, 1943–45', *International History Review*, 18 (1996), 28–47.

12. 16 Nov. 1944, TNA, CAB66/58 WP(44); and 10 Feb. 1945, TNA, CAB66/61 WP(45)89.

13. Satow and Sée, *The work of the Prisoner of War Department*, 9.

14. Donald McLachlan, *Room 39: Naval intelligence in action* (London: Weidenfeld and Nicholson, 1968), 176.

15. McLachlan, *Room 39*, 166–7, 181; Matthew Barry Sullivan, *Thresholds of peace: Four hundred thousand German prisoners and the people of Britain, 1944–1948* (London: Hamish Hamilton, 1979), 41; Vourkoutiotis, *Prisoners of war*, 193.

16. Sullivan, *Thresholds of peace*, 49–51.

17. S. P. MacKenzie, 'The shackling crisis: A case-study in the dynamics of prisoner-of-war diplomacy in the Second World War', *International History Review*, 17 (1995), 78–98; Jonathan Vance, 'Men in manacles: The shackling of prisoners of war 1942–1943', *Journal of Military History*, 59 (1995), 483–504.

18. S. P. MacKenzie, *The Colditz myth: British and Commonwealth prisoners of war in Nazi Germany* (Oxford: Oxford University Press, 2004), 245–8; David Rolf, 'The British government and POWs in Germany, 1939–1945', in Moore and Fedorowich (eds.), *Prisoners of war*, 56–60; Neville Wylie, *The politics of prisoners of war* (Oxford: Oxford University Press, forthcoming). For the raid on Sark, see Charles Cruickshank, *The German occupation of the Channel Islands: The official history of the occupation years* (7th edn.; Channel Islands, 1988), 240–1. For a detailed history of the shackling crisis, see S. P. MacKenzie, 'The Shackling Crisis', 78–98; and Vance, 'Men in manacles', 483–504. 8 Oct. 1942, Public Record Office (now part of TNA), CAB65/28 WM136 (42)2; 9 Oct. 1942, WM137(42)1; 12 Oct. 1942, WM139(42)1; 13 Oct. 1942, WM140 (42)2; 14 Dec. 1942, WM168(42)7.

19. Stories of German policies against Polish and later Soviet prisoners of war did cause some consternation in British military circles. Although never formally expressed, the evident German capacity for ignoring the Convention when it suited them undoubtedly informed British thinking at the time of the 'shackling crisis'.

20. Major General E. C. Gepp to Permanent Under-Secretary, War Office, 30 Dec. 1942, TNA, WO32/10720.
21. Major General E. C. Gepp to Permanent Under-Secretary, War Office, 30 Dec. 1942, TNA, WO32/10720.
22. See also 8 Oct. 1942, TNA, CAB65/28 WM136(42)2; 12 Oct. 1942, WM139(42)1.
23. In this regard, see the activities of the Spanish consul in South Africa. Bob Moore, 'Unwanted guests in troubled times: German prisoners of war in the Union of South Africa, 1942–43', *Journal of Military History*, 60 (2006), 63–90.
24. MacKenzie, *The Colditz myth*, 245; Bob Moore, 'The last phase of the gentleman's war: British handling of German prisoners on board HMT Pasteur, March 1942', *War and Society*, 17 (1999), 41–55.
25. Polish Ministry of Foreign Affairs, *German occupation of Poland: Polish White Book* (New York: Greystone, n.d.), 29–31. The conditions and food given to Polish prisoners of war was well below Convention norms, but civilianizing them allowed even poorer rations and conditions to be imposed.
26. The three workers for one prisoner deal was inequitable to begin with and widely resented by the prisoners, who saw the rich and the privileged exchanged while the most needy were left in captivity. See Gustave Folcher, *Marching to captivity: The war diaries of a French peasant, 1939–1945*, trans. and ed. Christopher Hill (London: Brassey's, 1996), 186; Sarah Fishman, *We will wait: Wives of French prisoners of war, 1940–1945* (New Haven, CT: Yale University Press, 1991), 36–8.
27. Folcher, *Marching to captivity*, 187–9.
28. Michael Wiesner, '"Wer die Macht hat, hat recht": De Belgische krijgsgevangenen in Duitsland en de Conventie van Genève, 1940–1945', M.Sc. thesis in History, Catholic University of Leuven, 2005, 28–9, 33–4.
29. Wiesner, 'Wer die Macht hat, hat recht', 54–5.
30. Pieter Jan Bouman, *De April-Mei Stakingen van 1943* ('s-Gravenhage: M. Nijhoff, 1950); Werner Warmbrunn, *The Dutch under German occupation, 1940–1945* (Stanford, CA: Stanford University Press, 1963), 113–18.
31. This included some 1,200 German paratroopers captured by the Dutch round The Hague after 10 May and shipped to the UK before the surrender.
32. Wiesner, 'Wer die Macht hat, hat recht', 70–3. Yoav Gelber, 'Palestinian POWs in German Captivity', *Yad Vashem Studies*, 14 (1981), 89–137. Vourkoutiotis notes that the Germans captured at least 1,500 Palestinian soldiers—the majority of them Jewish; see Vourkoutiotis, *Prisoners of war*, 189–90. Kochavi notes that the Germans were even prepared to return badly wounded Palestinian troops as part of POW exchanges in 1943; see Arieh J. Kochavi, *Confronting captivity: Britain and the United States and their POWs in Nazi Germany* (Chapel Hill: University of North Carolina Press, 2005), 125.
33. Mitchell G. Bard, *Forgotten victims: The abandonment of Americans in Hitler's camps* (Boulder, CO: Westview, 1994), 71–5.
34. David Killingray, 'Africans and African Americans in enemy hands', in Moore and Fedorowich (eds.), *Prisoners of war*, 187. Killingray estimates the number of captured *tirailleurs* at 80,000. Sheck estimates that there were between 1,500 and 3,000 *tirailleurs sénégalais* prisoners massacred by the Germans in 1940; see Raffael Sheck, *Hitler's African victims* (Cambridge: Cambridge University Press, 2006).
35. Clarence Lusane, *Hitler's Black victims: The historical experiences of Afro-Germans, European Blacks, Africans, and African-Americans in the Nazi era* (New York: Routledge, 2002), 150. Grundlingh notes that the POWs resented the film work as

they had to go naked all the time; see Louis Grundlingh, 'The participation of South African Blacks in the Second World War', D.Litt., Rand Afrikaans University, 1986, 217–18.

36. Grundlingh, 'The participation', 217. Kochavi notes that the Germans held 7,893 soldiers of the British Indian Army at the end of September 1943; see Kochavi, *Confronting captivity*, 53.

37. Satow and Sée, *The work of the Prisoner of War Department*, 12.

38. Vourkoutiotis, *Prisoners of war*, 190–1. The numbers of US Negro soldiers in German hands is subject to debate as official statistics give only 153, but other estimates suggest 3,000–4,000; see Lusane, *Hitler's Black victims*, 148. See also Robert W. Kesting, 'Forgotten victims: Blacks in the Holocaust', *Journal of Negro History*, 77/1 (1992), 31.

39. Lusane, *Hitler's Black victims*, 152. Kesting, 'Forgotten victims', 33.

40. Ian Gleeson, *The unknown force: Black, Indian and Coloured soldiers through two World Wars* (Rivonia: Ashanti, 1994), 203–6.

41. Dick van Galen Last, 'Black shame', *History Today*, 56/10 (2006), 14–21.

42. Bob Moore, 'Unruly Allies: British problems with the French treatment of Axis prisoners of war, 1943–1945', *War in History*, 7/2 (2000), 180–98.

43. Winston Churchill to Lord Ismay and Chiefs of Staff Committee, D142/1, 28 Apr. 1941, TNA PREM3/363/1.

44. Satow and Sée, *The work of the Prisoner of War Department*, 9.

45. Carl Mydans, *More than meets the eye* (New York: Harper and Brothers, 1959), 172, quoted in Gerald F. Linderman, *The world within war: America's combat experience in World War II* (Cambridge, MA: Harvard University Press, 1999), 123.

46. Matthew Barry Sullivan, *Thresholds of peace: German prisoners and the people of Britain, 1944–1948* (London: Hamish Hamilton, 1979), 2–4.

47. Arthur James Barker, *Behind barbed wire* (London: Purnell, 1974), 27–43.

48. Vourkoutiotis, *Prisoners of war*, 192.

49. Satow and Sée, *The work of the Prisoner of War Department*, 9.

50. Draft letter to Commanders, January 1943, ADM1/12656.

51. Tito to Churchill (Bari to Foreign Office, No. 52), 23 May 1944.

52. N. E. Nash to W St. C Roberts (FO), 15 June 1944; TNA, FO916/913.

53. Memorandum, V. Cavendish Bentinck (FO) to PWD-FO, 7 July 1944, TNA, FO916/913.

54. Sir Michael Palairet (FO) to General Gepp (DPW), 20 July 1944; Gepp to Palairet, 24 July 1944, TNA, FO916/913.

55. Gepp to Palairet, 24 July 1944, TNA, FO916/913.

56. Charles Peake (News Department, FO) to Sir Alexander Cadogan, 17 July 1944, TNA, FO916/913.

57. Linderman, *The world within war*, 108.

58. Ibid. 111.

59. Ibid. 119. Linderman notes that units often refused to take snipers prisoner on principle and cites several cases where such men were killed, often in groups.

60. Ibid. 112–14.

61. For the latest version, see James Bacque, *Crimes and mercies* (New York: Little, Brown, 1997), 41–63. For the rejoinder see Guenther Bischof and Stephen Ambrose, *Eisenhower and the German POWs: Facts against falsehood* (Baton Rouge: Louisiana State University Press, 1993).

62. See, for example, Christian Strauss, *Kriegsgefangenschaft und Internierung: Die Lager in Heilbronn-Böckingen* (Heilbronn: Stadtarchiv Heilbronn, 1998), 63–4. Edward N. Peterson, *The many faces of defeat: The German people's experiences in 1945* (New York: Lang, 1990), 32. This included a brutal internal regime run within camps by the Germans themselves.

63. Peterson, *The many faces of defeat*, 30.

64. Eugene Davidson, *The death and life of Germany* (London: Cape, 1959), 167.

8

The Treatment of Prisoners of War in the Eastern European Theatre of Operations, 1941–56

Rüdiger Overmans

About 9 million Germans, Finns, Italians, Slovaks, Croats, Spaniards, Poles, Hungarians, Romanians, Bulgarians, and Soviets fell into captivity on the *Ost-front* (eastern theatre of operations) during the Second World War. This is not to mention those who fought voluntarily despite the neutrality of their country, including Danes, Norwegians, Swiss, and many others. About 4 million of the total captured died in captivity, quite apart from the millions who fell during battle, died of their wounds, or died from illness. Thus, more soldiers died on the Eastern Front than in any other theatre during the Second World War, indeed in any conflict theatre in all of history. Describing this in its entirety goes beyond the scope of this chapter. The following remarks restrict themselves therefore to the main protagonists—the Germans and Soviets—regarding treatment of prisoners in their custody and attitude towards their own comrades in foreign hands.

The principles of warfare in the eastern theatre of operations differed funda-mentally from the western. In the former, neither side intended to apply the Hague Regulations of 1907 respecting the Laws and Customs of War on Land, or the Geneva Conventions on the treatment of prisoners and wounded. After the October Revolution of 1917, the Soviet government had explicitly refused to observe such treaties, which the previous tsarist government had signed. The same went for the 1907 Hague Regulations respecting the Laws and Customs of War on Land. The Soviet government did not enter the Geneva Convention relative to the treatment of prisoners of war (presumably fearing spies) since this treaty stipulated rights of visitation and inspection for protective powers and the International Red Cross in the country in which the prisoners were held. The second Geneva Convention of 1929 for the Amelioration of the Condition of the Wounded and Sick in Armies in the Field was, however, ratified by the Soviet Union, ostensibly because no oversight was foreseen. Since National Socialist Germany had participated in both conventions in 1934, a legally binding treaty existed between these two countries. Granted, the wording of The Hague Land Warfare Treaty was not binding, yet the principles of this treaty represented international humanitarian law which every state was obligated to uphold.[1] Therefore, every country, upon the opening of hostilities, and irrespective of concerns of mutuality, was obliged to carry out the following:

- Inform the enemy of the names of his dead, his ill, and his wounded now in the custody of the opposing country and issue death certificates.
- Leave medical personnel behind with the wounded to ensure their safe transfer to the enemy.
- Collect personal effects from fallen enemy soldiers and deposit them into state safe-keeping.
- Report to the enemy the names of organizations that had been mobilized for medical service.
- Treat the prisoners humanely at all times and protect them, particularly against acts of violence, insults, and public curiosity.
- Retain them in captivity only as long as necessary to prevent them from taking part in the hostilities.

When the invasion of the Soviet Union began on 22 June 1941, Germany was in the position to fulfil its obligations. Since the beginning of the Second World War, however, it had already field-tested its systems of handling POW matters in raids against Poland, France, Belgium, the Netherlands, Yugoslavia, and Greece. On 13 August 1941, the Soviet Union declared that it had set up an information centre. The diplomatic corps and other civilians, working in what was now enemy country, were transferred to their homeland without much trouble. The German ambassador in Moscow, Count Friedrich-Werner von Schulenberg, vacated his position by sending an elegantly worded telegram in French to Stalin. Therefore, to a certain degree the war started in a conventional manner.

Upon the suggestion of the International Red Cross, the Soviet Union expressed a willingness to exchange POW name lists on 27 June 1941, with the proviso that the exchange be mutual. In response to a query from the Swedish government asking whether the Soviet Union was prepared to comply with international law, the latter declared itself willing to abide by the Hague Convention with Respect to the Laws and Customs of War on Land, on 17 July 1941, again on the basis of reciprocity. The German Reich, contrariwise, answered negatively to the same question on 21 August, accusing the Soviet Union of breaking numerous provisions of international law in the first days of the war. An agreement with Germany would only be possible if the Soviet Union could prove that it had stopped committing offences in this regard. The United States tried especially hard to sway its future ally—the Soviet Union—to yield in matters of prisoners, but all efforts proved futile. Even the Pope and Prince Carl of Sweden tried in vain until 1943 to extract some concessions. Behind all these efforts loomed the concern, especially among the Americans, that such contempt for international law would spread to the western theatre. It was not only the Soviets who demonstrated a lack of interest in abiding by international law. On 11 March 1943, the Germans informed the Swedish government in no uncertain terms that they had no interest whatsoever in mediation on questions of international law.[2]

This declaration did not end matters for the German government. On the contrary, it faced a difficult situation. National Socialist ideology dictated that the individual counted for nothing compared to the well-being of the *Volksge-meinschaft* (people's community), but each person, as a member of this community, had a legitimate claim to state care. The armed forces expressed a willingness to provide this, fully cognizant that the highest echelons of both governments were not interested in coming to such agreements. The most pressing issue for the armed forces and the families of captured soldiers entailed determining who was still alive in Soviet custody. Furthermore, there was a desire to find ways to enhance the fate of the German POWs in the Soviet Union. This situation gave rise to a peculiar alliance. The *Wehrmacht* enjoyed support not only from the Foreign Office but also from Propaganda Minister Josef Goebbels, who recognized the great emotional importance this issue had for families of prisoners. Beyond that, countries allied with Germany expressed interest too. As a sign of goodwill, two delegates of the Red Cross, Edouard de Haller and Carl Burckhardt, were permitted to visit Stalag II F (315) Hammerstein, a special POW camp for Soviet non-commissioned officers and enlisted men, on 9 August 1941 in an unofficial capacity. In the autumn of 1941, name lists from several countries were submitted to Moscow through the Red Cross without, however, eliciting a reciprocal response. By early January 1942 Hitler had forbidden any further attempts to resolve the matter with the Soviets. This was based on two motives, as the German ambassador Karl Ritter notes in a report on a conversation with Hitler:

> One of the reasons was that he [Hitler] did not wish to spread a false impression among the troops on the Eastern Front, namely that they would, when captured, receive treatment in accordance with international law. The second reason was that a comparison with a list of names would allow the Russian government to establish that not all of the Russian soldiers who fell into German captivity were still alive.[3]

In reality, the Soviet Union had neither established the allegedly existent information centre, nor notified Germany of prisoners' names, nor attended to any of the other provisions stated in the Convention for the Wounded. The Soviet Union, like Germany, had no interest in submitting herself to international law during war. Instead, Stalin demanded in Order 270 that:

> [c]ommanders and political officers who rip their insignias off during battle, retreat to the hinterlands or give themselves up to the enemy are to be seen as malicious deserters, whose families, as families of law breakers and treacherous deserters, are subject to arrest. All superior officers and commissars are ordered to shoot such men on the spot...and when a commander or units of the Red Army prefer to surrender, then they are to be destroyed by any means necessary, such as ground or air attack. The families of captured Red Army personnel are to be denied any state assistance or support.[4]

With this it was obvious to Soviet soldiers that they could expect no mercy should they return home from German prison camps. Stalin's son Jacob committed suicide in such a camp on 14 April 1943, knowing that orders such as these from his father were not bluster but meant in deadly earnest. In many cases, returning POWs and forced labourers were sent to labour battalions or Gulags after the war's end. Whoever collaborated with the Germans had to reckon with death. Even those—mostly women—allowed to return relatively unmolested were treated as second-class citizens for the rest of their lives. Only an edict from the president of the Russian Federation on 24 January 1995 restored rights to former POWs and civilians who had suffered German imprisonment, thus ending discrimination. However, many veterans from the Second World War did not live to see that day.[5]

Soviet soldiers were not only threatened with the worst by their own government should they manage to survive captivity. POWs' existence in German hands was painted in the blackest colours with Soviet propaganda announcing to Red Army soldiers that they would not survive captivity. The government made use of the propaganda from the First World War, which had also portrayed German treatment of POWs as horrendous. The goal of all these orders and propaganda efforts was to make it abundantly clear to Soviet soldiers that there was no alternative but to fight to the death. Soviet soldiers' early experiences in the hands of the Germans—particularly those of commissars who were murdered on the spot—confirmed these messages. Draconian punishments and excessive use of firearms, especially in escape attempts, added to this impression. The experience of retreating German soldiers 'finishing off' immobile Soviet soldiers in full view of outraged villagers rounded off the picture. The reality of modern warfare, however, rarely offered soldiers the possibility of dying heroically in battle, as Stalin had demanded from them. More often units were cut off in encirclement battles, at the end of which they ran out of ammunition, food, and officers to lead them. In these situations soldiers would fall into captivity unless they committed suicide.[6]

Hitler painted a similar picture of captivity in Soviet hands as Stalin had of the Germans. Hitler's note from 21 August 1941, in which he rejected the application of the rules of war, was printed in the hundreds of thousands and distributed among the troops. In the note, he announced:

> Through the condition of dead German troops found during our advance and statements of German soldiers (sometimes wounded) having escaped from Russian clutches, one can establish that Soviet troops torture and murder, in a downright indescribable and bestial way, German POWs. Observations from the German side make it impossible for the *Wehrmacht* to speak of the Red Army as 'civilized'.

A central element of Hitler's argument was the concept of the *jüdisch-bolschewistische Kommissar* (Judeo-Bolshevik commissar) who spurred the simple Soviet soldier on to fight in a barbaric, 'Asiatic' manner. Hitler also recalled images from the First World War. Germans could remember how, after the October Revolution, Communist prisoners in Germany promoted agitation among their comrades and within German society at large. German POWs joined the October Revolution in Russia and fought on the Communist side during the civil war there. Some would become famous, for example Ernst Reuter, Roland Freisler, Bela Kun, and Imre Nagy. From then on, the image of the agitant Jewish-Bolshevik commissar resonated deeply in German consciousness. The National Socialists had but to activate it.[7]

Beyond this, captivity in Russia during the First World War for German soldiers really was the worst thing that could happen to them, short of death on the battlefield. The German public believed that 40 per cent of their POWs had died in Russian custody, although the actual death rate was closer to 20 per cent. Fridtjof Nansen, High Commissioner for the League of Nations, was able to retrieve the last German prisoners (through Vladivostok and the Pacific) only in 1926, such was the disarray of the Revolution. Edwin Erich Dwinger and others wrote best-selling novels about their experiences in the 'Hell of Tockoe' and other prison camps. The Swedish Red Cross helper, Elsa Brändström (well known as the 'Angel of Siberia'), confirmed as a quasi-neutral foreigner Dwinger's story in her book, *Among Prisoners of War in Russia and Siberia 1914/1920.*[8]

We can therefore deduce that the German soldier in 1941 feared the worst from captivity in the Soviet Union and from the behaviour of commissars. Hitler's demands on his troops left no room for doubt that each soldier must save the last bullet for himself, preferring death to surrender. This occurred, particularly among officers, much more frequently on the Eastern Front than on the Western. Field Marshal Paulus, who had been promoted just days before the end of the battle of Stalingrad, did not commit suicide and thereby did not meet Hitler's expectation that a German Field Marshal would never render himself to captivity. This refusal elicited the greatest contempt from Hitler:

> For in other cases one sets up a hedgehog defensive formation and saves the last bullet for oneself. If you just think to yourself that a woman has the pride to lock herself up and shoot herself, just for hearing a few insulting words, then I lose all respect for a soldier who enters captivity.[9]

Stalin's behaviour towards German POWs was far less emotional. It stood in marked contrast to his attitude toward the different ethnic groups in the Soviet Union, which Stalin regarded with hatred and mistrust bordering on paranoia. At the most he meted out harsh punishments for those who did not fight energetically enough against the Germans, but he felt no pity for the Soviet people who suffered at the hands of the Germans. Thus his posture toward captured enemy combatants, irrespective whether they were German, Finnish, or any other nationality, was not marked by hatred. He saw them primarily as a source of manpower which could rebuild the country. In a country that fought for its very existence, at first, this role for the prisoners held little relevance. Only about 100,000 German soldiers had entered Soviet captivity by the end of 1942, a great majority of whom died in short order, due to a mixture of widespread destruction of the already limited economic capacity of the Soviet Union and hatred for the occupying enemy force. Only about 5–10 per cent of this group survived POW camps. In early 1943, after a report indicated that very few of the 100,000 Germans captured at Stalingrad had survived, Stalin finally ordered the improvement of the supply conditions in order to maintain the ability of POWs to work. During the war years, the chances for survival improved, though the survival rate of German POWs in the Soviet Union approached a sufficient level only in 1947. During the war, Soviet camps filled with soldiers from other nations, such as Italy, Romania, and Hungary, who had switched to the Allied side in 1943 and 1944. Despite the fact that German, Finnish, and Japanese POWs were interned with those whose homelands were now allied with the Soviets, the Germans were treated no worse than the other prisoners and, in general, better than the civilian population. At the same time Stalin saw no reason to release those soldiers from what were now Allied countries—for him only manpower issues were of concern. This was also the reason which prompted him to deport about 200,000 German civilians in the spring of 1945 from eastern parts of Germany and the Balkans into forced labour camps in the Soviet Union.[10]

For all of these reasons it should come as no surprise that, as the war wound down, the Soviet Union was one of the driving forces against releasing German POWs, thereby breaking international laws of war. As the Allies, under pressure from the United States, arranged to repatriate German POWs by 1948, this decision ran into resistance from those states which had the most to lose by repatriating such a workforce—France and the Soviet Union. Unlike France, who had to bow to American pressure, Poland and the Soviet Union thwarted Allied agreements and began sending the greater part of their prisoners home only at the end of 1949. About 30,000 remained in the Soviet Union; some of those remained there until diplomatic relations were established with the Federal Republic in 1955. The last civilians deported to the Soviet Union during the war were repatriated only in the 1960s. Of the approximately 3 million Germans who were taken captive by the Soviets, just under 1 million lost their lives.[11]

The death rate of Soviets in German captivity was much higher. Before the opening of hostilities, Hitler made clear to his generals that the war that stood before them would be like no other. 'The Russian is, in the first and last, not a comrade' jotted the Chief of Army General Staff, four-star General Franz Halder, in his journal after Hitler's speech of 30 March 1941. There were scattered protests, most notably the statement made by the chief of the *Amt Ausland/ Abwehr* (Office Foreign Countries/Military Intelligence) Admiral Canaris, against Hitler's guidelines for the treatment of Soviet prisoners. He pointed out that the principles of international law during war posed an unalterable legal basis for treatment and that the policy outlined by Hitler would only fortify Soviet resistance, thereby rendering German occupation more difficult. But with few exceptions German soldiers followed Hitler's order without objection, if not willingly.[12]

As has already been explained, Hitler distinguished between two types of 'Russians': 'Judeo-Bolshevik commissars', who were subject to Hitler's exterminatory will, and the 'simple Russians'. Thus, his term for the Soviets was conditioned by the experience of the First World War, when there had been a Russian empire. Hitler's imagination was shaped by the experiences of the last war in which a million Russian POWs contributed substantially to German war production. Since that time, Russians figured in German imagination as belonging on a lower cultural plane. They were seen as being 'used to' surviving with considerably less and inferior quality food, and would work well so long as they were subject to harsh but just rules. The National Socialists reiterated this stereotype, but it was in any case deeply rooted in the German imagination.[13]

Initially the *Wehrmacht* had calculated that about a million POWs would fall into German hands. These would not, however, be transferred to the Reich proper but would remain in the operational area supporting German troops as per Hitler's orders. This figure stood in marked contrast to the state of the labour market in Germany. The number of open positions lay at 2.6 million by the opening of Barbarossa, whereas planners estimated that immediate needs for Soviet prisoners hovered around 700,000. Thus, by July 1941, the first contingents of Soviet prisoners had already been sent to Germany, contrary to Hitler's original order. Pressure from 'below'—the urgent need for manpower—forced Hitler to revise his point of view that October, allowing Soviet POWs to work in Germany. Altogether nearly 3 million of the total 5.3 million Soviet POWs were deported from operational areas.[14]

The orders which made the treatment of Soviet prisoners so different from the treatment of Western POWs can be divided into three types:

- The *Kommissarbefehl* (commissar order)
- The *Aussonderungsbefehle* (orders for sorting)
- The guidelines for the general treatment of POWs

From 6 June 1941, the *Kommissarbefehl* decreed that political commissars attached to the armed forces, along with those civil functionaries who actively resisted German troops, were, upon an officer's orders, to be separated from the regular troops and shot:

> Political commissars are the originators of barbaric, Asiatic fighting methods. Therefore one must proceed against them *immediately* and with all possible severity.
>
> They must be *immediately* sorted out and separated from the regular troops, i.e. while still on the battlefield. This is necessary in order to minimize any influence they might have on the captured troops. Commissars are not recognized as soldiers. The laws of war that protect POWs do not apply to them. These men, after sorted in their own group are to be finished off.[15]

The argument that political commissars attached to the military were not soldiers but agitators, who would spread communism among the other prisoners and even among the Germans, served the purpose of overcoming any legal or moral reservations the German soldiers might have had. In the end, and from the point of view of the German leadership, the *Kommissarbefehl* represented an immediate measure for which the troops themselves were responsible for carrying out. Even though the order stated that commissars were to be murdered in an inconspicuous manner, the Soviet side soon learned about it. By September 1941, the first attempt to rescind the order succeeded—not on moral grounds, but because as things stood, commissars fought to the end and shed German blood. But only on 5 May 1942 did the effort sway Hitler to suspend the *Kommissarbefehl*. According to the most recent research, the number murdered in this way lies in a high four-digit figure.[16]

The second type of order concerned the *Aussonderungsbefehle*, the separating of the prisoners in four basic groups:

- Prisoners from those regions of the Soviet Union that today form Russia were to remain in captivity.
- Prisoners who were to be released were those from the Baltic states, Finns, Russians of German descent, Ukrainians, and some Belarussians.
- Those prisoners who were to be handed over to the SD (Security Service) for liquidation included intellectuals, troublemakers, communists, and Jews.
- Anti-communists, Muslims, prisoners from the Caucasus, and others who could be collaborators.

Unlike the *Kommissarbefehl*, in this case, selection was not entrusted to the *Wehrmacht*. The *Sonderkommandos* (Special Detachments) from the SD (*Sicherheitsdienst*, Security Service) were responsible for this task. These men relied on denunciation and speculative presumptions because they had neither training nor experience to identify Jews, communists, or troublemakers. Muslims were 'sorted out' by the SD on the ignorant basis that they, like Jews, were circumcised. Prisoners selected for death were removed from *Wehrmacht* jurisdiction and murdered immediately at the nearest concentration camp. The number of victims of this measure has been estimated as up to 200,000—the majority of whom were Jews. In the end, a division of labour emerged which was observable in other situations too: the *Wehrmacht* was directly involved when it came to fighting communists, it assisted in the murder of Jews, but the 'dirty work' was left to the SS (*Schutzstaffel*, Protective Squadron).[17]

The 'other side' of this sorting process, namely the release or picking out of collaborators, has received little scholarly attention. Until the end of 1941, at least 270,000 prisoners were released, overwhelmingly ethnic Germans, Baltic peoples, and Ukrainians. Increasing demand for workers compelled a shift in thinking, so that from the end of 1941 prisoners were released only in a few exceptions; by the middle of 1942 this policy was ended altogether. Privileged groups among POWs were from then on used primarily as auxiliary forces or as assistant guard units to watch over their former comrades. By the end of the war, many fought as members of the Vlasov units or as auxiliary troops in *Flakeinheiten* (air defence units) of the *Wehrmacht* against the Soviet Union or the Western Allies. Those who volunteered for such work (and were accepted) were given privileged treatment in special camps run by the Reich ministry offices responsible for occupied territories in the east. In addition, they were educated to help in German occupation administration or for propaganda work. They were then deployed either in German prison camps for Soviet troops or for propaganda actions in the Soviet Union itself.[18]

The *Kommissarbefehl* and the *Aussonderungsbefehle* belonged to the central complex of orders contrary to the rules of war, but they do not explain the mass of deaths among Soviet POWs. The causes for this were the generally unsatisfactory standards of care provided for the prisoners. In addition to the fact that they were starved and given tattered clothing whilst in camps, many, particularly during the first part of the war, were forced to bivouac in the open, where they could at best dig holes in the ground during inclement weather. Medicinal care was supplied only when the Germans captured Soviet supplies and the insufficient attention to hygiene ensured epidemics. Rations were below the daily requirement, but this did not condemn the men to rapid death. During and after the war, broad swathes of the population in many countries had to make do with 1,500 calories at certain times. The real problem was that these rations depended on availability and that actual rations were lower. Added to this were the health effects of outside accommodation or living in unheated rooms with poor clothing.[19]

Death rates in camps began to rise as early as September 1941. German leaders had by that time discussed that the guarding, transport, housing (such as it was), and rationing (with its insufficiencies) were pointless when the presumed result was the death of the majority of the prisoners. To change this would have meant deciding to lower the rations of the German populace to support the Soviet POWs. National Socialist leadership, never as sure of its support among the population as it portrayed itself, rejected this. Memories of unrest resulting from hunger during the last war were too fresh and German rations had already been lowered in June 1941. Hitler and Göring would not consider a further reduction, meaning that Soviet prisoners received no increase in rations. When the death rate rose again in October, measures were implemented to improve the situation, still under the condition that German civilians' supply of foodstuffs would not be endangered.[20]

Death rates sank in March 1942, but by then about 2 million prisoners had died, been murdered, or been released. In recognition of the fact that more Soviet prisoners were required to be at the disposal of the increasingly demanding German war economy, orders were sent out to the effect that prisoners were to receive more humane treatment. The orders for Operation Citadel in 1943 marked the first time that one of the main goals of an operation was collecting prisoners. The situation improved, so that by the spring of 1945, Soviet prisoners were fed as well as any other—at least on paper. We need not assign too much concrete importance to this last measure, since Soviet prisoners, like Italians (after Italy's defection in 1943), were scorned by German society, and tended to be treated worse than other (especially Western Allied) prisoners. The death rate, though it never approached that of winter 1941–2, nevertheless remained high. About 2.5 million Soviet prisoners died out of a total of 5.2 million, the majority from hunger and sickness, not as victims of the *Kommissarbefehl* or the *Aussonderungsbefehle*.[21]

How can we explain a death rate which exceeded that of Western Allied prisoners in German hands by an order of ten or twenty? Did it have to do with premeditated murder, as Christian Gerlach's thesis of a 'Hunger Plan' posits?[22] A few of Hitler's statements about the fate of Soviet POWs have been handed down to us. By September 1941, Hitler is reported to have called for standards of care for prisoners sufficient to allow them to work. On 15 October of that year, Reich Leader Bormann informed Reich Minister Lammers:

> The *Führer* spoke yesterday about the necessary use of Russian POWs. It is necessary, said he, to get this very cheap labour force working as soon as possible. Since we have to feed them anyway, it would be senseless to have them loaf about in camps as useless eaters.[23]

On 31 October 1941, the *Wehrmacht* issued its first order to that effect. The following March, Hitler explained to Speer that he did not agree with the policy of low rations for the POWs. He issued directives concerning the employment of the labour force in Norway, in which he demanded a commensurate accommodation for Soviet POWs, concentration camp inmates, and Jews on work assignment. The rationale was not moral but material: however prisoners were neglected, they still consumed resources. Why not provide enough for them so they could work? Of course, should prisoners' needs conflict with those of the German army or the civilian population, then Hitler would automatically prioritize his own people. Thus, in December 1942, he ordered that the *Wehrmacht* 'strip the Soviet military and civilians from winter clothing' in order to cover the *Wehrmacht*'s needs.[24]

We find, therefore, that the reason for the deaths of so many Soviet prisoners must be taken in context rather than as an intentional act. First of all we must consider campaign planning, which did not devote enough attention to logistical demands. Had the Red Army been defeated within a few months and the majority of prisoners released shortly thereafter, as had occurred in earlier instances, then the situation which actually arose would never have occurred. In August and September 1941, however, as the numbers of prisoners swelled and deaths among them rose, the *Wehrmacht* experienced a logistical crisis. German leadership did not consider setting aside supplies and transport vehicles for Soviet prisoners. The urgent increase in rations necessary would have entailed a lowering of rations for German civilians, which was out of the question. Since Soviet prisoners were of the lowest priority, they accumulated all the deficits of an overstretched system. Nevertheless, we are left with the question whether the deaths of Soviet prisoners were actually due to quasi-technical mistakes. Doubt about this is not unreasonable—too many died, even after the winter of 1941–2. Above all, it may be mistaken to look to the highest echelons of power for an explanation. We must keep in mind the general attitude of German society towards 'Russians'. Despite much evidence that many did their best, there were more instances of mistreatment and neglect meted out at all levels of command, which would not have been directed towards prisoners from other countries. The 'Russian' was seen as someone who could survive in dugouts and with inferior provisions. An illustrative example of the effects resulting from such attitudes may be found in the fate of Italian internees, Italian soldiers who fell into German hands after the collapse of 1943. Although the German leadership actually demanded that they receive preferential treatment, the opposite transpired. The German population had already felt betrayed by the Italians after they had joined the Entente during the First World War. Switching sides a second time was deemed another betrayal and revenge was sought through German custody of Italian prisoners.[25]

Applying the findings from the eastern theatre of operations to the Second World War as a whole, one finds that the situation differed totally with respect to observation of the rules of war. In the west all countries had a vested interest in complying with international law, so that the principle of reciprocity—that is, treating prisoners reasonably well, lest the other side mistreat its prisoners— provided effective protection to POWs. The situation on the Eastern Front can, at best, be described as one of 'negative reciprocity': neither side wished to comply with international law. The German Reich could rationalize the deaths of countless Soviet prisoners only by signing off the fate of their own countrymen in Soviet captivity. The threat of mistreatment of German POWs could not move the Germans to alter their treatment of Soviet POWs. Thus, though compared to the west the policy was inverted, in the east a complementary situation existed. In the Pacific a more complex stance occurred. Western Allies held to international law while their opponents did not.

NOTES

1. This same obligation was derived, although restricted to the ill and wounded, from Article 2 of the Convention for the Amelioration of the Conditions of the Wounded and Sick in Armies in the Field, which ran: 'Except as regards the treatment to be provided for them in virtue of the preceding article, the wounded and sick of an army who fall into the hands of the enemy shall be prisoners of war, and the general provisions of international law concerning prisoners of wars hall be applicable to them.' See Levie Howard (ed.), *Documents on prisoners of war* (Newport, RI: Naval War College Press 1979), 176; Rüdiger Overmans, 'Die Kriegsgefangenenpolitik des Deutschen Reiches 1939 bis 1945', in Militärgeschichtliches Forschungsamt (ed.), *Das Deutsche Reich und der Zweite Weltkrieg*, 9/2 (München: Deutsche Verlags-Anstalt, 2005), 799–804.
2. Telegramm Reichsaußenminister Ribbentrop an die Gesandtschaft in Stockholm, Berlin, 11 March 1943, in *Akten zur deutschen auswärtigen Politik 1918–1945*, series E, vol. V (Göttingen, 1978), 388–9.
3. Aufzeichnung des Botschafters z.b.V. Ritter vom 9.1.1942, in *Akten zur deutschen auswärtigen Politik*, series E, vol. I (Göttingen, 1969), 193–4. From Goebbels' journal entry of 17 Dec. 1941: 'We have no binding agreement with the Soviets right now. We have well over 3 million of theirs in captivity, the Bolsheviks perhaps 30,000 of ours. Of course, we cannot leave these 30,000 men to their fate, so one searches through neutral channels (above all through Switzerland) to open a dialogue with the Soviets somehow.' See Elke Fröhlich (ed.), *Die Tagebücher von Joseph Goebbels*, part II, vol. 2 (München: Institut für Zeitgeschichte, 1996), 523–4.
4. Joseph Stalin, Order from Red Army High Command, 16 Aug. 1941, 'Der Befehl Nummer 270', *Osteuropa*, 39/11,12 (1989), 1035–7.

5. Pavel Polian, *Deportiert nach Hause* (München: Oldenbourg, 2001), 202–8; T. S. Dram'jan, 'Kto sprovociroval smet' starsego syna I.V. Stalina?, *Voenno-Istoricheskij Zhurnal*, 3 (2000), 78–87; Marian Jaworski, 'Stalin's Son in a War Prison', *Journal of Slavic Military Studies*, 5/2 (1992), 242–66.

6. Rüdiger Overmans, ' "Hunnen" und "Untermenschen"—deutsche und russisch/sowjetische Kriegsgefangenschaftserfahrungen im Zeitalter der Weltkriege', in Bruno Thoss and Hans-Erich Volkmann (eds.), *Erster Weltkrieg—zweiter Weltkrieg, ein Vergleich: Krieg, Kriegserlebnis, Kriegserfahrung in Deutschland* (Paderborn: Schöningh, 2002), 335–65.

7. Ernst Reuter, a leading Communist functionary during the Weimar Republic, was governor of Berlin during the blockade of 1948–9; Roland Freisler was president of the People's Court between 1943 and 1945, condemning the July 20th conspirators; Bela Kun was Foreign Minister of Hungary after the First World War; Imre Nagy was Prime Minister of Hungary during the revolt of 1956 and was executed for his part in it two years later; see Hannes Leidinger and Verena Moritz, *Gefangenschaft, Revolution, Heimkehr: Die Bedeutung der Kriegsgefangenenproblematik für die Geschichte des Kommunismus in Mittel- und Osteuropa 1917–1920* (Vienna: Böhlau, 2002), 533–634.

8. Elsa Brändström, *Unter Kriegsgefangenen in Russland und Sibirien 1914—20* (Leipzig: Koehler & Ameland, 1922); Edwin Dwinger, *Die Armee hinter Stacheldraht* (Jena: E. Diederich, 1923); Georg Wurzer, 'Das Schicksal der deutschen Kriegsgefangenen in Rußland im Ersten Weltkrieg: Der Erlebnisbericht Edwin Erich Dwingers', in Rüdiger Overmans (ed.), *In der Hand des Feindes: Kriegsgefangenschaft von der Antike bis zum Zweiten Weltkrieg* (Köln: Böhlau, 1999), 363–84.

9. 'Protokoll vom 1.2.1943', in Helmut Heiber (ed.), *Hitlers Lagebesprechungen* (Stuttgart: Deutsche Verlags-Anstalt, 1962), 124; Johannes Hürter, *Hitlers Heerführer: Die deutschen Oberbefehlshaber im Krieg gegen die Sowjetunion, 1941/42* (München: Oldenbourg, 2006), 360.

10. Andreas Hilger, *Deutsche Kriegsgefangene in der Sowjetunion: Kriegsgefangenenpolitik, Lageralltag und Erinnerung, 1941–1956* (Essen: Klartext, 2000); Rüdiger Overmans, 'Das Schicksal der deutschen Kriegsgefangenen des Zweiten Weltkriegs', in Militärgeschichtliches Forschungsamt (ed.), *Der Zusammenbruch des Deutschen Reiches 1945, Zweiter Halbband: Die Folgen des Zweiten Weltkrieges* (München: Deutsche Verlags-Anstalt, 2008), 402–6, 489–94.

11. With respect to the release of POWs, the Allies backed out of Article 75 of the POW Convention from 1929, which demanded release of prisoners after conclusion of a peace treaty. They did not think this article applied, since there was no peace treaty. But this position ignored a principle which the Allies themselves had hitherto abided by consistently and which had been endorsed by the International Military Tribunal in Nuremberg. Thus, one of the central tenets of international law stipulated that holding soldiers as prisoners, thereby depriving them of freedom, was justifiable only so long as conflict lasted. Enemy soldiers could be held for the duration of war, preventing them from taking further part in it, but no longer. This justification would end the very moment conflict definitively ends, which was obviously the case with Germany's capitulation in 1945. It is an irony of history that this position of law, which Admiral Canaris espoused through his motion to comply with international law in war against the Soviet Union in 1941, and was explicitly cited by the International Tribunal as a correct interpretation, was at the same time ignored by the Allies. See *Der Prozeß gegen die Hauptkriegsverbrecher vor dem Internationalen Militärgerichtshof Nürnberg*, 14 November

1945–1 October 1946, vol. I, Nürnberg 1949, 259f. See further Overmans, 'Das Schicksal der deutschen Kriegsgefangenen', 379–507, 499–502.

12. Hans-Adolf Jacobsen (ed.), *Kriegstagebuch*, II (Stuttgart: W. Kohlhammer, 1963), 334–8; *Der Prozeß gegen die Hauptkriegsverbrecher vor dem Internationalen Militärgerichtshof Nürnberg*, 14 November 1945–1 October 1946, vol. XXXVI, Nürnberg 1949, 317–22.

13. The most comprehensive order of the *Wehrmacht* in the handling of prisoners demanded: 'The reputation and honor of the *Wehrmacht* require that *every German soldier* maintains the greatest distance from Soviet POWs. Treatment must be cool but correct. Any leniency or even fraternization must be punished severely. The feeling of pride and superiority of the German soldier who is ordered to guard Soviet POWs must be identifiable to the public at any time.... Ruthless and energetic measures are hereby ordered, especially with Bolshevik agitators, even at the slightest sign of resistance.... Prisoners attempting to escape are to be shot on the run, *without calling "Stop!"* Warning shots are never to be fired. Heretofore valid provisions, particularly H.Dv. 38/11, side 13 and so forth are annulled. But any arbitrariness is forbidden. Caution and mistrust towards prisoners must never waver. Use of firearms against them is as a rule legitimate.' OKW/ AWA/ Kriegsgef. (I), Az. 2 f. 24.11, Nr. 3058/41 geh. vom 8.9.1941, Betr.: Anordnungen über die Behandlung sowjetischer Kr.Gef. in allen Kriegsgefangenenlagern, reprinted in Gerd Ueberschär and Wolfram Wette (eds.), *Der deutsche Überfall auf die Sowjetunion: 'Unternehmen Barbarossa', 1941* (Frankfurt: Fischer, 1999), 297–300; *Der Prozeß gegen die Hauptkriegsverbrecher vor dem Internationalen Militärgerichtshof Nürnberg*, 14 November 1945–1 October 1946, vol. XXVII, Nürnberg 1949, 65–9; Hürter, *Hitlers Heerführer*, 255, 261, 407.

14. Christian Gerlach, 'Die Ausweitung der deutschen Massenmorde in den besetzten sowjetischen Gebieten im Herbst 1941: Überlegungen zur Vernichtungspolitik gegen Juden und sowjetische Kriegsgefangene', in Christian Gerlach (ed.), *Krieg, Ernährung, Völkermord: Forschungen zur deutschen Vernichtungspolitik im Zweiten Weltkrieg* (Hamburg: Hamburger Edition, 1998), 53; Ulrich Herbert, *Fremdarbeiter: Politik und Praxis des 'Ausländer-Einsatzes' in der Kriegswirtschaft des Dritten Reiches* (Berlin/Bonn: J. H. W. Dietz, 1985), 137; Reinhard Otto, *Wehrmacht, Gestapo und sowjetische Kriegsgefangene im deutschen Reichsgebiet 1941/42* (München: Oldenbourg, 1998), 17, 42, 48.

15. Ueberschär and Wette, *Der deutsche Überfall*, 259–60.

16. In total this means, without a doubt, that we are talking about a great number of crimes. But compared to the circa 60,000 commissars deployed in the war against the Germans, there were astoundingly few identified commissars; see Felix Römer, *Der Kommissarbefehl: Wehrmacht und NS-Verbrechen an der Ostfront, 1941/42* (Paderborn: Schöningh, 2008).

17. POW camp commandants were permitted to carry out sorting independently, according to the criteria outlined above, only in camps of the operational area (i.e. regions east of the territory of the Reich) because *Wehrmacht* leadership wished to keep the SD as far from the operational area as possible. Only in October 1941 did the SD gain the right to judge the prisoners in these camps; s. Otto, *Wehrmacht, Gestapo und sowjetische Kriegsgefangene*, 48–86, 263–8; Hürter, *Hitler's Heerführer*, 403, 594; Christian Gerlach, *Kalkulierte Morde: Die deutsche Wirtschafts und Vernichtungspolitik in Weißrußland, 1941–1944* (Hamburg: Hamburger Edition, 1999), 839.

18. According to reports from the OKH about 350,000 prisoners were released all told, of which 270,000 by the end of 1941. OKW figures cite 530,000 for the total numbers of

men released; Gerlach, *Kalkulierte Morde*, 818; Hürter, *Hitler's Heerführer*, 360; 'OKW/ Abt. Kriegsgef. Org. (Id), Nachweisung des Verbleibs der sowj. Kr. Gef. nach dem Stand von 1.5.1944, 1.5.1944', in Ueberschär and Wette, *Der deutsche Überfall*, 310–11; Rolf-Dieter Müller, *An der Seite der Wehrmacht: Hitlers ausländische Helfer beim 'Kreuzzug gegen den Bolschewismus'*, *1941–1945* (Berlin: Ch. Links Verlag, 2007); Reinhard Otto, Rolf Keller, and Jens Nagel, 'Sowjetische Kriegsgefangene in deutschem Gewahrsam', *Vierteljahrshefte für Zeitgeschichte*, 56 (2008), 557–602.

19. Jacobsen, *Kriegstagebuch*, 35. Toomas Hiio, Meelis Maripuu, and Indrek Paavle, *Estonia, 1940–1945: Reports of the Estonian International Commission for the Investigation of Crimes Against Humanity* (Tallinn: Estonian Foundation for the Investigation of Crimes Against Humanity, 2006), 754; Gerlach, *Kalkulierte Morde*, 33.

20. Overmans, 'Die Kriegsgefangenenpolitik des Deutschen Reiches', 808–9.

21. Christian Gerlach, 'Die Verantwortung der Wehrmachtführung: Vergleichende Betrachtungen am Beispiel der sowjetischen Kriegsgefangenen', in Christian Hartmann and Johannes Hürter (eds.), *Verbrechen der Wehrmacht: Bilanz einer Debatte* (München: C. H. Beck, 2005), 43; Hürter, *Hitler's Heerführer*, 387, 392; Ernst Klink, *Das Gesetz des Handels: Die Operation 'Zitadelle'*, *1943* (Stuttgart: Deutsche Verlags-Anstalt, 1966), 296–301.

22. On Gerlach's 'Hungerplan' thesis, see Hürter, *Hitler's Heerführer*, 378–9.

23. Reichsleiter Martin Bormann an Reichsminister Dr. Lammers, 15 Oct. 1941, Bundesarchiv Berlin, record group R 43 II/670a.

24. 'Fernschreiben Führerhauptquartier an OKH vom 21.12.1941', in Percy E. Schramm (ed.), *Kriegstagebuch des Oberkommandos der Wehrmacht, 1940–1941*, 2 (Frankfurt: Bernhard & Graefe, 1965), 1085. On 22 March 1942, during a conference with Albert Speer, Hitler declared that he did not approve the mistreatment of the Soviet POWs; see Willi Boelcke (ed.), *Deutschlands Rüstung im Zweiten Weltkrieg: Hitlers Konferenzen mit Albert Speer 1942–1945* (Frankfurt: Athenaion, 1960), 86. On 7 February 1943, he ordered to feed up concentration camp prisoners and Jews before transporting them to Norway; see Boelcke, *Deutschlands Rüstung*, 234; Christopher R. Browning, *Die Entfesselung der 'Endlösung': Nationalsozialistische Judenpolitik, 1939–1942* (Berlin: Propyläen, 2003), 487.

25. Gerlach, 'Die Verantwortung der Wehrmachtführung', 48; Hürter, *Hitler's Heerführer*, 217, 392; Overmans, 'Deutsche Kriegsgefangenenpolitik', 836–8.

9

Japanese Culture and the Treatment of Prisoners of War in the Asian-Pacific War

Philip Towle

INTRODUCTION

Legal and moral restraints on warfare and violence evolve within particular cultures over long periods of trial and error. Their artificiality is more evident to outsiders than to those within a particular culture. Thus, John Glubb, serving with the British forces in the 1920s in what is now Iraq, was much impressed by the way in which Bedouin thieves would lurk outside the camp of another tribe hoping to steal their camels during the night. If they failed, they would calmly walk into the camp and ask for (and receive) hospitality, explaining to their intended victims that God had not favoured their enterprise.[1] During the same period, on the Northwest Frontier of India, rebels, who had previously served with British forces during the First World War, would sometimes call a halt to their attacks so that they could come and gossip with their former commander about their experiences.[2] Being warriors by tradition, they saw nothing wrong with their change of loyalty and expected the British to understand their feelings.

In the West, parallel conventions limiting violence are normally handed down from one generation to the next both orally by parents and teachers, and via the written word.[3] During the nineteenth century, people became more concerned about the protection of civilians, wounded soldiers, and prisoners in wartime, not least because society was becoming more socially conscious and democratic, and thus the loss of anyone, whatever their social class, became more important. At the same time, the development of the press and the growing tribe of war correspondents kept readers informed of the massacres, which occurred where restraints did not operate.[4] As a consequence, the formal and informal rules governing warfare were tightened, culminating in the promise at the 1907 Hague Peace Conference to try 'to diminish the evils of war, as far as military requirements permit' and agreeing that 'the inhabitants and belligerents remain [in wartime] under the protection of the law of nations, as they result from the usages established among civilised peoples, from the laws of humanity, and the dictates of the public conscience'.[5]

Before and during the Second World War, these cultural understandings, which Western governments had hoped to spread across the world, were under greater threat in the European heartland than they had been for hundreds of years. The Polish essayist and poet, Czeslaw Milosz, argued during the Second World War that severe shocks and particularly the experience of total war could numb this traditional moral sense and leave men feeling that human life had no value.[6] The democratic Weimar government established in Germany after the First World War was weakened from the beginning by the shocks of war and violence. The Nazis took advantage of the collapse of traditional mores 'to establish a new divinity, their own tribe, in the place of the over-thrown gods' and allowing those belonging to 'lesser' tribes or who stood in Germany's way to be obliterated. Individuals who would normally have behaved with humanity and restraint now joined criminals and sadists in killing and torturing the Jews, Poles, and Russians who fell into their hands.[7] The values inculcated by Christianity and the Enlightenment, which had under-pinned efforts to protect civilians and enemy prisoners during wartime, were consciously thrust aside.

JAPANESE CULTURE

The Japanese had also endured a succession of shocks after Commodore Perry forced the 'opening' of their reclusive country to outside trade and influence in the 1850s. The threat of Western aggression convinced members of the Japanese elite that the country would have to adopt Western technology and methods, but the country was deeply split about the benefits of accepting Western values and the international agreements in which they were incorporated. A senior British observer noted during the Russo-Japanese War:

> Already Bushido [the Japanese military code] stirs the antagonism of the foreign educated men who mean to try and rule Japan. These intellectuals regard military officers with greater dislike than a German professor displays towards a Prussian junker. They pine for the emancipation of women; they burn to humble the caste pride of the military and naval officers, and at all costs they are bent on democratising Japanese institutions in every direction.[8]

The strength of the opposition to the liberalizers was partly hidden from foreign governments before Pearl Harbor because Japan had signed international treaties relating to the law of war in general and POWs in particular, its leaders continued to insist that they would abide by such agreements, Japan had an active Red Cross, and it had treated Russian POWs in 1904–5 and German POWs in the First World War with dignity. The Japanese regulations for the treatment of prisoners laid down that 'a prisoner shall be humanely treated and in no case shall any insult or maltreatment be inflicted upon them'.[9] It seemed, therefore, that how-ever different Japanese history and experience had been, they were gradually accepting European ideas on the law of war, just as they were enthusiastically experimenting with Western technology. In the first decades of the twentieth century, they wanted to be regarded as one of the 'civilized peoples' referred to by the 1907 Hague Conference. They were determined to strengthen the alliance signed with Britain in 1902 and many members of the ruling elite were motivated by the humanitarian feelings which underpinned Western moves to reduce the destructiveness of warfare.[10]

However, the Japanese progressives were overawed and marginalized in the 1930s by those army officers who believed that Western attitudes towards warfare would undermine the Japanese military ethos and who wanted to challenge the Eurocentric world. This liberal defeat was precipitated by the Great Depression, but its fundamental cause was the predominance of nationalist, warrior values within the Japanese educational system. The schools had trained young men to believe that their lives were forfeit in wartime to the Emperor, and that defeat and surrender were unthinkable for a nation like Japan. Such values meant that during the Second World War the individual Japanese soldier was prepared to carry out operations which no other soldier of that period would have attempted, to die of starvation where he was fighting rather than to surrender, and to fight even though his transport had been torpedoed by US submarines more than once on the way to the battlefield.[11] The warrior ethic also encouraged Japanese commanders to take greater risks than their Occidental equivalents, such as moving air force squadrons rapidly between campaigns in different theatres.[12]

This warrior ethic represented a reversion to Japan's historic culture. Eleventh-century chronicles suggest that the *samurai* were ready to die in battle and were contemptuous of surrender. They hurled themselves at the enemy whatever the odds and however contrary to common sense. They revenged wrongs done to their family or lord in bloodthirsty vendettas and cut off their enemies' heads to prove that they had killed them. Rather than face dishonour by capture or in other ways, they were supposed to commit *seppuku*—a form of ritual suicide. Those foolish or cowardly enough to allow themselves to be taken alive could expect to be tortured, humiliated, and otherwise mistreated.[13] It is much easier for a warrior who was ready at any moment to sacrifice his own life to dismiss the sufferings of civilians and to regard surrendered enemy personnel with contempt.

The idea that war can only be fought in this way is still widespread in Japan and nowadays reinforces the emphasis there on peace and reconciliation. Studies comparing Japanese and British adolescents have found that:

> [Japanese] presented more protest and antiwar associations. ... The Japanese children referred more to reconciliation and respect and the Japanese adolescents used more peace symbols. In general, the Japanese children were more vehement in their protests against war and more preoccupied with international peace movements than English adolescents. [The researcher] assumed that these findings reflected cultural differences and the different experiences of the Japanese and English children.[14]

In 1978, the *Japan Times* published a collection of personal accounts by Japanese soldiers and civilians of the sufferings of the Second World War, which began:

> When man wages war, each side of the conflict seeks to convince its supporters that any sacrifice is warranted. Killing, burning, pillaging—all acts condemned by humanity under circumstances of peace—become acceptable in the cause of the moment, whatever it might be. Blindly accepting what their leaders say as true, large groups have committed mass suicide, mothers have abandoned their screaming infants, soldiers have turned weapons on their comrades.[15]

This aptly described Japanese experience in the Second World War, but it was in some ways unique even in that total conflict; nowhere else did people kill each other or commit suicide in any numbers to avoid capture; killing, burning, and pillaging were part of Nazi strategy to clear Eastern Europe for German settlers, but, Hitler's immediate associates apart, Germans did not commit suicide when their country surrendered. Moreover, burning and pillaging were not the norm during the Allied invasion of Italy and Germany at the end of the war.[16] Nor was it the way in which US occupation forces acted in Japan once that country had surrendered; Western soldiers committed serious crimes in Germany and elsewhere but these were not systematic and they were frequently punished.[17]

WESTERN AND EASTERN DEVELOPMENTS

In the West, democratization and the incorporation of all classes in the political nation made countries more sensitive about the fate of their soldiers.[18] In the pre-modern age, European nations had treated ordinary soldiers with some indifference. Captured officers had been ransomed but imprisoned soldiers had often been left to find their own way home after the war. The tens of thousands of British troops who died in the Caribbean of yellow fever during the French wars at the end of the eighteenth and beginning of the nineteenth centuries were largely forgotten except by their relatives.[19] In contrast, after the First World War, almost every British church had a plaque listing those of all ranks who had been killed and the nation still gathers together once a year to remember them. The French wars were commemorated in the triumphalist names given to Waterloo station and Trafalgar Square; the First World War is remembered at the Cenotaph.

Both Western and Japanese educational systems during the nineteenth century had tended to emphasize patriotic virtues and the superiority of their own nation. Indeed, as imperial rivalries increased, 'the generation of nationalist and imperialist attitudes in geography and history textbooks intensified'.[20] However, after the horrors of the First World War, the tide in the West began to flow in the opposite direction. There was a reaction against patriotic teaching, and geography and history became contested territory between those who continued to inculcate patriotic virtues and those who saw in the League of Nations the beacon to the future and wanted schools to preach the virtues of internationalism.[21] Influential figures, such as the imperial poet Rudyard Kipling, the novelist H. G. Wells, and the politician Lord Lansdowne renounced many of their earlier views and became much more anxious about the fragility of international society.[22]

Japan had not suffered to the same extent as the West during the First World War, and it did not experience the anti-war reaction which swept Britain and other Western states in the 1920s. When war came again, such sentiments encouraged pilots like Richard Hillary to despise overt nationalism, and the Labour politician, Denis Healey to rail against his patriotic Oxford tutors when he composed his memoirs many years after the Second World War.[23] Nevertheless, in order to make sure of excluding the socialist and liberal ideas steadily creeping into the country from the West, and to inculcate the warrior ethos, the Japanese government increased its control over schools and universities.[24] Until 1937, there was even a Thought Control Department in the Ministry of Education, though it was then renamed the Educational Affairs Bureau. These changes were made easier because civil society was comparatively weak in Japan; there had been no equivalent of the massive popular campaigns against the slave trade and for voting rights.[25] Most teachers accepted government direction of their work because it enhanced their influence in society, and those who refused to do so were weeded out. The goal of education thus became 'to grow and harvest people who would dedicate mind and soul to the cause of war. It was an easy step for Japanese youth, now invested with the spirit of sacrifice, to enthusiastically offer their bodies for the Great East Asian War.'[26] Of course, by no means all Japanese accepted nationalist teaching, any more than all Germans became ardent Nazis after Hitler's accession to power, and dissent was to grow when the war began to go against Japan. John Dower has shown how concerned the Japanese police became about dissent and has listed the anti-government and anti-war slogans they found daubed around the country.[27]

THE SECOND WORLD WAR

Nevertheless, the consequences of the early indoctrination were clearly visible in the astonishingly ambitious projects carried out by the Japanese armed forces during the Second World War and in their ideas as reflected, for example, in the diary kept by First Lieutenant Sugihara Kinryū during the fighting in Iwo Jima. The diarist mentions the appalling conditions only in asides, recalling the deaths of colleagues from malnutrition and the constant bombing without any of the feelings of shock or self-pity which might have affected a citizen soldier. Not that Kinryū was afraid to reveal his feelings; he was willing, for example, to record his satisfaction that his mother was recovering from some unspecified illness. But the diarist also shows how vastly different the Japanese view of the war was: 'Defilement of the Gods is a complete renunciation of the sublime rights of mankind. In other words, the plan of the enemy is to undermine the solid foundation of the state (human morality) and to insidiously weaken the solidarity of the people!'[28] The author was thus well aware of the intellectual depths of the struggle— everything his education and the Shinto religion had taught him to revere would be overthrown if he and his colleagues failed to defeat the Americans.

The brutality of Japanese military training and years of fighting against Chinese guerrillas had confirmed and honed this warrior ethos. Nothing infuriates a conventional army so much as trying to grapple with elusive insurgents who kill soldiers and then disappear into the countryside; nothing was more alien to the *samurai* ethic in which the courageous soldier stands and fights whatever the odds against him. Mao and his communist colleagues encouraged the peasantry to rise up against the Japanese in the sure knowledge that thousands of innocent Chinese would pay with their lives.[29] Only the severest discipline, publicity, and strong moral standards prevent acts of revenge by soldiers on civilians they suspect of supporting the guerrillas.[30]

Conditions were made all the worse for Asian civilians and Allied prisoners of war because of the gradual collapse of the Asian economy during the war years. The rapid Japanese advances in South-east Asia early in 1942 dislocated the regional economy. Rubber and sugar plantations destroyed during the invasion were not replanted. Tractors and expertise were not available to continue growing many crops. Shipping was inadequate to move goods from one country to another within the Japanese Empire, and the available vessels were so badly deployed that some travelled in ballast. It would have taken immense efforts to plan before December 1941 how the economy of the former Dutch East Indies, the Philippines, Burma, Thailand, Malaya, Korea, and Japan would somehow cohere to the best advantage of the Japanese and other Asian peoples. Planning of this nature was far beyond the resources of the Japanese bureaucracy.[31]

Allied attacks on Japanese shipping exacerbated the problem. At first the torpedoes in US submarines were ineffective but the problems were gradually remedied. They sank 172,000 tons of merchant ships in September 1943, 265,000 tons in November, and 321,000 tons in December the following year. There were 122,000 men in the Japanese merchant marine at the start of the war but during the course of the fighting 27,000 merchant seamen were killed and 89,000 wounded.[32] By the end of the war, the Japanese merchant fleet had been obliterated, and Asia had reverted to a subsistence economy. The Japanese population itself was on the brink of starvation; Japanese soldiers died of malnutrition in Okinawa and elsewhere. POWs could not have escaped the effect of this growing famine.

As it was, the POWs were seen by the Japanese command as an expendable source of labour in activities which were of vital importance to the Empire. Whether these tasks involved copper mining in Taiwan, coal mining, unloading ships and shipbuilding in Japan itself, or building the Thai-Burma railway, they were regarded as an essential part of the war effort and failure of the POWs to expend their utmost efforts were punished accordingly.[33] In the meantime, those who tried to escape were killed and those suffering from disease or malnutrition were often forced to work until they died.[34] Japanese soldiers were dying every-where in the Emperor's cause, why should enemy soldiers who were fortunate enough to have been spared on capture be treated in any other way? Ordinary Japanese soldiers knew nothing about international law.[35] It is also easy to see why the Japanese armed forces, stretched thinly across Asia, did not want to spend their time catching escaped POWs. Forcing the POWs to promise not to escape, and killing those who tried to do so, seemed the obvious solution.[36] Given the way in which Allied POWs were constantly trying to escape in Germany, Japanese ferocity over this question was understandable, however much it contra-dicted international law.

The Japanese perspective is well conveyed by Kazuo Tamayama's collection of accounts by their railway soldiers of their efforts to construct the line between Burma and Thailand. Here the deaths of POWs and indigenous workers are portrayed as sad examples of 'collateral damage'; Tokyo's orders were that the line should be built as rapidly as possible because maritime communications were becoming more difficult after the battle of Midway. Thus, the railway soldiers saw themselves as cogs in a vast machine; over and again they either failed to understand why the POWs were in such a bad condition and could labour no harder, or said that they had to obey orders to make them toil whatever the impact on the prisoners. They were not deliberately trying to work them to death in the way that the Nazis wanted Russian POWs to die, indeed their accounts stress their own difficulties and sufferings, their acts of kindness and those of their colleagues, the rarity of the brutal punishments recorded by POWs, and the gratefulness of the POWs for their general behaviour.[37]

It is hard to reconcile the Japanese and British accounts in such cases. More-over, there seems no doubt that many of the POWs' sufferings were dysfunctional for the Japanese Empire. Given the growing food shortages, the Japanese could not spare adequate food or any clothing for the POWs, but what did they gain from denying them Red Cross rations? Well-fed prisoners would have been better able to build railways or dig for copper. Moreover, Red Cross food would have taken some of the burden of feeding the POWs off their hands. What advantage was there in battening down the hatches on ships carrying POWs so that they could not escape if the ship were torpedoed? This would only reduce the number of survivors who could work for the Empire.[38] What benefit was there in refusing to provide rations for sick POWs?[39] What did they gain from conditions in the mines which made it impossible for the POWs to work there safely and effectively?[40]

But reasoning with the camp authorities was not usually wise or effective, and mentioning the laws of war, to which Japan had officially subscribed, was an invitation to the guards to attack or kill a prisoner. The point is an important one; the guards resented the arrogance of the Europeans, hence their insistence on prisoners admitting that Asians were superior.[41] The Europeans had lorded it over Asia for too long, now the Japanese, as Asian leaders, were in a position to take revenge and to assert that their historic *samurai* culture was superior to any Western regulations and conventions. In so far as Japanese officers were aware of their existence, international laws were part of the hated Western hegemony. Furthermore, Tamayama argues that Japanese brutality and indifference to the laws of war were a response to the killing of forty-eight Japanese POWs in the Featherston camp in New Zealand in February 1943.[42] The Japanese POW Control Bureau in Tokyo spread news of the incident to all the camps. According to Tamayama's account, conditions there then deteriorated and protests about breaches in international law were dismissed by reference to Allied behaviour on that occasion.[43] This may have exacerbated the situation in some cases, but mistreatment of POWs and infringements of the laws of war had begun well before February 1943.

Anti-Western or anti-European explanations for Japanese behaviour should not be pushed too far; the POWs were conscious that they were treated far better than their Asian counterparts. They had seen the way in which Chinese men, women, and children had been butchered on the beach after the fall of Singapore and how the population was terrorized during the wartime years.[44] POWs working on the Burma railway were only too conscious that tens of thousands of Malayan Indians, who had been tricked into agreeing to work on the railway, together with their families, were left to die there, of cholera and other diseases. Again a curiosity of Tamayama's account is that it minimizes these Asian sufferings and deaths, commenting mainly on the tendency of the local people to disappear from the railway camps at the first opportunity and thus the railway soldiers' general preference for employing POWs.[45]

AFTERMATH

All this has important implications for the Tokyo and other war crimes trials at the end of the Second World War and for international law in general. States will uphold the law if they perceive it to be in their interests and if the ideas which lie behind it are generally in accord with their culture. Japanese military leaders did not believe that supporting international law on the treatment of POWs and civilians was in their interests because they felt it would insidiously weaken their warrior ethic. As suggested above, this ethic often helped their war effort, although sometimes it undermined it. Many of the cruelties, summarized above, were counterproductive for the Japanese war effort because they weakened the prisoners, who were being treated as slaves. Moreover, although terrorizing civilians and obliterating villages in areas where guerrillas tried to operate appears to have been very largely effective at preventing nationalist insurgencies in Korea and Malaya, China was simply too large to make this possible.[46]

As far as the war crimes trials were concerned, the Japanese armed forces systematically breached the 1899 and 1907 Hague Regulations, which their country had signed, and the 1929 Geneva POW Convention, which they had said they would apply. The dissenting Indian Judge at the Tokyo Tribunal, Justice Pal, dismissed the resulting massacres at Nanking and elsewhere as typical of the sorts of events which happen in wartime.[47] This was partly true; as explained above, conventional armies have to be prevented by higher command if they are not to avenge themselves on the civilian population for guerrilla attacks. However, in the Japanese case (like the French in Algeria in the 1950s), such mistreatment was part of a deliberate and systematic tactic to terrorize conquered people into submission. Pal and the other judges also disagreed about whether Japanese leaders 'conspired' to wage aggressive wars. There would have been a consensus, however, that the Japanese had planned to drive the European colonialists out of Asia. The difference between the judges on this point was essentially political: Pal wanted the Europeans expelled and admired the Japanese for their efforts; the other judges, European, American, and Asian, did not.[48]

CONCLUSION

Milosz suggested that the violence of the First World War caused a loss of faith in Germany and elsewhere in civilization:

> Everything collapses; everything seems artificial and ephemeral in comparison with these elementary facts: the cruelty of human beings that is identical in its results with the cruelty of nature.... At such a moment all possible perspectives for contemplating man disappear; there remains but one—the biological perspective. The rest appears to be an unessential superstructure.[49]

If the horrors of war alone were enough to encourage this nihilism and subsequent state worship, then it should have caused similar results in all the former belligerents, which clearly it did not. Most of all, despair is much greater in defeated nations, even if the fruits of victory are also disappointing. Because of Britain's victory and the strength of British institutions, such nihilism was thus much less obvious there after the First World War than in Germany or Austria. Much of the old confidence in Britain's role in the world had disappeared, but the elites turned to idealism and faith in the League of Nations rather than nihilism and nationalism.[50] Furthermore, if Milosz had been right, the even greater bloodshed during the Second World War and the traumatic defeats inflicted on the Axis would have pushed their inhabitants yet further towards nihilism.

However, there were two essential differences between the atmosphere prevailing after 1918 and that after 1945, one in the realm of ideas and one in the confidence with which certain ideas and values were propagated. Ideologically, it was the biological perspective, the Social Darwinism of Hitler, Mussolini, and the Japanese leaders, which was so discredited in the Axis countries and elsewhere after 1945. The Second World War had laid bare the dangers of racism and extreme nationalism in the Holocaust, the battlefields of China and the eastern front, and the prisoner of war camps.[51] Secondly, the self-confident leadership provided by the United States set the moral standards for the post-war world, in the way that the weakened democratic states, led by Britain and France, were unable to do in the inter-war years.[52] Washington determined that the Axis leaders should be tried at Nuremberg and Tokyo for their war crimes; that the United Nations should be established in New York to replace the old Geneva-based League of Nations; that a free-trading system with fixed exchange rates should replace the protectionism of the inter-war years; and that the Atlantic powers should be bound together in an alliance.[53]

In contrast to the 1920s, the West has had the confidence since 1945 to defend the cause for which it fought. Indeed, as more information has gradually emerged about the nature of the Axis regimes, the Western consensus about the justice of the war has been strengthened. The vast pile of published accounts by POWs of their experiences in the Japanese camps has been part of this consensus-building. Like so much of the history of the Second World War, they revealed the depths of inhumanity of which nations are capable and validated the attempts to rein in these destructive impulses.

Japanese behaviour during the 1930s and the Second World War shows that the shocks of economic dislocation, like the shocks of defeat, can produce a conservative reaction against globalization, when this has already been insidiously undermined by educational institutions. Western observers often liked and admired Japanese society, and enjoyed socializing with their Japanese counterparts.[54] They also sympathized with Japanese pride at their economic and military achievements since the opening of their country but they paid insufficient attention to what was being taught in Japanese schools, and to the implications of the state worship being instilled, for the stability of the Asian international system.[55] Deeply nationalistic Japanese were shocked by the sufferings of their country during the Great Depression and the unwillingness of Europeans to accept what they saw as Japan's rightful position in its region; the consequences were the Second World War in Asia and the mistreatment of prisoners during that bitter struggle. In such circumstances, international law proved but a feeble protection for those who had fallen into the hands of their enemies.

NOTES

1. John Glubb, *Arabian adventures: Ten years of joyful service* (London: Cassell, 1978), 88. See also ibid. 74–5.
2. Charles Chenevix Trench, *The frontier scouts* (Oxford: Oxford University Press, 1986), 49.
3. Howard S. Levie (ed.), *Documents on prisoners of war* (Newport, RI: Naval War College Press, 1979), traces the evolution of the measures taken to protect prisoners of war over the centuries. For general attitudes towards the place of morality in warfare, see *The essays of Montaigne* (New York: Oxford University Press, n.d.), ii, 30; Oliver Morley Ainsworth (ed.), *Milton on education: The tractate of education* (New Haven, CT: Yale University Press, 1928), 55; Czeslaw Milosz, *Legends of modernity: Essays and letters from occupied Poland, 1942–1943* (New York: Farrar Straus Giroux, 2005), 80.

4. See, for example, Melton Prior, *Campaigns of a war correspondent* (London: Edward Arnold, 1912). For a powerful, later description of Balkan traditions see Milovan Djilas, *Land without justice: An autobiography of his youth* (London: Methuen, 1958).

5. 'Convention (IV) respecting the Laws and Customs of War on Land', signed at The Hague on 18 October 1907. SIPRI, *Arms control: A survey and appraisal of multilateral agreements* (London: Taylor and Francis, 1978), 55. For the previous situation, see L. (Lassa) Oppenheim, *International law: A treatise* (London: Longmans, Green, 1906), ii, ch. 4.

6. Milosz, *Legends of Modernity*, 80.

7. Ibid.

8. Sir Ian Hamilton, *A staff officer's scrap-book during the Russo-Japanese War* (London: Edward Arnold, 1906), ii, 31.

9. Article 2 of 'Regulation for the Treatment of Prisoners of War' in Levie, *Documents on prisoners of war*, 231–5. But note the following documents which show how the Japanese government undermined the objectives of the treaties; ibid. 236–48.

10. For the involvement of the Japanese Imperial family in the development of the Japanese Red Cross, see Margaret Kosuge, 'Religion, the Red Cross and Japanese treatment of POWs', in Philip Towle, Margaret Kosuge, and Yoichi Kibata, *Japanese prisoners of war* (London: Hambledon and London, 2000), 149ff.

11. There is a current debate about whether warriors are 'born', whether they are the product of national culture, or whether they can be created by military training. The Japanese example suggests that a very large segment of the population and the vast majority of a nation's armed forces can be instilled with a warrior ethos if culture and training combine to do so. See Christopher Coker, *Waging war without warriors* (Boulder, CO: Lynne Rienner, 2002), 1–3, 118–22; Bruce Newsome, 'The myth of intrinsic combat motivation', *Journal of Strategic Studies*, 26/4 (2003), 24–46.

12. A. D. Harvey, 'Army Air Force and Navy Air Force: Japanese aviation and the opening phase of the war in the Far East', in Jeremy Black (ed.), *The Japanese 1941–1945* [vol. 111 of *The Second World War*] (Aldershot: Ashgate, 2007), 151ff. British officers had noted the same willingness to take risks when they reported on the Russo-Japanese War; see Hamilton, *A staff officer's scrap-book*, i, 301, 338.

13. H. Paul Varley, with Ivan and Nobuko Morris, *The Samurai* (Harmondsworth: Penguin, 1974).

14. Amiram Raviv et al., *How children understand war and peace* (San Francisco, CA: Jossey-Bass, 1999), 164.

15. *Cries for peace: Experiences of Japanese victims of World War II*, compiled by the Youth Division of Soka Gakkai (Tokyo: Japan Times, 1978), 17.

16. Ulrike Jordan (ed.), *Conditions of surrender* (London: Tauris, 1997).

17. John Willoughby, *Remaking the conquering heroes: The postwar American occupation of Germany* (London: Palgrave, 2001), 16.

18. The French revolutionaries introduced a number of decrees intended to improve the treatment of ordinary POWs; see Levie, *Documents on prisoners of war*, 10–15.

19. The contrast with senior officers was stark; the eighteenth century saw the steady growth in the number of grandiose war memorials paid for by their wealthy relatives. See John Bonehill and Geoff Quilley (eds.), *Conflicting visions: War and visual culture in Britain and France, c.1700–1830* (Aldershot: Ashgate, 2005).

20. William E. Marsden, '"Poisoned history"—a comparative study of nationalism, propaganda and the treatment of war in the late nineteenth century and early twentieth century school curriculum', *History of Education*, 29/1 (2000), 29–47. For

British patriotic literature see also Michael Paris, *Warrior nation: Images of war in British popular culture, 1850–2000* (London: Reaktion, 2000).

21. Peter C. Gronn, 'An experiment in political education: "V.G.", "Slimy" and the Repton Sixth, 1916–1918', *History of Education*, 19/1 (1990), 1–21; Esmė Wynne-Tyson, *Prelude to peace* (London: C. W. Daniel, 1936).

22. On Kipling see Edmund Wilson, *The wound and the bow* (London: University Paper-backs/Methuen, 1961), ch. 2; on Wells see Edward Mead Earle, 'H. G. Wells, British Patriot in Search of a World State', in E. M. Earle (ed.), *Nationalism and internationalism* (New York: Columbia University Press, 1950); Lansdowne had been a firm supporter of Britain's declaration of war in 1914, but in 1917, he became the first senior British politician to call for a negotiated settlement; see Lord Newton, *Lord Lansdowne: A biography* (London: Macmillan, 1919), ch. 20.

23. Richard Hillary, *The last enemy* (London: Pan, 1956); Denis Healey, *Time of my life* (London: Michael Joseph, 1989).

24. For a contemporary view of changing views in the 1920s, see Sir Robert Craigie, *Behind the Japanese mask* (London: Hutchinson, 1945), ch. 3.

25. Nancy Bermeo and Philip Nord (eds.), *Civil society before democracy* (Lanham, MD: Rowan and Littlefield, 2000).

26. Yoshimitsu Khan, 'Schooling Japan's imperial subjects in the early Shōwa period', *History of Education*, 29/3 (2000), 218.

27. 'Sensational rumours, seditious graffiti, and the nightmares of the Thought Police', in John Dower, *Japan in war and peace: Essays on history, race and culture* (London: HarperCollins, 1995), 101 ff.

28. Stephen J. Lofgen, 'Diary of First Lieutenant Sugihara Kinryū: Iwo Jima', in Jeremy Black (ed.), *The Japanese War 1941–1945*, [vol. 11 of *The Second World War*] (Aldershot: Ashgate, 2007), 387ff.

29. Amleto Vespa, *Secret agent of Japan: A handbook of Japanese imperialism* (London: Victor Gollancz, 1938); Hugh Byas, *The Japanese enemy* (London: Hodder and Stoughton, 1942), 54.

30. For British reprisals against Palestinian civilians in the 1930s, see Arthur Lane, *One God, too many devils* (Stockport: Lane, 1989); on French troops' use of torture in Algeria in the 1950s, see Henri Alleg, *The question* (London: John Calder, 1958); General Paul Aussaresses, *The battle of the Casbah: Terrorism and counter-terrorism in Algeria, 1955–1957* (New York: Enigma Books, 2002), 121.

31. For a brilliant wartime analysis of Japan's difficulties, see Paul Einzig, *The Japanese new order in Asia* (London: Macmillan, 1941).

32. Clair Blair, *Combat patrol* (New York: Bantam, 1978); John Winton, *Convoy: The defence of sea trade* (London: Michael Joseph, 1983); Mark P. Parillo, *The Japanese merchant marine in World War II* (Annapolis, MD: Naval Institute Press, 1996); Jerome B. Cohen, *Japan's economy in war and reconstruction* (London: Routledge, 2000); Philip Towle, *From ally to enemy* (Folkestone: Global Oriental, 2006), ch. 10.

33. Ernest Gordon, *Miracle on the River Kwai* (London: Collins, 1963), 119.

34. Article 7 of the Japanese regulations laid down, 'prisoner of war who initially succeeds in escaping and is again captured shall not be liable to any punishment for his previous escape.' Levie, *Documents on prisoners of war*, 232.

35. Nagase Takashi and Watase Masaru, *Crosses and tigers* (Bangkok: Allied Printers, Post Publishing, 1990), 76.

36. R. Keith Mitchell, *Forty-two months in durance vile: Prisoner of the Japanese* (London: Robert Hale, 1997), 33.

37. Kazuo Tamayama, *Railwaymen in the war: Tales by Japanese railway soldiers in Burma and Thailand, 1941–47* (Basingstoke: Palgrave Macmillan, 2005).

38. There was one recorded occasion when a guard was killed by POWs who escaped when their ship was sunk, but this was bound to be rare. See Aidan MacCarthy, *A doctor's war* (London: Robson, 1989), 98.

39. Mitchell, *Forty-two months*, 189; Stanley L. Pavillard, *Bamboo doctor* (London: Macmillan, 1960); Thomas Pounder, *Death camps of the River Kwai* (Cornwall: United Writers, 1977); L. L. Baynes, *The other side of Tenko* (London: W. H. Allen, 1985 [orig. publ. as *Kept*, 1984]). Article 28 of the Japanese regulations on POWs made provision for the repatriation of sick POWs providing they gave their word not to bear arms again during the war.

40. John McEwan, *Out of the depths of hell* (Barnsley: Leo Cooper, 1999).

41. John Fletcher-Cooke, *The Emperor's guest, 1942–45* (London: Leo Cooper, 1994), 231.

42. Kent Fedorowich, 'Understanding the Enemy', in Towle, Kosuge, and Kibata, *Japanese Prisoners*, 61, 76, 79.

43. Tamayama, *Railwaymen*, 169–73.

44. For the beach massacre in Singapore see McEwan, *Hell*, 44–8. For the decapitation of Chinese for general crimes see Mitchell, *Forty-two months*, 52.

45. Tamayama, *Railwaymen*, 132, 139.

46. For an eyewitness assessment of the situation in Malaya, see F. Spencer Chapman, *The jungle is neutral* (London: Chatto & Windus, 1949).

47. Timothy Brook, 'The Tokyo judgement and the rape of Nanking', *Journal of Asian Studies*, 60/3 (2001), 686.

48. Ibid.

49. Milosz, *Legends of modernity*, 80.

50. R. B. McCallum, *Public opinion and the last peace* (London: Oxford University Press, 1944). See also Randall Thomas Davidson, Archbishop of Canterbury, *Occasions: Sermons and addresses delivered on days of interest in the life of church or nation* (London: Mowbray, 1925), ch. 1.

51. For classic early products of the post-1945 intellectual campaign against state worship see Karl R. Popper, *The open society and its enemies* (London: Routledge and Kegan Paul, 1945); Ernst Cassirer, *The Myth of the State* (New Haven, CT: Yale University Press, 1946).

52. A situation of which the Europeans were only too well aware; see Sir Charles Petrie, *Twenty years' armistice and after* (London: Eyre and Spotiswoode, 1940); Leopold Schwarzchild, *World in trance* (London: Hamish Hamilton, 1943).

53. On war crimes trials, see Henry L. Stimson, *On active service in peace and war* (New York: Harper Brothers, 1948), 584–90; on the UN, see Cordell Hull, *The memoirs of Cordell Hull*, vol. 2 (London: Hodder and Stoughton, 1948), 1292–307; for the origins of NATO in the ideas about alliances circulating in the United States during the Second World War see Walter Lippmann, *US Foreign Policy* (London: Hamish Hamilton, 1943), ch. 7; for the way in which the US imposed its economic ideas, see Robert Skidelsky, *John Maynard Keynes: Fighting for freedom, 1937–1946* (London: Penguin, 2000).

54. Captain Malcolm Kennedy, *The problem of Japan* (London: Nisbet, 1935); Major-General F. S. G. Piggott, *Broken thread: An autobiography* (Aldershot. Gale and Polden, 1950).

55. For the impact of education on young children see Geert Hofstede, *Cultures and organizations* (London: Profile Books, 2003), 4–6.

Part III

Detainees in Irregular Conflicts

10

Prisoners in Colonial Warfare: The Imperial German Example

Isabel V. Hull

COLONIAL WARFARE AND INTERNATIONAL LAW

Understanding the treatment of prisoners in colonial war poses several legal issues, for at base one is interested in discovering if colonial prisoners were worse handled than Europeans fighting among themselves. So, we must begin by asking what the legal baseline for European prisoners of war was in the late nineteenth century and how secure that legal foundation was in fact. Then we must ask whether those rules were held to apply to conflicts in the colonies.

'Military Necessity' Annuls International Law

Until the Hague Rules on land warfare (1899), no written international conventions covered prisoners of war in European conflicts. Nevertheless, custom and the precedent of the Geneva Convention on the treatment of the wounded (1864) encouraged most European powers, including Imperial Germany, to treat the unratified Brussels Declaration on Laws and Customs of War (1874) as reflecting international law.[1]

The Brussels articles held that captured soldiers were not to be killed; belligerents were forbidden from denying quarter; prisoners could work, but not in the war effort directed against their own state; their work was to be paid (minus their upkeep); they were not to be humiliated, or treated as criminals; they were instead to be treated as well as the soldiers of the capturing side.[2] The Hague Rules of 1899 (revised in 1907) added to the Brussels principles the admission of charitable gifts to prisoners of war and their right to exercise religion.[3] Both Hague Conventions were signed and ratified by Imperial Germany, and thus were part of German domestic law. If one were to judge only by the letter of the law, the situation for European prisoners of war seemed quite positive by the beginning of the twentieth century.

However, in dialectical relation with the codification and extension of the international law of war in the late nineteenth century, Imperial German jurists, statesmen, and military leaders developed a new, expansionary conception of 'military necessity'.[4] This view held that military necessity was a distillate of the nature of warfare itself. As one retired general wrote in 1877, '[w]ar interrupts explosively the legal condition of peace and to make possible its action suspends the entire legal norms completely on which peace is predicated. If the violence of war acknowledges duties, then it does so from the perfection of its own power—it cannot be forced to do so from the outside' (i.e. through law).[5] By 1908, the international legal jurist Christian Meurer was simply repeating the hegemonic German view that despite acceptance of the legality of the Hague Rules of 1907 no war act could be considered criminal 'if it is necessary to maintain the troops or to defend against a danger that threatens them and that cannot be stopped using other means, or in order to carry out a legal operation of war or to secure its success'.[6] For Imperial Germany, military necessity sharply curtailed the writ of international law. This 'strong' interpretation of military necessity led the international legal authority C. Lueder to write in 1889 in a leading German legal handbook that military necessity might permit the killing of wounded prisoners of war. The semi-official handbook on the laws of war, published by the German General Staff in 1902, opined that prisoners of war might lawfully be killed 'in a compulsive situation of necessity [*zwingender Notlage*] if other means of security are not available and the existence of a prisoner constituted a danger for one's own existence'.[7] The Imperial German concept of military necessity thus erased any absolute protections international law offered, even in European conflicts.

Did International Law Apply to the Colonies?

Despite widespread claims in the late nineteenth century that international law did not apply to the colonies, the matter was in fact confused. The violence of conquest seemed more and more to embarrass European states. Their practice of concluding treaties of protection with indigenous leaders—a novelty of the late nineteenth century—followed an international legal template that made colonial entities seem like independent, foreign states, and thus subjects (not merely objects) of international law. In a conflict with Europeans, therefore, captured warriors would have been entitled to consideration as prisoners of war, as the British Colonial Office, following its lawyers' advice, urged in the Ashanti War of 1900.[8] The alternative was punishment as rebels (against municipal or domestic law). In a large study of Europe's practices and legal argumentation regarding colonies from the early modern period to the present, Jörg Fisch has discovered that only for a brief time in the late nineteenth century can one find Europeans arguing that international law did *not* apply to colonies.[9] And throughout that time, there were voices arguing that it did, while others voiced no opinion.[10]

Despite the fact that Germany's colonies were 'protectorates', most of its legal writers did not recognize them as independent states, and thus they were not entitled to wage war by international standards (and their fighters were thus not protected by international law).[11] But the government and the *Reichstag* clashed repeatedly over this question. The government's position was inconsistent. Its spokesmen typically denied that colonial conflicts were 'wars' under international law, yet they used military language and concepts, such as 'war commander', 'courts martial', or 'spies', to justify brutal actions there. The *Reichstag*, especially the Social Democrats and Left Liberals, pressed to extend international legal protections to the colonies. In their struggle to hold colonial officials accountable for their deeds, *Reichstag* delegates cited every legal or quasi-legal principle they could think of, including international law, natural law, humanitarianism, and Christian morality. In his effort to cut through the opaque and frustrating legal situation, National Liberal Deputy, Dr Friedrich Hammacher, spoke for many when he said in 1896 that 'there is a natural law, a law which is so deeply rooted in the conscience and feeling of justice of mankind that the written law must conform to it'.[12]

The legal picture was unchanged in 1904 when Imperial Germany faced its largest colonial challenge: the Herero revolt, which 14,000 German troops were dispatched to suppress, and which lasted for three years. In the opinion of the Secretary of Justice, 'the revolt of natives cannot be regarded as a "war" against the German Empire'.[13] Nonetheless, Lieutenant General Lothar v. Trotha, who took command of the German troops in June 1904, followed the same legal procedures that the constitution mandated for the homeland in time of war with another state: he declared a wartime emergency (*Kriegszustand*) that suspended civilian administration and gave the military full executive power. At the same time, he followed the official line that colonial conflicts were not international wars. Herero fighters were rebels against domestic authority. As illegal combatants they were subject to summary execution. Following the Imperial Order of 28 December 1899 on 'Criminal Procedure in the Army in Wartime', Trotha gave every commanding officer (but not troops) the authority 'to shoot or hang without trial, according to the usual custom of war (*Kriegs-gebrauch*), coloured inhabitants whom German troops catch red-handed committing treasonous acts, for example all rebels, [and] those encountered bearing arms with warlike intention'.[14] Trotha warned troops that they would face criminal charges if they did the same, but he expressly permitted them to shoot to prevent prisoner escapes.[15] Trotha's order was part of a campaign of terror that ended in genocide.[16] The *Reichstag* again erupted in debate. The Socialist leader August Bebel excoriated the empire's 'barbaric war conduct, which is against all international law'. His remarks focused particularly on the treatment of prisoners. However, his colleague Matthias Erzberger of the Catholic Center Party denied that international law was applicable to colonial conflict: 'It is different in a war between civilized people and between whites and blacks', he argued.[17]

The conflict over the law remained until the outbreak of the First World War. In practice, the operative model was domestic, not international. Indigenous warriors were 'rebels', not soldiers, and their treatment was therefore punitive. Under the circumstances, neither international nor domestic law gave much protection to colonial fighters.

TREATMENT OF COLONIAL PRISONERS

By rights, this chapter should have presented a comparative overview of the treatment of prisoners in the European colonies. Such a synthesis is currently impossible. As I discovered while researching colonial war in German Africa, the secondary literature on the question tends to be unreliable: silent, anecdotal, or based on generalizing assumptions. Few studies focus on prisoners and difficult evidentiary problems hinder precision.[18] Colonial wartime practices, especially questionable ones, such as shooting women and children, massacres, orders to take no quarter, and rape, were often passed over in silence in the official documentary record. Courts-martial of misbehaving Europeans, which might provide good sources on this issue, seem to have been limited to the few cases which became public knowledge. In addition, the fate of prisoners depended largely on 'men on the spot' who were unevenly trained and experienced. One should expect a spectrum of different behaviour from them. In short, much work needs to be done. The following summary is based on research in German archives.[19]

Based on our current knowledge, one might distinguish between two models of prisoner treatment in the German colonies. The first, milder one occurred when military officials pursued limited war aims, because they were not existentially threatened by a rebellion (limited force seemed adequate to achieve acceptable ends), or they recognized the economic importance of keeping the indigenous population alive, or their military weakness dictated compromise. The second, harsher model happened when a revolt seemed (for whatever reason) to be a matter of national security or prestige. That perception placed the military at the centre of decision-making and made military considerations, routines, and assumptions the template for solving problems. In that case, a demonstrative victory of pure military force became the goal. It brought with it both a greater emphasis on punishment and higher standards for victory. The difficult fighting in jungle, brush, or desert made these harder to achieve, and the resulting frustration often fed a vicious cycle of violence.[20]

The first model was the usual one. It had five characteristics.

1. The number of prisoners taken during actual fighting was small; the greatest number surrendered upon general capitulation. These small numbers have fed the assertion—often found in the secondary literature—that no prisoners were taken at all in colonial conflicts. Even Governor Leutwein during the Herero revolt was under that mistaken impression.[21] Why were the numbers so small? The first reason is that Europeans were often simply unable to take many prisoners. Unfamiliar with the landscape, unused to fighting in jungles or deserts, far from their logistical infrastructure and thus often facing shortages of food, water, ammunition, and transport, European troops could rarely execute the mobile operations necessary to net large numbers of prisoners. In Africa, at least, indigenous inhabitants went to great lengths to avoid capture: they fled

their dwellings (which often were easy to rebuild), they exploited their knowledge of the terrain, and the wounded kept fighting even after European soldiers expected them to give up.

But German methods of colonial warfare also decreased the chances of capturing people alive. Burning villages, declaring rebel leaders outlaws, and putting a price on their heads would not have encouraged surrender. The difficulty in capturing Africans alive seems to have encouraged troops to shoot at all fleeing blacks indiscriminately. The Herero habit of not taking prisoners themselves and of killing the wounded raised the issue of reciprocity, which played such a large role in arguments against extending the protection of international law outside Europe and which was undoubtedly very important in determining how troops behaved in the field. Revulsion at Herero methods may also have influenced Trotha. Before he began his campaign, Trotha several times expressed outrage that Herero warriors mutilated dead German soldiers.[22] On the Germans' part, it appears that killing wounded African fighters was fairly common, though not ubiquitous, in colonial conflicts in South West Africa.[23]

It is very difficult to determine whether denying quarter altogether was also common. For the Herero campaign, I have discovered no such orders in the archives, though one usually reliable missionary claimed that transport troops in his district had received one.[24] Trotha's order for summary execution of armed rebels might have encouraged junior officers to interpret that as tantamount to 'no pardon'; this sort of operative drift is not uncommon in wartime.[25] German troops had several sources of encouragement along these lines. One was the Kaiser's public exhortation to troops leaving to quell the Boxer Uprising in China in 1900 to 'take no prisoners'.[26] Another was the widespread interpretation of 'military necessity' to excuse under certain circumstances killing prisoners or not taking them in the first place. Governor Leutwein seemed to be following that interpretation in his response to August Bebel's query in the *Reichstag* in 1904 as to whether such an order had been given. Leutwein told the Colonial Department that he had never done so. Nonetheless, he added: 'If Mr Bebel apparently believes that one is *obliged* to take prisoners in war, then he doesn't know international law.'[27]

2. Civilians (non-combatant women, children, and old people) were equally made prisoners alongside armed, adult males. This practice appears to have been ubiquitous in Africa, though not in the intervention against the Boxers in China. The assumption that civilians were wholly part of the war effort may partly have reflected African war customs. This assumption greatly increased the vulnerability of civilians to violence and death, but this danger was not limited to civilians in the colonial realm. General Helmuth v. Moltke had realized the centrality of civilians to the war efforts of modern nation states when the German states fought France in 1870.[20] His insight became commonplace in German military writings. The 1902 General Staff compendium *Kriegsbrauch* wrote that '[a]n energetic war cannot be waged merely against the combatants of an enemy state or against its fortresses. Rather, it must seek to

destroy in the same fashion the entire intellectual and material resources. Humanitarian considerations, such as protection of people and goods can only occur as the nature and goal of war permits.'[29] Nevertheless, *Kriegsbrauch* had mostly destruction, not internment, in mind, except in cases where a European population engaged in a *levée en masse*.[30] In the event, non-combatant prisoners—who in the colonies might easily make up the majority of captives— were then easily 'forgotten' by military commanders, who continued to think of all internees as 'prisoners of war', and to treat them according to those standards (see below).[31] Civilians also came under suspicion of spying, and the German military method of handling them, in Europe and in the colonies, was the same: execution, with trial if possible, but if 'the speedy motion of the war' did not permit, then without.[32]

3. Prisoners, combatant and non-combatant, were interned and held to forced labour (*Zwangsarbeit*).[33] Governor Leutwein's instructions for the surrendering Khauas-Khoi clan in May 1896 illustrate how this worked:

> The remainder of the Khauas-Hottentot tribe is to be brought under guard by the accompanying soldiers to an area as closed as possible and then busied as soon as possible in public works. Female prisoners can also be given to private persons to work, but must return each night to the tribe. All the measures taken should be done in consultation with the Witbooi foreman and the foreman of the Khauas Hotten- tots, Jakob Lambert. The surviving cattle [of the Khauas] are to be left with the tribe. I reserve later measures for my return in June.[34]

Although the Khauas revolt had 'brought the colony to the edge of disaster' in Leutwein's judgement, and throughout he referred to it as a 'war', he did not go to greater extremes in putting it down because German military presence was too weak and because he had reliable African allies (Hendrik Witbooi and Lambert). Therefore, their opinions were important in the treatment of the defeated Africans. One should also note that, though non-combatants were equally interned, gender made a difference in treatment. Women were more likely to end up in private hands, which generally (but not always) meant better working conditions than public works.[35] Nonetheless, the work was forced, usually unpaid, and reflected the German obsession with 'educating' the Africans to work.[36] Internment was often in a place removed from the prisoners' region, so it might amount to internal deportation. Finally, Leutwein's last sentence reminds us that the treatment of African prisoners was up to the Governor's discretion; it was not set or limited by legal regulation.

4. Prisoners, especially males, faced courts martial and condemnation. Prisoners identified as leaders were always tried. Depending on circumstances and on the German commander, investigations might extend to encompass many men. 'Ringleaders' faced charges of rebellion; their followers, murder and theft or property destruction. In the milder 'model', these trials were not designed to kill rebels by other means, but to demonstrate the colonizer's power and to coerce its acceptance by the defeated. That is, peace on the colonizer's terms was the goal. For this reason investigations and trials were often done by

mixed courts consisting of German officers and an equal number of reliable African allies, generally of other clans. The investigations were not necessarily trumped up. For example, one of the leaders of the Khauas revolt, Kahimemua Nguvauva, was at first left free, until 'the testimony of prisoners incriminated him more and more', and he was arrested, and later executed.[37] A decree of the Chancellor in 1896 forbade using any technique to extract confessions beyond those permitted in Germany itself.[38] To my knowledge no detailed study of courts martial in the colonies exists that would tell us how rules and reality measured up.

'Ringleaders', who were often the heads of clans, were typically condemned to death and executed. Sometimes, however, their death sentences were commuted, which illustrated the power of the colonizers to exercise grace, and also counter-manded overzealous officers-on-the-spot. Such was the case in German East Africa in 1896. In the wake of a successful 'punitive expedition' (then) Lieutenant Colonel Lothar v. Trotha had conducted 100 investigations, convicted eighty Africans, and sentenced seven to death. Governor Hermann v. Wissmann inter-vened and commuted all these sentences.[39] Other sentences meted out to defeated Africans might include collective fines, confiscation of cows (and, of course, guns), or taking Africans' land. Whipping was also a punishment that was designed to humiliate and demonstrate colonial superiority.

5. After internment, most prisoners were eventually released. When depended on the governor's discretion. Whereas Wissmann released the captives of v. Trotha quickly, Governor Leutwein refused to do so with the leaders of the Swartboi uprising, even seven years later.[40]

This first model of prisoner treatment in the colonies therefore differed strik-ingly from the written rules applying to European prisoners in European wars. After 1896 there were (some) legal guidelines from Berlin, and force of cir-cumstances and political goals might also limit the severity of treatment, but much was left to the governor's discretion. The parameters of confinement were largely set by three considerations: security, punishment (on a domestic model of rebellion that was the opposite of the international legal model of war and the *justus hostis*—the honourable, legal enemy whose status is equal to your own), and 'education' (i.e. exemplary treatment designed to demonstrate defeat and loss of status, and habituation to work for the interests of the colony). The first model looks moderate only when compared to the second model.

The second model was the purely military model which might develop where revolt seemed existential, or became symbolic of national prestige, or where its suppression became frustrating, as in guerrilla warfare, or because of the German military's very high standards of 'victory'. Its five characteristics are the same as in the first model, but more intensive and final.

1. Even fewer prisoners might be taken because the conduct of war was so extreme. Devastation of all housing and crops, slash and burn, as in German East Africa during the suppression of the Maji-Maji revolt (1905–8) pushed hundreds

of thousands of Africans away from the lines of march and left them to starve.[41] Lieutenant General v. Trotha's 'pursuit' of the Herero into the Omaheke desert resulted in their virtual annihilation by thirst. He accepted no prisoners and ordered Herero civilians to be driven from wells.[42]

2. Civilians, or non-combatants, were equally targets of imprisonment and of other war measures.

3. Adult male prisoners might be simply executed on the spot, or after such summary proceedings that they barely deserved the name. Trotha's order of June 1904 in South West Africa, permitting commanding officers without a trial to 'hang or shoot coloured inhabitants' caught red-handed or with arms, and to shoot escapees, fanned the usual flames of harsh treatment in battle. But even Trotha did not want shootings to get out of hand. He forbade common soldiers to do the same, and he set out rules for field courts that included African associate judges (*Beisitzer*) to handle Africans not captured in the above circumstances.[43] But typically he, too, added the escape clause reflective of 'military necessity': 'If the previous regulations cannot be applied, [if] a speedy judgment is pressingly necessary', then one could have summary proceedings followed by immediate execution. Trotha's abandonment of regular courts martial seems to have encouraged the wholesale shootings of male prisoners, and in the field, of all blacks whom the German troops encountered.[44]

4. Internment conditions in South West Africa (1904–7) were exterminatory; they amassed a death rate of at least 45–50 per cent, twice that of the notorious British camps in the Boer War.[45] The 'concentration camp', in its original meaning, was a colonial-military institution designed to intern and thus separate civilian populations from guerrilla fighters. None of the European countries operated these camps successfully. Death rates from disease were always high, because the military authorities were ill-trained to run permanent facilities for large numbers of civilians, whose needs were entirely different from those of healthy, young soldiers.

In December 1904, Berlin forced Trotha to accept surrendering Hereros of all ages and both sexes. They were at first housed in collection camps run by missionaries, who attempted to nurse them back to health before transferring them to camps set up and run by the military authorities. The military's prisoner of war camps were a horror. Inmates, including non-combatants, suffered starvation rations consisting of unaccustomed, poor quality food which they could not digest. They lacked the most basic clothing, shelter, and medical treatment. One of the camps, Shark Island in Lüderitz Bay, had a cold, wet climate—the reverse of the desert conditions to which its inmates were accustomed. Despite enormous death rates, military authorities, even after Trotha was removed from his post, did not improve conditions, citing security fears and the principle that the welfare of German troops trumped that of prisoners. In the end, it was not regular military officers from Germany, but an officer of the *Schutztruppe* (that is, a man with much experience in, and regard for, Africa and its people) who closed the camp and rescued the survivors. The exterminatory conditions in the military-run camps were primarily the result of policies designed to punish rebels. They proved impervious to improvement, even when the policy changed, because of the routines and inertia of military culture, the low priority of prisoners in wartime, incompetence, individual viciousness, and general 'lovelessness', in the words of a (military) critic.[46]

Other internees faced deportation from the colony. Leutwein deported 282 Herero to South Africa at the beginning of the rebellion. Deportation was also the fate of almost 100 Witbooi fighters who had helped German troops suppress the Herero revolt. Their leader, Hendrik Witbooi, then decided that his people, the Nama, should revolt, and the Witbooi soldiers were disarmed in October 1904 and shipped first to Togo and then to the Cameroons. In both places they were under civilian authority; the governors hoped to use them as labourers. But like Shark Island, Togo and the Cameroons featured a different climate, new diseases, and strange food. The Witboois sickened and died, despite the genuine efforts of the Cameroon authorities to help them. Until 1906, colonial authorities in South West Africa refused to take back the few survivors.

There were other new measures applied to prisoners. Trotha insisted that all prisoners be chained, because he lacked the manpower to guard them. That order was countermanded by the chancellor in Berlin.[47] He also intended 'to affix to prisoners of both sexes a nonremovable tin badge with the letters "G.H." [*gefangener Herero*, or Herero prisoner]'. Berlin let that idea stand, so long as it did not 'involve cruelty'. A similar idea had been floated in the civilian administration in 1900, but only in war could it become reality.[48]

Internees faced forced labour. The difference to the first model is that the miserable physical condition of the prisoners made even light work impossible. Inability to work did not move military authorities to improve conditions, however, whereas private employers seem to have responded better. When economics clashed with the punitive or security-oriented motives of the military, the latter always won. Economic need was never strong enough to overcome the ingrained habits and assumptions of the military.

Finally, there is evidence that female prisoners were victims of sexual violence or exploitation by German troops. It is unclear how much sexual exploitation was a regular feature of colonial life or of the first model. The increased number of German soldiers, the high number of detainees, and the length of the war all increased the likelihood that soldiers took advantage of African women. Of all the aspects of prisoner life, this is the perhaps the one most difficult to document.[49]

5. Release of the prisoners in South West Africa had to wait until military rule ended and civilian colonial administration resumed. But the prisoners were not released into a *status quo ante*. Deprived of their land, property, and political organization, they were destined to be a disposable labour force in a colony whose settlers had become intemperate, emotional racists bent on establishing an apartheid regime.[50]

RACISM AND CULTURE AS FACTORS IN
PRISONER TREATMENT

Racism certainly affected the treatment of prisoners in the colonies. Lothar v. Trotha, a self-declared racist, was a particularly striking example of a person who organized the world into biological–racial categories. But, as I have argued elsewhere, racism was not the only motive or cause for Trotha's extreme actions.[51] Nor was he the sole reason that military practice reached genocidal levels in South West Africa, much less in German East Africa, where he was not present during the Maji-Maji revolt. Racism is unfortunately too often a black box that substitutes for detailed analysis. Used in its most general sense, the term can be said to have characterized all Europeans at the turn of the century; yet for all their brutality, colonial policies, even military ones, differed from one another from place to place and time to time. Racism of particular individuals was often the product of their colonial experience, rather than the cause. Differentiating among types and degrees of racism would greatly benefit our understanding of how colonialism really worked.

Race-thinking, understood as a general predisposition to think in biological categories of difference with an assumption of European superiority, is visible on many levels of policy-making toward colonial prisoners. It is hard to believe, for example, that the state of lawlessness—or 'rightlessness'—that reigned in the German colonies would have been permitted to last so long if the inhabitants had been white or European. But it is useful to recall that other considerations cross-cut or pre-empted racism and race-thinking. The chancellor's order of 22 April 1896 regulating treatment of indigenous criminal prisoners forbade the whipping of women and the beating of youths under sixteen—thus gender and age modified racial precepts. Economic considerations could work the same way. And politics was a most important limiting influence. Concern for foreign opinion, moral censure from missionaries, and moral and legal criticism by *Reichstag* deputies had at least a periodic and punctual affect on harsh policies. So did humanitarian concerns privately held by leaders such as Chancellor Bernhard v. Bülow, who mentioned these first when he reined in Lieutenant General v. Trotha in 1904.[52] However, all of these considerations tended to be weaker than army leaders' arguments based on military necessity, and these were generated less by racism or race-thinking than by the habits and assumptions of military organizational culture.

Military culture was foundational in determining whether enemies were captured and how captives were treated, especially in the second model. A whole series of basic assumptions that derived from lessons learned in previous (European) wars and embedded in organizational routines and scripts underlay actual practices. From our perspective perhaps the most important of these assumptions was a characteristic that the German army shared with most others, though I would argue it had developed it to a greater extent: the single-minded focus on combat at the expense of all other considerations. That meant that prisoners (European or colonial) were a low priority. There was little advance planning, commanders were loath to expend manpower or resources on them, and officers and men put in charge of them were hardly the cream of the crop. There were few organizational incentives to handle prisoners correctly. In the European sector, reprisals therefore remained very important in determining the treatment of prisoners, as the First World War showed.[53]

When large numbers of non-combatants became captives it made matters worse. Militaries were used to the needs and resilience of young men, and their routines were cut to that cloth. Civilians were a nuisance and, in the German military's eyes, something of a lower species. Gender assumptions that coded civilians as feminine and soldiers as masculine did not help. No late nineteenth-century or early twentieth-century military that I am aware of treated interned civilians adequately. That required special training unlikely to be introduced until handling large numbers of civilians became a regular military task (which, in the age of humanitarian intervention, it finally did).

Late-nineteenth-century European military culture held several assumptions about honourable fighting that also profoundly affected the taking and treatment of prisoners. European militaries expected war to be among organizations like their own: organized by a state, commanded by recognizable officers, clad in uniforms, wielding industrialized weaponry, and fighting in units in the open. As the premier land power, Germany had the highest expectations of regularized warfare. The main arguments during the codification of the laws of war after 1871 ranged Imperial Germany against smaller or island nations, which insisted that militias and even armed citizens should be recognized as proper soldiers. Germany profoundly disagreed and brought its high standards to the colonies. There, it met opponents who fought with what they had at hand: with bullets made of melted glass or shredded lead, munitions apparently forbidden by the Hague Rules on Land Warfare.[54] They fought without uniform (or, worse, in captured German uniforms); their command structure was indecipherable; and, with some exceptions, they fought guerrilla-style, rather than out in the open. The Hereros, in addition, took no prisoners and clubbed downed German soldiers to death. Despite the Germans' regular use of military terms to describe colonial conflicts and the recurring reference to 'prisoners of war', African fighters were thought of as 'rebels'—a category that added to the dishonour accruing to them by virtue of their style of fighting.

Colonial fighters therefore mostly failed the Europeans' reciprocity test. In the late nineteenth century, reciprocity, in the form of shared custom, was thought to be the foundation on which international law had developed (among Europeans).[55] With codification and the development of recognized human rights, reciprocity was just beginning to lose its power in favour of absolute rules that withstood even flouting by one side. Some German writers, including the author of *Kriegsbrauch*, which reflected General Staff opinion, believed, on the contrary, that reciprocity was absolute; where it did not exist, there was no international law—there was only the law of force.[56] But probably most European writers of the time felt that reciprocity remained a cornerstone of international law. Thus, a panoply of practice-based, military-cultural expectations directly affected how law was interpreted and whether it was followed. These were commonly assimilated into the racialized epithet of 'civilized' versus 'uncivilized.' These cultural expectations, deriving from history, military culture, and ideology, were important in denying to colonial peoples the legal protections being worked out at the conferences in Europe.

NOTES

1. C. Lueder, 'Krieg und Kriegsrecht im Allgemeinen,' in Franz von Holtzendorff (ed.), *Handbuch des Völkerrechts* (Hamburg: A. G. Richter, 1889), 323–5; C. Lueder, 'Das Landkriegsrecht im Besonderen,' in Holtzendorff *Handbuch des Völkerrechts*, iv, 381, 432–43.
2. Leon Friedman, *The law of war: A documentary history* (New York: Random House, 1972), i, 194–203.
3. James Brown Scott (ed.), *The proceedings of the Hague Peace Conferences: Translation of the official texts; the conference of 1899* (New York: Oxford University Press, 1920), 474–83.
4. Isabel V. Hull, ' "Military necessity" and the laws of war in Imperial Germany', in Stathis Kalyvas, Ian Shapiro, and Tarek Masoud (eds.), *Order, conflict, violence* (Cambridge: Cambridge University Press, 2008), 352–77.
5. Julius von Hartmann, 'Militärische Nothwendigkeit und Humanität: Ein kritischer Versuch', *Deutsche Rundschau*, 13–14 (1877–8), 124.
6. Christian Meurer, *Das Kriegsrecht der Haager Konferenz*, [vol. 2 of *Die Haager Friedenskonferenz*] (Munich: J. Schweitzer, 1907), 14.
7. German General Staff, *Kriegsbrauch im Landkriege* [vol. 31 of *Kriegsgeschichtliche Einzelschriften*] (Berlin: E. S. Mittler, 1902), 16.
8. Sam C. Ukpabi, 'The British Colonial Office approach to the Ashanti War of 1900,' *African Studies Review*, 13/3 (1970), 376.
9. Jörg Fisch, *Die europäische Expansion und das Völkerrecht* (Stuttgart: Steiner, 1984), 288. His study does not concentrate on the laws of war, but it has implications for them.
10. Charles Edward Callwell, *Small wars: Their principles and practices* (1906; 3rd edn. repr.; London: EP Publishing, 1976) is silent on international law.
11. Wallace-Bruce has argued cogently that Europeans misinterpreted the state-like qualities that many African groups actually had formed prior to colonization. Nii Lante Wallace-Bruce, 'Africa and international law—the emergence of statehood,' *Journal of Modern African Studies*, 23/4 (1985), 575–602.
12. *Sten. Ber.*, 9t. Legisl. Per., Sess. IV, 1895–1896, vol. 2, 60. Sitz. 14 March 1896, 1454.
13. Rudolf Arnold Nieberding to Colonial Dept. of the Foreign Office, Abschrift K. 7421, Nr. 1436, Berlin, 19 May 1905, BA-Berlin, R 151 F, Film Nr. FC 4712, D.IV.L.2. Bd. 4, pp. 72–4.
14. Gerd Hankel, *Die Leipziger Prozesse: Deutsche Kriegsverbrechen und ihre strafrechtliche Verfolgung nach dem Ersten Weltkrieg* (Hamburg: Hamburg Edition, 2003), 215, 228–40. On 'Kriegsbrauch' see 228–40.

15. Order of June 1904, Namibian National Archives, Windhoek, ZBU Geheimakten IX.Z. Bd.1, B.1b, cited in Jürgen Zimmerer, 'Kriegsgefangene im Kolonialkrieg: Der Krieg gegen die Herero und Nama in Deutsch Südwestafrika (1904–1907)', in Rüdiger Overmans (ed.), *In der Hand des Feindes: Kriegsgefangenschaft von der Antike bis zum Zweiten Weltkrieg* (Cologne: Böhlau, 1999), 282; and in Conrad Rust, *Krieg und Frieden im Hererolande: Aufzeichungen aus dem Kriegsjahre 1904* (Leipzig: L. A. Kittler, 1905), 344–5.

16. Isabel V. Hull, *Absolute destruction: Military culture and the practices of war in Imperial Germany* (Ithaca, NY: Cornell University Press, 2005).

17. Bebel: *Sten. Ber.*, XI. Legisl. Per., 1st Session, 62nd Sitzung, 19 March 1904, Bd. 199, 1967C; Erzberger, ibid., 2nd Session, 5th Sitzung, Bd. 214, 2 Dec. 1904, 111.

18. For two recent studies, see Zimmerer, 'Kriegsgefangene' and Joachim Zeller, '"Wie Vieh wurden hunderte zu Tode getrieben und wie Vieh begraben": Fotodokumente aus dem deutschen Konzentrationslager in Swakopmund/Namibia 1904–1908', *Zeitschrift für Geschichtswissenschaft*, 49/3 (2001), 226–43.

19. Hull, *Absolute destruction*, chs. 1–3, 6.

20. Trutz v. Trotha offers a different, chronological model in which 'pacification' is the first and most violent phase. Trutz von Trotha, *Koloniale Herrschaft: Zur soziologischen Theorie der Staatsentstehung am Beispiel des 'Schutzgebietes Togo'* (Tübingen: J. C. B. Mohr, 1994), 5–16.

21. Hull, *Absolute destruction*, 14–15.

22. Trotha diary entry of 16 July 1904, Trotha Family Archives, Lothar v. Trotha Papers, Nr. 315, p. 20; Hull, *Absolute destruction*, 30, 33.

23. Hull, *Absolute destruction*, 20; but Leutwein to Chancellor, draft, Okahandja, 8 June 1896, BA-Berlin, R 151 F, Film Nr. FC 4704, D.IV.C., Vol. 1, 124–34.

24. Hull, *Absolute destruction*, 21.

25. Operative drift was made more likely by the German army's 'mission tactics': see Hull, *Absolute destruction*, 115–17.

26. Hull, *Absolute destruction*, 135; Featherstone claims British troops gave no quarter in China: Donald Featherstone, *Colonial small wars, 1837–1901* (Newton Abbot: David & Charles, 1973), 207.

27. Leutwein to Colonial Department of Foreign Office, Nr. 395, Windhoek, 17 May 1904, BA-Berlin, R 1001 Nr. 2115, 64.

28. Stig Förster, 'The Prussian triangle of leadership in the face of the people's war: A re-assessment of the conflict between Bismarck and Moltke, 1870/71', in Stig Förster (ed.), *On the road to total war: The American Civil War and the German wars of unification, 1861–1871* (New York: Cambridge University Press, 1994), 138.

29. German General Staff, *Kriegsbrauch im Landkriege*, 2.

30. Ibid. 13.

31. Hull, *Absolute destruction*, 86, referring to Colonel v. Deimling in Southwest Africa.

32. German General Staff, *Kriegsbrauch im Landkriege*, 31. The Hague Rules on Land Warfare required trials, regardless of circumstances; see Art. 30.

33. Governor Leutwein's phrase: Leutwein to Chancellor, draft, Okahandja, 8 June 1896, BA-Berlin, R 151 F., Film Nr. FC 4704, D.IV.C., Bd. 1, 124–34. On forced labour: Jan Bart Gewald, *Herero heroes: A socio-political history of the Herero of Namibia, 1890–1923* (Athens: James Currey, 1999), *passim*.

34. Leutwein to Lt. Governor, Omuramba camp, 15 May 1896, in Gewald, *Herero heroes*, 170.

35. Hull, *Absolute destruction*, 81.

36. Jürgen Zimmerer, *Deutsche Herrschaft über Afrikaner: Staatlicher Machtanspruch und Wirklichkeit im kolonialen Namibia* (Hamburg: Lit-Verlag, 2001), ch. 5.

37. Leutwein to Chancellor, draft, Okahandja, 8 June 1896, BA-Berlin, R 151 F: Film Nr. FC 4704, D.IV.C. Bd. 1, 124–34. See also Gewald, *Herero heroes*, 102–9.

38. 'Verfügung des Reichskanzlers, betreffend der Gerichtsbarkeit über die Eingeborenen in den afrikanischen Schutzgebieten', 27 Feb. 1896, in Otto Kolisch (ed.), *Die Kolonialgesetzgebung des Deutschen Reichs mit dem Gesetze über die Konsulargerichtsbarkeit* (Hanover: Helwing'sche Verlagsbuchhandlung, 1896), 77.

39. Report Nr. 1003, Dar-es-Salaam, 9 Nov. 1896, BA-Berlin R 1001, Nr. 6467, Bl. 188–90.

40. Leutwein to Bezirksamtmann Kliefoth, 3.6.1902 R 151 F, Film Nr. FC 4706 D.IV.F. Bd. 2, Bl. 384 v&r.

41. Modern estimates of death range from 250,000–300,000 Africans; see John Iliffe, *A modern history of Tanganyika* (Cambridge: Cambridge University Press, 1979), 200.

42. Hull, *Absolute destruction*, 55–63.

43. Order of June 1904.

44. Hull, *Absolute destruction*, ch. 2.

45. Ibid. chs. 3, 8.

46. Ludwig von Estorff, *Wanderungen und Kämpfe in Südwestafrika, Ostafrika und Südafrika, 1894–1910* (Wiesbaden: Private publication of Christoph-Friedrich Kutscher, 1968), 118. On the standard practices of internment, see Hull, *Absolute destruction*, 149–57.

47. Hull, *Absolute destruction*, 70–1.

48. Ibid. 73; Zeller, 'Wie Vieh wurden hunderte zu Tode getrieben', 238 n. 37; Zimmerer, *Deutsche Herrschaft*, 73 n. 56.

49. Hull, *Absolute destruction*, 150–1.

50. Helmut Bley, *South-West Africa under German rule, 1894–1914*, trans. and ed. Hugh Ridley (Evanston, IL: Northwestern University Press, 1971), 170–283; Gesine Krüger, *Kriegsbewältigung und Geschichtsbewußtsein: Realität, Deutung und Verarbeitung des deutschen Kolonialkriegs in Namibia 1904 bis 1907* (Göttingen: Vandenhoeck & Ruprecht, 1999); Zimmerer, *Deutsche Herrschaft*; Jürgen Zimmerer and Joachim Zeller (eds.), *Völkermord in Deutsch-Südwestafrika: Der Kolonialkrieg (1904–1908) in Namibia und seine Folgen* (Berlin: Ch. Links Verlag, 2003).

51. Hull, *Absolute destruction*.

52. Ibid. 64.

53. Heather Jones, 'The enemy disarmed: Prisoners of war and the violence of wartime, Britain, France and Germany, 1914–1920', Ph.D. thesis, University of Dublin, 2006 [forthcoming Cambridge University Press].

54. Theodor Leutwein, 'Die Kämpfe der Kaiserlichen Schutztruppe in Deutsch-Südwestafrika in den Jahren 1894–1896, sowie die sich hieraus für uns ergebenden Lehren', Vortrag gehalten in der Militärischen Gesellschaft zu Berlin am 19 February 1898, *Beiheft zum Militär-Wochenblatt*, 1 (1899), 14. Art. 23e forbade states 'to employ arms, projectiles, or material calculated to cause unnecessary [*superfluous*] suffering.' The 1899 Hague Declaration III Concerning Expanding Bullets did likewise. Adam Roberts and Richard Guelff (eds.), *Documents on the laws of war* (3rd edn.; Oxford: Oxford University Press, 2000), 63–6, 77.

55. The standard narrative, see L. (Lassa) Oppenheim, *International law: A treatise*, ed. H. Lauterpacht (8th edn.; London: Longmans, Green, 1958), ii, paras. 26–9; Karl Gareis, *Institutionen des Völkerrechts: Ein kurzgefasstes Lehrbuch des positiven Völkerrechts in seiner geschichtlichen Entwicklung und heutigen Gestaltung* (2nd edn.; Giessen: Emil Roth, 1901), para. 10.
56. Lueder, 'Krieg und Kriegsrecht im Allgemeinen', 255; German General Staff, *Kriegsbrauch im Landkriege*, 2–3, 5, 40.

11

The French in Algeria: Can There be Prisoners of War in a 'Domestic' Operation?

Raphaëlle Branche

THE ALGERIAN WAR OF INDEPENDENCE

The Algerian war of independence lasted almost eight years, and it has dramatically changed Algerian society. The losses were high on the Algerian side: of a population of 8 million,[1] around 300,000 to 400,000 people, mostly civilians, were killed.[2] The ratio of overall deaths relative to the total population is comparable to the deaths in France in the First World War. The war was a highly asymmetrical one, fought on Algerian soil. The French military suffered about 23,000 casualties, from a force size of approximately half a million at the peak of the war. As a whole, 1.7 million men fought in the war on the French side, 1.2 million of them conscripts.

France fought a protracted war in Indochina (1946–54) that ended in disaster. Still shocked by this failure, French leaders tried to preserve the remaining parts of the French empire by reforming the relationship between the *Métropole* and her colonies. In North Africa, the protectorates of Morocco and Tunisia were granted independence on 2 March and 20 March 1956 respectively. Algeria then became the focus of French attention.

For the French, Algeria was a very special territory, officially composed of departments and therefore to be defended like France itself. As the first country conquered by France in the nineteenth century, Algeria was made a colony for settlers. Its population was discriminated against due to its religion, despite the fact that they were 'French'. Alongside these statutory discriminations, huge disparities existed in living conditions.

The first modern political expressions of nationalist aspirations arose between the two World Wars within the migrant community in the *Métropole* and in Algeria itself. However, until the 1950s, they gave priority to legal means of action, given the fact that French authorities showed some evidence of a more liberal spirit after the Second World War. Until 1955–6, most nationalists remained committed primarily to tactics inspired by the French workers' movement: they favoured the use of petitions, strikes, demonstrations, and elections—regardless of how obviously these were rigged in Algeria. Only a small minority favoured armed struggle. By the end of the 1940s, they had formed the Special Organization (OS), which was dismantled in 1950. In 1954, some ex-OS members founded the National Liberation Front (FLN), which was brought into being with a series of attacks during the night of 31 October 1954. The guerrilla fighters were qualified as 'rebels', 'outlaws', and 'terrorists' by the French. The General Government's communiqués evoked acts 'committed by small groups of terrorists', whereas the attacks themselves were identified as 'criminal intrigues or acts'.[3]

The FLN's tactical evolution reinforced the position of those who wished to play down the importance of its action as criminal acts and refused to consider their political use and significance. Indeed, by spring 1956, the guerrilla warfare tactics had evolved into acts of mere terrorism and blind attacks. Deadly attacks took place in Algiers from that September. These acts of terrorism were carried out by members of the FLN and its bombing networks in particular. However, guerrilla fighters remained in the countryside and were able to build an army named the National Liberation Army (ALN). From summer 1956 onwards, it became organized according to the administrative divisions the FLN had imposed upon Algeria (mainly inspired from French administrative divisions: a *préfecture* becoming a *wilaya*). Each *wilaya* had a pyramidal organization and at its head a committee. The heads of the five (later six) *wilayas* were supposed to meet when important decisions had to be taken, but the *wilayas* mainly fought by themselves. They were also supposed to keep in touch with the FLN leaders who, as of 1957, were based abroad: imprisoned in France or settled in Tunis or Cairo.[4] Moreover, the ALN had bases in Morocco and Tunisia. In that respect, these countries were part of the picture.

In any case, guerrilla fighters were closely associated with the political organization. Political commissars accompanied the so-called *maquisards* and most of the directives were signed FLN/ALN. Hence a political reading of the ALN's actions is inevitable. In this context, it is relevant to enquire about the manner in which the issue of prisoners was used by the FLN/ALN as much as by the French government and armed forces.

Although the two sides were unevenly matched, they had a similar stake in the matter, since the question of recognition of war, and therefore of the status of those involved in war, was inherently linked to the recognition of the application of international humanitarian law to the conflict under way. The same can be said of the use of prisoners of war in psychological warfare, in which prisoners and the treatment they receive delivers powerful messages to public opinion, beyond the reach of authorities.

Yet the adversaries did not face the same challenges regarding the issue of prisoners. France was the overwhelming power and the only internationally recognized state. I will start by presenting the French position on international law with respect to prisoners of war, followed by a study of the situation on the ground. Following this, and given that the FLN attitude towards the prisoners was much more of a response to the French than a genuine position, the case of French soldiers being held prisoner by the nationalists will then be scrutinized.

FRANCE'S INTERPRETATION: A DOMESTIC
AFFAIR, NOT A WAR

The specific political situation of Algeria made it easier for the French authorities not to recognize a state of war. They acknowledged only an internal affair and wanted other countries to stay out of it. Recognition of a state of war would mean admitting the existence of a civil war within France—or, alternatively, the legitimacy of Algerians' nationalist claims. And so, for eight years, French armed interventions in Algeria were officially referred to as 'police operations' aimed at 'maintaining order' on French territory.

Because the legal means ordinarily available in peacetime would not suffice to subdue those disturbing the colonial order, successive French governments had to opt for exceptional and renewable measures. Six months after the outbreak of the revolt, a 'state of emergency' was declared in some areas of Algeria and then gradually extended to apply to the entire Algerian territory.[5] The law allowed for exemptions from common law on two levels. Civilian authorities received the right to limit inhabitants' liberties, and could go as far as putting them under house arrest or interning them in camps. The army, meanwhile, saw its judicial powers increased in order to accelerate judicial processes in a context qualified as a 'fight against terrorism'.

Later, in March 1956, the new government went further and asked the members of parliament (MPs) to grant special powers for Algeria. Contrary to what a state of emergency involved, this did not mean specific powers, but that the legislature recognize the principle of the executive's omnipotence in Algeria. These special powers constituted the legal framework for the entire war which, in the end, was almost exclusively in the hands of the executive branch of government. This also led to giving significant weight to the military and to their interpretation of reality. Indeed, the armed forces led the way by imposing most of their views upon the civil authorities, especially under Robert Lacoste's rule in Algeria (from 1956 to mid-1958) and then under General Salan (June to December 1958). The refusal to recognize the Algerian guerrilla fighters as prisoners of war was one of the most obvious signs of collusion between military interpretations and political interests. The army had been brought in to keep order and did not consider itself bound by the international legal framework of war.[6]

What about the French authorities? France had signed the Geneva Conventions and ratified them by June 1951. The war in Algeria was the first opportunity to test, over a period of time, the validity of these Conventions and to test France's willingness to apply them. French authorities were very reluctant to consider that the Conventions were relevant to the situation in Algeria. Nonetheless, the Third Geneva Convention was partly applicable to the situation. If not a war, it was a non-international armed conflict and the Third Convention provided some protection for victims in this kind of conflict. Therefore, attempts were made to convince the French authorities to let the International Committee of the Red Cross (ICRC) delegates do their job.

As a result, Pierre Mendès France, the head of the French government, entangled the ICRC within very strict limits and its delegates were ordered to concern themselves with one matter only—the conditions under which prisoners were detained. But they were forbidden to name them 'prisoners' under the Third Convention. France thus found herself in a paradoxical situation. The 'events' taking place in Algeria warranted the treatment of prisoners, under the Third Convention, as prisoners taken in armed conflict, yet the applicability of the Third Convention was not officially recognized. Hence, it was still deemed permissible to turn a blind eye to any contraventions. Moreover these same 'events' were not supposed to justify the application of the First Convention to those wounded on the battlefield, or the Fourth Convention to civilian populations. As far as these other conventions were concerned, peace officially reigned in Algeria—although the tacit recognition of the Third Convention indicated a state of war.

Although officially irrelevant to the situation in Algeria, the ICRC managed to set up nine inspections in the country during the war, between February 1955 and December 1961. Each time, delegates spent around six weeks in Algeria, visiting several camps and carrying out duties including talking to prisoners in private. Even though they failed to encompass the wider picture and get to know the situation endured by prisoners in Algeria in depth, the ICRC's reports gave an insight into prisoners' experiences.

A TWISTED LEGALITY TO FIT THE WAR'S DENIAL AND ILLEGAL VIOLENCE TOWARDS PRISONERS

To understand the autonomy the army had in carrying out the war on the ground, we must refer to the rules the military had to comply with. Though they were prescriptive, almost all the directives or instructions advocating certain approaches were ambiguous. The key terms used to designate the enemy or techniques of violence were vague enough to leave those implementing them considerable latitude in doing so. This was expressed quite directly by some senior officers, as the following description of morally exhausted officers at the end of 1957 demonstrates:

> Indeed, many consider that the ends do not justify the means; on the other hand, they have to accomplish their mission. Thus, the conscience of a large number of leaders and intelligence officers must choose between efficiency and moral revulsion toward the use of methods that have been condemned many times in other circumstances.... To determine what their attitude should be, they only have directives and insufficient legislation that is too vague, and that requires too much initiative from them in an area that involves the entire nation's responsibility. They need codified legal means, or at least total support from the military authorities and state officials.[7]

Further on, he added: 'It does not suffice to prescribe the destruction of the rebels' political-administrative infrastructure. The right approach and the means for doing so must be specified, and defined in legal terms. Otherwise, those who carry this out only have a choice between inefficiency and illegality.'[8]

Indeed the French authorities were reluctant to give precise instructions that could be considered explicit orders to carry out unlawful actions. Yet, from the first year of the war they issued a text that gave leeway for the worst act: they granted the possibility to shoot on sight every suspect trying to escape.[9] The recommendation was crystal-clear: 'Any rebel using a gun, seen holding one or committing acts of violence, will be shot immediately, ... fire must be opened on any suspect attempting to escape.'[10] Nowhere were the notions of 'rebels' and 'suspects' precisely defined. Then from that date on, anyone running away was a potential suspect and any suspect was a potential runaway, who could be killed. This text undeniably involved an a priori legalization of summary executions, under the cloak of lexical camouflage, turning summary executions into 'escape attempts' or 'shooting runaways'. Far from being directly involved in violent practices and organized in terrorist cells or armed bands, Algerian 'suspects' formed a huge group with notably blurred boundaries. The order made no distinction between civilian and military, or even between armed and unarmed persons. Simply to take flight was to render one suspect.

This earlier text made very explicit the degree to which any Algerian, or any civilian for that matter, could be arrested and killed. An even earlier principle, stemming from operations in the spring of 1955, acknowledged the principle of collective responsibility: if an attack took place, the nearest village was considered collectively responsible, and the ensuing reprisals might include executing hostages.[11] In short, the population was granted no particular protection against the army.

Aside from these various methods of getting rid of their enemies, which formally implied at least some lexical camouflage, the military did arrest people while fighting. These prisoners formed a minority of all prisoners the military had to deal with. At least for the first four years of the war, they were treated similarly to any person suspected and arrested. Hence they were very likely to be subject to torture and to be detained in camps.

Torture could be used on the battlefield. Even though torture was officially prohibited, a special group was established during the war to function as a secret service and specialize in the torture and eventual execution of prisoners. This organization—the *Détachement Opérationnel de Protection* (DOP)—came to specialize in the most difficult cases. They had a particular responsibility for former guerrilla fighters who had decided to rally round the French. Their willingness was put to a severe test, to say the least. At the same time, torture was practised within regular military units, notably by teams from the *Deuxième Bureau*, the office charged with gathering intelligence information. At the beginning of the war, a decision was indeed made to create intelligence teams at every military level down to the sector (the basic administrative military unit). Alongside these teams, other soldiers might also be induced to torture prisoners, especially when the prisoners were to be interrogated immediately after capture—a process they were instructed to follow. In fact, soldiers were pressured to view the search for information as their greatest priority. Torture— rarely explicitly recommended but often quietly suggested—was one important way of obtaining it.[12]

Torture was also prohibited theoretically, explicitly, and officially; its perpetrators, too, were liable in principle to be punished under the French codes and statutes. In reality, however, torture enjoyed a much more ambiguous status; it was both prohibited and authorized. At the end of the day, torturers in Algeria went unpunished. The logic of war appeared to justify torture, so it would have been illogical to punish it.

Indeed, beyond the direct victims, these acts of violence formed part of a political lexicon aimed against the Algerian population as a whole. The central place of torture in the system of control was clear: the population was both a source of information and the target of psychological warfare. It was necessary for the French to keep the Algerian people off-balance, while confronting the nationalists operating in their midst. Torture was not, therefore, simply one means of obtaining information. It was an essential weapon, allowing the French to fulfil their fundamental war aims. Torture was not merely a weapon against terrorists, but also a political weapon. Torture was used not only to force people to talk, but to make them understand, and to remind them, who wielded power.

Torture contributed to an important strategic reorientation of the French army, which claimed to have borrowed its enemy's methods in order to fight it.[13] In fact, torture was effectively adapted to the new form of warfare that the army faced in Algeria. However, this was not because the war demanded more intelligence gathering than other conflicts; it was because it required control over the civil population.

Another way of controlling the population was to force rural people into camps. The policy of 'concentration camps' (*camps de regroupement*) was meant to separate the FLN from the population, as the 'fish' from the 'water'.[14] In doing so, the military intended to gain vast room for manoeuvre in order to definitively quell the ALN. Eventually more than 2 million people—a quarter of the population—had to move and live in these new settlements.

Alongside these concentration camps, special camps were created for the 'suspects' waiting for interrogation or simply kept under surveillance for security reasons. These military-run camps were housing guerrilla fighters as well as civilians, without any distinction (at least until March 1958). First created and then legalized, these camps were born out of military necessity. They could consist of a simple block in a military camp, or an actual camp devoted to the prisoners. The longer the war lasted, the more the military imposed their view on this internment issue. These camps were called '*centres de tri et de transit*' (CTT): the military designated three categories of prisoners, each with a different fate. These categories were firstly those who where 'to be released'; secondly, the 'unwanted', whose fate was to be detained for a longer period in the CTT or in a civilian-run camp called a *centre d'hébergement*; and thirdly, the 'criminals' who were sent to trial under common law (with charges such as 'criminal association', as no specific charge had been created at that time to deal with the nationalists).

Although, in theory, the prisoners were not to be detained in the CTTs for longer than one month, this detention status was later made renewable up to three times. Some prisoners would be there for much longer than three months, sometimes even for years. Indeed, the military proved skilful at twisting the light veil of legality covering their methods of putting people under pressure. Interrogation was a primary activity within these camps. The prisoners were granted no rights, and it very often led to torture.

The fragile legalization of the camps in April 1957 came after scandalous revelations on the use of torture in Algeria.[15] But this legalization provided only weak protections for the internees, since there was no real intent to test the military severely at that time. Indeed, it might have prompted the military to make some prisoners 'disappear'; in other words, to kill them without keeping an official record of their deaths. In fact, these camps could be considered as signs of both the growing power of the military during the war, and the inability of the civilian authorities, at least up to 1959–60, to ensure respect for certain elementary rights for prisoners.

Each military sector was supposed to have one CTT and only one. In reality, this was not the case. Some locations were used as a CTT but not declared as such. Others were considered as annexes of the sector's CTT and, moreover, some were merely clandestine camps (particularly when used by the DOP).[16] This reality was well known, particularly because of the ICRC's inspections, but there was no improvement until as late as 1960. A financial investigation on behalf of the new civilian authority in charge of Algeria at the beginning of 1960 counted 113 declared CTTs for less than eighty military sectors.[17] Even though the military declared 19,950 food rations, they were not supposed to detain more than 17,440 persons.[18] The inspectors found not only annexes but also clandestine camps in order to keep some prisoners in the hands of the military as long as considered necessary. They also discovered the habit of interrogating suspects for one day or two, and then releasing them without even officially registering their identity. They wrote straightforwardly that this underestimation was meant to dissimulate deliberately how numerous the detainees were in some areas. The worst situation was no doubt faced by people in the DOP's hands, which a note dated May 1959 estimated to be around 20 per cent of people arrested.[19] This same official report counted approximately 10,000 persons per month in the CTTs.

For some military at least, the prisoners were not only sources of information or targets on which torture could be used in order to terrorize; they could also be submitted to what was called *action psychologique*. Some centres for re-education (CDR) were settled on the basis of CTT rules. The detainees were submitted to a three-phase process. During the first phase, they were not allowed any mail or visits. They had to work eight to ten hours a day. They could not speak or smoke while working. At night, there were calls where guilty mottos were shouted. Officers in *action psychologique* addressed them before they could move to the second phase called *mise en confiance* (winning the trust) and then the third (*détente* or relaxation phase).[20]

The prisoners were considered to be a fishpond to which the military could apply their new method of warfare allegedly derived from the Indochina experience: psychological warfare. Alongside civilians and the French military, this doctrine had the prisoners as a third target. A specific branch of the army was created in March 1955, which developed into a *Cinquième Bureau* (the fifth of the headquarters' six branches). It was assigned the task of organizing this activity, derived from the new doctrine, which was progressively dominant in Algeria in 1956–60.[21] Each army corps, each military zone, and each military sector was given a *Cinquième Bureau* in order to fulfil the aims of the 'counter-revolutionary war' France was supposed to be waging in Algeria.[22]

Throughout the war, the men in charge kept complaining about the fact that not enough means were provided to achieve good 'psychological' work with the prisoners. Except for some of them, they did not take into account the fact that the French camps or detention centres where the prisoners spent weeks or months might turn the so-called suspects into truly convicted nationalists. Thus, even those who might not have been part of the nationalist struggle were liable to become engaged in it after their detention.

As the war deepened, the boundaries of gender and age blurred. Women, the elderly, and children, traditionally considered to be protected by the French soldiers, fell under increasing suspicion.[23] Children could be arrested and tortured because of their relatives' activities, being sometimes submitted to ill-treatment in front of a father or a brother. They could also be suspected of being used as *choufs* (watchers) by the FLN/ALN—a mission some of them carried out for the 'revolution'. In that case, soldiers made no distinction and the light protection provided by youth disappeared when the life of French soldiers was considered to be at stake. One of the first testimonies published on torture by a whistle-blower soldier mentioned this extreme situation.[24] On 28 January 1956, he wrote in his diary:

> The pig squealing that we heard yesterday evening at around 9 pm was actually coming from a kid. They had him on the magneto. The method is simple: a wire on a testicle, another on the ear and you switch the power on. They didn't use the usual method on the kid: they fixed a wire on his wrist and his ear. The kid—they say—admitted he went to warn four men armed with hunting guns who were waiting for the [French] soldiers... Yesterday evening I first thought it was coming from the jackals, but it lasted, so I went out in my pyjamas and listened. Voices and moans came out of the lieutenants' tent... I came back, once more, crippled by nausea, I was thinking of the kid who, I figured, was being terrorised at the rear of the trailer. And yet, it was the kid they were torturing. This morning, I feel completely broken.... I can't go and talk to the kid, comfort him. He won't understand since he doesn't speak French.

Although this kind of situation was extreme, it was not uncommon, especially for teenagers. Much more frequent was the use of violence against women, who were increasingly taken prisoners as the war deepened and the men left for the *maquis* or for France if they had not been taken prisoner before. The longer the war went on, the more aggressive and blatant the repression became. At first considered victims, women gradually became part of the 'suspect' category and could be arrested and detained. They were therefore submitted to the same treatment as the men, yet their presence made some of the men in charge ill at ease. The need for a special camp was discussed. In the eastern part of Algeria, the solution was envisaged to send them to a unique CTT as had been done in the west: the CTT of Rio Salado in the Oran Army Corps (West of Algeria) was a female CTT. But in the vast majority of cases, women had to share detention in CTT with men. In any case, of the hundreds of detainees in one CTT, there were never more than a few dozen women. After the CTT, they were sent to Tefeschoun, one of the two biggest internment camps, located in northern Algeria, with a female section.[25] Women from across Algeria were sent there as soon as the local CTTs were done with them. Djamila Amrane, a former nationalist militant, arrested when she was sixteen, recorded the testimony of a woman concerning her time at Tefeschoun:

> There were about 200 women from all over the country. Some of them had never even left their village, never seen the sea. Tefeschoun is located on the coast. They told us: 'they've brought us here to throw us into the sea'. They came directly from where they had been interrogated and tortured. Their clothes had been torn to pieces; some of them had their heads shaved. Upon their arrival, we asked the kitchen for huge tubs of hot water, helped them wash and got some clothes ready for them. After that, we cleaned and mended their clothes. If you only knew what they had been through...you could write a book on every single woman...We asked the administration for their address (they were illiterate) and we wrote letters on their behalf. They received letters and parcels in return, sometimes even from France where they had relatives. They were happy. They were from all over Algeria, from Kabylia [centre of Algeria], from the Aurès [east of Algeria] from Maghnia [north of Algeria], from all over.[26]

The women arrested who were not transferred to Tefeschoun were either transferred to prison to be trialled, or—in some very rare cases—transferred to a *Centres Militaires d'Internés* (CMI). The CMI were internment camps designed to house 'PAMs' (*pris les armes à la main*—individuals 'captured while armed'). From 'outlaws' and 'rebels' to 'PAMs', France had progressively come as near as possible to a definition of what could be considered a 'prisoner of war'. Although it was still deemed impossible to qualify the prisoners on the battlefield as POWs, this new kind of camp, created in March 1958, was a first move in that direction. Indeed, the vocabulary had been carefully chosen and officials were warned to name the centres 'military internment camps' and not 'camps for military inmates'. It was again claimed that the Third Convention did not apply to the detainees in these camps. Yet, their creation was a slight acknowledgment of these prisoners' specificity. If it could be proved that they had not been involved in terrorism, they were put in separate camps and, finally, accorded some recognition as combatants.

These camps made explicit a distinction that France was forced to recognize between terrorist acts and military operations. Thus, a note by General Salan, head of the Army in Algeria, dated November 1957, stated:

> The attitude of rebels who have been taken prisoner in combat and who have not participated in any exaction does not bear the same hideous characteristic as banditry and terrorism. Therefore one must treat them according to this fundamental difference. They should be granted treatment as close as possible to that which is accorded to prisoners of war by civilized states committed to engagements in this region.[27]

It was, regardless of the wording, close to a prisoner-of-war-like status—except for the 'psychological' re-education they sometimes had to endure.

As the war came close to an end, their situation improved. Whereas the French orders of 1958–9 were still to ignore the Geneva Conventions, from 1960 onwards it became more common to find documents urging the officers in charge of some camps to take the Geneva Conventions into account, if not strictly to comply with them. Nevertheless, compared to over 100 CTTs existing in Algeria, the CMI were very few: there were seven by August 1960. At that time, they housed 3,000 prisoners.[28]

ON THE ALGERIAN SIDE

From Autumn 1958 onwards, the self-declared Provisional Government for the Algerian Republic (GPRA) was using all its diplomatic skills to put pressure on France. The recognition of the Geneva Conventions in 1960 was part of this diplomatic offensive. The GPRA agreed to respect the Conventions in the context of negotiations with the French government. Thus, by adopting a position commonly reserved for a state, it intended to affirm its own legitimacy and Algeria's proto-statehood. Nevertheless, the legal aspect should not have raised unreasonable expectations. The recognition or non-recognition of the status of prisoner of war was an important element, but even when recognized, this status often concerned only a small number of people.

Indeed, the Geneva Conventions were not a main concern for the GPRA or the FLN. The issue would be raised or emphasized as long as some benefit was to be expected. In the first years of the war, the FLN decided to publicize French violations of these Conventions, but this was done on a very specific agenda that reveals how political this claim for the Geneva Conventions to be respected really was. The emphasis was launched with an offensive on the international community, with the UN General Assembly becoming a battleground.[29] However, although, from 1957 onwards, the FLN insisted on putting the Algerian issue on the UN General Assembly's agenda, it put no emphasis on the prisoners' situation. What was mostly publicized was the situation for Algerian civilians. Their situation was also a great opportunity for the FLN to talk about genocide, concentration camps, and so on. Indeed the situation of Algerian prisoners, including the fact that they were subjected to ill-treatment, torture, and exposed to summary execution, was considered to be collateral damage of the war. The revolution they were striving for deserved the sacrifice of these combatants, who were celebrated as martyrs (*chouhada*) if they were killed.

Yet, after some resistance, the FLN tried to use the ICRC in order to strengthen its international position. ICRC delegates were invited to meet some prisoners and representatives from *el Moudjahid*, the FLN newspaper, in order to be photographed and to have their picture published alongside an interview with French soldiers expressing how thankful they were for the way the FLN treated them.[30]

Alongside this diplomatic arena, the National Liberation Army (ALN) knew how to use the issue of prisoners to its advantage.[31] At first, the ALN did not have a precise doctrine on the treatment of prisoners. In August 1956, guidelines were provided and the *maquisards* were told to take prisoners (not to kill them) and to treat them well. Some documents mentioned the project to set up a specific department to take care of the prisoners in every zone (the level under the *wilaya*). However, the FLN did not have the power to impose its view on the combatants. The reiteration of the ban from killing prisoners tends to prove how common killing was. Nevertheless, real attention was given to them as the war went on.

The *maquisards* took their prisoners with them. The prisoners had to endure the same life as they did: a severe wound or inability to cope with the harsh conditions of living would mean death. The fate of the French military prisoners depended on more ordinary factors, such as their ability to walk as fast as the *maquisards*, or their resistance to hunger and tiredness. They were watched carefully and therefore might have been permanently chained.[32] Prisoners would send letters to their parents to force the French government into action (e.g. to encourage them to consider the FLN as real enemies and not as rebels on outlaws).

Apparently, at some point, the ALN was able to secure a zone in some areas in order to set up camps for the prisoners. A likely case for this arrangement was Kabylia, a traditionally rebellious mountainous region located in the centre of the country (and therefore quite isolated), which had witnessed the biggest insurrection in nineteenth-century Algeria. The Djurdjura might have been one of these areas in 1956. Yet most of the time prisoners were kept alongside the *maquisards* and, from 1957 onwards, were more likely to be driven to Tunisia where the FLN had camps at the border.[33] Some places in Algeria, even some villages, might have been used as temporary meeting points in order to set up the exit to Tunisia. The French intelligence service was aware that at least three camps still existed in the spring of 1958. They were located in the Djurdjura, the Djebel Louha (south of Medea), and by the Aït Zikki (north-north-west of Akbou).[34]

As the war went on, prisoners were often used as targets for psychological warfare. On the one hand, some might have genuinely felt some admiration or thankfulness for the *maquisards*. Sometimes, liberations were overly publicized, aiming at increasing the FLN's international audience and respectability. This was, for example, the case in December 1958: eight prisoners were liberated in the presence of Princess Lalla Aïcha in Rabat. But on the other hand, prisoners could also be used as bargaining chip. The ALN could do so by warning the French authorities that it would kill its prisoners unless they ceased executing condemned nationalists. The same kind of warning could be expressed by a specific leader of the ALN in any given region, or by the GPRA itself. Some prisoners were indeed executed. Their deaths were publicly presented as a judicial execution. The FLN thereby claimed the legal authority to execute their French prisoners as war criminals.[35] In any case, the prisoners' fate was very fragile and subject to great variations according to the context, the individuals in charge, and the balance of power between the *maquisards* and the politicians, or between the FLN and the GPRA.

Taking prisoners was above all a political issue, meant to be part of the internationalization of the conflict that the FLN was trying to promote. Whether this was sought in the existence of detention centres outside Algeria, by the insistence on the need to make use of a third territory to exchange prisoners or release them, in the reference made to the Geneva conventions, French prisoners were never considered as individual soldiers but as small chips of power grabbed from France.

In March 1962, the war culminated in a ceasefire agreement. The prisoners were to be freed immediately on both sides. Camps and prisons in France and Algeria opened their gates and people were allowed to return home. Everyone was to forget his or her supposed guilt or suspected link with what was no longer called a rebellion but a fledgling state. Yet about 200 people had been officially sentenced to death and executed by the French as 'criminals' and many more had been killed summarily or had endured fierce treatment under torture. The total figure would certainly be tens of thousands of people at least. The amnesty enclosed in the ceasefire agreement granted France and its soldiers a blanket pardon for this. Nothing was to be remembered and nothing was to be asked. The amnesty was officially twofold. The same applied to the FLN, and nothing would be asked about the 200 prisoners or so who never came back.[36]

Of course, there is no point in comparing the sorrows and the pains. The quest for missing relatives still haunts families on both shores of the Mediterranean Sea. But suffice to say, memories of the detention are indeed very unequal; this reflects to this day the inequalities of the last French colonial war.

NOTES

1. The Algerian population was 9 million in 1960. Approximately a million were of European descent. I use the term 'Algerian' here in a sense restricted to the 'natives', people officially referred to as French Muslims by the French officials.

2. On the difficulties of assessing the casualties see Kamel Kateb, *Européens, 'indigenes' et juifs en Algérie (1830–1962): représentations et réalités des populations* (Paris: INED, 2001).
3. Communiqué from the general government, quoted in Mohammed Harbi, *1954: La guerre commence en Algérie* (Brussels: Complexe, 1985).
4. For a more extensive description of the FLN, see Gilbert Meynier, *Histoire intérieure du FLN: 1954–1962* (Paris: Fayard, 2002).
5. The state of emergency was first voted on 3 April 1955 and extended on 22 August 1955.
6. See Raphaëlle Branche, 'Entre droit humanitaire et intérêts politiques: les missions algériennes du CICR,' *Revue Historique*, 609 (1999), 101–25.
7. Report on the morale of the 7th *Division Mécanique Blindée* (DMR) [a light armoured division] and of the battalions of the Ain Taya sector, 1957, Service Historique de la Défense (SHD), Vincennes, 1H 2424.
8. Ibid.
9. The text asked 'everyone to use their imagination in order to apply the most appropriate means compatible with [their] conscience[s] as soldier[s]'.
10. Directive from the Minister of National Defence and the Minister of the Interior, dated 1 July 1955, Service Historique de la Défense (SHD), Vincennes, 1H 2896/1.
11. Although this was officially prohibited, and condemned on several occasions in the French National Assembly, it was explicitly recommended by some military leaders, and tacitly implemented by others.
12. On the status of torture at that time and its practice by French military, see Raphaëlle Branche, *La torture et l'armée pendant la guerre d'Algérie, 1954–1962* (Paris: Gallimard, 2001).
13. This reorientation corresponded to the arrival of Raoul Salan to the post of Commander-in-Chief, and an increase in urban terrorism. It led to the redefinition of the army's duties; from then on, the military included fighting urban terrorism within its realm of intervention. Algiers became its main field of experimentation as of January 1957, during what was called the 'battle of Algiers.'
14. The military French doctrinaires were great readers of Mao. The quotation of his *Aspects of China's anti-Japanese struggle* (1948) was very common: 'The people are like water and the army is like fish.'
15. Decree by the Minister of Algeria, 11 April 1957, Service Historique de la Défense (SHD), Vincennes, 1H 2750/1.
16. Although the DOP were regularly renamed during the war, they kept on using the same methods, mostly out of any authority's reach.
17. Report on the camps' management by MM. Rouvillois and Mailley, 2 April 1960, SHD, Vincennes, 1H 1100/2.
18. These figures dated from January to August 1959.
19. Note to General Challe by General Boyer-Vidal on the CTT, 30 May 1959, SHD, Vincennes, 1H 3617/1.
20. According to the ICRC report on the Center for Re-education of Ksar-Thir near Sétif, December 1957, Institut Pierre Mendès France (IPMF), Paris, PMF XIV-A.
21. The *Cinquième Bureau* was disbanded in 1960 because some of its officers were exercising too much freedom and were suspected of fighting their own 'parallel' war. Yet the activities of the *Bureau* continued: they were executed by other staff under different supervision.
22. See Marie-Catherine et Paul Villatoux, *La République et son armée face au péril subversif: Guerre et action psychologique en France (1945–1960)* (Paris: Les Indes savantes, 2004).

23. For an extraordinary document on children see Saïd Ferdi, *Un enfant dans la guerre* (Paris: Le Seuil, 1981). This autobiographical work shows the fate of a teenage boy detained for years in a French 'camp'.

24. The author, Stanislas Hutin, was a seminarist at that time. His diary was sent to the head of the French state and parts of it were published anonymously at the beginning of 1957. A full version of the diary was published in 2002. See Stanislas Hutin, *Journal de bord. Algérie novembre 1955–mars 1956* (Toulouse: Université de Toulouse Le Mirail, 2002).

25. Tefeschoun camp could house 1,500 persons, whereas the other internment camps had a capacity of 150 to 900.

26. Fatma Baïchi interviewed by Djamila Amrane in 1980, translated from dialect in Djamila Amrane, *Des femmes dans la guerre d'Algérie* (Paris: Khartala, 1994), 111–23.

27. Note by General Salan, 24 November 1957, SHD, Vincennes, 1H 3799/2.

28. In comparison, internment camps had a capacity of a maximum of 10,000 detainees. This capacity was reached in Spring 1959.

29. Matthew Connelly, *A Diplomatic Revolution: Algeria's fight for independence and the origins of the post-cold war era* (Oxford: OUP, 2002).

30. *El Moudjahid* [FLN newspaper], issue 17 (1 February 1958).

31. French soldiers were not the only ones to be taken prisoner. Soldiers from the Foreign Legion as well as Algerian conscripts serving in the French army, or even Algerian auxiliaries, were also taken. Civilians could also be taken prisoner for certain reasons. This chapter only deals with French military prisoners. Their number was considerably lower than that of Algerian prisoners captured by the French.

32. This is what some prisoners freed from the FLN told the Intelligence Bureau. See « Informations obtenues des prisonniers libérés en mai 1959 », SHD, Vincennes, 1H2592/2*.

33. Morocco had once sheltered such camps in 1956, but from 1957 onwards Tunisia was much more welcoming to FLN activities.

34. Note from the Intelligence Bureau, 20 March 1958, SHD, Vincennes, 1H1511/1*.

35. This was the case in April 1958: the execution of French prisoners was cited as the incident that sparked the May 1958 crisis—a coup in Algiers that successfully brought General de Gaulle back to power as the last *Président du Conseil* of the Fourth Republic.

36. While the author is currently working on this topic, no study on the French prisoners of the FLN has been completed to date. For a first account, mainly based on testimonies by former prisoners, see Yves Sudry, *Guerre d'Algérie: les prisonniers des Djounoud* (Paris: L'Harmattan, 2005).

12

Detention and Interrogation in Northern Ireland, 1969–75

Huw Bennett

INTRODUCTION

At 4.30 a.m. on 9 August 1971, British soldiers and the police launched Operation Demetrius, arresting 342 people throughout Northern Ireland for internment without trial.[1] Between 11 August and 18 October fourteen men, in two batches, underwent up to a week's interrogation in depth at Ballykelly airfield, being subjected to noise, sleep deprivation, a restricted diet, wall-standing, and hooding.[2] Quickly exposed and denounced as torture, the five techniques were eventually ruled by the European Court of Human Rights to constitute inhuman and degrading treatment.[3] Immediately after Demetrius, disputes broke out as to whether the damage inflicted on the Irish Republican Army (IRA) justified the infringed freedoms and increased violence. These events represented the nadir in British security policy in Northern Ireland, a descent into state-sanctioned criminality that destroyed all remaining legitimacy in the minority community. Thinking about what befell fourteen men in 1971 leads to wider questions concerning the role of detention in the conflict. Reliant upon a statute—the 1922 Civil Authorities (Special Powers) Act—forming a major grievance in the civil rights movement's agenda, detention practices were inevitably politicized. With the army replacing the discredited Royal Ulster Constabulary (RUC) in Catholic areas during this period, military policy is the focus, as it formed the centrepiece in the state's response to Republicanism until moves towards Ulsterization in late 1975.[4] This chapter examines the army's detention and interrogation policies, analysing their strategic purpose and their perceived consequences. Initially operating in aid to the civil power in Stormont, whilst subordinate to London, the formula for democratic control over the armed forces fluctuated in response to the changing strategic environment. Thus, detention practices are here analysed in the context of wider security policy, which ultimately also conditioned the putatively independent legal restraints on military behaviour. Detention policy evolved in three broad phases in the militarized period of the Troubles. From their first deployment in 1969 to around August 1971, the army tried to keep the peace and had minimal involvement in detentions, only sporadically arresting rioters. By the second phase, starting in August 1971 when the government decided to launch mass internment and selective deep interrogation, security policy was escalating in an effort to defeat Republican militants. After this proved politically controversial, the government de-escalated from March 1972, although the extent of the restraint is contestable. Even after significant reforms to security policy, detention and interrogation remained highly controversial and attempts at depoliticization through adopting the criminalization approach achieved limited success in a society unwilling to return its lost legitimacy to the state.

MILITARY INTERVENTION IN NORTHERN IRELAND, AUGUST 1969–AUGUST 1971

The British Army was deployed on 14 August 1969 after the Northern Ireland government's failure to satisfy the civil rights movement resulted in inter-communal violence. Expected to act as temporary peacekeepers replacing the police, the army's neutral status increasingly came into question as it was drawn into pursuing controversial security policies.[5] A close working relationship with Stormont obscured the formally independent position held by the General Officer Commanding (GOC), allowing a burgeoning IRA to present the army as an extension of Unionist dominance based upon discrimination.[6] Security policy failed to recognize the deficit in the Northern Irish state's authority to govern, proceeding on the assumption that military operations within law of any kind produced legitimacy.[7] Legality is less likely to be equated with legitimacy when a democracy departs from commonly accepted standards.[8] The long-term normalization of emergency powers in Northern Ireland promoted exactly such a deviation. The Special Powers Act granted the Minister of Home Affairs almost unrestricted powers to issue regulations.[9] Amidst over a hundred other regulations, number twenty-three permitted indefinite detention of persons suspected of acting, having acted, or being about to act in a 'manner prejudicial to the preservation of the peace and the maintenance of order'.[10] Regulation eleven was the one most prolifically exercised by the army, granting powers to arrest on suspicion, and without a warrant. These provisions were denounced as 'a complete and effective abrogation of the rule of law'.[11] The government considered international rules irrelevant to a domestic law and order matter, refuting the applicability of Common Article 3 of the 1949 Geneva Conventions.[12] Instead, whatever repressive elements existed in the Special Powers Act were theoretically counter-balanced by the ordinary law's supremacy over the security forces and normal citizens alike.[13]

Evidence on how arrest policy operated within this legal framework in the first few years is limited. The army primarily concerned itself with riot control, seeking to halt sectarian violence and engaging in low-level cooperation with Catholic community defence groups. By March 1970 the army were operating a policy of snatch arrests of rioters in Derry. Bystanders were sometimes grabbed and convictions against them secured on the strength of a soldier's uncorroborated testimony.[14] The change in military approach from peacekeeping to counter-insurgency began on 3 April 1970, when the GOC, Lieutenant General Sir Ian Freeland, announced a 'get tough' policy following the wounding of thirty-eight soldiers in riots.[15] This sanctioned the use of lethal force against petrol bombers, and had a limited impact on arrest policy. Arresting rioters was not easy, as youths familiar with the cities ran away and escaped chasing soldiers. The army reluctantly assumed policing duties, and thought arrests an un-military task. Forty-seven arrests from 31 March to 4 April resulted in only sixteen imprisonments and five fines. Such returns seemed a wasted effort.[16] Aside from individual arrests, some larger cordon-and-search operations took place to gather intelligence, although with limited results and at the price of widespread alienation.[17] The July 1970 Lower Falls curfew in Belfast, intended to show army domination, produced forty-one arrests, some arms and ammunition, and a boost to IRA recruitment.[18] Overall, the 3,107 house searches conducted throughout 1970 may be taken as an approximation for the limited extent of arrest activity.[19] In October 1970 the Provisional IRA launched a bombing campaign against commercial premises, and in early 1971 authorized retaliatory attacks on soldiers following Catholic casualties.[20] Lord Carrington, the Secretary of State for Defence, informed the Cabinet in February that the violence was developing from inter-communal disturbances into armed conflict.[21] The army adopted a more aggressive policy on 24 March, setting its priorities as bringing to justice 'all subversive elements', reasserting the rule of law, and capturing arms and explosives. Desperate to avoid the war on two fronts threatened by a Protestant backlash, British policy increasingly aimed to placate Stormont.[22] Brian Faulkner, Northern Ireland Prime Minister from 23 March 1971, insisted on a hard line.[23] Mass arrests proceeded under Operation Linklater on 23 and 27 July, bringing up to a hundred people into detention.[24] A general increase in security force activity is indicated by the rise in house searches in 1971 to 17,262.[25] Security policy developed from the individual arresting of rioters to mass arrests intended to dominate the minority population. The change in emphasis derived from desperation about the worsening violence and an almost complete dearth of intelligence required for a more discriminate response.

When interrogating prisoners, the military were guided by a document authorized by the Joint Intelligence Committee (JIC): the 1967 Joint Directive on Military Interrogation in Internal Security Operations Overseas. This generic doctrine required adherence to Common Article 3 of the 1949 Geneva Conventions. It prohibited '[v]iolence to life and person, in particular mutilation, cruel treatment and torture', and 'outrages upon personal dignity, in particular humiliating and degrading treatment'.[26] Later on, the contradiction between these admonitions and the document's call for 'psychological attack' caused grave difficulties.[27] Whether the protections afforded by the Directive extended to police questioning was never clear.[28] The Judges' Rules and Administrative Directions to the Police prohibited ill-treatment and required that evidence be given voluntarily if it were to be accepted in court.[29] How far the army indulged in interrogations in this period is unknown.

Legal oversight promised to control violence by enhancing state legitimacy through due process being consistently applied. Despite most court cases being 'dealt with fairly and without discrimination', a minority of unfair cases received disproportionate attention, leading to a sense of 'structural bias' against Catholics.[30] Although judges threw out confessions obtained under oppressive conditions, intensive interrogations aimed at producing operational intelligence rather than convictions proceeded regardless. Because the Special Powers Act permitted the security forces to make arrests without having to account for the decision to a court, judicial oversight of arrest policy was limited. Soldiers brought before the courts were likely to be acquitted because the judiciary sympathized with them and the vast majority of jurors were Protestants due to a property qualification rule.[31] Such prosecutions in any case proved rare, with only twenty-nine soldiers tried for offences against civilians from December 1970 to May 1973.[32] A resulting impunity may have influenced operational planning.[33] The judiciary's power to enforce military compliance with the law was qualified by the reliance upon weak investigatory agencies. The refusal to investigate the deaths of Séamus Cusack and Desmond Beattie in Derry in July 1971 alienated Catholic moderates and prompted increased violence.[34] A statement by the senior military police officer responsible for investigations unveils the prevailing mentality:

> The RMP [Royal Military Police] investigator was out for information for managerial, not criminal, purposes, and using their powers of discretion, it was unlikely that the RUC would prefer charges against soldiers except in the most extreme of circumstances.[35]

Thus, soldiers may well have acted with impunity, knowing that indiscipline would be concealed by their superiors.[36] The reluctance exhaustively to investigate and prosecute all allegations also stemmed from the feared damage this would do to military morale. A widespread belief that accusations originated from a sustained Republican propaganda campaign enhanced the institutional refusal to take abuses seriously.[37] The IRA certainly conducted propaganda, and senior commanders, and even the JIC in London, repeatedly complained about media misrepresentations.[38] However, these sentiments exaggerated IRA influence, dismissing moderate voices as essentially identical to the militants and denying anything but benevolence in military behaviour. Popular perceptions mattered, a truism subsumed in the rush to defeat rising Republican violence.

DESTROYING THE IRA: INTERNMENT AND DEEP INTERROGATION

After Brian Faulkner assumed the premiership, planning for internment began in April 1971.[39] Under pressure from his own party, introducing internment would ensure his government's survival, and seemed the last measure available in a desperate bid to out-escalate the IRA.[40] In his valedictory report as Commander of Land Forces, Major General Anthony Farrar-Hockley advised that internment could remove the IRA leadership and harvest valuable intelligence. At the decisive Cabinet meeting on 5 August, Lieutenant General Tuzo, the GOC, and General Carver, the Chief of the General Staff, opposed Farrar-Hockley's view. Despite recognizing the likelihood of increased IRA recruitment in the aftermath, Home Secretary Reginald Maudling was in favour, and along with Faulkner and RUC Chief Constable Shillington persuaded Heath to approve it.[41] On 9 August, army arrest teams swept up men identified by Special Branch, taking them to Regional Holding Centres at Ballykinler, Magilligan, and Girdwood Park. Here a Special Branch interview decided whether to detain or release them. Those selected for detention went from Ballykinler and Magilligan to the specially adapted *HMS Maidstone*, moored in Belfast lough; and from Girdwood Park to Crumlin Road jail. Out of 464 arrests, 342 detention orders were issued.[42] Some detainees alleged ill-treatment, including beatings, during the arrest process.[43] Arrest operations continued after August. By mid-February 1972 the number arrested for internment had risen to 2,447.[44] From early 1972 army units frequently screened the population in their areas. Suspects were arrested, taken to a local screening centre, processed by military police, medically examined, questioned by an intelligence team, given another medical exam, and then released or handed to the police. As the army worked mainly in Catholic areas, they suffered more screening than Protestants.[45] The effect of internment cannot be distinguished from the immense impact dealt by interrogation in depth.

Preparations began on 24 March 1971, when the Joint Services Interrogation Wing (JSIW), part of the School of Service Intelligence, agreed to train the RUC Special Branch, instructing officers the following month in Belfast.[46] Drawing on colonial experience, the sensory deprivation techniques originated in Communist practice in the Korean War.[47] They may have been deemed appropriate in Northern Ireland because the armed forces used them in their own training to resist enemy questioning.[48] The Parker Inquiry (discussed later) claimed that the five techniques were practised without Cabinet authorization.[49] Many studies follow Parker's conclusion, presuming ignorance amongst senior figures including the Chief of the General Staff, Lieutenant-General Tuzo and Lord Carrington.[50] Recent archival studies challenge this interpretation.[51] On 9 August, the Vice-Chief of the General Staff (VCGS) wrote to Carrington summarizing the JIC interrogation directive, and explained that supporting methods would be used. These included isolation, fatigue, white sound, and deprivation of a sense of place and time. The interrogations would be conducted by Special Branch, with the JSIW providing technical advice. When Carrington and Maudling discussed the matter neither disagreed with the VCGS's note.[52] On passing details of the procedures to the VCGS, the army's senior intelligence officer in Whitehall recommended the Secretary of State be briefed in case of 'possible complaints from such organisations as Amnesty International'. The techniques exploited 'the contrast between the very harsh and the kind and gentle interrogator, in circumstances designed to heighten the subjects [*sic*] desire to communicate'.[53] On 11 August, Faulkner was 'extensively briefed by the Director of Intelligence in

Northern Ireland on the techniques of interrogation'. He then authorized the transfer of twelve people to the interrogation site under the Special Powers Act, following advice from the RUC.[54] The Northern Ireland Attorney General was never consulted on deep interrogation's legality.[55]

The rationale behind deep interrogation raises two questions: why did the government authorize it, and why only on fourteen people out of hundreds in internment? The answer to the first point is that the expected intelligence thereby produced would save many lives.[56] The assertion that politicians agreed to measures because they were not believed to cause suffering is undermined by the concerns about Amnesty International, and later attempts to portray their purpose in a positive light.[57] Furthermore, the army's desire for the RUC to conduct the actual interrogations when 'it would be neither desirable nor politically acceptable for JSIW to be physically involved in interrogation', suggests unease about the legal position. The army wanted the intelligence reward without the expected 'inevitable recrimination'.[58] On the second point, the fourteen men went to Ballykelly because information showed that they held senior positions in the IRA, and were thought unlikely to confess in normal questioning.[59] The GOC explained the relationship between interrogation in depth and normal questioning:

> The lurid and exaggerated stories told by those questioned in Op Calaba after their release, or transfer to prison or internment camp, were eagerly taken up by the Republican press. The possibility of being interrogated in depth provided a further encouragement to talk, to those being questioned in PHC's [Police Holding Centres]. . . . The relationship between PHC's and Op Calaba is thus a complementary one, and neither can be considered in isolation in the present situation. The interrogation in depth provided by Op Calaba is not necessary for all suspects, nor it is desirable [sic], practical or economical to provide it for all. It takes (much) longer than PHC questioning and many suspects will now give much information to a PHC questioner, particularly if it is known that interrogation in depth is available for recalcitrant persons.[60]

Deep interrogation started on 11 August under twenty Special Branch interrogators, twelve JSIW advisers, and twenty-six RUC guards. Initially, twelve individuals were interrogated: James Auld, Joseph Clarke, Michael Donnelly, Kevin Hannaway, Patrick McClean, Francis McGuigan, Sean McKenna, Gerald McKerr, Patrick McNally, Michael Montgomery, Patrick Shivers, and Brian Turley. They were questioned until 11.30 a.m. on 17 August, and then moved to Crumlin Road jail. The Special Branch sought information on imminent operations, the location of people, arms, and explosives, and future IRA intentions. Detainees had to stand at a wall for between four and six hours at a time, and guards forced them to resume the position when they collapsed. Sometimes violence was inflicted to enforce compliance. Total times at the wall varied: nine hours for Turley and Donnelly, twenty hours for Hannaway, and forty-three hours for Auld. Bread and water was offered every six hours, until 15 August, when normal rations were issued. Medical records showed all the detainees lost weight.[61] At some point in September, Lord Balniel, the Minister of State for Defence, visited a training exercise to observe the five techniques.[62] The following month Lieutenant General Tuzo reported Calabar's resumption, assuming 'as before, that there is full Ministerial support... and that all concerned are ready to field the various missiles which may well come towards us'.[63] William Shannon was transferred to Hut 60 on 11 October, where Liam Rodgers joined him the following day. They underwent the same techniques as the earlier group until their release on 18 October.[64]

The security forces viewed interrogation in depth as a success. An assessment stated ten of the men provided 'large quantities of information of great value to the security forces'. Approximately three-quarters of the arms and explosives discovered after internment came from interrogation in depth.[65] Lieutenant Colonel J. R. Nicholson, the senior military officer at the interrogation centre, categorized the results into four areas. Firstly, six summaries were produced detailing possible IRA operations, arms caches, safe houses, supply routes, and wanted persons. Secondly, over forty sheets were written up on the IRA's order of battle. Thirdly, the detainees generated approximately 500 personality cards. Finally, over forty major past incidents were solved. However, the two unproductive sources indicated incorrect selection, and Nicholson argued the facility would work best with no more than six detainees at once.[66]

Were these gains worth the resulting violence, which reached unprecedented levels? By the end of the first day of internment, over a hundred houses had been set on fire as inter-communal violence broke out, and ten people were killed.[67] In the six months before internment, twenty-five people died; in the six months afterwards, 185.[68] Thus, while senior officers thought the intelligence outcome a success, some commanders deplored the consequences on the ground.[69] Moderate Catholic politicians withdrew from Stormont in protest and launched a civil disobedience campaign.[70] Meanwhile, financial support for the Provisionals and recruitment increased substantially in the north and the Republic.[71] Internment seriously disrupted Special Branch's understanding about ongoing IRA activities, and diverted manpower into clerical work administering the detainees.[72] On their release, some men found themselves subjected to 'intensive debriefing' by IRA units keen to discover what had been disclosed and how the Special Branch functioned.[73] The Cabinet declared its Northern Ireland policy 'in ruins' on 30 September.[74] In October 1971, PIRA announced an all-out offensive in response.[75] Hennessey claims that notwithstanding the short-term increase in violence, internment succeeded in the long run.[76] Cabinet records suggest though that the failure of internment prompted the beginning of a change in British strategy, moving towards de-escalation.[77] The claim that the five techniques in particular caused decades of violence cannot be verified.[78] It cannot be disaggregated from internment, and should be seen in the context of other important events, such as the Bloody Sunday massacre in January 1972. Similarly, the effectiveness of deep interrogation in comparison with other intelligence gathering methods cannot be properly assessed until fuller archival material is available.

A press scandal erupted very shortly after the introduction of internment.[79] The Association for Legal Justice and Archbishop Conway of Armagh called for an inquiry into brutality.[80] Several inquiries resulted, constituting a series of retrospective political controls on detention and interrogation policies, and formulating new rules for future operations. Reginald Maudling announced an inquiry on 21 August 1971, with a remit to investigate allegations 'of physical brutality while in the custody of the security forces prior to either their subsequent release, the preferring of a criminal charge, or their being lodged in a place specified in a detention order'.[81] Sir Edmund Compton agreed to chair the inquiry, accompanied by Edgar Fay QC and Dr Ronald Gibson.[82] Internal investigations occurred simultaneously, as B. T. W. Stewart visited Ulster in October, reporting to the Cabinet's Intelligence Coordinator, Dick White. Stewart advised Ministers should be able to say a review found the techniques appropriate given the terrorist threat, and avoid scapegoating the RUC 'for something which they were trained and encouraged to do by British Officers'. Public protest necessitated reducing the interrogation period, but not abandoning it altogether.[83] The GOC concurred on the time limits, whereas Lieutenant Colonel Nicholson suggested soundproof cells to eliminate the requirement for white noise, and enforcing hood wearing and wall-standing for a maximum of two hours at a time.[84] The Intelligence Coordinator's wider-ranging report recommended detainee handling, including interrogations, should remain under the guidance of the 1967 JIC doctrine, and overall control stay with the police. Interrogators needed more information on detainees before selecting them. Medical scrutiny and record-keeping required improvement, and changes in the centre's layout needed carrying out. However, the 'three special techniques' (forgetting sleep deprivation and reduced rations) should be retained. They might well effect the detainee's will to resist, but the stipulated reasons must relate to security, such as hiding the centre's location, protecting individual identities, preventing violence against the guards, and stopping detainees communicating.[85] Brigadier Bremner, Commandant of the Intelligence Corps, defended the 'operational requirement for the "offensive" use' of the special techniques.[86] The Ministry of Defence noted the General Staff's belief in keeping the techniques 'as part of the whole process of imposing discipline on internees and making them more amenable to successful interrogation'.[87] Lord Carrington decided to await the independent inquiry's results before adjudicating on these contrasting ideas.[88]

The Compton Inquiry reported on eleven detainees on 3 November, finding no evidence of physical brutality, but designating the interrogation techniques as 'illtreatment'. Two further reports, on 14 and 15 November, concluded that the other three people received the same ill-treatment.[89] Omitting mental suffering compromised the Compton inquiry's credibility.[90] Compton uncritically took soldiers at their word. John McGuffin, himself interned, criticized the inquiry on other grounds: it sat in secret, Compton was not a senior judge as convention demanded, he had close connections to the Unionist party, witnesses could not be compelled to attend, neither could documents be demanded, and detainees were denied legal aid.[91] A legal analysis criticized Compton's conclusion that brutality did not occur because those inflicting the treatment lacked evil intentions, arguing the perpetrator's intention was irrelevant to the nature of the interrogation. Furthermore, the ban on complainants cross-examining witnesses and having access to transcripts of evidence were serious shortcomings.[92] In providing the inquiry with operational records, the army made helpful annotations correcting some 'factually inaccurate statements'. The military police interviewed personnel involved in internment and deep interrogation before the inquiry.[93] Whether an agreed-upon narrative emerged is unknown, but should not be ruled outside the bounds of possibility. The Cabinet Office aimed to present evidence favourably, removing references to fatigue, downplaying the softening-up benefits of the techniques, and stressing the security reasons.[94] Ultimately they only succeeded in presenting the techniques as motivated by security concerns.

Because Compton failed to exonerate the security forces, the government needed to deflect ongoing criticism and depoliticize the decision about future policy. On 3 November the Cabinet Committee on Northern Ireland agreed upon another inquiry, mandated to consider whether interrogation procedures required modification, composed of three Privy Counsellors, one nominated by the Opposition.[95] The Home Secretary finalized the membership on 30 November as Lord Parker of Waddington (a former Lord Chief Justice) in the chair, accompanied by Lord Gardiner (the Opposition member, a former Lord Chancellor) and Mr John Boyd-Carpenter, a Conservative MP. The Ministry of Defence resumed the debate on how to present the techniques, opting to portray them as security measures.[96] The Intelligence Corps made plain their concern that the techniques be maintained for their vital contribution towards creating an atmosphere of 'strict discipline'. Such influences apparently proved effective on 'the type of detainee encountered in revolutionary warfare today [who] has rarely, if ever, had any discipline imposed upon him'.[97] The final submission to Parker advocated ministerial approval for interrogation and handling methods, using hooding and wall-standing for only up to two hours with any exceptions requiring a report from the commanding officer, and full record-keeping, including videotape recordings.[98]

A leak from the Committee's secretary forewarned the government that Lord Gardiner was likely to write a dissenting report declaring the five techniques illegal.[99] Lord Carrington thought this automatically meant permanently abandoning deep interrogation. Legalizing the methods, by a new Bill in Parliament, adjusting the Special Powers Act, or permitting continued practice and exempting interrogators from prosecution were deemed legally difficult and not 'practical politics'.[100] Lord Parker delivered his report, and the minority report from Lord Gardiner, on 31 January. The government stalled publication while reflecting on the right response. Passing an Act of Indemnity covering security force activities might imply illegal acts spread wider than at Ballykelly. It would 'be unjust to remove all legal redress from those who had undergone deep interrogation and it was therefore agreed that the legislation should only prevent either criminal prosecutions or actions for tort being brought against individuals, and that actions against the Crown would be allowed to lie'.[101] If detainees brought civil actions against anyone, 'the Crown could be expected in any event to stand by its servants'.[102] The GOC and his Director of Intelligence warned that abandoning the methods would damage intelligence collection and benefit IRA propaganda.[103] Indeed, ever since suspension of the techniques following Compton, routine police questioning had failed to deliver an adequate product.[104] On 25 February the Cabinet Secretary passed his final submission to the Prime Minister on the Parker Inquiry, asking him to choose one of four courses of action. Edward Heath selected Option D—accepting the majority report, but banning the five techniques for interrogation, allowing wall-standing for a very short period during searches, and keeping the techniques in special forces' resistance to interrogation training.[105]

RECALIBRATING SECURITY POLICY FROM MARCH 1972

The Chief of the General Staff sent an order banning the five techniques to Northern Ireland on 1 March.[106] The move comprised part of government's wider attempt to calm the worsening violence which had spiralled even further out of control after Bloody Sunday. On 22 March, the Cabinet recognized that a military victory was impossible, and decided to de-escalate the conflict.[107] Following the imposition of direct rule from London, the new Northern Ireland Secretary, William Whitelaw, began releasing those interned.[108] Accordingly, HQ Northern Ireland issued a new directive on arrest policy in April. It instructed those arrested be delivered to the police 'with the minimum disturbance', and soldiers remembering that suspects 'are not necessarily guilty'.[109] On 22 June, the Provisional IRA declared its intention to begin a ceasefire on the 27th if the government reciprocated, and Whitelaw accepted.[110] Headquarters reacted rapidly in revising orders to desist arresting people simply for interrogation. Arrests would take place under the criminal law, not the Special Powers Act.[111] The army halted offensive operations against the IRA, reverting to peacekeeping. Soldiers only acted if they caught a 'wrongdoer red-handed', before handing them over to the RUC.[112] PIRA and the government failed to reach an accommodation, and the change in the rules governing detentions left a legacy of confusion about exactly what was permitted.[113]

Another change in detention policy attended the assault on the IRA heralded by Operation Motorman on 31 July, when over 30,000 troops cleared barricades in Derry and Belfast, reclaiming formerly 'no-go' areas from Republican control.[114] Motorman's success encouraged the GOC to request authorization for Special Branch interrogations in police offices at Ballykelly, Castlereagh, and Armagh.[115] Between March and August neither the army nor the police conducted any interrogations aside from those related to criminal prosecutions.[116] Thus, the scandal caused by deep interrogation substantially damaged the security forces' ability to carry out normal interrogations. The Ministry of Defence supported the police offices idea, but worried that 'despite all the safeguards ... there may well be allegations of rough treatment, and some of the mud thrown may hit the Army'.[117] Removing suspects to special sites for lengthier questioning might lead people to conclude the five techniques had returned to Northern Ireland.[118] London allowed interrogation under strict guidelines based on the revised JIC directive, issued with an expansive annex, offering some interesting insights into the process. Detailed questioning, always conducted within the law, was required for the small minority privy to important information. Depending upon the subject's personality, interrogators chose from four basic techniques, deviation from which was prohibited to ensure proper treatment. These were:

- A harsh approach in which the questioner will frequently raise his voice.
- A monotonous approach in which without changing his tone of voice the questioner relentlessly pursues his questioning.
- An apparently unprofessional approach in which the questioner appears to allow the subject to dominate.
- A friendly approach in which the questioner is calm and logical.[119]

The RUC received similar guidelines, covering interrogation for intelligence, rather than prosecution, where the Judges' Rules still applied. The Special Branch controlled the three special police offices, carrying out questioning, with the army in a supporting role. Persons arrested under the Special Powers Act were held for up to seventy-two hours before being released, charged, or issued with a detention order.[120] In September 1972, the Northern Ireland Secretary requested the army arrest around 200 senior IRA officers for prosecution.[121] By the end of the month, the government held 170 people in internment and 70 on detention orders.[122] On 6 November, the government introduced the Detention of Terrorists Orders, whereby the Secretary of State authorized applications for the detention of PIRA officers for up to twenty-eight days, pending referral to a commissioner. Whitelaw would sign orders related to Official IRA and Protestant terrorists if they posed a serious security threat.[123] The number detained without trial rose to over 500 in early 1973, and many were held for five or six months.[124] This arose because the Special Powers Act contained no formal time limit— seventy-two hours was merely an 'administrative rule'.[125] A review in late November instructed soldiers to leave a 'White Card', telling relatives how to obtain information about detainees. Soldiers handed prisoners to a military police arrest team as soon as possible, who in turn passed them on to the police. The army could only hold detainees for four hours.[126] The first loyalists were interned in February 1973, years too late for many in the Catholic community.[127] The July 1973 Northern Ireland (Emergency Provisions) Act reaffirmed the detention periods of four hours by the army and seventy-two hours by the police.[128]

Although the Parker Inquiry brought about notable changes in policy, complaints did not disappear altogether, and the legal system provided avenues for seeking redress and imposing further restraints. When Heath banned the five techniques, twenty-five civil actions were pending against the Crown.[129] Reflecting the earlier attitude towards critics, the GOC repudiated these cases as 'a propaganda exercise'.[130] Notwithstanding such complacency, London worried about ongoing police brutality, in June 1972 despatching J. T. Ellis from HM

Chief Inspector of Constabulary to investigate. He believed assurances from officers, yet found: 'inducements are made such as affording protection, ... and occasionally references are made to the necessity to interview close members of the family'.[131] The government decided to appoint an independent Director of Public Prosecutions. The Attorney General stated that although the Director was independent, potential prosecutions of the security forces should be referred to London for a final decision. By June 1972, 180 civil claims against the Crown were in process, and he was dealing with them thus:

> Where the claim relates to unlawful arrest, my present policy is to advise a settlement.... Where the claims involve allegations of physical assault or ill-treatment, I have asked for the cases to be referred to me before advising settlement.[132]

The Attorney General proposed to deny (with exceptions) criminal proceedings against security forces personnel who killed or wounded civilians during the course of their duty.[133] This disjuncture in attitudes towards punishing assaults and killings may have influenced an alleged 'shoot to kill' policy in the early 1980s, encouraging certain units to kill suspects rather than arrest them.[134] Legal control relied upon the police investigating themselves and passing on case files to the Director. The Northern Ireland Office lamented the RUC's lack of progress in pursuing brutality complaints.[135] In November 1972, the Director of Public Prosecutions ordered all allegations against the security forces to be passed directly to him.[136] Between March 1972 and November 1974, 1,078 cases of assault by the army were investigated by the Director of Public Prosecutions.[137] In total, from April 1972 to the end of January 1977, the DPP prosecuted 218 security force personnel for assault, of whom 155 were convicted.[138] As late as June 1978 Amnesty International alleged ill-treatment of detainees.[139] However, even critics acknowledged a sharp decrease following Heath's ban, despite continued abuses.[140]

CONCLUSION

Detention and interrogation constituted an integral dimension to the government's military strategy for at first moderating inter-communal animosity, and then defeating Republican militant opposition. From the outset the legal regime occupied a contested zone ignored by a counter-insurgency doctrine insufficiently concerned with problematizing the state's legitimacy and acting cautiously to ensure its enhancement. Thus, the set of laws potentially capable of circumscribing executive power in fact permitted significant scope for deploying repressive practices. Rather than checking the escalating violence, the laws governing detention and interrogation became subject to policy-makers' intentions. Only in the case of the adoption of Lord Gardiner's dissenting report did principle notably triumph over political expediency. Matters improved a great deal when the government appointed an independent Director of Public Prosecutions to oversee the impartial application of legal restraints on the armed forces. Although this went some way to remedy flaws in the previous self-investigatory position, complaints of abuses continued.

Enacting deep interrogation in Northern Ireland, despite warnings about the consequences from military advisers, proved a hugely symbolic moment in alienating an entire community. Once allowed the notorious five techniques by their political masters, military commanders were reluctant to give them up, devising elaborate schemes for retaining them in the face of widespread political outrage in Britain and abroad. This was because they were deemed highly effective, both in producing intelligence from the small group subjected to the cruel methods, and in instilling fear into a much larger group of people placed under arrest. Comprehensively assessing deep interrogation's effectiveness is not fully possible until further archive document releases enable a comparative understanding of the various other types of intelligence-gathering operations in place at the time. However, internment and deep interrogation certainly contributed towards a large increase in violence, and new evidence suggests it also undermined Special Branch's capabilities. Ultimately, the abandonment of the techniques and the decline in the numbers interned shows the government itself thought the measures on balance to be undesirable. Subsequently, major reforms in tightening up detention and interrogation practices tried to prevent any future criminal acts by the state. But having earlier unleashed security force personnel, restraining them proved difficult, and civilian attitudes towards the state could not be reoriented simply by issuing a new directive on detention policy. The memory of internment and inhuman treatment lingered long after the firearms impounded in August 1971 were destroyed.

NOTES

1. Thomas Hennessey, *The Evolution of the Troubles 1970–72* (Dublin: Irish Academic Press, 2007), 131.
2. Letter from Sir Edmund Compton to Sir Philip Allen, 15 Nov. 1971, The National Archives, United Kingdom [all cited documents from this source], CJ 3/119; Hennessey, *Evolution of the Troubles*, 158.
3. For the judgement of 18 Jan. 1978, see <http://cmiskp.echr.coe.int/tkp197/viewhbkm. asp?sessionId=7308599&skin=hudoc-en&actio>.
4. John Newsinger, 'From counter-insurgency to internal security: Northern Ireland 1969–1992', *Small Wars and Insurgencies*, 6/1 (1995), 99.
5. Paul Dixon, *Northern Ireland. The politics of war and peace* (Basingstoke: Palgrave, 2001), 82–97; Peter R. Neumann, *Britain's long war: British strategy in the Northern Ireland conflict 1969–1998* (London: Palgrave Macmillan, 2003), 51–2.
6. Paul Bew, *Ireland: The politics of enmity, 1789–2006* (Oxford: Oxford University Press, 2007), 496.

7. Fionnuala Ní Aoláin, *The Politics of force: Conflict management and state violence in Northern Ireland* (Belfast: Blackstaff Press, 2000), 14.
8. Colm Campbell and Ita Connolly, 'A model for the "War against terrorism"? Military intervention in Northern Ireland and the 1970 Falls Curfew', *Journal of Law and Society*, 30/3 (2003), 347.
9. Kevin Boyle, Tom Hadden, and Paddy Hillyard, *Law and state: The case of Northern Ireland* (London: Martin Robertson, 1975), 38.
10. Laura K. Donohue, *The cost of counterterrorism: Power, politics, and liberty* (Cambridge: Cambridge University Press, 2008), 36–7.
11. Tom Hadden and Paddy Hillyard, *Justice in Northern Ireland: A study in social confidence* (London: Cobden Trust, 1973), 28, 31.
12. Letter from Tony Hetherington, Attorney General's Department, to Sir Kenneth Jones, 7 Jan. 1972, CJ 4/118.
13. Draft memo by Attorney General, 8 June 1972, CJ 4/435/1.
14. Niall Ó Dochartaigh, *From civil rights to armalites: Derry and the birth of the Irish troubles* (Basingstoke: Palgrave Macmillan, 2005), 151, 189.
15. Peter Taylor, *Brits: The war against the IRA* (London: Bloomsbury, 2002), 45.
16. Thomas Hennessey, *Northern Ireland: The origins of the troubles* (Dublin: Gill and Macmillan, 2005), 335.
17. Neumann, *Britain's long war*, 56.
18. Rod Thornton, 'Getting it wrong: The crucial mistakes in the early stages of the British army's deployment to Northern Ireland (August 1969 to March 1972)', *Journal of Strategic Studies*, 30/1 (2007), 87; Campbell and Connolly, 'Military intervention in Northern Ireland', 355.
19. Paul Dixon, 'Counter-insurgency in Northern Ireland and the crisis of the British state', in Paul B. Rich and Richard Stubbs (eds.), *The counter-insurgent state: Guerrilla warfare and state building in the twentieth century* (Basingstoke: Macmillan, 1997), 193.
20. M. L. R. Smith, *Fighting for Ireland? The military strategy of the Irish Republican Movement* (London: Routledge, 1997), 95.
21. Neumann, *Britain's long war*, 54.
22. Dixon, *The politics of war and peace*, 128.
23. Henry Patterson, *Ireland since 1939: The persistence of conflict* (Dublin: Penguin Ireland, 2006), 220.
24. Hennessey, *Evolution of the Troubles*, 112–15.
25. Kevin Boyle, Tom Hadden, and Paddy Hillyard, *Ten years on in Northern Ireland: The legal control of political violence* (London: Cobden Trust, 1980), 28.
26. Michael O'Boyle, 'Torture and emergency powers under the European Convention on Human Rights: Ireland v. The United Kingdom', *American Journal of International Law*, 71/4 (1977), 676–7.
27. Donohue, *Cost of counterterrorism*, 50.
28. Letter from Michael Herman, Secretary of the JIC, to Brigadier J.M.H. Lewis, Brigadier General Staff (Intelligence), Ministry of Defence (MoD), 6 Apr. 1972, WO 32/21726.
29. Boyle, Hadden, and Hillyard, *Ten years on in Northern Ireland*, 36.
30. Hadden and Hillyard, *Justice in Northern Ireland*, 63.
31. Boyle, Hadden, and Hillyard, *Law and state*, 40–1, 51, 90; Robin Evelegh, *Peacekeeping in a democratic society* (London: C. Hurst, 1978), 86.
32. Boyle, Hadden, and Hillyard, *Law and state*, 139–42.

33. Aoláin, *The politics of force*, 96–117.
34. Ó Dochartaigh, *From civil rights to armalites*, 232–5.
35. Cited in Hennessey, *Evolution of the Troubles*, 302.
36. Boyle, Hadden, and Hillyard, *Law and state*, 35.
37. Desmond Hamill, *Pig in the middle: The army in Northern Ireland, 1969–1984* (London: Methuen, 1985), 79.
38. Eunan O'Halpin, '"A poor thing but our own": The Joint Intelligence Committee and Ireland, 1965–72', *Intelligence and National Security*, 23/5 (2008), 670.
39. Taylor, *Brits: The war against the IRA*, 64.
40. Neumann, *Britain's long war*, 56; Ó Dochartaigh, *From civil rights to armalites*, 230.
41. Hennessey, *Evolution of the Troubles*, 120–9.
42. Ibid. 130–1.
43. Ibid. 156.
44. Donohue, *Cost of counterterrorism*, 37.
45. Boyle, Hadden, and Hillyard, *Law and state*, 43–7.
46. Hennessey, *Evolution of the Troubles*, 152–3.
47. Hamill, *Pig in the middle*, 66.
48. Hennessey, *Evolution of the Troubles*, 166.
49. Laura K. Donohue, *Counter-terrorist law and emergency powers in the United Kingdom 1922–2000* (Dublin: Irish Academic Press, 2001), 120.
50. For example: Taylor, *Brits: The war against the IRA*, 65; Hamill, *Pig in the middle*, 67.
51. Neumann, *Britain's long war*, 57.
52. Hennessey, *Evolution of the Troubles*, 154.
53. Minute from Brigadier J.M.H. Lewis, BGS(Int) to VCGS, 9 Aug. 1971, CAB 163/173.
54. Minute from A.P. Hockaday to Private Secretary to the Defence Secretary, 9 Nov. 1971, CAB 163/171.
55. Letter from Mr Kelly, NI Attorney General, to Sir Peter Rawlinson, UK Attorney General, 12 Jan. 1972, CJ 4/118.
56. Taylor, *Brits: The war against the IRA*, 73.
57. Michael Dewar, *The British army in Northern Ireland* (London: Arms and Armour, 1985), 55.
58. Letter from Brigadier Lewis to H.D. Eastwood, Director of Intelligence, HQ Northern Ireland, 6 Aug. 1971, DEFE 24/744.
59. Minute by C.H. Henn, 8 Nov. 1971, DEFE 13/1115.
60. Paper by GOC Northern Ireland on 'Interrogation in Northern Ireland: An assessment', 24 Nov. 1971, DEFE 24/745.
61. Hennessey, *Evolution of the Troubles*, 155–8.
62. Letter from J.M. Parkin, Ministry of Defence, to J.T. Williams, Northern Ireland Office, 8 Feb. 1973, CJ 4/1744.
63. Letter from Lieutenant General Sir Harry Tuzo to General Sir Michael Carver, 12 Oct. 1971, CJ 4/95.
64. Letter from Sir Edmund Compton to Sir Philip Allen, 15 Nov. 1971, CJ 3/119.
65. Hennessey, *Evolution of the Troubles*, 217–18.
66. Report by Lieutenant Colonel J.R. Nicholson, 26 Aug. 1971, CAB 163/173.
67. Donohue, *Cost of counterterrorism*, 38.
68. Neumann, *Britain's long war*, 57.
69. Hamill, *Pig in the middle*, 63.
70. Hennessey, *Evolution of the Troubles*, 146–50.
71. Patterson, *Ireland since 1939*, 221.

72. Minute from RUC HQ to Special Branch, August 1971, CAB 163/170.
73. Minute from Lieutenant Colonel. F.G. Allardyce to J.A.T. Howard-Drake, 27 Oct. 1971, CAB 163/171.
74. Neumann, *Britain's long war*, 47.
75. Smith, *Fighting for Ireland*, 95.
76. Hennessey, *Evolution of the Troubles*, 221.
77. Neumann, *Britain's long war*, 63.
78. Donohue, *Cost of counterterrorism*, 34.
79. O'Boyle, 'Torture and Emergency Powers', 675.
80. Hennessey, *Evolution of the Troubles*, 157.
81. MoD press release, 21 Aug. 1971, CJ 4/95.
82. Hennessey, *Evolution of the Troubles*, 160–1.
83. Report by B.T.W. Stewart, 22 Oct. 1971, CAB 163/173.
84. Minute from B.T.W. Stewart to Intelligence Coordinator, 28 Oct. 1971, CAB 163/171.
85. Report by the Intelligence Co-ordinator, 2 Nov. 1971, WO 32/21776.
86. Letter from Brigadier Bremner to Brigadier Lewis, 24 Nov. 1971, DEFE 24/745.
87. Minute from Sir James Dunnett to Secretary of State for Defence, 30 Nov. 1971, DEFE 24/743.
88. Letter from A.W. Stephens to B.M. Norbury, 8 Nov. 1971, DEFE 24/744.
89. Letter from Sir Edmund Compton to Sir Philip Allen, 15 Nov. 1971, CJ 3/119.
90. Hennessey, *Evolution of the Troubles*, 163.
91. John McGuffin, *The guineapigs* (Harmondsworth: Penguin, 1974), 51, 79, 83, 87.
92. O'Boyle, 'Torture and emergency powers', 675.
93. Letter from Colonel D.A. Barker-Wyatt, HQ Northern Ireland, to Sir Edmund Compton, 11 Sep. 1971, CJ 4/113.
94. Memo from Sir Burke Trend to Sir James Dunnett, 25 Oct. 1971, CJ 4/95.
95. Note by Chairman of the Cabinet Northern Ireland Committee, 3 Nov. 1971, CAB 163/171.
96. Note of a meeting held by PUS, MoD, 23 Nov. 1971, CAB 163/172.
97. Report by the Intelligence Centre, 1 Dec. 1971, DEFE 24/743.
98. MoD memo, 7 Jan. 1972, CJ 4/118.
99. Letter from Noel Moore to C.A. Whitmore, 4 Jan. 1972, DEFE 23/160.
100. Minute from R.C. Kent to PUS, MoD, 12 Jan. 1972, DEFE 23/160.
101. Note of a meeting held at MoD, 3 Feb. 1972, DEFE 24/209.
102. Letter from Treasury Solicitor's Office to DUS(Army), MoD, 14 Feb. 1972, DEFE 24/743.
103. Minute from R.C. Kent to PS/PUS, MoD, 9 Feb. 1972, DEFE 24/209.
104. Record of meeting held by VCGS, 15 Feb. 1972, DEFE 24/209.
105. Minute from Sir Burke Trend to Prime Minister, 25 Feb. 1972, CJ 4/118.
106. Signal from CGS to GOC Northern Ireland, 1 Mar. 1972, CJ 4/118.
107. M.L.R. Smith and Peter R. Neumann, 'Motorman's long journey: Changing the strategic setting in Northern Ireland', *Contemporary British History*, 19/4 (2005), 419–21.
108. Donohue, *Cost of counterterrorism*, 42.
109. Order from HQ Northern Ireland to 3 Bde, 8 Bde, and 39 Bde, 24 Apr. 1972, CJ 4/1744.
110. Hamill, *Pig in the middle*, 107.
111. Letter from J.T.A. Howard-Drake, Northern Ireland Office, to John Howe, Civil Adviser to GOC Northern Ireland, 23 June 1972, CJ 4/458.
112. Commander Land Forces Directive for Future Internal Security Operations, 24 June 1972, CJ 4/458.

113. Minute to Sir William Nield from J.T.A. Howard-Drake, 25 July, 1972, CJ 4/458.
114. Smith and Neumann, 'Motorman's long journey', 414.
115. Minute from Major R.H. Swinburn, MA to VCGS, to PS to Secretary of State, 2 Aug. 1972, DEFE 13/1116.
116. Minute from R.C. Kent, DUS(Army), to VCGS, 3 Aug. 1972, DEFE 13/1116.
117. Minute from D.R.J. Stephen, AUS(GS), to APS/Secretary of State, 4 Aug. 1972, DEFE 13/1116.
118. Letter from R.J. Andrew to T.C. Platt, 7 Aug. 1972, DEFE 13/1116.
119. Letter from VCGS to Brigadier R.M. Bremner, 8 Aug. 1972, DEFE 13/1116.
120. Letter from J.T.A. Howard-Drake to Sir Graham Shillington, 16 Aug. 1972, CJ 4/1744.
121. Letter from William Whitelaw to Lieutenant-General Tuzo, 1 Sep. 1972, DEFE 24/824.
122. Minute from A.W. Stephens to BGS(Int), 26 Sep. 1972, DEFE 24/871.
123. Letter from William Whitelaw to Lieutenant-General Tuzo, 6 Nov. 1972, DEFE 24/824.
124. Boyle, Hadden, and Hillyard, *Law and state*, 32, 63.
125. Letter from J.T.A. Howard-Drake to J.T. Williams, 28 Nov. 1972, CJ 4/458.
126. Letter from John Walter, MoD, to P.G. Fullerton, Northern Ireland Office, 30 Nov. 1972, CJ 4/458.
127. Dixon, *The politics of war and peace*, 124.
128. Boyle, Hadden, and Hillyard, *Law and state*, 40.
129. Letter from Peter Jeffery, PS/Minister of State for Defence, to C.W. Roberts, PS/Prime Minister, 1 Mar. 1972, CJ 4/118.
130. Notes of a meeting between the Prime Minister, CGS and GOC, 1 Mar. 1972, CJ 4/118.
131. Report by J.T. Ellis, 2 June 1972, CJ 4/435/1.
132. 'The Legal Picture in Northern Ireland. A Note by the Attorney General', 2 June 1972, CJ 4/435/1.
133. Extract from draft memo by the Attorney General for circulation to Gen 79, 8 June 1972, CJ 4/435/1.
134. Christopher Tuck, 'Northern Ireland and the British approach to counter-insurgency', *Defense and Security Analysis*, 23/2 (2007), 174.
135. Minute from N.F. Cairncross to Northern Ireland Secretary, 15 June 1972, CJ 4/435/1.
136. Hennessey, *Evolution of the Troubles*, 302.
137. O'Boyle, 'Torture and emergency powers', 679.
138. Donohue, *Cost of counterterrorism*, 56.
139. Donohue, *Counter-terrorist law and emergency powers*, 121.
140. Boyle, Hadden, and Hillyard, *Law and state*, 50.

13

The Status and Treatment of Detainees in Russia's Chechen Campaigns

Bettina Renz

Tensions leading to armed conflict between Russian federal forces and Chechen separatists in the post-Soviet era can be traced far back into the history of relations between the two sides. Following decades of resistance, the North Caucasus, including the territory of contemporary Chechnya, was incorporated into the Russian empire in the nineteenth century, and became a part of the Russian Soviet Federated Socialist Republic (RSFSR) after the Bolshevik revolution. Recurrent rebellion against Soviet authority was forcefully suppressed, culminating in the deportation of the Chechen nation to Central Asia and Siberia in 1944, which was justified by fears over the defiant nation's collaboration with fascist Germany.[1] By the time of the collapse of the Soviet Union in 1991, a 'monochronic' reading of Chechnya's relationship with Russia as one characterized by permanent suppression and suffering was appropriated by Chechen separatist groups. Such a reading of history demanded nothing but full independence from Russia as a remedial right resulting from centuries of suffering. It precluded other negotiated outcomes from the outset and goes far in terms of explaining the protracted nature of a conflict which has no end in sight.[2]

The first application of large-scale armed force in the post-Soviet era (in 1994) intended to bring the separatist Chechen Republic back into line with other Russian Federation subjects. Although Chechnya's declaration of independence following the collapse of the Soviet Union in 1991 had not been recognized by Russia, or by the international community, the Republic enjoyed a period of de facto self-rule until the onset of the 'first Chechen campaign', which had the objective of restoring constitutional order to the troubled Republic. The campaign lasted until 1996, when a ceasefire agreement was signed by the Russian and Chechen leaderships which delayed a decision about the Republic's status until 2001. Following the withdrawal of Russian forces from the Chechen Republic and another period of de facto self-rule, a negotiated decision was pre-empted by the onset of the 'second Chechen campaign' in September 1999. The renewed use of armed force followed a number of terrorist attacks on Russian territory and the incursion of Chechen fighters into the neighbouring Republic of Dagestan. Rather than an operation aimed at restoring constitutional order, the second campaign was framed as an anti-terrorist operation from the outset.[3]

With regard to both the first and second Chechen campaigns, the international community accepted Russia's just recourse to using armed force in order to defend its territorial integrity and national security. However, the justness of the conduct of the operations in both cases was widely questioned by Western governments, media, and international organizations, for its excessiveness in terms of the scale and means of force employed by the Russian military.[4] Critics specifically objected to the discrepancy between the portrayal of the conflicts as consisting of limited and targeted operations, and the harsh reality of the campaigns with all their consequences. These included the large-scale bombardment of densely populated areas in the early stages; a large number of refugees and displaced persons; a 'leave or die' ultimatum issued to the population of Grozny in December 1999; and a high number of casualties, both civilian and military, including conscripts.[5] Human rights abuses in Chechnya, including disappearances, indiscriminate and arbitrary detentions, and ill-treatment, torture, and extrajudicial executions of detainees, have been widely documented by both Russian and international human rights organizations. They are at the heart of much of the criticism levelled against Russia for its conduct of the Chechen campaigns and are also the subject of this chapter.

This chapter assesses the legal status and treatment of Chechen detainees by Russian federal forces and seeks to trace the major explanatory factors for their ill-treatment during both campaigns. Whilst it is by no means the intention to justify human rights abuses committed by Russian federal forces, the chapter argues that such abuses during both campaigns need to be understood within the wider framework of post-Soviet transition. Incomplete reforms of the Russian legal and penitentiary systems, as well as problems associated with reforms of the military and law-enforcement agencies in the aftermath of the Soviet collapse, have not only facilitated the ill-treatment of detainees in Chechnya, but have had grave consequences for the human rights situation in the Russian Federation more broadly. *Dedovshchina*—the brutal hazing of conscripts—as a widespread problem within the Russian armed forces is relevant here. Equally relevant are the excesses of police officers throughout Russia whose actions, despite repeated efforts to reform and modernize the Interior Ministry (MVD) in the post-Soviet era, continue to be characterized by a lack of 'democratic tradition and familiarity with basic human rights notions on an institutional level'.[6] The chapter suggests that human rights abuses and the ill-treatment of detainees in Chechnya are not officially sanctioned strategic decisions, but rather have been due to a wide variety of factors, often related to the uncertainties and chaos of the transitional period that have affected all aspects of legal, political, and social life in post-Soviet Russia.

THE LEGAL STATUS OF DETAINEES IN THE CHECHEN CAMPAIGNS

The ill-treatment of detainees during both campaigns was facilitated in part by the fact that their legal status was never clearly identified. In both cases uncertainties in definition were due to the ambiguity of the legal grounds on which military force was applied. According to the Russian Constitution, martial law and individual restrictions on rights and freedoms can be introduced throughout the country or in individual locations thereof, in the form of a state of emergency declared by presidential decree.[7] Having declared a state of emergency in 1991, following the Chechen declaration of independence, President Boris Yeltsin saw his decree annulled by the Parliament on the same day in the face of strong political opposition. At the onset of military operations in 1994, Yeltsin did not attempt to impose emergency rule, as this was seen as too costly in political terms.[8] The application of military force in the first Chechen campaign occurred in a legal vacuum, resulting in widespread criticism within Russia itself. Protest included the resignation of high-ranking military officers unwilling to use force against their compatriots.[9]

Similarly, at the onset of the second Chechen campaign in 1999, no state of emergency was declared. Instead, the use of armed force, and restrictions on rights and freedoms of the Chechen population, were justified with reference to the Russian federal law 'On the fight against terrorism', which had been adopted in 1998.[10] In contrast to the declaration of a state of emergency, an invocation of the terrorism law required the President to seek neither initial sanction, nor periodical reconfirmation by the Parliament, thus presenting less potential for political controversy and opposition.[11] However, the legality of applying terrorism law to the context of long-term and large-scale military operations in Chechnya has been questioned subsequently, both in Russia and internationally. Whilst the adequacy of the legal act per se was not seen as problematic, concerns were voiced with regard to its arbitrary and broad interpretation in relation to its use within the framework of the second Chechen campaign. Legal experts have cautioned that the law was intended for localized and short-term use in the case of a large-scale terrorist attack, but did not allow for the imposition of emergency rule over an entire federal region for several years.[12] A new terrorism law adopted in 2006 did away with this ambiguity, no longer restricting the zone of counter-terrorist operations to limited locations with specified boundaries, but allowing the conduct of operations on territories with a 'considerable population'.[13]

Legally speaking, due to the absence of a declaration of martial law or state of emergency during both Chechen campaigns, the situation in the Republic was 'ordinary' in both instances,[14] making it difficult to define the status of individuals detained by Russian federal forces for their involvement in armed hostilities. During both Chechen campaigns, the Russian government did not concede the applicability of Additional Protocol II to the Geneva Conventions, which makes a clear distinction between civilians, on the one hand, and individuals taking direct part in hostilities and therefore subject to lawful targeting, on the other. Instead, armed insurgents were treated as criminals or terrorist suspects and usually detained with reference to relevant criminal law.[15] After the start of the first Chechen campaign a group of Russian parliamentarians challenged the constitutionality of the federal government's actions in the Constitutional Court. Although the Court did not pronounce the campaign as unconstitutional, it determined that Protocol II was binding for both sides of the conflict and that the federal forces' conduct in Chechnya violated Russia's international obligations. At the same time, however, it excused Russia's non-compliance with the Protocol due to the fact that it had not yet been incorporated into the country's legal system.[16]

The lack of a clear legal definition and associated guidelines for the treatment of Chechen detainees made them particularly vulnerable to abuse by Russian federal forces. According to a Russian human rights organization, the Memorial Human Rights Centre, in the early stages of the first campaign Chechen individuals suspected of being party to armed hostilities were detained without any legal grounds for their detention or official documentation of the detentions ever having taken place. Reportedly, detentions were documented only two months into the conflict, most of them with reference to violations of presidential decrees, 'On measures to prevent vagrancy and begging' and 'On urgent measures to defend the population from banditry and other manifestations of organised crime'.[17] Both decrees permitted the detention of individuals without charge or judicial decision for nine and thirty days respectively, circumventing the forty-eight hour limit enshrined in Article 22 of the Russian Constitution. Following widespread criticism the decrees were repealed by 1997.[18] During the second Chechen campaign individuals were detained under the Criminal Procedural Code allowing detention without charge for up to ten days and up to thirty days with reference to terrorism-related legislation.[19]

THE TREATMENT OF CHECHEN DETAINEES AND POST-SOVIET REFORMS

Incomplete post-Soviet reforms of the Russian legal and penitentiary systems have also facilitated the ill-treatment of detainees in both conflicts. The adoption of a new Criminal Procedural Code in 2002 was a big step towards the regularization of the treatment of detainees in the Russian Federation, including in Chechnya. However, this Code was not implemented until long after the military phase of the second campaign had been declared over in mid-2000. Until its implementation, pre-trial detention of individuals was unrestricted, often lasting for years. According to the new Code detainees can be interrogated only in the presence of a lawyer. This requirement was introduced in order to avoid detainee torture or enforced confessions.[20] In another important move, the new Code deprived the Federal Security Service (FSB) and the Interior Ministry (MVD) of their right to issue their own warrants for the search or arrest of an individual without the approval of a magistrate or judge. Until the adoption of the new Code this state of affairs had often led to the arbitrary arrest of individuals and their prolonged detention without charge or trial.[21] It is worth noting here that military operations in Chechnya were conducted not only by the regular armed forces, but in conjunction with military personnel under the jurisdiction of the FSB and MVD. It is these law-enforcement agencies that have been the focus of allegations about the ill-treatment and torture of detainees.[22]

Incomplete reforms of the Russian penitentiary system contributed to the absence of safeguards against the ill-treatment of Chechen detainees during both conflicts. Large-scale reforms of the Russian prison system were not implemented until 1998, when the system was transferred from the jurisdiction of the militarized MVD to the Justice Ministry. This reform was implemented in response to a request by the Council of Europe, which Russia joined in 1996, to comply with European prison rules.[23] In the aftermath of these reforms the Committee for the Prevention of Torture (CPT) recorded noticeable improvements in the treatment and conditions of detainees throughout the Russian Federation. During its subsequent visits to the Chechen Republic it reported that 'hardly any allegations were received of ill-treatment by staff working in the Ministry of Justice establishments.'[24] In an important initiative President Vladimir Putin signed into law the transfer of all pre-trial detention centres to the Justice Ministry in 2006.[25] Despite marked improvements of the situation, however, in 2007 the CPT continued to express concern about the ill-treatment of detainees in unofficial places of detention run in Chechnya by the MVD.[26]

Another aspect, relating to incomplete reforms of the Russian legal and penitentiary systems, exacerbated instances of illegal detention and torture of individuals in Chechnya. According to the Memorial Human Rights Centre, Russian prosecutors dealing with detention matters during the second Chechen conflict in particular were unable to deal with the sheer number of cases assigned to them. Having failed to interrogate detainees or to develop criminal cases against them, many detainees were released on amnesty within six months. This failure of the Russian justice system to cope with the demands of large-scale military operations, and not a limited anti-terrorist campaign as the conflict was officially termed, caused some federal military and law-enforcement personnel to take the law into their own hands to ensure that detainees did not escape the punishment that they, in their eyes, deserved.[27]

In addition to ambiguities regarding the legal status of detainees and the issue of incomplete reforms, the failure of law-enforcement agencies to follow due legal process involved in the detention of individuals has further exacerbated detainees' vulnerability to ill-treatment and abuse. As mentioned earlier, particularly in the early stages of the first Chechen campaign, detentions were not officially documented. Moreover, in many instances, detainees were denied access to lawyers and medical attention, and their families were not informed about their arrest and whereabouts.[28] The arbitrary arrest and subsequent disappearance without a trace of Chechen nationals—up to 5,000 between 1999 and 2005 alone, according to Human Rights Watch—has been another variant of ill-treatment of detainees in both campaigns. Reportedly, large numbers of individuals, often unarmed civilians including male youth, were abducted by federal law-enforcement personnel in their own homes during so-called *zachistki* (sweep-up) operations and at military checkpoints especially in the period from 1999 to 2000. In some cases victims of unacknowledged detention were later released, whilst in other cases relatives were only able to recover the bodies.[29] Reports by human rights groups and international organizations active in Chechnya contain much credible evidence of the use of torture to extract confessions and information, as well as of extrajudicial executions of Chechen detainees by federal law-enforcement personnel.[30] Much concern continues to be expressed with regards to the existence of 'unofficial' detention centres in Chechnya, which are the focus of allegations of torture and ill-treatment and are hard to access by international observers due to the fact that their existence is not officially acknowledged.[31]

A trend towards the increasing brutalization of Russian forces as a by-product of incomplete military reforms in the post-Soviet era is a probable contributing factor to instances of ill-treatment and torture of Chechen detainees, particularly during the first campaign. The brutal treatment of conscripts in the Russian armed forces, sometimes resulting in serious injury or even death, has been well documented.[32] The tradition of hazing or *dedovshchina* in the Russian armed forces dates back to the Soviet era, but worsened in the post-Soviet era due to the authorities' increasing inability to recruit conscripts from a cross-section of Russian society. By 2003 only about 10 per cent of those eligible for military service were drafted. These were predominantly men with little education and an addiction to alcohol and drugs, whereas healthy, educated young men evaded military service in increasing numbers through bribes or enrolment in higher education institutions.[33] Whilst in 1999 efforts were made to attract contract soldiers and professional forces to fight the second Chechen campaign, poorly paid and trained conscripts made up the bulk of federal forces fighting in Chechnya from 1994 to 1996. Being accustomed to brutal treatment by superiors, in addition to having to face combat situations with often as little as six months of military training, is likely to have diminished the threshold of soldiers to engage in the abuse and ill-treatment of detainees in their custody.[34] Having said this, a general deficiency in the training, discipline, and morale of Russian troops, including of professional and contract soldiers deployed to Chechnya during the second campaign, is seen to have been a major contributing factor to the excessive levels of human rights abuses committed against the local population.[35]

THE TREATMENT OF CHECHEN DETAINEES— RACISM AND REPRISAL

A variety of factors unrelated to incomplete reform processes deserve attention as potential reasons for the widespread ill-treatment of Chechen detainees. One such factor often held responsible for Russian federal forces' human rights abuses in Chechnya, particularly by many Western authors, is one of racism and the general demonization of the Chechen nation.[36] Whilst racism as a motivating factor behind the actions of some Russian military and law-enforcement personnel in Chechnya cannot be discarded entirely, it is in itself too simplistic an explanation. Since the official phase of military operations in Chechnya was declared over by mid-2000, responsibility for upholding security in the Republic has been gradually returned to local law-enforcement agencies as part of a broader policy of 'Chechenization'. According to Human Rights Watch, by 2007 ethnic Chechen forces were responsible for the majority of systematic ill-treatment and torture, negating the issue of race and culture as a fundamental explanatory factor for the abuse of detainees in Chechnya.[37] Moreover, although ethnic minorities, including Chechens, detained by federal forces in Chechnya appear to be particularly vulnerable to ill-treatment whilst in detention,[38] ethnic Russians have also been subject to ill-treatment in police custody, pre-trial detention facilities, and prison colonies across the Russian Federation.[39]

The issue of reprisal serves as a further explanatory factor for the motivation behind the engagement of Russian military and law-enforcement personnel in the ill-treatment and torture of Chechen detainees. It has been widely acknowledged that not only Russian soldiers have been guilty of violating the human rights of their opponents, but that Chechen militants, too, have 'committed unspeakable acts of terrorism in Chechnya and other parts of Russia'.[40] Graphic attacks by Chechen fighters on Russian troops were filmed and distributed on videotape,[41] prisoners were used as human shields,[42] and the execution of Russian prisoners in some instances was announced on the Internet.[43] According to the Memorial Human Rights Centre, particularly during the first military campaign, the Chechen separatist leadership maintained its own detention centres holding captured Russian military personnel. Conditions in these centres were brutal and included torture, extrajudicial executions, and mass killings of detained Russian servicemen.[44]

The kidnapping of hostages for ransom money, including Russian soldiers, has been a tactic employed by Chechen fighters. Not unlike the practice of other sub-state military groups and terrorist organizations, kidnappings were used to demand the release of Chechen fighters from Russian prisons, and ransom money was utilized for the purchase of weapons and equipment. It has to be noted, however, that the taking of hostages for ransom money in Chechnya and other parts of the North Caucasus is not merely a symptom of post-Soviet conflicts with Russia, but part of an ancient tradition that continued even under tsarist and Soviet times.[45] It is likely that such kidnappings and ill-treatment of hostages and Russian soldiers on behalf of Chechen militants contributed to retaliatory crimes committed by Russian forces. On the other side of this coin, kidnapping rackets for financial gain accounted for a considerable number of arbitrary detentions of Chechens by Russian forces at military checkpoints.[46]

THE TREATMENT OF CHECHEN DETAINEES— STRATEGY OR BY-PRODUCT OF AN UGLY WAR?

According to Amnesty International, information and confessions extracted from detainees under duress have led, and continue to lead to, the instigation of criminal cases against individuals in Chechnya and in other parts of the Russian

Federation. The Chechen Ombudsman for Human Rights asserted in 2006 that a large number of the 12,000 Chechens in Russian prisons had been falsely accused on the basis of forced confessions.[47] Having said this, evidence suggests that the Russian political and military leadership has judged the ill-treatment of detainees with the view to extracting information to be counter-productive to the achievement of its strategic objectives in the Chechen campaigns, at least in theory. A document issued by the Russian military command to soldiers fighting in Chechnya in 1995 warned soldiers to refrain from human rights abuses as this would 'discredit the country, encourage the enemy, and lead to unpredictable results'.[48] The new Criminal Procedural Code adopted in 2002 included articles intended to eliminate ill-treatment and abuse of detainees to extract confessions. It introduced the requirement of having a lawyer present during interrogations and allowed defendants to retract confessions, particularly if they had been coerced.[49] In an interview with the Western media in 2004 Putin acknowledged the occurrence of human rights violations in Chechnya, but pointed out that, like the treatment of detainees by US soldiers in Abu Ghraib in Iraq, such events were not sanctioned from the top, but the result of 'ugly processes which have their own logic'.[50]

In condemning the ill-treatment of Chechen detainees at the hands of Russian federal forces, human rights groups, international organizations, and governments have stopped short of accusing the Russian government of pursuing an official policy of systematic torture and abuse. However, criticism pertaining to insufficiently resolute and systematic actions aimed at rooting out human rights abuses in Chechnya continues to be levelled against the Russian political and military leadership at the highest level.[51] In addition to aforementioned reforms of the Russian legal and penitentiary systems, some official and concrete efforts were made during both Chechen campaigns to curb human rights abuses committed by Russian federal forces, including the ill-treatment of detainees. As mentioned above, in February 1995 the Russian military command issued its soldiers with a document outlining their relations with the local population and ordering compliance with international humanitarian law. It warned that only military objects were legitimate targets and that violence against civilians would incur severe punishment. The document's release, however, clearly was not followed up with resolute enforcement, as reports of widespread ill-treatment of Chechen detainees continued to appear.[52]

During the second campaign attempts were made in the form of a military order to curb instances of arbitrary arrest and the subsequent disappearance of Chechens detained during *zachistki* operations. In 2002, the commander of the Combined Group of Russian Forces in Chechnya, Lieutenant General Moltenskoi, signed Order No. 80 that aimed to 'lessen the [number of] unlawful acts committed against the local population and to increase trust between the soldiers and civilian authorities'. Moltenskoi admitted that this order was necessary because 'there are facts showing that innocent and not-so-innocent people have gone missing during special operations—either through the fault of individual commanders or others who conducted the operations'.[53] The order required Russian federal military and law-enforcement personnel involved in *zachistki* operations to identify themselves (where they had previously worn masks), to record any detentions, notify relatives, and take any measures necessary to safeguard civilians from abuse. Order No. 80 was complemented by the Procurator General's Order No. 46, which required the presence of a procurator during all *zachistki* operations carried out in Chechnya. Whilst these efforts to curb the number of disappearances were acknowledged and welcomed internationally,[54] concerns were raised subsequently about the fact that the orders were not strictly enforced and were violated in many instances. According to a report by the CPT, senior members of the Chechen administration indicated in 2003 that the number of disappearances had not decreased substantially following the release of these orders. A number of *zachistki* operations continued to be carried out at night by masked law-enforcement personnel without prior notification of local military commanders and prosecutors, who were subsequently unable to gather information about the perpetrators' identity or the whereabouts of individuals detained during such raids.[55]

Crucially, attempts by the Russian authorities to bring to justice those responsible for the ill-treatment, torture, or murder of Chechen detainees have been judged internationally to be 'largely unproductive'.[56] Whilst large numbers of criminal cases into disappearances of Chechen detainees were opened by prosecutor's offices (as many as 1,814 between 1999 and 2005 alone),[57] only a small proportion of cases resulted in judicial proceedings and 'very few' have ever led to sentences.[58] Most cases were closed after several months, as the identity of the accused could not be established.[59] As late as 2007 the CPT criticized the Russian authorities for being reluctant and slow at instigating investigations into allegations of ill-treatment and torture at a variety of military facilities in Chechnya. Despite the partially effective reforms of the Russian legal and penitentiary systems over the past decade, it concluded that civilian and military prosecutors in Chechnya still lacked the 'staff, resources and facilities necessary for the effective investigation of cases involving allegations of ill-treatment, illegal detention and disappearances'.[60]

Concerns were also raised about the way in which investigations were conducted. In particular, a lack of promptness led to the loss of important evidence in many investigations scrutinized by the CPT. Often, forensic medical examinations of detainees that were the object of an investigation were not carried out until possible traces of ill-treatment had disappeared. Although the CPT noted that considerable investments had been made into a functioning forensic medical establishment in Chechnya by 2007, it concluded that the institution's work continued to be slow and ineffectively managed. Moreover, in the aftermath of several visits to the Chechen Republic the CPT raised concerns that, in some cases, detainees whose allegations of ill-treatment in Russian military installations had led to an investigation were later returned to the same institution where the alleged ill-treatment had occurred. This made them vulnerable to possible further abuse, and the CPT assessed such a situation as 'totally inadmissible'.[61]

In 1998, Russia ratified the Council of Europe Convention for the Protection of Human Rights and the Convention for the Prevention of Torture. Since the conventions entered into force for Russia in September 1998, a CPT delegation has visited detention facilities in the Russian Federation, including Chechnya, on a yearly basis. The Russian leadership has repeatedly expressed its commitment to improving the human rights situation in Chechnya in cooperation with the international community.[62] Despite verbal commitments to cooperation, however, the Russian Federation has been criticized by some of the international organizations in question for not fully engaging in such cooperation in practice. Regardless of Putin's assurance that 'Russia is not interested in hiding anything',[63] according to Amnesty International, Russia is the only member of the Council of Europe that does not agree to the established (yet not obligatory) practice of publishing the CPT's periodic and detailed reports on its findings in the country.[64]

The Council of Europe concluded that Russia's engagement with the CPT has been uncooperative, causing it to take the unusual step of issuing three public statements on the problems it encountered with regard to Russia's compliance with the Convention for the Prevention of Torture. The first statement, published in 2001, followed the Russian authorities' unwillingness to provide information requested by the Committee with regards to the investigations into specific allegations of ill-treatment. It judged Russia's decision to withhold the information—Russia did not see this matter as falling within the CPT's purview—as evidence of the country's failure to cooperate with the Committee. At the time of the second and third public statements in 2003 and 2007, the CPT noted the positive efforts Russia had made to control the conduct of federal forces in Chechnya and to restore the legal system in the republic. However, it felt compelled to make public its concerns about what it saw as the Russian authorities' insufficient commitment to bringing to justice those responsible for the ill-treatment of detainees and the 'token responses' it had received to previous recommendations. The Committee cautioned that an unambiguous formal warning to military and law-enforcement personnel in Chechnya about severe sanctions for human rights abuses, coming from the highest political level, was crucial, but this has yet to be delivered.[65]

In conclusion, no single factor can account for the widespread instances of human rights abuses and ill-treatment of detainees in Chechnya by Russian federal forces during both campaigns. Whilst the Russian authorities can be criticized for insufficient rigour in rooting out human rights abuses by military and law-enforcement personnel, and for failing to bring those responsible to justice, an officially sanctioned policy of torture and ill-treatment as a strategic tool is improbable. Evidence suggests that the chaos of post-Soviet transition and incomplete reforms in a variety of spheres have contributed much to the severity of the situation. The ambiguous status of detainees, due to the uncertain legal grounds on which military force was applied, made individuals particularly vulnerable to abuse when detained by Russian military personnel. As evidenced in chapters elsewhere in this volume, Russia has not been alone in negating the applicability of Protocol II for an internal conflict in order to deny the enemy legitimacy as a powerful actor under international law. The practice of referring to domestic law of questionable relevance in order to justify the use of military force and restrictions on civil liberties has also been observed elsewhere. The situation in Chechnya, however, was exacerbated due to the fact that the conflict, the first campaign in particular, occurred amidst the uncertainty of Russia's early years of post-Soviet transformation. A number of legal acts and procedures intended to regulate the situation of detainees in Chechnya were only recently adopted, making their prompt implementation unattainable. Incomplete reforms to the legal sphere, the prison system, and military and law-enforcement organizations, made a transparent and legitimate detention regime next to impossible. Most importantly, whilst democratic norms and notions of human rights were codified in the Russian Constitution in 1993, they were not automatically and instantaneously established as the basis for attitudes and conduct of military forces, law-enforcement personnel, and, arguably, politicians.

NOTES

1. John Dunlop and Rajan Menon, 'Chaos in the North Caucasus and Russia's future', *Survival*, 48/2 (2006), 103–4.
2. Richard Sakwa, 'Introduction: Why Chechnya', in Richard Sakwa (ed.), *Chechnya: From past to future* (London: Anthem Press, 2005), 5, 14.
3. Edwin Bacon and Bettina Renz, *Securitising Russia: The domestic politics of Putin* (Manchester: Manchester University Press, 2006), 48.
4. Mike Bowker, 'Western views of the Chechen conflict', in Sakwa (ed.), *Chechnya: From past to future*, 223–38.
5. Bacon and Renz, *Securitising Russia*, 56.
6. Amnesty International, 'Russian Federation: Torture and forced 'confessions' in detention', 2006, AI Index EUR 46/056/2006, 4.
7. The Russian Constitution, Article 56. Full translation available in Richard Sakwa, *Russian politics and society* (4th edn.; Abingdon: Routledge, 2008).
8. Boris Kalashnikov and Bruno Coppieters, 'The first Chechen war, 1994–1996', in Bruno Coppieters and Nick Foiton (eds.), *Moral constraints on war: Principles and causes* (Oxford: Lexington Books, 2002), 193.
9. Robert Barylski, *The soldier in Russian politics: Duty, dictatorship and democracy under Gorbachev and Yeltsin* (New Brunswick, NJ: Transaction Publishers, 1998), 313.
10. Full translation available on the Federation of American Scientists website: <http://www.fas.org/irp/world/russia/docs/law_980725.htm>; accessed May 2008. The 1998 law was replaced in 2006 with a new law on counter-terrorism.
11 Alexander Cherkasov and Dmitry Grushkin, 'The Chechen wars and the struggle for human rights', in Sakwa (ed.), *Chechnya: From past to future*, 142.
12. Ibid.
13. Otto Luchterhand, 'Das Neue Terrorismusbekaempfungsgesetz', *Russlandanalysen*, 99 (2006), 5 [online edition]: <http://www.laender-analysen.de/russland/pdf/Russlandanalysen099.pdf>; accessed June 2008.

14. Frederico Speretto, 'Law in times of war: The case of Chechnya', Human Rights and Human Welfare Working Paper no. 47, University of Denver, 2007, 3: <http://www.du.edu/gsis/hrhw/working/2007/47-sperotto-2007.pdf>; accessed May 2008.
15. William Abresch, 'A human rights law of internal armed conflict: The European Court of Human Rights in Chechnya', *European Journal of International Law*, 16/4 (2005), 754.
16. Paola Gaeta, 'The armed conflict in Chechnya before the Russian constitutional court', *European Journal of International Law*, 7/4 (1996), 568.
17. Memorial Human Rights Centre, 'Conditions in detention in the Chechen republic conflict zone: Treatment of detainees', Moscow, 1995: <http://www.memo.ru/hr/hotpoints/chechen/filter/eng/>; accessed May 2008; and Amnesty International, 'Russian Federation: Torture and ill-treatment', 1996, AI Index EUR 46/46/96.
18. United Nations Committee Against Torture, 'Consideration of reports submitted by states parties under Article 19 of the Convention', 2001, CAT/C/34/Add.15.
19. Amnesty International, 'Russian Federation: Torture and forced "confessions"', 12.
20. Mark Kramer, 'Rights and restraints in Russia's criminal justice system', *PONARS Policy Memos*, 289 (2003): <http://www.csis.org/media/csis/pubs/051111_pm_0289.pdf>; accessed May 2008.
21. Ibid.
22. Bacon and Renz, *Securitising Russia*, ch. 3.
23. Bettina Renz, 'Russia's force structures and the study of civil–military relations', *Journal of Slavic Military Studies*, 18 (2005), 569.
24. Council of Europe Committee for the Prevention of Torture and Inhuman or Degrading Treatment or Punishment, 'Public statement concerning the Chechen Republic of the Russian Federation', 2003, CPT/Inf (2003) 33.
25. Amnesty International, 'Russian Federation: Torture and forced "confessions"', 2.
26. Council of Europe Committee for the Prevention of Torture and Inhuman or Degrading Treatment or Punishment, 'Public statement concerning the Chechen Republic of the Russian Federation', CPT/Inf (2007), 2007, 17.
27. Alexander Cherkasov, '"Informal" penitentiary system in the Chechen Republic', Memorial Human Rights Centre, Moscow, 2003: <http://www.memo.ru/hr/news/turma/eng/index.htm>; accessed May 2008.
28. Amnesty International, 'Russian Federation: Preliminary Briefing to the UN Committee against Torture', 2006, AI Index EUR 46/014/2006, 2.
29. Human Rights Watch, 'Worse than a war: "Disappearances" in Chechnya—a crime against humanity', HRW briefing paper, 2005: <http://hrw.org/backgrounder/eca/chechnya0305/chechnya0305.pdf>; accessed May 2008.
30. Anatol Lieven, 'Morality and reality in approaches to war crimes: The case of Chechnya', *East European Constitutional Review*, 10/2–3 (2001) [online edition]: <http://www.law.nyu.edu/eecr/vol10num2_3/special/lieven.html>; accessed May 2008.
31. International Helsinki Federation for Human Rights, 'Unofficial places of detention in the Chechen Republic, 2006 [online report]: <http://www.ihf-hr.org/documents/doc_summary.php?sec_id=58&d_id=4249>; accessed May 2008.
32. See, for instance, *Journal of Power Institutions in Post-Soviet Societies*, Special issue 1 (2004): <http://www.pipss.org/sommaire190.html>; accessed May 2008; or Françoise Dauce and Elisabeth Sieca-Kozlowski (eds.), *Dedovshchina in the post-Soviet military* (Stuttgart: Ibidem Verlag, 2007).
33. Dale Herspring, 'Vladimir Putin and military reform in Russia', *European Security*, 14/1 (2005), 140.

34. Sophie Lambroschini, 'Chechnya: Draft avoidance rises as Russia ponders professional army', Radio Free Europe/Radio Liberty Special Report, 2000: <http://www.rferl.org/features/2000/07/F.RU.000714143952.asp>; accessed May 2008.
35. Mark Kramer, 'Guerrilla warfare, counterinsurgency and terrorism in the North Caucasus: The military dimension of the Russian–Chechen conflict', *Europe–Asia Studies*, 57/2 (2005), 220–1.
36. See, for instance, John Russell, 'Mujahedeen, mafia, madmen . . . : Russian perceptions of Chechens during the wars in Chechnya, 1994–1996 and 1999–to date', *Journal of Postcommunist Studies and Transition Politics*, 18/1 (2002), 73–96.
37. Human Rights Watch, 'Testimony for the International Commission of Jurists eminent jurists' Panel on Terrorism, Counterterrorism and Human Rights in Russia', 2007: <http://ejp.icj.org/IMG/HRW_testimony.pdf>; accessed May 2008.
38. Mark Kramer, 'Rights and restraints', 4.
39. Amnesty International, 'Russian Federation: Preliminary briefing'.
40. Human Rights Watch, 'Worse than a war', 2.
41. Susan B. Glasser and Steve Coll, 'The web as a weapon', *Washington Post*, (9 August 2005): <http://www.washingtonpost.com/wp-dyn/content/article/2005/08/08/AR2005080801018_pf.html>; accessed May 2008.
42. Kalashnikov and Coppieters, 'The first Chechen war', 199.
43. Lieven, 'Morality and reality'.
44. Cherkasov, '"Informal" penitentiary system'.
45. Nabi Abdullaev, 'Foreigners beware: Kidnappers are still operating in the North Caucasus', *Jamestown Foundation – Prism*, 7/2 (2001) [online edition]: <http://www.jamestown.org/publications_details.php?volume_id=8&&issue_id=442>; accessed June 2008.
46. Lieven, 'Morality and reality'.
47. Amnesty International, 'Russian Federation: Torture and forced "confessions"', 3.
48. Kalashnikov and Coppieters, 'The first Chechen war', 199–200.
49. Kramer, 'Rights and restraints', 3.
50. Jonathan Steele, 'Angry Putin rejects public Beslan inquiry', *Guardian* (7 September 2004): <http://www.guardian.co.uk/world/2004/sep/07/russia.chechnya>; accessed June 2008.
51. Council of Europe Committee for the Prevention of Torture, 'Public statement, 2003', 5.
52. Kalashnikov and Coppieters, 'The first Chechen war', 199–200.
53. The Jamestown Foundation, 'Zachistki goes bureaucratic', *Chechnya Weekly*, 3/1 (2002): <http://www.jamestown.org/chechnya_weekly/>; accessed May 2008.
54. United Nations Committee against Torture (2002), 'Conclusions and recommendations of the Committee against Torture: Russian Federation', 2002, CAT/C/CR/28/4, section B/f.
55. Council of Europe Committee for the Prevention of Torture, 'Public statement, 2003', 4.
56. Ibid. 5.
57. Human Rights Watch, 'Worse than a war', 17.
58. Council of Europe Committee for the Prevention of Torture, 'Public statement, 2003', 5.
59. Human Rights Watch, 'Worse than a war', 18.
60. Council of Europe Committee for the Prevention of Torture, 'Public statement, 2003', 5.

61. Council of Europe Committee for the Prevention of Torture, 'Public statement, 2007', 11–15.
62. President of Russia Official Web Portal, 'Excerpts from a talk with German and Russian media', 7 April 2002: <http://www.kremlin.ru/eng/text/speeches/2002/04/07/0000_type82915type82917_150406.shtml>; accessed May 2008.
63. Ibid.
64. Amnesty International, 'Russian Federation: Preliminary briefing, 2006', 17.
65. All CPT statements and reports on the Russian Federation are available on the CPT website: <http://www.cpt.coe.int/en/states/rus.htm>; accessed May 2008.

Part IV

Contemporary Problems and Challenges

14

Private Military Personnel as Prisoners of War

Chia Lehnardt

The presence of non-state actors participating in military operations in an environment of armed conflict poses difficult challenges to a legal regime premised on the assumption that states fight wars with their armed forces. Private military companies (PMCs) are no exception. The magnitude of this challenge has grown immensely in the past fifteen years as more military functions are delegated to such companies, resulting in a significant shift both in numbers and range of outsourced activities. This development has been most visible in Iraq, after the US invasion in 2003,[1] but also in other conflicts in Africa, Europe, Asia, and the Americas.[2] Services offered include not only rather mundane activities, for example the building and maintenance of barracks, the feeding of troops, or the transport of supplies, but also more sensitive areas such as intelligence gathering on both the strategic and the tactical level; the training of state armies; and, importantly, activities potentially including the lethal use of force: staffing of checkpoints, protection of personnel and military assets, and sometimes combat functions. Those services are provided to both states and non-state actors, such as transnational corporations, individuals, or non-governmental organizations (NGOs) operating in unstable environments.

In principle, the level of protection international humanitarian law (IHL) offered to individuals in an international armed conflict depends on the classification of the individual as a combatant or as a civilian. As functions previously carried out by the state military pass from the public to the private sphere, PMCs challenge this neat schema, raising questions as to whether IHL is an adequate tool to regulate the environment these companies operate in. It is frequently asserted that it is not. Publicity surrounding specific scandals such as the involvement of PMCs in the abuses in Abu Ghraib or indiscriminate shootings of civilians, and the apparent impunity of the perpetrators, has lent credence to claims that PMCs operate in a legal vacuum, or that they fall through the cracks of existing norms. Others concede that rights and obligations of private military personnel can be determined in one way or another, but suggest the law is no longer sufficient or 'practical'.

Underlying such claims is often a widely shared perception that PMCs are problematic from a moral perspective.[3] By contrast, prisoner of war (POW) status implies a certain legitimacy of those entitled to it. Therefore, the question of whether private military personnel benefit from POW status, and thus from a very high level of protection offered to persons in captivity, is arguably a prism through which can be scrutinized the merit of concerns that IHL is no longer an adequate governing tool of these new actors.

The first section of this chapter examines the question of whether PMC personnel are entitled to POW status under the laws of international armed conflict, followed by a discussion of the consequences following from their status. The legal situation in non-international armed conflicts is much less detailed and thus only briefly explored in the second section. It will be shown that PMC personnel contracted by states and operating in an international armed conflict designated as civilians accompanying the armed forces can in principle benefit from POW status—subject, however, to the condition that they refrain from participating directly in hostilities. In the end, therefore, the key question is how 'direct participation in the hostilities' is interpreted.

PRIVATE MILITARY PERSONNEL IN CAPTIVITY IN AN INTERNATIONAL ARMED CONFLICT

The question of status of private military personnel under IHL arises first and foremost in a situation of an international armed conflict. The following analysis is therefore pertinent to two situations: where a conflict is fought between two states (Common Art. 2(1) of Geneva Conventions I–IV [hereafter GC], Art. 1(3) of Additional Protocol I [hereafter AP]); and in a situation of occupation (Common Art. 2(2) of GC I–IV, Art. 1(3) of AP I).

Status of Private Military Personnel Under IHL

It is a fundamental tenet of IHL that war is a conflict between states, not between individuals.[4] The consequences of this assumption are twofold. First, as states exercise force against the enemy through their organs, only members of armed forces have the right to fight.[5] Second, military operations shall be conducted only against armed forces and military objectives.[6] Accordingly, IHL identifies essentially two categories of persons in international armed conflict, each of which implies a distinct level of protection. Members of armed forces are as combatants entitled to POW status (Art. 44(1) AP I, Art. 4 GC III) and may not be prosecuted for their participation in hostilities unless they violated the laws of war. Generally they shall be released and repatriated after the cessation of active hostilities (Art. 118 GC III). As will be seen, while all combatants are entitled to POW status, not all individuals entitled to POW status are combatants.

Civilians, by contrast, do not have the right to participate directly in hostilities and are protected from attack by enemy forces as long as they refrain from doing so (Art. 51(2), (3) AP I). According to Art. 50(1) AP I, PMC personnel who have not committed hostile acts shall in case of doubt be treated as civilians immune from attack. This immunity, however, may be forfeited if PMC employees take 'a direct part in the hostilities', in which case, lacking combatant privilege, upon capture they may be treated as criminals under the domestic law of the captor.

The proximity of PMC employees to the armed forces, combined with an appearance that is often indistinguishable from their military counterparts, has sometimes led to the assumption that they are combatants and thus entitled to treatment as POWs. Yet, from an international law perspective, there are only two ways of acquiring combatant and POW status, both depending on the affiliation to a party of the conflict.

Art. 4A(1) GC III determines that the following category of persons is entitled to POW status as a consequence of de iure combatant status:

> Members of the armed forces of a Party to the conflict, as well as members of militias or volunteer corps forming part of such armed forces.

whereas subparagraph (2) addresses de facto combatant and POW status:

> Members of other militias and members of other volunteer corps, including those of organized resistance movements, belonging to a Party to the conflict and operating in or outside their own territory, even if this territory is occupied, provided that such militias or volunteer corps, including such organized resistance movements, fulfil the following conditions:
>
> (a) that of being commanded by a person responsible for his subordinates;
> (b) that of having a fixed distinctive sign recognizable at a distance;
> (c) that of carrying arms openly;
> (d) that of conducting their operations in accordance with the laws and customs of war.

Art. 43(1) AP I encompasses both categories of combatants and supplements Art. 4A GC III to the extent applicable:

> The armed forces of a Party to a conflict consist of all organized armed forces, groups and units which are under a command responsible to that Party for the conduct of its subordinates, even if that Party is represented by a government or an authority not recognized by an adverse Party. Such armed forces shall be subject to an internal disciplinary system which, inter alia, shall enforce compliance with the rules of international law applicable in armed conflict.

No doubt exists that private military personnel have combatant status if they are formally incorporated into a state's armed forces. The means of incorporation—conscription, enlistment, or even a contract[7]—is a matter for the internal law of the state, although it must be clear to other states who belongs to the armed forces (s. 43(3) AP I). Typically private military personnel are not contracted into the military; they operate separate from and alongside it. Indeed, integration would be at variance with the very rationale of outsourcing military tasks and is therefore unlikely. Thus, instances where private military personnel can be seen as *de iure* combatants, and as such benefit from POW status, will be rare.

If a formal incorporation into the armed forces is absent, will private military personnel qualify as de facto combatants? First, the individual must belong to an organized group, a condition easily met by employees of PMCs. The second criterion in Art. 4A GC III, that the group must belong to a party to the conflict, requires the company to be associated with a state party. The International Committee of the Red Cross (ICRC) commentary notes that the crucial criterion for determining whether a group belongs to a state is a de facto relationship between the party to the conflict and the group, the threshold question being whether the group—the private military company—is 'fighting on behalf of a party to the conflict'.[8] It is unclear when precisely that is the case. It seems at least not sufficient to actually fight the enemy of the state. In principle, given the historical origin of the provision, this requirement should not be construed too narrowly.[9] Tacit agreement would therefore suffice,[10] and a contract between the state and the company is generally capable of meeting this requirement. More complicated is the case where the company is subcontracted, for instance when company X is under contract with the state and subcontracts company Y to fulfil its obligations. The best view is probably that such a situation would not prevent the subcontractor from acquiring de facto combatant status as long as his activities are integral to contract performance.[11]

It should be noted that, although the wording of the requirements of 'belonging to a Party to the conflict' and 'armed forces of a Party' as such do not exclude contractors who are not contracted to fight but nonetheless armed—for example, security guards—the provisions should be understood more narrowly. It is doubtful whether the provisions granting de facto combatant and POW status were intended to cover persons contracted by a state on the basis of a commercial contract for purposes other than war fighting. Of course, PMCs could not be taken into account when the rules granting POW status were relaxed in 1949 and 1977.[12] Nevertheless, even when provisions are interpreted in a dynamic manner, as is proposed here, the purpose and history of a provision should be taken into account when determining its scope. At the time the Geneva Conventions and the Additional Protocols were drafted, discussions focused on the question whether partisans and other guerrilla forces fighting for their country, but structurally independent of the state military, should be viewed as legitimate and thus entitled to POW status in the case of capture.[13] It would be very difficult to assert that commercial providers contracted to fulfil functions falling short of combat functions have anything in common with such groups[14] and that they should receive the same treatment. Rather, it appears that their inclusion is outside the narrow purpose of these provisions.

Moreover, as stated above, classification as combatant implies not only POW status but also authorization to fight (Art. 43(2) AP I). Where a state has made it clear that a person is not entitled to fight, there is no room for any deviating interpretation of his or her status. This is so because it is the sovereign right of states to organize their armed forces.[15] In most cases, private military personnel are excluded from combatant status on the grounds that they were not contracted for that purpose. If PMC employees are given the status of civilians accompanying the armed forces—as discussed later—or if the contracting state makes it otherwise clear that the company is contracted for 'defensive services' only, these are strong indications that the state did not authorize them to fight. While it is clear that PMC employees in fact authorized to fight—for example, by contract or tacit agreement—can qualify as combatants regardless of the formal status given to them by the contracting state,[16] the fact alone that a PMC employee ultimately does take part in hostilities does not make him or her combatant,[17] but is a separate question pertinent to his or her individual criminal accountability. Consequently, by way of teleological interpretation the provisions granting de facto combatant status should be understood more restrictively. Private military personnel contracted both legally and factually for civilian purposes fall outside their scope[18] and do not benefit from POW status linked to de facto combatant status.

Provided the PMC employee is contracted by a state to fight, he or she must be under the command of a person, civilian or military,[19] responsible for his subordinates and in a position to ensure adherence to the rules applicable in armed conflict.[20] If the employee is subject to a supervisory chain ensuring discipline in a manner similar to military command,[21] it is still questionable whether contractual liability in the case of non-performance of the contract would make the superior 'commanding' PMC employees 'responsible' to the state. It could be argued that this requirement calls for the latter's criminal or civil jurisdiction.[22] In the end, however, given the historical origin of the norms granting de facto combatant and POW status, the requirement should not be understood too restrictively. Furthermore, PMC personnel must have a fixed distinctive sign recognizable from a distance, and carry their arms openly. These requirements have been relaxed in Art. 44(3) AP I. The last criterion is compliance with the laws of war, which does not require each individual to act lawfully in every instance, but does require the company or group to which the PMC employee belongs to respect the law generally.[23] Private military personnel contracted to fight can generally meet these requirements and thus benefit from POW status.

Consequences

In view of the teleological restriction applied to the wording of the provisions granting de facto combatant status, and the numerous conditions to be met if they do apply in principle, most military contractors contracted by states fall into the category of civilians. Moreover, since the crucial factor for determining the primary status of private military personnel is their affiliation to a state that is party to the conflict, the question of combatant and POW status does not arise with regard to all PMC employees working for other non-state actors, such as corporations or NGOs. It is therefore clear that a large number of private military personnel are civilians.

As stated above, in principle, as civilians PMC personnel are not entitled to POW status. Instead they benefit from the protection provided by the Fourth Geneva Convention and the First Additional Protocol or at least, depending on their nationality,[24] by Art. 13 GC IV and Art. 75 AP I.[25] In addition, customary international law establishes the guarantees enshrined in common Art. 3 GC I–IV as a minimum standard to be respected by the detaining power.[26] Where applicable the captor state must also respect the human rights of the PMC employee.

To accommodate potential security concerns the detaining power has various possibilities to restrict the rights of PMC employees who were caught fighting. They may be interned or imprisoned following regular procedures if presumed to have committed a crime (Art. 68 GC IV) or for imperative security reasons (Art. 41–43, 78 GC IV). In that case they shall be released as soon as possible after the close of hostilities (Art. 133(1) GC IV), in any case 'as soon as the reasons which necessitated his internment no longer exists' (Art. 132(1) GC IV). Art. 5 GC IV allows the detaining power to restrict further the rights of 'unprivileged belligerents' in comparison to peaceful civilians. However, in such cases PMC personnel are still entitled to a minimum standard of protection, including humane treatment and the right to a fair and regular trial. In case of doubt as to the status of a captured PMC employee who has taken direct part in hostilities, Art. 5 GC III and Art. 45 AP I create a presumption of his or her entitlement to POW status.

Entitlement to POW Status as Civilians Accompanying the Armed Forces

Art. 4A(4) GC III provides an exception from the principle that only combatants are entitled to POW status, stipulating that persons falling into the following category are POWs:

> Persons who accompany the armed forces without actually being members thereof, such as civilian members of military aircraft crews, war correspondents, supply contractors, members of labour units or of services responsible for the welfare of the armed forces, provided that they have received authorization from the armed forces which they accompany, who shall provide them for that purpose with an identity card similar to the annexed model.

The US Department of Defense[27] and the UK Ministry of Defence[28] consider the PMC personnel working for them as falling within this category. As civilians they are still prohibited from participating directly in hostilities[29] and would lose their immunity from attack if they did. But would such activity also result in loss of POW status? Admittedly, while the majority of persons listed in Art. 4A(4) GC III typically have a non-combat role, the inclusion of 'civilian members of military aircraft crews' seems surprising. Not only are they closer to the heart of a military operation than the other categories mentioned, it would also be difficult to think of a scenario in which a military aircraft, as a legitimate target, would be attacked and civilian members on board spared, making the distinction between persons directly attacked and incidentally killed in this case particularly artificial. Thus, it could be argued that abstention from hostilities is not a prerequisite for POW status pursuant to Art. 4(4) GC III. On closer inspection, however, the better arguments speak for treatment as ordinary civilians in that regard.[30] In particular, it would be surprising if Art. 4A(4) GC III created a category of persons with combatant privileges without having to meet the conditions laid out in Art. 4A(2) or (6) GC III.[31] Consequently, in accordance with UK doctrine,[32] and contrary to the US position,[33] if they take direct part in hostilities, they lose not only immunity from attack but also entitlement to POW status.

Loss of POW Status I: Private Military Personnel Taking Direct Part in Hostilities?

Whether PMC employees designated as civilians accompanying the armed forces can claim the protection afforded by POW status depends therefore on the following question: under what circumstances do they take direct part in hostilities? The clear-cut case of a PMC employee using conventional arms and weapons in order to cause direct harm to the enemy will be rare. With the advent of high-tech weapon systems, however, states have begun to outsource not only their maintenance but also their operation to PMCs.[34] For example, contractors have operated US Global Hawks and Unmanned Aerial Vehicles (UAVs) in Afghanistan and Iraq[35] and have been contracted to provide information on warfare techniques.[36] These activities would clearly result in loss of POW status.

If IHL is to keep pace with changes in warfare, however, the notion of direct participation cannot be limited to actual fighting;[37] that is, to those activities that are the immediate cause of harm inflicted upon a party to the conflict. The vagueness of the term makes it susceptible to an interpretation that takes such changes into account. The flip side is that its ambiguity results in great uncertainty as to what activities short of actual fighting result in a loss of protection. Military operations depend on a multitude of activities from producing weapons and ammunitions or feeding and sheltering troops to the actual launching of the operation. While it is acknowledged that the first two do not amount to direct participation and the last one does, there is disagreement over nearly every function in-between.[38] Particularly problematic are two major sources of business for PMCs: so-called support functions—the provision of intelligence, technical support, and maintenance of military equipment and systems—and the provision of close security. The Conventions and Additional Protocols are silent on whether such activities are prohibited. The only textual clues can be found in Art. 49(1) AP I and Art. 4A(4) GC III.

With regard to security services provided by PMCs, the first provision makes clear that both defensive and offensive actions can constitute an attack, meaning that such qualification is irrelevant for the purposes of determining what constitutes direct participation. If, however, PMC personnel engage in conduct covered by the right to individual self-defence or help to others, they make use of a right they have regardless of status. The exercise of these rights therefore does not constitute 'direct participation'.[39] They presuppose an unlawful attack, the existence of which is determined by reference to IHL. The crucial distinction to be made here is based on the character of the guarded object. As IHL permits the targeting of military objects, including combatants (Art. 48(1) AP I), the use of force against military operations attacking such targets would constitute direct participation. Accordingly, civilians defending military objects are precluded from relying on the right to self-defence or defence of others as long as there is a nexus between the hostile act and the armed conflict. With regard to the guarding of civilian objects or civilians, the line is between use of force that is necessary for the purposes of self-defence on the one hand and what goes beyond the necessary on the other. This line can be difficult to establish, particularly in an environment of armed conflict.

The second textual hint can be found in the Third Geneva Convention. As Art. 50(1) AP I stipulates that anyone not falling under Art. 4A(1), (2), (3), and (6) GC III is a civilian, and as civilians are not entitled to fight, the persons mentioned in the remaining paragraphs of Art. 4A GC III typically do not engage in fighting.[40] The list of activities provided for in Art. 4A(4) GC III is not exhaustive. The ICRC commentary notes, somewhat unhelpfully, that the provision could also cover 'other categories of persons or services who might be called upon, in similar conditions, to follow the armed forces'.[41] Instructions issued by the US Department of Defense on the use of civilians accompanying the armed forces prohibit the hiring of contractors for 'unique military functions'.[42] Such references, however, beg the question.[43]

In an attempt to provide an abstract definition, the ICRC characterizes direct participation as 'acts of war which are intended by their nature or their purpose to hit specifically the personnel and the *materiel* of the armed forces of the adverse Party'.[44] Taken by itself, this definition is rather broad. Thus, in addition there must be 'a direct causal relationship between the activity engaged in and the harm done to the enemy at the time and the place where the activity takes place'.[45] The crucial term 'direct' leaves, of course, considerable room for different interpretations. In view of the complexity of military operations it should be understood not only to cover those acts inflicting immediate harm on their own but also acts that, only in conjunction with other acts, hit the adverse party.[46] Thus, if PMC personnel carry out an activity which is an indispensable part of a military operation causing direct harm they take a direct part in hostilities.[47] This would include technical support to the extent that advice is provided during ongoing operations in order to make a weapon system operable or more effective.[48] Similarly, while the collection and provision of intelligence on a strategic level merely contributes to the war effort, on the tactical level, where information provided is directly relied upon to direct attacks, it becomes an indispensable requirement for launching an operation.[49] In all these cases the PMC employees involved would lose their POW status and be treated like civilians who were caught fighting.[50]

Loss of POW Status II: Private Military Personnel Taking Direct Part in Hostilities for Financial Gain—Mercenaries?

The fact that private military personnel provide services involving the use of force in exchange for financial compensation has prompted claims that they are 'modern day mercenaries'.[51] Yet from an international law perspective, it is very unlikely that they fall under the definition of a mercenary, as its scope is extremely narrowly drawn. Art. 47(2) AP I lists no less than six cumulative conditions that must be met for someone to be considered a mercenary:

A mercenary is any person who

(a) is specially recruited locally or abroad in order to fight in an armed conflict;

(b) does, in fact, take a direct part in the hostilities;

(c) is motivated to take part in the hostilities essentially by the desire for private gain and, in fact, is promised, by or on behalf of a party to the conflict, material compensation substantially in excess of that promised or paid to combatants of similar ranks and functions in the armed forces of that party;

(d) is neither a national of a Party to the conflict nor a resident of territory controlled by a Party to the conflict;

(e) is not a member of the armed forces of a party to the conflict; and

(f) has not been sent by a state which is not a party to the conflict on official duty as a member of its armed forces.

Each of the criteria can be problematic. For example, although PMC personnel might ultimately take direct part in hostilities, most contractors are not recruited specifically for that purpose,[52] which would exclude them from the scope of the provision by virtue of condition (a). Moreover, proving someone fights for financial gain, in accordance with due process standards, can be very difficult. Apart from these technical flaws that render the provision unworkable,[53] however, it is hard to see as a matter of principle why a PMC employee from state A, which is not a party to the conflict, should be treated differently from a colleague contracted for the same activity by state B, which is, provided both employees fight for money. The definition excludes the latter from its scope by virtue of condition (d). More importantly, however, is that the provision is, in terms of legal consequences, not only less harsh than one would expect, but also redundant. Mercenaries are live ordinary civilians not authorized to participate in hostilities not entitled to POW status, but they may be treated as such if the captor state wishes to do so (Art. 47(1) AP I).

PRIVATE MILITARY PERSONNEL IN CAPTIVITY IN NON-INTERNATIONAL ARMED CONFLICTS

The IHL regime applicable in a non-international armed conflict—including the intervention of a state in a conflict in another state with the latter's consent[54]—is much less detailed than the law governing international armed conflicts, leaving many questions to domestic law. In particular, it is silent on the question of whether a person is a combatant or otherwise entitled to fight. Thus, although the Colombian FARC (*Fuerzas Armadas Revolucionarias de Colombia*—Revolutionary Armed Forces of Colombia) refers to its hostages, including the three contractors freed in July 2008, as prisoners of war,[55] as a matter of law the question of POW status does not arise in non-international armed conflicts unless the parties thereto agree otherwise. In the absence of such agreement, or another agreement granting PMC employees immunity from domestic jurisdiction, private military personnel are subject to the domestic law of the detention state. The guarantees enshrined in common Art. 3 GC I-IV and, to the extent applicable, Art. 4 AP II, including the prohibition of murder, torture, as well as inhuman and degrading treatment, provide a minimum standard of protection to captured PMC employees who do not take part in hostilities or have ceased to take part in hostilities. As for a conflict between a state and non-state actors that goes beyond that state's territory, the US Supreme Court has held that at least common Art. 3 GC I–IV affords some minimum protection for such situations as well.[56] Both states and non-state actors, such as insurgent or rebel groups fighting the government, are subject to these principles. In addition, PMC employees captured by a state benefit from protection provided by human rights law to the extent it is applicable, at least from those which may not be suspended even in times of war.[57]

REINTERPRETATION, RETHINKING, OR REVISION OF THE CATEGORY OF COMBATANTS?

The earlier analysis has shown that PMC personnel hired by states can not only be entitled to POW status but simultaneously, as civilians, also be protected from attack. Some commentators have come to the conclusion that their protection as civilians is inadequate and that they should be considered combatants, with the consequence that they enjoy POW status regardless of activity and are subject to attack at all times. For example, it is sometimes argued that combatant status should be determined on the basis of actual activity: anyone carrying out combat functions should be considered a combatant,[58] or that affording PMC employees who are voluntarily close to the battle space the same level of protection against attack as ordinary civilians is unrealistic and in any case not deserved.[59] Such arguments are based on the observation that private military personnel are crucial to the success of a military operation, and that they are 'civilians in name and garb only'.[60]

Although it is not always clear whether these authors argue for a rereading of existing categories of IHL or for their complete revision, it is important to bear in mind that while there are considerable uncertainties regarding the interpretation of key notions of the laws of war, in the case of armed conflict the application of

IHL is not a matter of choice. The factual circumstances on which combatant and POW status can be based are listed in Art. 4A(2) GC III, Art. 43(1) AP I. To the extent that these provisions are deemed applicable in principle to private military personnel, it is doubtful, in the absence of additional arguments, how a determination of that status could be based on an additional and entirely different criterion. Second, the right to fight follows from combatant status. To claim that combatant status should be based on actual fighting is a circular argument and neglects the clear wording of Art. 43(2) AP I and Art. 51(3) AP I. According to these provisions, while civilians do not have the right to take direct part in hostilities, the consequence of their doing so is not a change in their status, but the temporary loss of certain protections civilians enjoy.[61] The fact that they can no longer claim non-combatant immunity in such cases also demonstrates that concerns that PMC personnel, as 'dangerous' individuals, are unduly protected and unwarranted: when they do become dangerous by participating directly in the fighting, they lose protection from attack and cannot claim POW status if captured.

CONCLUSION

Private military personnel are, as commercial providers of military services, frequently perceived as illegitimate actors in armed conflict. It might therefore appear counter-intuitive to afford them benefits of both combatant and civilian status—the entitlement to POW status and protection from attack. Furthermore, while it is not wholly unlikely that PMC personnel, if captured in an international conflict, will in fact be denied POW status on the ground that they are mercenaries, the legal definition of a mercenary is much more narrow than the generic use of that term. At first glance these findings seem to imply that there is a discord between the general rejection of the idea of private force on the one hand and the law on the other. On closer inspection, however, they rather suggest an inconsistency between the perception of private military personnel as 'fighters' in a war and a narrow interpretation of the notion of 'direct participation'. As has been shown, whether PMC personnel enjoy both POW status and protection from attack depends on their refraining from participating directly in the conflict: their protection under IHL comes with restrictions on the range of activities they can engage in. The particular problem with regard to private military personnel is that a great number are contracted for functions that are not those of the typical civilian as envisaged when the Geneva Conventions and Additional Protocols were drafted. This, however, is not a result of an inherent deficiency of the applicable law.

The lack of terminological precision in the Geneva Conventions and the Additional Protocols, and the resulting ambiguity of applicable provisions, have often been criticized. Yet the open wording of key provisions holds out the possibility to interpret the law applicable in armed conflict in a manner that takes changes in warfare into account. In the past, IHL has been responsive to such developments.[62] Its effectiveness and ability to regulate the conduct of war adequately despite the emergence of private contractors as significant military actors crucially depends on state practice, which ultimately determines how applicable norms are interpreted.[63] It is likely that state practice with regard to PMCs will differ. Those states relying extensively on private military contractors have an interest in interpreting the term 'direct participation' rather narrowly, while states facing civilians carrying out functions integral to military operations are likely to advocate a lower threshold.

Either way it is important to bear in mind that the questions discussed in this chapter arise from a general trend that increasingly sees non-state actors involved in armed conflict. It is clear, therefore, that any interpretation of IHL as applied to the PMC context has ramifications beyond the issue at hand. Conversely, efforts to tailor the laws of war to perceived needs of fighting terrorism cannot be made in isolation from the discussion on PMCs. The establishment of double standards would severely damage the legitimacy and acceptance of IHL as a legal regime providing a neutral framework for the conduct of hostilities. Perhaps a starting point for a consistent approach is to accept also in the commercial private military context that the fewer civilians present in the theatre, the lesser will be the ambiguities that arise with regard to their status and protection. There is a strong case for leaving essential military functions to the armed forces. This general approach would strengthen the prescriptive effect of the principle of distinction, which serves the protection of civilians and is a cardinal principle of humanitarian law.

NOTES

Many thanks to Jeannine Drohla, Georg Nolte, Christian Schaller, Sibylle Scheipers, and participants at the conference on 'Prisoners in War' in Oxford in December 2007 for helpful discussions and comments on a previous draft.

1. Jennifer K. Elsea, Moshe Schwartz, and Kennon H. Nakamura 'Private security con-tractors in Iraq: background, legal status, and other issues' (25 August 2008), <http://www.fas.org/sgp/crs/natsec/RL32419.pdf>.

2. See overview in Peter W. Singer, *Corporate warriors: The rise of the privatized military industry* (Ithaca, NY: Cornell University Press, 2003), 9–15, 93.

3. Sarah Percy, 'Morality and regulation', in Simon Chesterman and Chia Lehnardt (eds.), *From mercenaries to market: The rise and regulation of private military companies* (Oxford: Oxford University Press, 2007), 11.

4. See Christopher Greenwood, 'Historical development and legal basis', in Dieter Fleck (ed.), *The handbook of humanitarian law in armed conflict* (2nd edn.; Oxford: Oxford University Press, 2008), 20.

5. Art. 43(2) AP I.

6. Art. 51(2) AP I.

7. For an opposite view see Christian Schaller, 'Private security and military companies under the international law of armed conflict', in Thomas Jäger and Gerhard Kümmel (eds.), *Private military and security companies: Chances, problems, pitfalls and prospects* (Wiesbaden: VS Verlag, 2007), 345, 347.

8. Jean Pictet (ed.), *Geneva Convention relative to the treatment of prisoners of war* [vol. III of *The Geneva Conventions of 12 August 1949: Commentary*] (Geneva, International Committee of the Red Cross, 1952–60) [hereafter *Commentary GC III*], 57; Michael Bothe, Karl Josef Partsch, and Waldemar A. Solf, *New rules for victims of armed conflict: Commentary on the two 1977 protocols additional to the Geneva Conventions of 1949* (The Hague: Martinus Nijhoff Publishers, 1982), 234.

9. Yet the ICTY Appeals Chamber found that this criterion required control over the individual by a party to the conflict, interpreting the notion of control by reference to the principles of state responsibility; *Prosecutor v. Tadic*, IT-94–1, judgement, 15 July 1999, paras. 95.

10. Pictet, *Commentary GC III*, 57.

11. Michael Schmitt, 'Humanitarian law and direct participation in hostilities by private contractors or civilian employees', *Chicago Journal of International Law*, 5/2 (2004–5), 527.

12. Schmitt, 'Humanitarian law and direct participation', 531.

13. Pictet, *Commentary GC III*, 52–6; Bothe, Partsch, and Solf, *New rules for victims*, 234.

14. Louise Doswald-Beck, 'Private military companies under international humanitarian law', in Chesterman and Lehnardt, *From mercenaries to market*, 137.

15. Bothe, Partsch, and Solf, *New rules for victims*, 232; Schaller, 'Private security and military companies', 348.

16. Knut Ipsen, 'Combatant and non-combatants', in Fleck, *The handbook of humanitarian law*, 82.

17. See also *infra* text accompanying note 62.

18. See Emanuela-Chiara Gillard, 'Business goes to war: private military/security companies and international humanitarian law', *International Review of the Red Cross*, 88/863 (2006), 534–5; Schmitt, 'Humanitarian law and direct participation', 527.

19. Pictet, *Commentary GC III*, 59.

20. See Art. 43(1) AP I; Pictet, *Commentary GC III*, 59.

21. Schmitt, 'Humanitarian law and direct participation', 525.

22. Doswald-Beck, 'Private military companies', 121.

23. Schmitt, 'Humanitarian law and direct participation', 531.

24. Art. 4 GC IV.

25. See Art. 45(3) AP I, which is considered customary international law; Jean-Marie Henckaerts and Louise Doswald-Beck (eds.), *Customary international humanitarian law* (Cambridge: Cambridge University Press, 2005), 299; European Commission for Democracy through Law [Venice Commission], 'Opinion on the possible need for further development of the Geneva Conventions', Opinion no. 245/2003, para. 40.

26. ICJ, case concerning military and paramilitary activities in and against Nicaragua (*Nicaragua v. United States*) (Merits), ICJ Reports 1986, 14, at 114; Yoram Dinstein, *The conduct of hostilities under the law of international armed conflict* (Cambridge: Cambridge University Press, 2004), 32.

27. US Joint Chiefs of Staff, 4–0 Doctrine for Logistics Support of Joint Operations, Apr 6 2000, V-6, <www.dtic.mil/doctrine/jel/new_pubs/jp4_0.pdf>; US Department of Defense, Instruction No. 3,020.41, Oct. 3 2005), para. 6.1.1, <http://www.dtic.mil/whs/directives/corres/html/302041.htm>.

28. Gillard, 'Business goes to war', 539.
29. Art. 50 (1), Art. 51 (3), 43 (2) AP I.
30. Ipsen, 'Combatants and non-combatants', 107; Doswald-Beck, 'Private military companies', 124; Gillard, 'Business goes to war', 538; ICRC/Asser Institute, 'Report on the third expert meeting on the notion of direct participation in hostilities', October 2005, 81; J. Ricou Heaton, 'Civilians at war: Reexamining the status of civilians accompanying the armed forces', *Air Force Law Review*, 57 (2005), 174.
31. University Centre for International Humanitarian Law, 'Expert meeting on private military contractors: status and state responsibility for their actions', Geneva, 2005, 15.
32. UK Ministry of Defence, *The manual of the law of armed conflict* (Oxford: Oxford University Press, 2004), para. 4.3.7.
33. US Department of Defense, Instruction No. 1,100.22 [updated on April 6 2007], note 19.
34. See US General Accounting Office (GAO), 'Military operations: contractors provide vital services to deployed forces but are not adequately addressed in DoD plans', GAP-03–695, 2003, 8–9, 16.
35. Heaton, 'Civilians at war', 190.
36. Dawn S. Onley, 'Air Force picks information warfare contractors', *Government Computer News* (28 August 2003) [online article], <www.gvn.com>.
37. Yves Sandoz, Christophe Swinarski, and Bruno Zimmermann (eds.), *Commentary to the Additional Protocols of 8 June 1977 to the Geneva Conventions of 12 August 1949* (Geneva: International Committee of the Red Cross, 1987) [hereafter *Commentary AP I*], 516, 619.
38. Nilz Melzer, *Targeted killing in international law* (Oxford: Oxford University Press, 2008), 334–44; ICRC/Asser Institute, 'Report on the third expert meeting'; Henckaerts and Doswald-Beck, *Customary international humanitarian law*, 23.
39. Melzer, *Targeted killing*, 343.
40. Schmitt, 'Humanitarian law and direct participation', 532.
41. Pictet, *Commentary GC III*, 64. Art. 3 of the Regulations Respecting the Laws and Customs of War on Land, Annexed to Hague Convention (II) of 1899 and Hague Convention (IV) of 1907 reads: 'Individuals who follow an army without directly belonging to it, such as newspaper correspondents and reporters, sutlers and contractors, who fall into the enemy's hand and whom the latter thinks expedient to detain, are entitled to be treated as prisoners of war, provided they are in possession of a certificate from the military authorities of the army which they were accompanying.'
42. DoD Instruction 3020.41, para. 6.3.5.
43. DoD Instruction 3020.41 explicitly permits contractor personnel to support contingency operations through the 'indirect participation in military operations, such as by providing communications support, transporting munitions and other supplies, performing maintenance functions for military equipment, providing security services . . . and logistic services such as billeting, messing, etc.' DoD Instruction 3020.41, para. 6.1.1.
44. Sandoz et al., *Commentary AP I*, 516. See also ICRC, Interpretive guidance on the notion of direct participation in hostilities under international humanitarian law.
45. Sandoz et al., *Commentary AP I*, 516.; similarly Hans-Peter Gasser, 'Protection of the civilian population', in Fleck (ed.), *The handbook of humanitarian law*, 262; and Israeli Supreme Court, *The Public Committee against Torture in Israel et al. v. Government of Israel*, Judgement, 11 December 2005, HCJ 769/02, para. 35.
46. Melzer, *Targeted killing*, 343.
47. Michael E. Guillory, 'Civilianizing the force: Is the United States crossing the rubicon?', *Air Force Law Review*, 51 (2001), 134. For an opposite view see Lisa L. Turner and Lynn G. Norton, 'Civilians at the tip of the spear', *Air Force Law Review*, 51 (2001), 28.

48. Guillory, 'Civilianizing the force', 128.
49. Gasser, 'Protection of the civilian population', 262; W. Hays Parks, 'Air war and the law of war', *Air Force Law Review*, 32 (1990), 134.
50. See *supra* text accompanying notes 33, 34.
51. See, for example, Abdel-Fatau Musah and J. Kayode Fazemi (eds.), *Mercenaries: An African security dilemma* (London: Pluto Press, 2000).
52. See *supra* at 8–9.
53. Francoise J. Hampson, 'Mercenaries: Diagnosis before prescription', *Netherlands Year-book of International Law*, 22 (1991), 31. Another commentator has stated that 'any mercenary who cannot exclude himself from this definition deserves to be shot—and his lawyer with him!' Geoffrey Best, *Humanity in warfare: The modern history of the international law of armed conflicts* (London: Weidenfeld and Nicolson, 1980), 328.
54. The characterization of a particular conflict at a particular point of time can be inordinately difficult, as the examples of Iraq and Afghanistan—two main sites of PMC operations—illustrate.
55. Simon Romero, 'Colombian guerrilla leader reported dead', *New York Times* (25 May 2008).
56. US Supreme Court, *Hamdan v. Rumsfeld*, judgment, June 29 2006, 126 S.Ct. at 2795 (2006). While holding that such conflicts are governed by common Art. 3 GC I–IV, the Court left their classification open; Eran Shamir-Borer, 'Revisiting Hamdan v. Rumsfeld's analysis of the laws of armed conflict', *Emory International Law Review*, 21 (2007), 601.
57. Art. 4 International Covenant on Political and Civil Rights; Art. 15 European Convention on Human Rights; Art. 27 American Convention on Human Rights.
58. ICRC/Asser Institute, 'Report on the third expert meeting', 77; Miriam Saage-Maass and Sebastian Weber, '"Wer sich in Gefahr begibt, kommt darin um..."—zum Einsatz privater Sicherheits- und Militärfirmen in bewaffneten Konflikten', *Humanitäres Völkerrecht—Informationsschriften* (2007), 174, arguing that 'More practical is a wider interpretation of the notion of combatant.... If private military personnel carry their arms openly or wear uniforms, they should be treated as combatants until the opposite has been proven' [author's translation]; Daphne Richemond-Barak, 'Private military contractors and combatancy status under international humanitarian law', conference paper, Jerusalem, 1–3 June 2008, 16; <http://law.huji.ac.il/upload/Richmond_Barak_Private_Military_Contractors.pdf>.
59. Saage-Maass and Weber, 'Wer sich in Gefahr begibt', 173–5; Richemond, 'Private military contractors', 12, 13.
60. Parks, 'Air war', 32.
61. Israeli Supreme Court, *The Public Committee against Torture in Israel et al. v. Government of Israel*, para. 31.
62. Michael Schmitt, 'The principle of discrimination in 21st century warfare', *Yale Human Rights and Development Law Journal*, 2 (1999), 145–6; Adam Roberts, 'The law of war in the war on terror', *Israel Yearbook on Human Rights*, 32 (2003), 240.
63. See also the 'Montreux Document on Pertinent International Legal Obligations and Good Practices for States Related to Operations of Private Military and Security Companies During Armed Conflict', 17 September 2008, which aims, *inter alia*, at recalling 'certain existing international legal obligations of States regarding private military and security companies'; <http://www.icrc.org/web/eng/siteeng0.nsf/htmlall/montreux-document-170908/$FILE/Montreux-Document.pdf>.

15

Child Prisoners in War

Matthew Happold

Children frequently participate in contemporary armed conflicts. At present, some 250,000 children[1] are reported to be serving as soldiers in over thirty 'situations of concern' worldwide.[2] And although children have always taken part in armed conflict, in recent years the roles which they have been called upon to play have changed. Children continue to be used where their size and agility is useful, but increasingly they participate in hostilities as combatants. A number of states' armed forces recruit from their national school-leaving age when it is below eighteen, but the most egregious recent uses of children to take part in hostilities have been by non-state actors. To take a particularly current example, insurgents in Afghanistan and Iraq have used children as suicide bombers.[3]

In recent years children's recruitment and use to participate in hostilities have become a matter of increasing international concern.[4] Yet the rules specifically governing their participation, including those regulating their treatment when captured by an adverse party to a conflict, are sparse. This might be thought surprising, considering, in particular, the detailed codes regulating the treatment of prisoners of war and civilian detainees in the Third and Fourth Geneva Conventions. The best explanation for this may be found in Protocol I Additional to the 1949 Geneva Conventions, which in Article 77 refers to captured child soldiers as 'exceptional cases' because the article substantially restrics the recruitment of children. A disinclination to face the fact that, despite the increasingly stringent legal prohibitions governing children's recruitment into armed forces and groups, they continue to take part in hostilities may consequently lie behind the paucity of legal rules governing their participation. Moreover, the fact that most uses of child soldiers takes place in non-traditional armed conflicts by non-state actors, can give rise to difficulties regarding the rules applicable to such conflicts and the legal status of child combatants within them. This chapter will analyse the current legal regulation of the treatment of child prisoners in war, before examining how child soldiers have in practice been treated in the ongoing 'global war against terror'. It should be noted, however, that the detention of children because of their associations (or alleged associations) with armed groups in violation of the applicable international standards is a more general problem, with recent instances reported in Burundi, Colombia, the Democratic Republic of Congo, Iraq, Israel, Myanmar, and the Philippines.[5]

INTERNATIONAL LAW AND CHILD PRISONERS IN WAR

A patchwork of treaties now exists restricting the recruitment of children by armed forces and groups, and their use to participate in hostilities: the two Protocols Additional to the 1949 Geneva Conventions,[6] the Convention on the Rights of the Child,[7] the African Charter on the Rights and Welfare of the Child,[8] ILO Convention 182 on the Worst Forms of Child Labour,[9] and the Optional Protocol to the Convention on the Rights of the Child on the Involvement of Children in Armed Conflict.[10] These treaties move from requiring state parties to take all feasible measures to prevent children under fifteen from participating directly in hostilities (including by refraining from recruiting them into their armed forces),[11] to prohibiting all forcible or compulsory recruitment of children;[12] they do so by raising the minimum age at which children can volunteer for military service to sixteen;[13] prohibiting the recruitment and use of child soldiers by armed opposition groups;[14] requiring state parties to take all feasible measures to ensure that child volunteers in their armed forces do not take a direct part in hostilities;[15] and even, in one case, prohibiting all recruitment and use of child soldiers.[16] In consequence, a state's obligations regarding children's involvement in armed conflict can vary considerably according to which treaties it is party to.

However, because the rules are not directed at the children themselves, but at their recruiters, child combatants, providing they fulfil the relevant criteria, benefit from the same protections as other similarly situated persons. Their age alone does not make them 'unlawful combatants'.[17] Child soldiers who are members of the armed forces party to an international armed conflict are combatants entitled to participate directly in hostilities.[18] They benefit from 'combatant privilege' and cannot be punished for bearing arms and taking part in hostilities, providing, of course, that their actions are in accordance with international humanitarian law. If captured, they are entitled to prisoner of war (POW) status and all the protections set out in the Third Geneva Convention (hereafter GC III).[19] GC III, however, says nothing about child POWs. The only provisions in the 1949 Geneva Conventions specifically dealing with children appear in the Fourth Geneva Convention (hereafter GC IV) on the protection of civilians in wartime.[20] The first international humanitarian law provisions regulating children's participation in hostilities and the consequences thereof were in the two 1977 Protocols Additional to the 1949 Geneva Conventions (hereafter AP I and AP II).[21]

AP I includes several provisions covering children involved in international armed conflicts. Article 77 provides that:

> 1. Children shall be the object of special respect and shall be protected against any form of indecent assault. The Parties to the conflict shall provide them with the care and aid they require, whether because of their age or for any other reason.
>
> 2. [. . .]

3. If in exceptional cases, despite the provisions of paragraph 2, children who have not attained the age of 15 years take a direct part in hostilities and fall into the power of an adverse Party, they shall continue to benefit from the special protection accorded by this Article, whether or not they are prisoners of war.

4. If arrested, detained or interned for reasons related to the armed conflict, children shall be held in quarters separate from the quarters of adults, except when families are accommodated as family units as provided in Article 75, paragraph 5.

5. [...]

Article 77(1), first sentence, complements Article 76(1) AP I, which declares that women are the object of special respect. The two provisions filled what was perceived as a lacuna in Article 16 GC IV, in which the wounded and sick, the infirm, and expectant mothers, but not women and children per se, were declared to be objects of 'particular protection and respect', but seems only to import a general obligation that children will be treated with particular consideration in all circumstances. Article 77(1), however, also requires that children be protected against 'any form of indecent assault'. In the context of children's detention or internment, this would oblige the party holding the children to protect them from indecent assault not only from its own forces but also from the children's own comrades, both adults and children, and anyone else who might wish to cause them such harm. At a minimum, systems to deter such behaviour should be put in place, probably including some segregation of children and adults on the one hand, and boys and girls on the other (this would also mesh with the obligation set out in Article 77(4) to hold children arrested, detained, or interned for reasons relating to an armed conflict in quarters separate from those of adults), as well as mechanisms for the investigation, prosecution, and punishment of offenders. As for the obligation to provide the aid and care children require in Article 77(1), second sentence, at the least this would appear to require that child detainees and internees be provided with medical attention directed towards their particular needs, with appropriate foodstuffs, and with schooling.[22] Article 77(3) deals specifically with the detention and internment of child soldiers. It makes clear that child soldiers continue to benefit from the protections set out elsewhere in Article 77, regardless of whether their recruitment or use to participate in hostilities was illegal or not. It also makes explicit that child soldiers can be POWs. Finally, Article 77(5) states that the death penalty cannot be executed on persons for crimes related to an international armed committed before the perpetrator's eighteenth birthday. However, there are no other provisions in the Protocol regarding the prosecution and punishment of child offenders.

AP II, covering non-international armed conflicts above a certain degree of intensity, goes into less detail than AP I. Article 4(3) provides that children 'shall be provided with the care and aid they require', which is specifically said to include education. Article 4(3)(d) mirrors Article 77(3) AP I by stating that the special protection provided by the Article shall remain applicable to children under fifteen who take a direct part in hostilities and are captured. Article 5(2)(a) provides that women detained or interned for reasons related to any internal armed conflict shall be accommodated separately from men, but, unlike AP I, there is no provision requiring child detainees or internees to be accommodated separately from adults. However, Article 37(c) of the Convention on the Rights of the Child (hereafter CRC) does impose such a requirement 'unless it is in the child's best interest', and as no party to AP II is not also a party to the CRC, the omission, even if deliberate, would appear to be immaterial. Finally, Article 6(4) prohibits the pronouncement of the death penalty for offences related to an internal armed conflict on persons who were under eighteen years of age at the time of the offence but, as with AP I, there are no other provisions dealing with the prosecution and punishment of child offenders.

As regards the recruitment and use of child soldiers, the Convention on the Rights of the Child largely mirrors AP I. However, although the Convention says nothing specific about how child soldiers should be treated when detained, it has much to say about the treatment of child detainees generally.[23] State parties must treat every child deprived of liberty 'with humanity and respect for the dignity of the human person, and in a manner which takes into account the needs of persons of his or her age'.[24] Other articles of the CRC, such on those regarding the child's right to the highest attainable standard of health, to an adequate standard of living and to education,[25] and the obligations incumbent on state parties to protect children from violence, sexual abuse, and exploitation,[26] would seem to add detail to the rather general provisions in the two APs. Article 37(b) of the Convention, however, provides that: 'The detention or imprisonment of a child . . . shall be used only as a measure of last resort and for the shortest appropriate period of time.' The primary purpose of the detention of POWs or the internment of civilians during an armed conflict or belligerent occupation is incapacitation. POWs can be held for the duration of the conflict, as they are being held to prevent them rejoining the fighting. Similarly, civilian internees can be held for long as necessary for security reasons. In neither case is their confinement punitive in purpose, but it is the detaining power's interests that are paramount in determining its duration. The animating principle of the CRC, on the other hand, is the best interest of the child.[27]

It can consequently be concluded that international law mandates a number of protections for child prisoners in war. However, the relevant provisions are scattered across a number of treaties. This might not, of itself, be a problem, as all but two states in the world are parties to the CRC, which might be seen as setting minimum standards. However, reconciling what international humanitarian law permits and what the CRC mandates is not always unproblematic. Space does not permit a full examination of the extent to which international human rights law applies in situations of armed conflict. However, a few brief points can be made.

First, there seems no objection to applying the CRC to interpret the provisions in AP I and AP II dealing with children detained or interned for reasons relating to an armed conflict[28] or to regulate issues not covered by international humanitarian law. The issue is whether the CRC has anything to say about the legality of their detention and whether it imports additional procedural rights.[29] A pragmatic way to manage this issue might be to seek to utilize mechanisms already in existence in international humanitarian law. For example, under Article 109 of GC III, parties to a conflict remain free to conclude agreements for the repatriation of POWs prior to the cessation of hostilities or for their internment in some willing neutral state. Similarly, Article 78 of GC IV speaks of internment or 'assigned residence', which might be more appropriate in certain circumstances and/or be used to permit earlier release of child internees. However, there is little sign that such options have been considered.

The issue cannot be avoided, however, as regards the Optional Protocol to the Convention on the Rights of the Child (hereafter OP). There is no doubt that the OP applies in situations of armed conflict. Moreover, Article 6(3) of the OP provides that:

> States parties shall take all feasible measures to ensure that persons within their jurisdiction recruited or used in hostilities contrary to the present Protocol are demobilized or otherwise released from service. States parties shall, when necessary, accord to such persons all appropriate assistance for their physical and psychological recovery and their social reintegration.

Article 6(3) seems to be modelled on Article 39 of the CRC, which requires state parties to that Convention to 'take all appropriate measures to promote physical and psychological recovery and social reintegration' of child victims of various forms of abuse and ill-treatment. The question is whether it applies to illegally recruited child soldiers[30] serving in the forces of an adverse party to a conflict who have fallen into the hands of a State party to the OP. To put it another way: are such persons within the State's 'jurisdiction'? It might be thought that they are. Certainly the term, as used in other human rights treaties, has been interpreted to include persons in a state's custody, even when held outside its territory.[31] If this interpretation is correct, it would seem to impose considerable positive obligations on parties to the OP and raise large questions as to circumstances in which illegally recruited child soldiers can be detained lawfully. There is, however, little state practice of applying the provision.

Before moving to consider the question of compliance, however, one final issue needs to be examined: whether, and, if so, in what circumstances, can child soldiers be prosecuted and punished for their activities? Child soldiers are most often used in internal armed conflicts, where there is no concept of lawful combatancy granting immunity from prosecution for actions relating to the conflict, or in various roles that render them 'unlawful combatants'. In some cases, children are recruited specifically because their lack of maturity and consequent suggestibility makes them more easily persuaded or coerced into committing atrocities.[32] A number of cases have been reported when child soldiers have been prosecuted under national law for their actions in armed conflicts[33] and prosecutions for crimes under international law are not unknown either.[34]

International law lays down no minimum age of criminal responsibility. The APs are silent on the issue, and although the CRC requires that states establish a minimum age of criminal responsibility (rather than determining legal responsibility on an individual basis by reference to the accused's personal characteristics), it does not purport to tell them what that age should be.[35] Indeed, the Committee on the Rights of the Child has gone no further than to state that any minimum age of criminal responsibility below the age of twelve is not 'internationally acceptable'.[36] What does seem clear, however, is that if tried for offences related to an armed conflict, children are entitled to both the protections provided by international humanitarian law and those set out in the CRC. For example, when drafting the Statute of the Special Court for Sierra Leone, the only international criminal tribunal whose statute explicitly envisages trying persons for crimes committed whilst they were children, the Secretary General of the United Nations, the Security Council, and the Government of Sierra Leone all agreed that defendants should be treated 'in accordance with human rights standards, including the rights of the child'.[37] Indeed, contemporary international opinion seems largely to have set its face against prosecutions of child soldiers.[38] It seems inconsistent with seeing child soldiers as victims and difficult to reconcile with the increasing emphasis on their rehabilitation and reintegration into society.[39] Thus, although the Special Court's Statute permits the prosecution of persons for crimes committed when aged over fifteen, and child soldiers committed numerous atrocities in the conflict in Sierra Leone, early in his tenure the Court's Prosecutor stated that as a matter of policy he did not intend to indict any person for crimes committed when a child.[40]

CHILD PRISONERS IN THE 'WAR AGAINST TERROR'

US actions in its 'war against terror' starkly illustrate the legal problems discussed earlier. To begin with, how the conflict is to be categorized is disputed. The original position of the US administration was that its struggle against al-Qaeda was an international armed conflict, but that as it was not a conflict between states it was not regulated by the GCs.[41] Detainees captured in the struggle were categorized as 'unlawful combatants' entitled to neither the protections accorded to POWs nor to civilians. Subsequently, in *Hamdan v. Rumsfeld*[42] the US Supreme Court held that, at a minimum, Common Article 3 applied to the conflict. The US Administration has since adopted this characterization,[43] although Common Article 3 provides that it applies when the conflict occurs 'in the territory of one of the High Contracting Parties', which does not seem accurately to describe the 'global war against terror' (although it might describe some aspects of it). Adding even more uncertainty, at least with regard to the treatment of child prisoners, is the fact that the United States is a party to neither the two APs, nor to the CRC, although it is a party to the OP and ILO Convention 182.

A number of child soldiers fell into US hands during Operation Enduring Freedom in Afghanistan in 2001–2 and were transferred to its detention camp at Guantanamo Bay. In a letter dated 3 September 2004 to Judge Green, Senior US District Judge for the DC Circuit, written in response to a request from the Judge for information concerning minors at Guantanamo and any special accommodations accorded them, Thomas R. Lee, Deputy Assistant Attorney General, wrote:

> The law of armed conflict does not define with precision the age at which a combatant is considered a child or an adult. Generally accepted norms in the field, including the Geneva Conventions and other international protocols to which the United States is a party, while not specifically addressing the issue of combatants who are minors, recognize that during a time of war civilians and individuals under the age of 15 are accorded differential treatment than persons who are older. As a matter of policy, the Department of Defense has treated individuals assessed upon their arrival at Guantanamo Bay to be younger than age 16 in a manner appropriate to their age and to the military mission.[44]

Three Afghan detainees transferred to Guantanamo aged between thirteen and fiteen were placed in a separate detention facility, 'Camp Iguana', and received care appropriate to their age provided by trained personnel. According to a Pentagon spokesperson:

> We recognize the special needs of juvenile detainees and the unfortunate circumstances surrounding their young lives. Every effort was made to provide them a secure environment free from the influences of older detainees.[45]

They were taught Pashto, English, Arabic, mathematics, science, art, and Islam; played football, basketball, and volleyball; watched films; and even learned to snorkel; although they also were interrogated about their knowledge of al-Qaeda and the Taliban. The three detainees were released and repatriated to Afghanistan in January 2004 and in subsequent interviews to journalists spoke favourably about their time in captivity.[46]

Further press reports, however, indicated that other child detainees were being held in the Guantanamo general prison population, with no allowances being made for their age.[47] In a letter to the *Guardian* in July 2008, Cori Crider, a lawyer at the NGO Reprieve, which is representing a number of Guantanamo detainees, claimed that prisoner lists released following a US Freedom of Information Act request and a Department of Defense admission put the number of detainees aged under eighteen on their arrival at Guantanamo at twenty-two,[48] of which four were still imprisoned there.[49] The US administration, however, asserts that it has held no more than eight children at Guantanamo, including the three aged under sixteen who were held at Camp Iguana and released in January 2004, and another three aged between sixteen and seventeen, who were released in 2004, 2005, and 2006.[50] It seems undisputed, however, that two remaining detainees were originally detained when they were children, and that both of them are now being prosecuted for war crimes before US military commissions.

The first, Omar Khadr, was detained by US forces in Afghanistan in July 2002 when he was fifteen years old.[51] He was held at Bagram Airbase until after he had passed his sixteenth birthday and only then transferred to Guantanamo, where he has subsequently been treated as an adult. Khadr was subjected to prolonged interrogation and, it is alleged, suffered serious abuse, amounting to torture, at the hands of his interrogators.[52] The original criminal proceedings brought against Khadr were discontinued as a result of the US Supreme Court's judgment in *Hamdan v. Rumsfeld*, but following the enactment of the Military Commissions Act (hereafter MCA)[53] charges of murder in violation of the law of war, attempted murder in violation of the law of war, providing material support for terrorism, and spying were sworn against him and referred to a military commission in April 2007. His trial is set to begin in January 2009. The other defendant is Mohammed Jawad, who was sixteen or seventeen years old when captured in Afghanistan and transferred to Guantanamo. Jawad has suffered periods of solitary confinement and sleep deprivation at Guantanamo, and it is alleged that while detained at Bagram Airbase he was subjected to abuse amounting to torture.[54] After his second period of solitary confinement, he attempted suicide. Charges of murder in violation of the law of war and intentionally causing serious bodily injury were sworn against Jawad and referred to a military commission in November 2007. Proceedings against him are also continuing.

In both cases, no allowances have been made to take account of the fact that the defendants were children when they allegedly committed the crimes with which they are charged. Indeed, the military commission rules do not specifically provide for any such accommodations. An attempt by Khadr to have the charges against him dismissed on the ground that the military commission lacked jurisdiction under the MCA over crimes committed by child soldiers failed. In particular, the commission held that:

> Neither customary international law nor international treaties binding upon the United States prohibit the trial of a person for alleged violations of the laws of nations committed when he was 15 years of age.[55]

However, the issue before the commission was solely whether it was entitled to try Khadr. The commission also stated that: 'the [defence] arguments and positions concerning the need to protect a child and a child's incapacity to understand his/her actions relate to issues which may be presented to the finders of fact at this commission'.[56] It did not rule on issues of intent and capacity, the existence and ambit of possible defences, or potential mitigating circumstances. The defence has subsequently applied to have all evidence of statements that Khadr allegedly made to the US authorities, or at least those allegedly made prior to his eighteenth birthday, suppressed on the ground that his detention as an 'unlawful combatant' violated the OP, which obliged the United States 'to classify him as a captured child soldier and to provide him with the special protection for children required by the Protocol',[57] in particular under Article 6(3).[58] The prosecution has argued that the OP is irrelevant to issues of the admissibility of evidence,[59] but as yet the military commission has not ruled on the matter (or, at least, any such ruling has not yet been published). However, in its earlier ruling the commission stated: 'Whether or not being tried for alleged crimes is rehabilitative is not a question before the commission.'[60] This *dictum* might indicate that the commission sees the issue as one for the Executive, not for itself.

However, although the child detainees at Guantanamo have been the subject of considerable media coverage and NGO agitation, recent figures released by the US administration reveal that they make up only a small proportion of the number of children detained by US forces in the global 'war against terror'. In a written response to questions asked by the Committee on the Rights of the Child, the State Department stated that since 2002 the United States had held around 2,500 persons under eighteen years of age at the time of their capture, detaining them at Guantanamo, in Afghanistan, and in Iraq. Since 2002, the United States has held approximately ninety children in Afghanistan, with around ten being held at Bagram as of April 2008. Since 2003, the United States has held around 2,400 children in Iraq, with about 500 being held as of April 2008. According to the US Response, these children have been detained because they have actively participated in hostilities against United States and Coalition forces. Because the United States considers itself to be in an ongoing conflict with al-Qaeda and the Taliban, it asserts the right to hold enemy combatants for the duration of the conflict, although it also claims that it 'has a number of policies in place that attempt to limit the length of time a juvenile is held in detention'.[61]

In Iraq, detainees are held as 'imperative threats to security' pursuant to the authorization given the Multinational Force in Security Council resolution 1546, which permits internment when 'necessary for imperative reasons of security'.[62] A detainee's status is reviewed, in the first instance, by the detaining unit, to decide whether he is an 'imperative security threat'. It appears that some 50 per cent of those initially detained are released at the unit location. Those who are determined to be such a threat are transferred to the Theater Internment Facility, where another review is undertaken by a Magistrate Cell, which recommends either release, transfer to the Iraqi courts (if there are grounds for criminal prosecution), or referral to the Combined Review and Release Board (CRRB). The CRRB conducts a third-tier review, allegedly consistently with Article 78 GC IV.[63] According to the Response, the majority of child detainees have been released within six months and few are detained for longer than twelve months.

In Afghanistan, child detainees are detained subject to Department of Defense Directive 2310.01E.[64] The Directive applies to all armed conflicts, regardless of their characterization, and provides that detainees shall be treated humanely and in accordance with international humanitarian law (at a minimum, consistently with Common Article 3). Where there is doubt as to a detainee's legal status, his status shall be determined by a 'competent authority'. A competent authority must also periodically review the basis for the detention of detainees who are not POWs. 'Unlawful enemy combatants', who do not enjoy POW status, are defined in the Directive as including any individual 'who is or was part of or supporting Taliban or Al Qaeda forces or associated forces that are engaged in hostilities against the United States or its coalition partners'.[65] In Afghanistan, a detainee's unlawful combatant status is assessed upon capture, reassessed within seventy-five days of entry into Bagram, and thereafter at six-month intervals. The Response did not specifically touch on how long children were being held in

Bagram, only stating that the average length of detention was less than twelve months.

In all cases, however, once it has been determined that a detainee is a child, which is usually following a medical assessment, he is separated from the adult detainee population and afforded 'special protections and programs'.[66] Child detainees receive medical attention from 'professionals, who recognize that because their need, they require special care'.[67] In Afghanistan, child detainees have access to a Mental Health Unit, although none have availed themselves of its facilities.[68] In August 2007, a Juvenile Education Center was opened at Camp Cropper in Iraq, which provides educational instruction, to a curriculum designed in consultation with the Iraqi Ministry of Education, to all child detainees:

> All juvenile detainees are offered attendance in basic educational programmes in grades 1–6, with a core curriculum of six subjects: Arabic reading, writing, and language skills; math instruction from simple addition through algebraic equations; history and social studies beginning with those of Iraq and then the world; earth science and biology; civics instruction in the structure of the Iraqi government and basic citizenship; and, instruction in English numbers, letters, and phrases.
>
> The education centre features classrooms, a library, a medical treatment facility, and four soccer and athletic fields. Juveniles are afforded the chance to exercise, to paint, and to participate in activities appropriate for persons of their age.[69]

However, matters are different in Afghanistan. It appears that '[s]pace constraints [at Bagram] have limited the ability to offer detainees educational, religious and vocational programs', as well as restricting opportunities for recreation, although the Response claims that it is planned to provide such programmes and facilities in the future.[70]

What is clear is that the United States has promulgated no general policy on how its forces should treat child prisoners in war.[71] This may not be unusual. However, the consequences are apparent in the ad hoc and varied reactions of various units of the US armed forces and the US administration to the different situations where child soldiers have fallen into US hands. There appear to have been instances of good practice, such as with regard to Camp Iguana and the new Juvenile Education Center at Camp Cropper (although it might be recalled that US forces have been detaining children in Iraq since 2003). But elsewhere things have been less satisfactory. Space constraints can hardly excuse the lack of educational and recreational facilities for child detainees at Bagram. The prosecution of the former child soldiers Khadr and Jawad before military commissions, particularly given how long they have already been held and the treatment to which they have allegedly been subject, is difficult to square with the United States' obligations under the OP and ILO Convention 182. Indeed, one might ask why they are being prosecuted at all, given their status as 'foot soldiers'. The conclusion must be that it is largely for publicity purposes. Unlike the other original defendants, who were prosecuted for involvement in a criminal conspiracy, Khadr and Jawad had been captured whilst engaged in combat with US troops; that is, 'with blood on their hands'.

Nor, one might consider, has the situation been helped by the lack of clarity in the applicable legal rules. Article 6(3) of the OP, in particular, is so general as to provide little concrete guidance. To return to a theme from the beginning of this chapter, international disapprobation for children's involvement in armed conflict has led to a refusal to contemplate—and regulate—the consequences of their participation in hostilities. More recent provisions in human rights treaties do not always mesh easily with the rules set out in earlier humanitarian law conventions. It might be thought that this area suffers from too much, rather than too little, law-making. However, some guidance, taking account of both children's rights and military exigencies, would be welcome.[72] At the least, states should consider publishing their own policies.

NOTES

This chapter was written in 2008 prior to the ending of the mandate of the Multilateral Force in Iraq and the inauguration of US President Obama.

1. This chapter will follow the convention of defining children as all persons under eighteen years of age; see Article 1 of the Convention on the Rights of the Child, 1577 UNTS 3 (1989) [hereafter CRC]. See also *Roper v. Simons* 543 US 551 (2005), 573: 'The age of 18 is the point where society draws the line for many purposes between childhood and adulthood.'
2. Report of the Special Representative to the Secretary-General for Children and Armed Conflict, UN Doc A/61/275, 17 August 2006, para. 11. See also Coalition to Stop the Use of Child Soldiers, *Child soldiers: Global report 2008*.
3. Martin Chulov, 'Raid uncovers Al-Qaida network of child suicide bombers in Iraq', *Guardian* (4 December 2008); and David Smith, 'When death calls in the killing fields of Afghanistan', *Observer* (14 December 2008), reporting the killing of four Royal Marines by a thirteen-year-old suicide bomber.
4. Recent discussions of children's participation in armed conflict include Rachel Brett and Irma Specht, *Young soldiers: Why they choose to fight* (Boulder, CO: Lynne Rienner, 2004); Alcinda Honwana, *Child soldiers in Africa* (Philadelphia, PA: University of Philadelphia Press, 2006); David M. Rosen, *Armies of the young: Child soldiers in war and terrorism* (New Brunswick, NJ: Rutgers University Press, 2005); and Peter Warren Singer, *Children at war* (New York: Pantheon, 2005).
5. See Report of the Secretary-General on children and armed conflict, 21 December 2009, UN Doc. A/62/609-S/2007/757, para. 9; and Coalition to Stop the Use of Child Soldiers, *Child soldiers*, 18–19.
6. Protocol Additional to the Geneva Conventions of 12 August 1949 and Relating to the Protection of Victims of International Armed Conflicts, 1125 UNTS 3 (1977) [hereafter AP I]; and Protocol Additional to the Geneva Conventions of 12 August 1949 and Relating to the Protection of Victims of Non International Armed Conflicts, 1125 UNTS 609 (1977) [hereafter AP II]. As of 15 December 2008, 168 states were parties to AP I and 164 to AP II.
7. Convention on the Rights of the Child, 1577 UNTS 3 (1989). As of 15 December 2008, 193 states were parties to the CRC.

8. African Charter on the Rights and Welfare of the Child, 1990, OAU Doc. CAB/LEG/ 24.9/49. As of 15 December 2008, thirty-seven states were parties to the Charter.

9. ILO Convention 182 Concerning the Prohibition and Immediate Action for the Elimination of the Worst Forms of Child Labour (1999) 38 ILM 1207 [hereafter ILO Convention 182]. As of 15 December 2008, 169 states were parties to the Convention.

10. Optional Protocol to the Convention on the Rights of the Child on the Involvement of Children in Armed Conflict, GA res. 54/263 of 25 May 2000; (2000) 39 ILM 1285 [hereafter OP]. As of 15 December 2008, 125 states were parties to the OP.

11. Article 77(2) AP I and Article 38 CRC. Article 4(2)(c) AP II prohibits the recruitment and use of children under fifteen to take (any) part in hostilities.

12. Articles 1–3 ILO Convention 182 and Article 2, OP.

13. Article 3 OP.

14. Article 4 OP.

15. Article 1 OP.

16. Article 22(2) African Charter on the Rights and Welfare of the Child.

17. See Richard R. Baxter, 'So-called "unprivileged belligerency": Spies, guerrillas and saboteurs', *British Yearbook of International Law*, 28 (1951), 323; and Knut Dörmann, 'The legal situation of "unlawful/unprivileged combatants"', *International Review of the Red Cross*, 85/849 (2003), 45–74.

18. Article 43 AP I.

19. See Article 77(3) AP I.

20. Indeed, looking at the provisions of GC IV, it appears that its drafters took a rather different view of when childhood ends and adulthood begins than is now current. When an age limit is given, the Convention sets it at fifteen: see Articles 14, 23, 24, 38, and 50, Geneva Convention (IV) relative to the protection of civilians in time of war of 12 August 1949, 75 UNTS 973 (1950).

21. For a full examination of the provisions, the context of their adoption, and negotiating history, see Matthew Happold, *Child soldiers in international law* (Manchester: University of Manchester Press, 2005), 57–69.

22. Interestingly, although Article 77(1) AP I does not specifically refer to children's education, Article 4(3)(a) AP II does, listing education as an aspect of the care and aid required by children.

23. The African Charter on the Rights and Welfare of the Child does not go beyond the CRC in any relevant respect.

24. Article 37(c) CRC.

25. See Articles 24, 27, 28, 29 CRC.

26. Articles 19, 34, and 36 CRC.

27. Article 2(1) CRC.

28. See Article 31(3)(c) Vienna Convention on the Law of Treaties (1969) 1155 UNTS 331.

29. Article 37(d) CRC requires that all children deprived of their liberty have the right to prompt access to legal assistance and to challenge the legality of their detention before a court or other competent independent and impartial authority.

30. See text to endnotes 11–16. A similar situation arises with regards to the provisions in Article 5 of ILO Convention 182 requiring state parties to the Convention to 'provide the necessary and appropriate direct assistance for the removal of children from the worst forms of child labour and for their rehabilitation and social integration; ... [and] ensure access to free basic education, and, wherever possible and appropriate, vocational training, for all children removed from the worst forms of child labour',

which category includes children who have been compulsorily or forcibly recruited for use in armed conflict.

31. See, for example, *Al-Skeini v. Secretary of State for Defence* [2007] UKHL 27.
32. See, in particular, the comments in Rachel Brett and Margaret McCallin, *Children: The invisible soldiers* (revised edn.; Stockholm: Rädda Barnen, 1998), 153–4; and Ilene Cohn and Guy S. Goodwin-Gill, *Child soldiers: The role of children in armed conflicts* (Oxford: Clarendon Press, 1994), 6.
33. See the examples given in Matthew Happold, 'The age of criminal responsibility in international criminal law', in Karin Arts and Vesselin Popovski (eds.), *International criminal accountability and children's rights* (The Hague: Hague Academic Press, 2006), 69.
34. See *Trial of Johannes Oenning and Emil Nix*, British Military Court, Borken, Germany, 21 and 22 December 1945, XI LRTWC 74; and *Trial of Alois and Anna Bommer and their daughters*, Permanent Military Tribunal at Metz, judgment of 19 February 1947, IX LRTWC 62.
35. Article 40(3)(a) CRC.
36. Committee on the Rights of the Child, General Comment No. 10 (2007), *Children's rights in juvenile justice*, UN Doc. CRC/C/GC/10, 25 April 2007, para. 32.
37. Article 7(1) Statute of the Special Court for Sierra Leone, Annex, 'Agreement between the United Nations and the Government of Sierra Leone on the establishment of the special court for Sierra Leone', signed on 16 January 2002.
38. See the Paris Principles, endorsed by fifty-eight states, which provide that: 'Wherever possible, alternatives to judicial proceedings must be sought': Principle 3.7, Paris Principles and Guidelines on Children Associated with Armed Forces and Armed Groups, February 2007.
39. Ibid. Principle 3.6.
40. Public Affairs Office, Special Court for Sierra Leone, press release, 'Special court prosecutor says he will not prosecute children', 2 November 2002.
41. Memorandum for the vice-president: Humane treatment of al Qaida and Taliban detainees, signed by President George Bush on 7 February 2007.
42. 548 U.S. 557 (2006).
43. Memorandum on the Application of Common Article 3 of the Geneva Conventions to the Treatment of Detainees in the Department of Defense, signed by Gordon R. England, the Deputy Secretary of Defense, on July 7 2006.
44. Letter from Deputy Assistant Attorney General Thomas R. Lee to the Honourable Joyce Hens Green, September 3 2004.
45. Quoted in Sonia Verma, 'Boy, 12, recounts days as terror inmate', *San Francisco Chronicle* (13 February 2004).
46. Verma, 'Boy, 12'; Andrew North, 'Boy praises Guantanamo jailers', *BBC News* (2 February 2004), <http://news/bbc.co.uk/go/pr/-/1/hi/world/south_asia/3488175.stm>; and James Astill, 'Cuba? It was great, say boys freed from US prison camp', *Guardian* (6 March 2004).
47. See Neil. A. Lewis, 'Some held at Guantanamo are minors, lawyers say', *New York Times* (13 June 2005); and Severin Carrell, 'The children of Guantanamo Bay', *Independent* (26 May 2006).
48. Cori Crider, 'Guantanamo children', *Guardian* (19 July 2008). See also Jo Becker, 'The war on teen terror', *Salon.com* (24 June 2008), which also states that: 'according to government records obtained by the Associated Press under the Freedom of Information Act, more than 20 detainees under the age of 18 have been brought to the prison

camp since 2002' [information published online by *Washington* Post: <http://projects.washingtonpost.com/guantanamo/#afghanistan>].

49. Becker, 'The war on teen terror', writes of three remaining prisoners, listing Mohammed Jawad, Mohammed el Gharani, and Omar Khadr, but not Faris Muslim al Ansari. The difference may be because of the uncertainty about al Ansari's age.
50. Bureau of Democracy, Human Rights and Labor, US Department of State, United States Written Response to Questions Asked by the Committee on the Rights of the Child, A to Q 12(a).
51. For the circumstances of Khadr's capture, see Isabel Vincent, 'The good son', *National Post* (28 December 2002).
52. See Jeff Tietz, 'The unending torture of Omar Khadr', *Rolling Stone* (10 August 2006).
53. Pub. L. No. 109–366, 120 Stat. 2600, 17 October 2006.
54. See Jo Becker, 'American credibility on trial', *Salon.com* (20 August 2008).
55. *US v. Khadr*, D-022, Ruling on defense motion for dismissal due to lack of jurisdiction under the MCA in regard to juvenile crimes of a child soldier, 30 April 2008, 6.
56. Ibid. 7.
57. *US v. Khadr*, Defense motion to suppress evidence of statements (violation of child soldier protocol), 29 May 2008, 1.
58. Ibid. 4.
59. *US v. Khadr*, Government's response to the defense's motion to suppress evidence of statements (violation of child soldier protocol), 6 June 2008.
60. *US v. Khadr*, D-022, Ruling on defense motion for dismissal due to lack of jurisdiction under the MCA in regard to juvenile crimes of a child soldier, 30 April 2008, 6.
61. Bureau of Democracy, Human Rights and Labor, US Department of State, United States Written Response to Questions Asked by the Committee on the Rights of the Child, A to Q 12(b).
62. SC res 1,546 of June 8 2004: see op. para. 10 and annexed letter from US Secretary of State Colin L. Powell to the President of the Security Council, at p. 11. The authorization mirrors the wording of Article 78 GC IV.
63. For more details about the procedures, see *Munaf v. Geren* 128 S. Ct. 2,207 (2008).
64. United States Department of Defense, DoD Directive 2310.01E, 5 September 2006.
65. Ibid. E2.1.1.2.
66. Bureau of Democracy, Human Rights and Labor, US Department of State, United States Written Response to Questions Asked by the Committee on the Rights of the Child, A to Q 12(d).
67. Ibid. A to Q 12(e).
68. Ibid.
69. Ibid. A to Q12(e).
70. Ibid.
71. This can be inferred from the Declaration of Ms Sandra L. Hodgkinson, Deputy Assistant Secretary of Defense for Detainee Affairs, 3 July 2008, attached to *US v. Khadr*, Government response to defense request for the production of MS Hodgkinson to testify regarding D062, 5 August 2008. See, in particular, her statement at para. 12: '[T]here is no existing law or Department policy that requires detainees under the age of 18 to be separated from the general detainee population'.
72. The Paris Principles and Guidelines on Children Associated with Armed Forces and Armed Groups, February 2007, provide for the release of all child soldiers. It is suggested that this goes beyond what international law requires and is unrealistic, even impracticable.

16

Legal Issues Related to Armed Conflict with Non-state Groups

John B. Bellinger III

The US Department of State's Office of the Legal Adviser has undertaken extensive bilateral and multilateral efforts designed to develop a common approach to a range of legal questions arising out of the fight against transnational terrorism. One of the mistakes the United States made after 11 September 2001 was not discussing with its allies the reasoning and legal basis behind the steps taken to combat al-Qaeda. Not surprisingly, many of our discussions have been retrospective, attempting to explain the legal basis for the actions taken by the United States after the terrorist attacks of September 11.[1]

The major accomplishment of these discussions has been the increasing number of legal experts who now acknowledge that the legal framework for conflicts with transnational terrorists like al-Qaeda is not clear.[2] The Organization for Security and Co-operation in Europe (OSCE) Parliamentary Assembly Special Representative Anne Marie Lizin's report from July 2006 recognized that 'there is incontestably some legal haziness' regarding the legal status of members of international terrorist organizations.[3] Indeed, she recommended the formation of an international commission of legal experts to examine the question.[4] Likewise, at the 2006 US–EU summit, the then Austrian Chancellor Wolfgang Schüssel acknowledged that we face 'legal gray areas' regarding detention of terrorists.[5] Most recently, the Foreign Affairs Committee of the UK House of Commons wrote that the Geneva Conventions dealt inadequately with the problems posed by international terrorism, and called on the UK government, in connection with state parties to the Geneva Conventions and the International Committee of the Red Cross (ICRC), to work on updating these Conventions for modern problems.[6]

Some critics of this effort have suggested that the goal of the United States is to discard the existing rules or to try and find gaps in existing law to place detainees beyond the protection of the law. In fact, the gaps described in this chapter are real and recognizing this fact does not mitigate the obligation of states to comply with international law, nor does it justify placing persons beyond the protection of the law. The Geneva Conventions were designed for traditional armed conflicts between states and their uniformed military forces, and do not provide all the answers for detention of persons in conflicts between a state and a transnational terrorist group.

Given the growing acknowledgment that the Geneva Conventions do not provide a satisfactory set of rules for contemporary conflicts, it is important to identify areas where they fall short. Common Article 2 of the Conventions restricts the scope of applicability of most of the Conventions' provisions to conflicts between High Contracting Parties.[7] However, as we are seeing throughout the world, contemporary conflicts often do not have more than one High Contracting Party to the Conventions involved. Some of these conflicts occur within the boundaries of one country, like Sri Lanka's conflict with the Tamil Tigers. Increasingly, however, conflicts cross national boundaries, like Israel and Hezbollah or the ongoing conflict between the United States and its allies and al-Qaeda. In cases such as these, we are left in a situation where Common Article 3, and, depending on a state's treaty obligations and the nature of the non-state actor, Additional Protocol II, provide the only treaty-based rules governing detention of unprivileged combatants.[8]

It should be noted here that it was not always clear to the US government that Common Article 3 applied as a treaty-law matter to a conflict between a state and non-state actors that transcended national boundaries. While the US Supreme Court decision in *Hamdan v. Rumsfeld* (2006) held that the conflict with al-Qaeda, as one not between states, is a non-international conflict covered by Common Article 3, many international legal scholars would question that conclusion. Textually the provision is limited to armed conflict 'not of an international character' occurring 'in the territory of *one* of the High Contracting Parties', suggesting the scope of the provision is limited to conflicts occurring in the territory of a single state. Indeed, other states, such as Israel, have concluded that conflicts with terrorist organizations outside the state's borders are international armed conflicts not falling within the scope of Common Article 3. I make these points not to relitigate the *Hamdan* case, or to disregard the view of many that Common Article 3 is customary international law, but rather to note that, in some cases, not even Common Article 3 may apply as a treaty-law matter to conflicts with transnational terrorist groups.

But even assuming that Common Article 3 does cover contemporary transnational conflicts of this sort, it is striking just how little guidance Common Article 3 in fact provides. The one area where Common Article 3 does provide good detail is with respect to the treatment of detainees once in custody. Treatment protections include the prohibition against torture and cruel, humiliating, and degrading treatment, and a requirement that those criminally tried in relation to the conflict be provided judgement by 'a regularly constituted court affording all the judicial guarantees considered essential by civilized peoples'. Depending on a state's treaty-law obligations these treatment protections can be supplemented in certain circumstances by Additional Protocol II. Many would also argue that Article 75 of Additional Protocol I provides other relevant protections if it is interpreted as customary international law applicable in non-international armed conflict.[9]

But, quite clearly, the meaning of particular treatment protections may be subject to different interpretations. Common Article 3 was not designed with the precision of a criminal statute. Indeed, the International Criminal Tribunal for the former Yugoslavia acquitted a defendant of violation of Common Article 3's prohibition on 'violence to life and person' because the term lacked a sufficiently precise definition under international law.[10] The United States has also wrestled with how to implement this article in our criminal law, especially since the *Hamdan* court ruled that it governs our operations in the conflict with al-Qaeda. For example, 'outrages upon personal dignity' is defined in Pictet's Commentary on Common Article 3 as capturing only those acts that 'world public opinion finds particularly revolting'.[11] But reasonable people can and do differ about what behaviour that phrase captures. It was this concern that led the Bush administration and Congress to agree in the Military Commissions Act to amend the War Crimes Act to clarify which specific violations of Common Article 3 are criminally sanctionable.[12]

More importantly, though, Common Article 3 does not address at all four central questions that I believe must be answered with respect to conflicts with non-state groups. Each of these questions will be discussed in what follows: first, who may a state detain in a conflict with a global non-state actor? Second, what processes must a state provide detainees to determine whether they can be detained? Third, when are hostilities over in armed conflict with a non-state group? And fourth, what legal obligations do states have in connection with repatriating detainees at the end of the conflict?

THE GAPS ARE NOT ALREADY FILLED

A frequent response to these questions is that we are looking in the wrong place for their answers. Critics respond that other treaties or customary international law fill these gaps. It is not clear, however, that they do.

First, some argue that Additional Protocol II to the Geneva Conventions was designed to address the limited scope of Common Article 3 by providing additional rules for non-international armed conflict. President Reagan submitted Additional Protocol II to the Senate seeking advice and consent to ratification in 1987, but the Senate has not acted on the treaty to date, meaning its provisions do not bind the United States as a matter of treaty law. But even for states that have become party to Additional Protocol II, such as the United Kingdom, the Protocol does not provide a satisfactory answer to the questions posed. While Additional Protocol II expands on the treatment protections provided in Common Article 3, it has a more limited scope of application defined in Article 1, and its provisions do not squarely address any of the four questions.

Second, some have suggested that customary international law can be used to fill gaps in treaty law. As explained above, the conclusion that Article 75 of Additional Protocol I is customary international law applicable in all armed conflicts would add to the treatment protections in non-international armed conflict provided by Common Article 3. But, as a general matter, states need to be careful to adhere to proper methodology before describing particular provisions of treaty law as custom. Many commentators assert customary international law as they would like it to be, rather than as it actually is. The US government sent a letter to ICRC President Jakob Kellenberger noting concerns with the methodology employed by the ICRC International Humanitarian Law (IHL) Customary International Law Study, in deeming treaty provisions customary international law.[13] Although it may seem attractive as a policy matter to import rules developed in international armed conflict to other situations, we must be careful not to describe rules as custom when there is an insufficient basis to do so. Providing unprivileged combatants the same or greater protections and rights as those provided to prisoners of war risks rewarding illegal actions, ultimately placing innocent civilians at greater risk.

Third, human rights groups and some European states argue that human rights law fills the gap wherever IHL is insufficiently specific to address a particular situation. It is important to remember here that states have different obligations under different treaties. US obligations under the International Covenant on Civil and Political Rights (ICCPR) apply only on US territory, while European states are parties to human rights instruments with protections that extend outside national borders. So when we talk about human rights law, we need to be sure we are taking into account different national circumstances.

But even where states do have human rights obligations, it is fair to ask proponents of this approach what particular human rights provisions they would apply to activities arising in the conduct of armed conflict, and how they would apply them in practice. For example, Article 9 of the ICCPR requires states to provide any detained individual the right to bring their case before a judge without delay to determine the legality of the detention.[14] Would it be practical to expect states detaining tens of thousands of unprivileged combatants in a non-international armed conflict to bring them before a judge without delay? This is not something states must do even for prisoners of war under the Third Geneva Convention. If the answer is that the state should derogate from Article 9 if the exigencies of a civil war so demand, then what contribution has human rights law made to answering questions regarding the procedures owed to combatants in non-international armed conflict? Some rights deemed non-derogable by the ICCPR, such as the right to life, would clearly be displaced by more specific law of war rules that govern as the *lex specialis*.

In the end, it is submitted, the gaps identified in the rules regarding detention of combatants in non-international armed conflict are real, and that simply labelling international armed conflict rules as custom in non-international armed conflict or importing human rights law does not satisfactorily resolve these difficulties. Through the course of my dialogue as Legal Adviser, more and more Europeans have been willing to acknowledge that the existing rules were not designed for, and are in fact not well suited for, the threat posed by transnational terrorism.

DETENTION SCOPE AND PROCEDURES

Having established that the issues identified with Common Article 3 are not easily resolved by resort to other treaties or customary international law, each of the four major unaddressed issues will now be explored in turn. These issues do not form an exhaustive list of areas where further dialogue and legal development are needed, but are perhaps the most important issues I have faced as Legal Adviser. The first question is how states should define the category of persons that can be detained in non-international armed conflict. With respect to combatants, trad-itional international armed conflict has a relatively easy answer: a state detains enemy forces. These forces usually wear uniforms, are in clear command and control structures, and conduct their operations in accordance with the laws of war. But in contemporary conflicts determining the legal contours of the category of 'combatant' can be extremely difficult.

Clearly, Taliban militants captured on the battlefield in Afghanistan, as many of those at Guantanamo were, would fall within the scope of persons that can be detained for the duration of hostilities. So too would an al-Qaeda terrorist in Iraq with a strapped-on suicide vest headed to a civilian area to detonate. But what about the person who made the explosive-laden vest? The financier whose money laundering for al-Qaeda made the suicide operation possible? The religious leader who knowingly inspired the suicide bomber to embark on his mission? This issue has been a difficult one for the United States with regards to al-Qaeda, and has been a source of tension with our European allies, some of whom are concerned that our definition of combatant is over-inclusive. But where exactly to draw the line here is unclear. Although it may seem reasonable to say that only those like the suicide bomber or vest maker should be detained as combatants, it may be the financier's broad operations that in fact pose the greatest threat to a state.

Of course, the law of war envisions that a state will detain both combatants and civilians during armed conflict. The laws of war have long permitted the deten-tion of supporters of hostile forces during armed conflict, including civilians connected to armies such as labourers, messengers, guides, scouts, and civilians transporting military supplies and equipment in proximity to the battlefield. Article 42 of the Fourth Geneva Convention clearly contemplates security intern-ment of protected persons, 'where the security of the Detaining Power makes it absolutely necessary'.[15] The Israeli Supreme Court in the Public Committee against Torture case concluded that combatants not in regular armies or militias that meet the requirements of Article 4A (2) of the Third Convention were in fact civilians, who lost their comprehensive protections against attacks, 'for such time as they take a direct part in hostilities'.[16]

It is worth noting here that the term 'direct part in hostilities' in Article 51, paragraph 3, of Additional Protocol I, has been a difficult phrase to define. For years, a group of forty law-of-war experts have grappled with this issue in a series of expert meetings co-organized by the ICRC and the TMC Asser Institute. More centrally, though, we should query what the relevant differences are between categorizing some as unprivileged combatants (al-Qaeda, for example) and other civilians who may be the object of direct attack but only for such time as they take a direct part in hostilities. In each case, a state can detain these persons for the duration of the conflict, and must treat individuals involved in a non-international armed conflict consistently with Common Article 3.

This question of whom a state may detain relates to the second major question to be discussed: what procedures must a state use before deciding someone may be detained in non-international armed conflict? In international armed conflict, normally no process is used to determine whether or not soldiers from the opposing army may be detained. Such detained combatants, usually prisoners of war, who are not criminally charged are not entitled to counsel or judicial review. After 9/11, the US government took the view that Taliban and al-Qaeda militants that were picked up on the battlefield were subject to detention under the law of war. As with traditional conflicts, these combatants were not provided lawyers nor afforded judicial review of the legality of their detention. But while this practice may make sense with respect to clearly identifiable soldiers, how should a state decide whether to detain non-state actors who often lack identifiable indicia of being a combatant? Is it sufficient to treat them as the law of war treats traditional combatants, or does something about their non-traditional status make further process necessary?

The US Supreme Court clearly felt uncomfortable with applying the traditional rules to these unprivileged combatants. In its *Hamdi* decision in 2004, the Court ruled that US citizens picked up on the battlefield and detained in the United States are entitled to an administrative review process to determine whether they are in fact combatants.[17] In the companion *Rasul* decision, the Court extended statutory habeas corpus rights to alien detainees held at Guantanamo.[18] The issue in *Boumediene* was whether the right to common law habeas corpus protected by the Suspension Clause extends to the Guantanamo detainees.[19] Ultimately, the United States appears to have arrived at a place where it is unquestioned, as a general matter, that administrative review of combatant status, and often subsequent judicial review of the legality of detention, accompanies extended detention in non-traditional conflicts.

It may be that we may have arrived at rules not that different from the rules set out for internment of civilian Protected Persons in Article 43 of the Fourth Geneva Convention. That article states, in part, 'Any protected person who has been interned or placed in assigned residence shall be entitled to have such action reconsidered as soon as possible by an appropriate court or administrative board designated by the Detaining Power for that purpose.' The US government is currently following this procedure in Iraq, where it adheres to the Fourth Convention as a policy matter with civilian security internees. But it also meets this standard with combatants who are detained at Bagram in Afghanistan or Guantanamo. While questions remain as to whether it makes sense to classify al-Qaeda members as civilians as opposed to unprivileged combatants, as the Israeli Supreme Court and others have suggested, the added procedural protections afforded interned or detained civilians may provide a model for appropriate rules for the detention of unprivileged combatants.

END OF THE CONFLICT?

Along with these two questions surrounding initiation of detention, Common Article 3 and other applicable IHL do not provide clear answers to two questions regarding termination of detention in contemporary conflicts. Even if one acknowledges that al-Qaeda militants may be lawfully detained as unprivileged enemy combatants, when must detained persons be released? Again, traditional IHL principles provide a simple answer: upon the cessation of active hostilities. In traditional conflicts it is obvious why this is the case. Could anyone imagine Allied forces during the Second World War releasing before the end of the conflict German soldiers who could return to the fight? And during the US conflict in Vietnam, captured US military personnel were held by the North Vietnamese for up to nine years without any idea as to when they might be released or repatriated. At the same time this answer seems deeply unsatisfactory to some in the current conflict with al-Qaeda. Critics ask fair questions when they query how the United States will identify the end of hostilities. Although it would have been difficult for those living in London during the Blitz to identify when hostilities would have ended, at least there was a sense of what an end to the conflict might look like. It is highly unlikely this conflict will end with the signing of a formal surrender document on a battleship.

But what are the consequences of the conclusion that it will be difficult to identify when the conflict may end? Does this mean we should just release everyone we are holding now? This option is unpalatable given that many of the people released would immediately return to the fight. As of December 2007, the Defense Department believes that more than thirty released Guantanamo detainees have already returned to the fight. Presumably, releasing the more dangerous individuals still detained at Guantanamo would result in an even greater number of recidivists. Or could it mean that states should, after some period of time, release detainees or subject them to trial? I have in the past given lengthy explanations of the difficulties Western legal systems have faced in criminally prosecuting terrorists—from the challenges posed by extraterritorial and retroactive legislation to difficulties in collecting admissible evidence in battlefield and intelligence settings.

The better answer may be to conceptualize the end of the conflict differently, possibly looking to principles found in the Fourth Geneva Convention. Article 43 of the Fourth Convention contemplates twice-yearly reviews of security internment of protected persons by a court or administrative board. In situations where the end of the conflict is as uncertain as it is with the conflict between the United States and al-Qaeda, administrative reviews could be used to determine whether the conflict has ended with respect to a particular detainee. Two leading legal experts, Curt Bradley and Jack Goldsmith, have written on this point, arguing that the unique characteristics of the war on terrorism require an individualized determination on end of the conflict.[20] They suggested that such a determination could take into account the detainee's past conduct, level of authority within al-Qaeda, statements and actions during confinement, age and health, and psychological profile.

At Guantanamo, the US government has implemented annual Administrative Review Boards (ARBs), in which a panel of military officers considers whether an individual detainee can be released or transferred in a manner that would not threaten the security of the United States or its allies. In a sense, this is an assessment of whether or not the conflict can be viewed as having ended with respect to the detainee in question. Perhaps there should be a consideration as to what changes to the ARB process might be warranted to pursue this concept further.

The fourth and final question to be addressed is what should be done with detainees we no longer have a reason to hold in these non-traditional conflicts. Common Article 3 does not answer this question. The Third Geneva Convention offers a simple answer with respect to prisoners of war. Article 118 states: 'Prisoners of war shall be released and repatriated without delay after the cessation of active hostilities.' Traditional state practice has been to return these detainees to their states of nationality. But although this traditional rule has been easier to apply in conflicts involving a limited number of states, it becomes far more challenging to apply when there are nationals of many states involved in the conflict. At Guantanamo, for example, the US government has detained nationals from more than forty countries. This has raised numerous practical problems. Rather than negotiate one bulk repatriation, as envisioned in Article 118, the US government has been forced to negotiate separate agreements with every country whose nationals have been detained in the conflict. Needless to say, this has delayed the repatriation process significantly.

This problem grows in magnitude when the detainees we wish to repatriate express fears of mistreatment or persecution upon return. Although this is not a new problem, Article 118 is conspicuously silent on what states should do when those they wish to return do not wish to go back due to their concerns about treatment upon return. In the Second World War, many thousands of Soviet nationals who had taken up arms for Germany, and who expressed fears of returning to the Soviet Union, were forcibly repatriated by the United States and United Kingdom in compliance with the 1945 Yalta Agreement. Christiane Shields Delessert's book on this topic details the brutal treatment these prisoners received after being returned to Soviet custody, including relocation to forced labour camps in Siberia and in some cases execution.[21] In Korea and again in the first Gulf War, Allied forces used a different approach with prisoners not wishing to be repatriated, eschewing forcible repatriation in favour of third-country resettlement. In the current conflict with al-Qaeda, the United States has looked to human rights law as a non-binding guide for determining when to repatriate prisoners to third countries, establishing the firm policy not to turn over detainees where it is more likely than not that they will be tortured. This policy, central as it is to Western values, has meant that dozens of detainees who cannot be repatriated, such as the Uighurs to China, have remained at Guantanamo for years after the US has wished to transfer them. This is an area where the US government has asked its European partners and other allies to assist in the humanitarian resettlement of these individuals.

It is suggested that this problem is only likely to grow. In the conflict with al-Qaeda, for example, the majority of detainees are nationals of countries with poor human rights records. The problem is even more acute than in traditional armed conflict, because these governments are often harshest towards the very group of citizens that are being detained—people considered to be terrorists. This is less true when those being repatriated are a state's own soldiers. Exacerbating the problem is the lack of available third countries to resettle those detainees expressing credible fears. Unlike in previous conflicts when those detained may have had no ideological disagreement with the detaining power beyond the current conflict, and who may be expected to live peaceful lives once resettled, terrorists such as those at Guantanamo have the training and ideological desire to pose a continuing threat once resettled. Not surprisingly, third countries, including the United States, have not been willing to accept this risk.

Ultimately, I would posit that the solution is going to require a greater pragmatism in approaching this question. Although groups like Human Rights Watch have argued against the use of diplomatic assurances as the basis for repatriations, I would suggest that such groups need to think about what alternative tools exist to manage humane treatment concerns in states that mistreat their citizens. Not only can assurances be effective when properly obtained and monitored, but taking a principled stand against assurances results in detainees being marooned in detention facilities years after they might otherwise have been released. For those detainees who come from countries where even assurances do not sufficiently mitigate the risk of mistreatment, the West is going to need to consider what realistic options exist to allow for third-country resettlement.

CONCLUSION

I hope it has been demonstrated that Common Article 3 and other applicable international legal rules do not answer important questions related to both the initiation and the termination of detention in armed conflict with transnational terrorist groups. While there may be a range of reasonable policy answers, none are dictated by international law. I hope that the scholarly debate in this area will move beyond assertions that all that is needed is better implementation of existing law, and instead work will begin in earnest on addressing the difficult challenges identified here. It is very easy for all of us to agree that the fight against transnational terrorism must be conducted in accordance with the rule of law, but it is much harder to say what the law exactly is, and how it should be applied in this context.

NOTES

1. See John B. Bellinger III, 'Legal issues in the war on terrorism', Address at the London School of Economics, London, 31 Oct. 2006 (providing a comprehensive account of the legal basis for various decisions the United States took after September 11).

2. See Jack Goldsmith, 'The global convergence on terror', *Financial Times* (1 August 2007).

3. Anne Marie Lizin, *Report on Guantanamo Bay*, OSCE Parliamentary Assembly, 30 June 2006, 13.

4. Ibid. 16.

5. Remarks by Austrian Chancellor Wolfgang Schüssel in press availability with President George W. Bush and EU Commission President Jose Barroso, 21 June 2006 ('But our discussion today went far beyond closing Guantanamo, because we have a legal problem, we have gray areas. And there should be no legal void, not in the fight against terrorists...').

6. House of Commons, Foreign Affairs Committee, 2nd Report, 'Visit to Guantanamo Bay', 2006–07, 10 Jan. 2007, para. 85.

7. Geneva Convention Relative to the Treatment of Prisoners of War (Geneva Convention III), Art. 2, 12 Aug. 1949, 75 U.N.T.S. 135.

8. Ibid. Art. 3; Geneva Protocol II Additional to the Geneva Conventions of 12 August 1949, and Relating to the Protection of Victims of Non-International Armed Conflicts (Additional Protocol II), 8 June 1977, 1125 U.N.T.S. 609.

9. Geneva Protocol I Additional to the Geneva Conventions of 12 August 1949, and Relating to the Protection of Victims of International Armed Conflicts (Additional Protocol I), 8 June 1977, 1125 U.N.T.S. 3.

10. *Prosecutor v. Vasiljevic* [29 Nov. 2002] Case No. IT-98–32-T, Judgment, 193–204.

11. Jean Pictet (ed.), *Geneva Convention relative to the treatment of prisoners of war* [vol. III of *The Geneva Conventions of 12 August 1949: Commentary*] (Geneva, International Committee of the Red Cross, 1952–60), 39.

12. Military Commissions Act of 2006, Pub. L. No. 109–366, §6(b), 120 Stat. 2600, 2633 (2006).

13. John B. Bellinger III and William J. Haynes II, Joint letter to Dr Jakob Kellenberger, President, International Committee of the Red Cross, regarding Customary International Law Study, *International Legal Materials*, 46/3 (2007), 514.

14. International Covenant on Civil and Political Rights, Art. 9, 16 Dec. 1966, 999 U.N. T.S. 171.

15. Geneva Convention Relative to the Protection of Civilian Persons in Time of War (Geneva Convention IV), Art. 42, 12 Aug. 1949, 75 U.N.T.S. 287.

16. *Public Committee Against Torture in Israel v. Israel* [2005] Israel Supreme Court, HCJ 769/02.

17. *Hamdi v. Rumsfeld* [2004] 542 U.S. 507.

18. *Rasul v. Bush* [2004] 542 U.S. 466.

19. The Supreme Court issued its decision subsequent to these remarks. See *Boumediene v. Bush* [2008] 128 S. Ct. 2229.

20. Curtis Bradley and Jack Goldsmith, 'Congressional authorization and the war on terrorism', *Harvard Law Review*, 118/7 (2005), 2123–7.
21. See Christiane Shields Delessert, Release and repatriation of prisoners of war at the end of active hostilities: A study of Article 118, paragraph 1 of the 3rd Geneva Convention relative to the treatment of prisoners of war (Zurich: Schulthess, 1977).

17

Detainees: Misfits in Peace and War

Adam Roberts

For centuries, wars and peacetime emergencies have resulted in the detention of an extraordinary variety of people: the Boers held in the first modern 'concentration camps' in the Boer War (1898–1902), the Japanese-Americans interned in the United States in the Second World War, terrorist suspects in Northern Ireland from 1971 onwards, and the individuals of many nationalities detained in many countries in the 'war on terror' since 2001. These are merely a few of the many examples—some well known, some obscure—of the holding of people who were not prisoners of war (POWs) in the normal sense, nor had been convicted for a specific offence, yet who were nonetheless prisoners of a kind. Whether called detention or internment (the terms are largely synonymous), what the cases have in common is that security grounds were the stated reason for detaining the people concerned. Hence they will be referred to in this chapter as 'security detainees'.

These people have been misfits in two senses. First, they have often been viewed—at least by their adversaries—as social misfits. Second, their international legal status was often unclear: they didn't exactly fit the category of prisoner of war, but if not, what were they, and how were they to be treated? This second aspect of the 'misfit' problem particularly suggests the need for a set of rules to apply to them.

The status and treatment of such detainees is always emotionally and politically controversial. It cannot be otherwise when large numbers of individuals are held without charge or trial—and usually on a basis related to their ethnicity, nationality, or political religious affiliation. In many cases the detainees are interrogated—with ill-treatment and even torture an ever-present possibility. The questions raised by such detentions are moral, political, and strategic as well as legal. Time and again, the status and treatment of detainees has itself become a major issue of domestic and international debate, and has become part of the polemic of war.

This survey looks at the heterogeneous class of security detainees in a wide variety of circumstances, including in international wars, civil wars, and internal emergencies that fall short of civil wars. It explores some of the issues surrounding them in the following six parts:

1. Security detainees as a distinct category.
2. Moral, political, and strategic dimensions of the subject.

3. International legal provisions regarding detainees.
4. Detainees in the US-led 'war on terror' since 2001.
5. The muddle in Afghanistan.
6. A new international agreement?

SECURITY DETAINEES AS A DISTINCT CATEGORY

In the evolution of thinking about rules governing armed conflict, the category of security detainees was anything but obvious. Partly this was because, at a time when rules about prisoners of war were at best rudimentary, the very idea of a special category of non-POW detainees would have lacked meaning. In his great work *De Jure Belli ac Pacis*, Hugo Grotius (who had direct experience of prison and of escape therefrom) entitled a chapter 'Moderation in regard to prisoners of war', but the definition of prisoners of war was vague, apparently encompassing 'the captured subjects of the enemy', and the default assumption about them was that captivity normally meant enslavement.[1] To modern eyes it is not one of Grotius' better chapters, and it is seldom cited today. Yet it is a true reflection of the fact that our assumptions today about how prisoners should be treated were not shared in earlier centuries. The important and troublesome distinction between prisoners of war and other kinds of security detainees has emerged slowly and incompletely. A necessary precondition was the process, which gathered pace in the nineteenth century, of securing agreement on which people qualified for prisoner-of-war status, and what the standards of detention for POWs were to be. Where did this leave other classes of detainees?

The camps established by the British in the Anglo-Boer War in South Africa of 1899–1902 were a harbinger of things to come. They introduced the grim term 'concentration camp' into English and international usage;[2] they were the subject of much propaganda both during and after the war; and they had multiple purposes, ranging from protective to punitive. They were created as a response to the conflicting pressures placed on farmers by the ongoing anti-British guerrilla campaign in the Transvaal. The order establishing the camps stated that the British sought to remove 'all men, women and children and natives from the Districts which the enemy's bands persistently occupy'. It then specified that there would be two classes of detainees:

> The women and children brought in . . . should be divided in two categories, viz., 1st: Refugees, and the families of neutrals, non-combatants, and surrendered Burghers. 2nd: Those whose husbands, fathers and sons are on commando. The preference in accommodation etc., should of course, be given to the first class.
>
> It should be clearly explained to Burghers in the field that, if they voluntarily surrender, they will be allowed to live with their families in the camps until it is safe for them to return to their homes.[3]

This variety of the purposes of the concentration camps in the Boer War points to a larger problem in treating detainee operations in war as a single category. The circumstances in which people have been detained, even though they were not uniformed members of an adversary's armed forces, have been numerous. Such circumstances can arise in peacetime emergencies—for example, if there is civil strife or a terrorist campaign that does not amount to an armed conflict; and they can also arise in both civil and international wars.

- In peacetime emergencies (including in counter-terrorist operations), and in ongoing civil wars, colonial wars, and insurgencies, governments have historically been reluctant to accord the status of 'combatant' to their adversaries and have, with some notable exceptions, tended therefore to deny them prisoner-of-war status. In addition, governments have sometimes arrested and detained individuals or whole populations suspected of some degree of association with, or support for, the rebels.

  In addition, in civil wars and insurgencies many people have been relocated, whether compulsorily or voluntarily, to new villages guarded by the government, or to camps in a different part of the country, for the stated purposes of protecting them from pressure to join in or assist the insurgency, and separating them from any insurgents in their midst.

- In international wars there may be several distinct types of security detainees. In wars that give rise to the occupation of territory, detentions have often been particularly widespread and severe, and can have many of the same stated purposes as do detentions in civil wars.

  There can be another important group of security detainees: those who are living in one belligerent state, but have common links of ethnicity, religion, or nationality with an adversary state—and are believed to constitute a security threat to the state in which they live.
  In addition, some participants in an international war (e.g. certain spies or saboteurs) may fail to satisfy the criteria for treatment as prisoners of war, and yet also fail to fit the category of civilian. There may be a case for treating them as prisoners of war, but such a case would be based more on ethics, or on policy considerations, than on a strict interpretation of the law. Whether these people are called 'unlawful combatants', 'unprivileged belligerents', or something else, if they are captured, they may be viewed as one class of security detainees.

- In one UN-authorized use of force—the US-led Multinational Force in Iraq from 2004 onwards—there has been explicit Security Council authorization of internment.[4]

There is a further class of people who can only too easily end up as, in effect, security detainees: refugees who have fled their country, and internally displaced persons (IDPs) who have fled their homes but remain in their own country. Both groups often find themselves in camps being in effect 'warehoused' in circumstances similar or identical to security detainees.

The stated reasons for initiating systematic detentions can be varied. They can include safe provision of food and shelter to people who might otherwise lack such basics; protecting people from pressure from violent factions seeking to recruit them for a rebel cause; protecting vulnerable minorities from the wrath of the majority community; incarcerating individuals who are believed to be actually or potentially involved in terrorist activities; and holding individuals who are believed to have knowledge of enemy activities in order to interrogate them.

These reasons should not always be taken at face value. There are often other motives for incarceration: a desire to punish a particular group, or to send out a warning *pour encourager les autres*. There have been many cases of mass internments and detentions that have been exposed, either at the time or subsequently, as lacking in justification and causing lasting disruption and misery. Indeed, some have been based on little more than ethnic, political, or religious prejudice.

Just as the circumstances in which people are detained, and the stated reasons and motives for holding them, can vary greatly, so can the international legal rules that should govern their status and treatment. All of these many types of security detainees are subject to basic provisions of international human rights law, whether regional or global. These rules not only have particular applicability to the relations between citizens and their own government, but also have some application to other situations. In addition, some security detainees are also subject to other legal regimes. For example, civilians interned in belligerent states during war, and also those interned in occupied territory, are, as discussed later, subject to the provisions of the 1949 Geneva Convention IV on civilians; and refugees are subject to the body of rules based on the 1951 Convention on Refugees.

The very fact that the stated reasons and underlying motives for holding security detainees can be so varied, and so questionable, actually reinforces the case for considering them as a category of people whose status and treatment needs to be taken seriously and to involve common standards. A plethora of different circumstances and legal standards creates opportunities for loopholes. Various forms of ill-treatment of security detainees often aggravate conflicts.

MORAL, POLITICAL, AND STRATEGIC DIMENSIONS

In the 'war on terror', official documentation on the status and treatment of security detainees has for the most part been framed in legal terms. The US government memoranda on the non-applicability of the Geneva Conventions, and those justifying torture, were written by lawyers, mainly in the US Department of Justice. The narrowly legalistic approach that they adopted, discussed later, suffers from an obvious weakness. It focuses attention more on abstruse interpretations of the meaning of words and phrases than on moral, political, and strategic dimensions of the problem. Legalism can easily drive out common sense and the lessons of experience.

The moral difficulties raised by the holding of security detainees can be summarized quite simply. On the one hand, most societies that have been faced with certain types of serious security threats, especially those involving terrorism, have resorted to one form or another of detention without trial. Yet on the other hand, the holding of people who may have committed no offence, for an indefinite period, often with little or no international supervision or right of appeal, runs contrary to basic norms of justice, and creates extraordinary opportunities for abuse of power by the detaining authority. It risks being, or being seen as, the 'practice of arbitrary imprisonments' that was memorably condemned by Alexander Hamilton as 'the favourite and most formidable instrument of tyranny'.[5] The situation offends against moral codes that are common to many different cultures and legal systems; and it easily gives rise to rumours and reports of abuse. Controversies about detention without trial, and mistreatment of detainees, are all too common in guerrilla and counter-terrorist campaigns. This is not just a US problem.

These moral difficulties have political and strategic consequences. If people are detained who are believed in their communities to be innocent, then many hearts and minds are likely to be antagonized. In counter-insurgency or counter-terrorist campaigns, the central strategic purpose of the exercise—the drying up of the pool of support on which insurgents rely—will have been undermined. This consequence is even starker if and when it becomes known that ill-treatment or torture was used against detainees. Indeed, some terrorist movements have claimed, with a degree of plausibility, to be reacting to oppressive regimes that torture their adversaries.

Just as a belligerent in an armed conflict may encourage defections among the adversary's forces if conditions for prisoners of war are known to be reasonable, so a regime of detention that is known to be humanely managed may have the purpose of encouraging defections from guerrilla or terrorist movements—as was indicated in Lord Kitchener's memorandum of December 1900 cited earlier. Many such movements, in their internal propaganda, portray the adversary government as a regime of torturers precisely in order to reduce the risk of defections.

Examples of the adverse political and strategic effects of maltreatment are not hard to find. In the United Kingdom, the conditions of detention and interrogation of those suspected of terrorism in the course of the Northern Ireland Troubles from the late 1960s onwards provide an instructive example. Curiously, this episode is not mentioned in the generally comprehensive UK *Manual of the Law of Armed Conflict*, published in 2004;[6] nor does it appear to have been emphasized by the UK government in its thinking about the 'war on terror' since September 2001. Yet it has had a considerable impact on the thought and practice of the army in comparable situations. The Northern Ireland case is considered in detail elsewhere in this volume.[7] A brief summary of key aspects of detainee treatment in 1971–2 is needed here because it illustrates a central theme of this chapter: the need to be seen to work within a clear legal framework even if the circumstances of the case are different from those spelt out in relevant treaties.

In 1971, the UK government and the authorities in Northern Ireland responded to a situation of increasing violent unrest by introducing a policy of internment and interrogation of those suspected of involvement in terrorism. Their approach to internment and interrogation was widely perceived as both legally unsound and politically disastrous. The official policies and practices did not appear to work, could not be defended robustly because of their numerous weaknesses, and caused huge and continuous controversy. After some years, the UK government changed track and followed a different policy. So far as interrogation was concerned, it in effect applied basic legal principles derived from the laws of war in a situation to which the laws of war did not technically apply. It also accepted the application of the European Convention on Human Rights. This episode illustrates how responses to terrorism need to be shaped by moral and legal principle. The key document was the minority report, by Lord Gardiner, in the report of a three-man committee of Privy Councillors on interrogation procedures.[8] This was accepted by the government in a House of Commons statement on 2 March 1972. The Leader of the Opposition, Harold Wilson, made a comment on this decision that indicated a prudential consideration that may have lain behind it—namely that observance of such limitations can help to stop the further inflammation of an explosive political situation:

> It is a wise announcement in all the circumstances, and it may make more than a marginal difference to the possibility of stabilizing and improving the situation in Northern Ireland.[9]

This decision provided one useful basis for developing policy in a less inhumane and controversial direction than had prevailed up to 1972. However, no one could claim that it finally solved the question of treatment of detainees in Northern Ireland. This continued to be extremely difficult, as the large number of Northern Ireland cases relating to detention that went to the European Court of Human Rights showed. Although it might have been expected that such appeals to a court outside the United Kingdom would cause resentment, it has been suggested that officials in the Ministry of Defence and Northern Ireland Office regarded the process 'although painful and hard fought all the way, as ultimately beneficial.'[10] Overall, the episode contributed positively to the United Kingdom taking legal considerations seriously in the course of the struggle in Northern Ireland.

INTERNATIONAL LEGAL PROVISIONS REGARDING DETAINEES

W. C. Fields, when found on a film set reading the Bible, and asked why, replied: 'Looking for loopholes.' Many governments have approached the question of international law governing detention operations in the same spirit. Loopholes have not been hard to find.

The two bodies of international law that have a bearing on detention are human rights law and the laws of war. Human rights law has particular importance because it starts from a position of criticism of detention. As Article 9 of the International Covenant on Civil and Political Rights states: 'No one shall be subjected to arbitrary arrest or detention.' Also the Covenant places great emphasis on judicial guarantees, particularly in Article 14. However, the effect of these provisions is weakened by the fact that they are among the many articles from which states can derogate 'in time of public emergency which threatens the life of the nation.'

As far as the law of armed conflict (also called international humanitarian law) is concerned, a main problem has always been that many operations involving mass detentions have not been in the context of international war. They have taken place in colonial wars against internal rebellions, in civil wars, and in international counter-terrorist operations. Granted these basic facts, two possibilities arise as regards the application of the laws of armed conflict:

1. The full range of rules should be applied by analogy, as the set of rules most appropriate to the situation that is faced, even if the formal conditions of application have not been met. Under this approach, detainees might be held either as prisoners of war in accord with the 1949 Geneva Convention III, or as civilian detainees in accord with 1949 Geneva Convention IV.

2. Within the laws of war certain basic rules can be identified that apply to all detainees, irrespective of the precise characterization of the armed conflict. Under this approach, the 'minimum kit' of any detention regime would include common Article 3 of the 1949 Geneva Conventions (which applies to 'armed conflict not of an international character') and Article 75 of 1977 Geneva Protocol I (which is discussed further below).

Both of these approaches have the merit that they acknowledge that international legal rules contained in the laws of war must apply to detention operations. Yet there are not many precedents for these approaches. As regards the first approach, a pioneering document of the laws of war, the 1863 US Lieber Code, was prepared for use in the US civil war, and was clear that a wide range of enemies should be treated as prisoners of war. Thus, it might appear that the idea of applying the rules in a situation other than war between recognized sovereign states has a persuasive and respectable precedent. However, Article 67 of the Lieber Code appeared to take it for granted that the treatment of prisoners of war was connected to their status as being in the service of a state:

> The law of nations allows every sovereign government to make war upon another sovereign state, and, therefore, admits of no rules or laws different from those of regular warfare, regarding the treatment of prisoners of war, although they may belong to the army of a government which the captor may consider as a wanton and unjust assailant.[11]

When specifically addressing the problem of civil war and rebellion, the Lieber Code suggested that disloyal citizens, and also whole areas in revolt, could be subjected to a harsher regime than non-combatant enemies have to suffer in regular war; and Lieber went so far as to state that the commander 'may expel, transfer, imprison, or fine the revolted citizens who refuse to pledge themselves anew as citizens obedient to the law and loyal to the government'.[12] There is no mention here of POW status. Thus, at least as regards detainee issues, the Lieber Code offers no precedent for the proposition that the full range of international rules should be applied by analogy even in a situation differing from standard international war.

The frequently asked legal question about status is: should a given class of detainees be considered prisoners of war? Or civilians? Or something different? The existence of a possible third category is controversial. Forgetting for a moment the special questions raised by the 'war on terror', there is obviously some room for a third category. For example:

- In the case of a non-international armed conflict, or a terrorist campaign not reaching the level of a civil war, there are likely to be detainees, yet the 1949 Geneva Conventions do not apply fully, if at all, in such situations.

- In addition, 1977 Protocol I, Article 75 acknowledges that even in international armed conflicts certain detainees may have a status that is different from those of POWs and civilians under the 1949 Geneva Conventions III and IV. This article, which is almost a mini-convention in its own right, begins by stating that 'persons who are in the power of a Party to the conflict and who do not benefit from more favourable conditions under the Conventions or under this Protocol shall be treated humanely in all circumstances and shall enjoy, as a minimum, the protection provided by this Article . . .'.

The crucial issue is not whether there is sometimes a 'third' category, but what is done with that category, and in particular what body of law is seen as applying to it—both as regards determination of status, and as regards treatment. That is where serious mistakes have been made, and continue to be made, in the 'war on terror'.

Two problems that arise particularly with detainees in terrorist campaigns— and that are generally less serious in international wars—are:

- *The evidence on which detention is based.* It is well known that in counter-terrorist campaigns many innocent people have been detained and even convicted, so the question of whether and how detention can be challenged is serious.

- *The decision-making processes for ending detention in particular cases.* Since a 'war on terror' may last for decades, and may not have a determinate ending, the need for a process for ending detention is evident.

These problems are touched upon very inadequately in existing agreements on the laws of war.[13] As a result, it is important that principles embodied in the international law of human rights should be one part of an international regime on detainees. This is because, to a greater extent than the law of armed conflict, human rights law contains strong provisions about judicial guarantees—important if the position of detainees is to be reviewed robustly by an appropriately qualified body. In addition, the domestic laws of states are often of great importance in the management of a detention regime, and much can be learned from them. In a few states, detainee matters are addressed in the constitution.[14]

DETAINEES IN THE US-LED 'WAR ON TERROR' SINCE 2001

In the years between 11 September 2001 and the end of the administration of President George W. Bush in January 2009, the United States came up with a distinctive approach to the issue of the holding of detainees in an anti-terror campaign that was an object lesson in how not to manage such issues.

While in certain conflicts in the 'war on terror' the US government accepted the application of the laws of war, and recognized its adversaries as entitled to POW status, it pursued a different policy in respect of those suspected of involvement in terrorism. This policy particularly concerned the treatment of non-US citizens, and it had two main aspects:

- *Detention at locations whose existence is acknowledged*, and that are subject to some degree of supervision by the International Committee of the Red Cross. Guantanamo is the most conspicuous of these, and was chosen precisely because US law does not, or does not fully, apply there. Although there was an ICRC presence from 18 January 2002 onwards, the key US policy statement, issued by the White House on 7 February 2002, stated that neither Taliban nor al-Qaeda detainees at Guantanamo were entitled to the status of POW but they would be 'provided with many POW privileges as a matter of policy.'

- *Detention at secret locations*, of which certain US-run establishments in Poland and Romania appear to be the clearest examples. This category also includes the secret transfer of detainees to foreign prisons (e.g. in Syria and Morocco). Their existence and management, and the practice of extraordinary rendition to them, were not acknowledged by the Bush administration as being covered by international law: neither the law of armed conflict nor the law of human rights was deemed applicable.

On 17 October 2006 President Bush signed the 2006 Military Commissions Act, which provided a clearer legal framework than before for trying non-US citizens deemed to be 'unlawful enemy combatants'. However, this law contained controversial elements. It denied habeas corpus rights to detainees who have not been charged with any offence. Bush emphasized that it allowed the Central Intelligence Agency to continue its programme for questioning key terrorist leaders and operatives: at the signing ceremony he said that this was 'one of the most successful intelligence efforts in American history. It has helped prevent attacks on our country.'

Meanwhile, the prison at Guantanamo remained a matter of acute controversy. So, too—and increasingly—was the extraordinary rendition of detainees to locations where not too many questions would be asked about the conditions of their detention and interrogation—a matter that was the subject of detailed reports in 2006–7 by the Council of Europe,[15] the US Congressional Research Service,[16] and the European Parliament.[17] While the US government issued numerous statements that US military personnel must not use torture, it did not face up to the evidence that some of the officially sanctioned practices in the 'war on terror'—especially as applied by certain US intelligence personnel— amounted to torture. Moreover, attempts by the US and its allies to clear up the mess caused by past failures of detainee policy are themselves problematical, and have led to a Babel-like set of arrangements and agreements in present-day Afghanistan, discussed in the next section.

One unexpected consequence of the US policy on detainees has been the difficulty of putting them on trial, and the failure to do so in practically all cases. Two factors have been involved. First, at least until 2006, the Bush admin-istration had laid down procedures for trial by military commissions that had little chance of being viewed as legitimate by any international body or by any US appellate body—or indeed by some of the officers who would have been in charge of the commissions: so it was inhibited from initiating the very trials that it had claimed to want. Second, numerous interrogators, increasingly fearful of claims or revelations that they had used torture, have been, and remain, afraid to give evidence.

The moral muddle and practical confusion surrounding detainee issues led to increasing pressure to sort out questions relating to the status and treatment of the detainees. A key landmark was the decision of the US Supreme Court in June 2006 in *Hamdan v. Rumsfeld,* which laid down that some provisions of the 1949 Geneva Conventions—in particular those in their common Article 3—applied to detainees in the 'war on terror'. This decision was not free of problems: many were surprised at the Court's interpretation of Article 3's scope of application—'armed conflict not of an international character occurring in the territory of one of the High Con-tracting Parties'— as encompassing the international campaign against terrorism. What was important in the Court's decision was the open acceptance that the United States had to act within the framework of international law. No longer was it a matter of the US government stating that it would implement certain provi-sions on an optional basis: the Supreme Court made it clear that this was a matter of legal obligation. In particular, there was a clear prohibition on cruel treatment and torture, and a requirement that, if detainees are put on trial, it could not be by the military commissions planned by President George W. Bush, but must be in a better-constituted court. Also the Supreme Court judgement mentioned Article 75 of 1977 Protocol I.

How was it that the US government had handled the policy on detainees so disastrously? What was the process of US government decision-making that led to extensive torture and to international public revulsion? It appears to have been the pressures on the US military in Iraq, at the time of growing insurgency in summer 2003, that led to the use of torture. In an e-mail in mid-August 2003 a captain in military intelligence said of detainees classified as unprivileged belligerents: '[W]e want these individuals broken. Casualties are mounting and we need to start gathering info to help protect our fellow soldiers from any further attacks.'[18]

Other factors influenced the weak policy-making on detainees. There is simply no evidence of a robust process of discussion at the highest levels of the US government, in which the full range of moral, political, and strategic considerations relating to the status and treatment of detainees was explored.[19] In addition, the US decision-making process was procedurally odd, often leaving out of the loop departments that might have had some sensitivity to the complexities of detainee issues. It is noticeable how some of the key memos from the Department of Justice were simply not copied to State. There was a direct line from the Department of Justice to Alberto Gonzales (at that time Counsel to the President), occasionally (but by no means always) including the Department of Defense.

There have been over ten major official investigations into allegations of prisoner and detainee abuse in Iraq, Afghanistan, and Guantanamo. The reports of these investigations suggest that a distinction can be drawn between the part of the torture which was a reflection of unprofessional and frequently incompetent behaviour, not linked in any way to serious interrogation, and the other part of the torture that was part of a programme of intelligence collection. The first was symbolized by the horrific photos taken in Abu Ghraib. The second represents what may be a more sinister and enduring problem.

There is a need for fuller discussion on such matters as:

1. How did the argument that ill-treatment would yield good intelligence develop in certain parts of the US government and armed forces? In particular, was this a classic case of 'bogus realism' based on lazy thinking and no evidence, or was there a serious basis for it? Was there an obsessive focus on the utterly exceptional but much-cited case of the ticking nuclear time-bomb as justification for torture? Was there ever a serious discussion within the US government of the numerous reasons for questioning the assumption that ill-treatment results in good intelligence, and even more that it is a way to help end insurgency?

2. Is there something peculiar to US legal culture that can take seriously such arguments as those in the notorious memorandum sent from the Justice Department to the White House on 1 August 2002? This memo (which had to be withdrawn in 2004) had stood the plain meaning of words on their head when it redefined torture in such a way as to allow a huge range of cruel and inhuman treatment to escape the definitional net of United States and international legislation against torture. It had also indicated that the President had total and unfettered discretion to ensure that prisoners were effectively interrogated, even to the point of authorizing torture.[20]

3. Why were the officials and others dealing with these issues so prone to arguing abstractly, without any reference to historical events and to previous cases of torture? Did the alleged uniqueness of the al Qaeda threat, and of the US struggle, mean that all historical evidence was deemed irrelevant?

The verdict on US policy regarding detainees has been mainly negative. In an article in July 2007, Jack Goldsmith, US Assistant Attorney General from October 2003 to June 2004 with particular responsibility for advising President Bush regarding the legal framework of the 'war on terror', reached this grim conclusion:

> Nearly six years after 9/11, the US government's system for detaining terrorists without charge or trial has harmed the reputation of the country, disrupted alliances, hurt it in the war of ideas with the Islamic world and been viewed skeptically by U.S. courts.[21]

It is not enough, however, to conclude with easy criticism. It is also necessary to recognize the complexity of the issue with which the United States was faced, and to consider the practical problems of how to bring to an end a dreadful episode in US history. President Obama has declared that Guantanamo will close. Earlier, the UK government indicated that it wanted it closed, and President Bush had even indicated the same. However, it was hard to resolve who would be prepared to accept the actual people. No country wants to take over the responsibility for any significant portion of them, and no American state wants them on its territory. Guantanamo, in short, is proof of the proposition that a bad policy is one that creates a situation from which there is no easy escape.

THE MUDDLE IN AFGHANISTAN

The case of Afghanistan, and in particular the attempts to develop a detainee regime there, illustrates how even eight years into the 'war on terror' there is wasteful effort and ongoing policy confusion on a vital issue. The treatment of detainees in that country has long been problematic, resulting in many disturbing events, including the prison revolt at Qala-e Jhangi Fort near Mazar-e Sharif in the period 25 November–1 December 2001, and in the cases of mistreatment and killing of prisoners in the area of Shebarghan from December 2001 onwards.

The NATO-led International Security Assistance Force (ISAF) in Afghanistan has from the beginning operated within a framework of commitment to human rights. This is evident in the Security Council resolutions defining its mission, starting with Resolution 1386 of December 2001 which contained a reference to 'inalienable rights' to be enjoyed by all Afghans.[22] It is also clear from the Military Technical Agreement concluded in January 2002, on the basis of Resolution 1386, between ISAF and the Interim Administration of Afghanistan.[23]

The extensive roles of foreign forces in Afghanistan, coupled with awareness of the potential of detainee issues to cause political disaster, have added salience and urgency to the question of treatment of detainees that the various units comprising ISAF (or indeed the US-led coalition forces) may take in the course of their operations. The issue is particularly delicate because detainees have to be handed over to the Afghan authorities. There has been an obvious requirement for a coherent integrated approach on the handling of detainee matters. As a result of considerable attention being devoted to this matter, there have been two kinds of policy outcomes:

1. Bilateral agreements were made between individual ISAF- or coalition-participating governments and the government of Afghanistan in 2005 and 2006. At certain times it has been possible to find some of these agreements on web sites of the governments concerned. These include the agreements made by Denmark, referring to 'the relevant provisions of international law, including providing humane treatment';[24] by Canada, requiring detainees to be treated in accord with Geneva Convention III;[25] by the Netherlands, with different but clear stipulations on detainee treatment;[26] and the United Kingdom, drawing on 'basic standards of international human rights law such as the right to life, and the prohibition against torture and cruel, inhumane and degrading treatment'.[27]

2. Some pronouncements and agreements of a more general nature have been concluded: for example, an ISAF Standard Operating Procedure on detainee issues was adopted in May 2006. Paragraph 1 of this document is notable for its joint appeal to the rival gods of law and strategy when it states:

   Commanders at all levels are to ensure that detention operations are conducted in accordance with applicable international law and human rights standards, and that all detainees are treated with respect and dignity at all times. The strategic benefits of conducting detention operations in a humanitarian manner are significant. Detention operations that fail to meet the high standards mandated herein will inevitably have a detrimental impact on the ISAF Mission.[28]

The Afghan government would be entitled to be bemused by the complexity of the legal arrangements for classification and treatment or detainees, consisting as they do of an extraordinary variety of different documents from different states. It is especially noteworthy that the dialogue on these matters with the United States, despite its almost baroque complexity, fails to put any emphasis on the application of human rights law. Nor is there a clear and agreed line on what are the relevant and applicable rules of the laws of war. Canada says bluntly that the standards of Geneva Convention III must be followed, but others place emphasis on human rights law. There are serious concerns that some detainees handed over to the Afghan authorities on the basis of these agreements have been maltreated.[29]

It is puzzling to many students of the laws of war that the historical tendency, particularly pronounced since the mid nineteenth century, to secure agreement on a uniform set of internationally agreed rules on such basic matters as treatment of prisoners should have been stood on its head in Afghanistan, with a plethora of different rules and precious little uniformity.

A NEW INTERNATIONAL AGREEMENT?

To criticize the records of the United States and other NATO governments, whether in Afghanistan or elsewhere, is not to say that the laws of war or of human rights, as at present constituted, offer a sufficient framework, nor that there are simple answers to all the legal, practical, and policy issues involved. It is widely accepted that the international legal regime on detainee issues, while far from non-existent, does lack clarity and specificity, especially when the detention is not in the context of an international armed conflict. There is a need for a set of procedural principles and safeguards that should—as a matter of law and policy—be applied as a minimum to at least those cases of deprivation of liberty for security reasons not covered by the 1949 Geneva Conventions.

International lawyers with experience of detainee issues have increasingly recognized this. For example, Jelena Pejic of the ICRC has proposed such an approach.[30] Similarly, Bruce Oswald of the Melbourne Law School has suggested that existing legal regimes are 'fragmented and inadequate' and that there is 'a need to develop a special regime that deals with detention'.[31]

An objection to such a proposal could be that security detention is a form of arbitrary imprisonment, and that the proper position would be to insist on habeas corpus rights for all: detainees should be either charged or released. This view is persuasive in many situations but runs up against the fact that certain forms of detention without trial are widely accepted, including of course the status of prisoner of war. The case for developing a special regime is that if some detentions without trial of people other than POWs are inevitable, much needs to be done to address issues which regularly arise. However, the solution does not necessarily lie in the direction of granting habeas corpus rights to all detainees.

Questions to be tackled in any negotiation include: what should be the procedures, criteria, and safeguards regarding the initiation of detention? What should be the decision-making process for deciding to release individuals from detention—an issue that is proving especially troublesome in the 'long war' against terrorism? What forms of oversight, by ICRC or other bodies, would be appropriate in detention facilities? And if in certain cases extraordinary rendition is considered necessary—for example to take a detainee out of a country where the government is too terrorized by its opponents to be able to release anyone to foreign justice—what safeguards can be put in place to ensure that such rendition does not lead to secret prisons and abuse against individuals, nor does it become a more generalized practice? Other issues, such as the critically important one of re-education of detainees suspected of involvement in terrorism, may more appropriately be handled by individual countries in accord with their own legal systems and cultural or religious frameworks.

It might seem logical that such an agreement should be negotiated in the framework of the United Nations. All these issues relate to the United Nations for a variety of reasons.

- The UN General Assembly, and bodies that have been created under it, has been deeply involved in drawing up and monitoring the implementation of a range of closely related treaties in the field of human rights, including the 1984 UN Convention on Torture.
- The UN Security Council has assumed a degree of responsibility for addressing terrorism issues, and has stressed that states, in taking measures against terrorism, must 'comply with all of their obligations under international law, in particular international human rights law, refugee law, and humanitarian law'.[32]

However, UN conferences involve well-known problems of delay and grandstanding. There is an argument for preliminary work being done first by other bodies with expertise and interests in this field. The ICRC is one such body, and its record of preparing texts for negotiation is impressive. Even though detainee status and treatment is an issue not tied exclusively to armed conflict, there is a strong enough connection for the ICRC role to be entirely legitimate. There is also a case for NATO getting its act together first.

The main existing initiative in the field, the Copenhagen Process on the Handling of Detainees, has involved NATO, the UN, the ICRC, and more than twenty countries around the world, of whom the majority are NATO members. This Danish initiative started in 2006 to establish detainee standards for a UN-mandated coalition acting abroad (whether in international armed conflict, an internal one, or violence short of armed conflict) has made progress, but has not yet resulted in a unified solution to the problem either in general or in respect of the case that provoked the initiative—Afghanistan.[33]

The status and treatment of detainees is not just a US problem but a more general one, for the United Kingdom, the United Nations, and others. It is a perennial problem, which long pre-dates the 'war on terror' and Afghanistan. It encompasses, but is not confined to, the sphere of military operations that is the subject of the Copenhagen Process. It is inherently difficult to resolve by general international negotiation. Yet unless and until some resolution is found, detainees will continue to be misfits in more ways than are necessary.

NOTES

1. Hugo Grotius, *De Jure Belli ac Pacis Libri Tres* (Paris, 1625), book III, ch. XIV. In the *Classics of International Law* edition, 761–9.
2. 'Concentration camp: a camp where non-combatants of a district are accommodated, such as those instituted by Lord Kitchener during the South African War of 1899–1902; one for the internment of political prisoners, foreign nationals, etc., esp. as organized by the Nazi regime in Germany before and during the war of 1939–45.' *Oxford English Dictionary online*, accessed 18 May 2009.

3. Lord Kitchener, memorandum to General Officers Commanding, Pretoria, 21 December 1900. Text in A. C. Martin, *The concentration camps 1900–1902: Facts, figures, and fables* (Cape Town: Howard Timmins, 1957), 7.
4. United Nations Security Council, S/RES/1546 (2004), adopted by the Security Council at its 4,987th meeting, on 8 June 2004.
5. Alexander Hamilton, 'Certain general and miscellaneous objections to the Constitution considered and answered', *The Federalist*, no. 84 (28 May 1788).
6. UK Ministry of Defence, *The manual of the law of armed conflict* (Oxford: Oxford University Press, 2004).
7. See Huw Bennett, 'Detention and interrogation in Northern Ireland, 1969–1975', in this volume.
8. Report of the Committee of Privy Counsellors appointed to consider authorized procedures for the interrogation of persons suspected of Terrorism, Cmnd. 4,901, Her Majesty's Stationery Office, London, March 1972. Report available at <http://cain.ulst.ac.uk/hmso/parker.htm>.
9. *Hansard*, House of Commons, 2 March 1972, col. 744.
10. Lord Lester of Herne Hill, speaking in the House of Lords debate on the International Criminal Court Bill. Lord Archer of Sandwell, one of the Law Officers at the time of the ECHR Northern Ireland cases, stated on this point: 'I totally agree.' *Hansard*, House of Lords, 8 March 2001, col. 371. Available at <http://www.publications.parliament.uk/pa/ld/ldse0001.htm>.
11. 'Instructions for the Government of the Armies of the United States in the Field', prepared by Francis Lieber and promulgated at General Orders No. 100 by President Lincoln, 24 April 1863, Article 67. Text in Dietrich Schindler and Jiri Toman (eds.), *The laws of armed conflicts: A collection of conventions, resolutions and other documents* (3rd rev. and completed edn.; Dordrecht: Martinus Nijhoff, 1988), 3–23.
12. Lieber Code, Article 156.
13. 1949 Geneva Convention IV, Articles 43 and 132; 1977 Geneva Protocol I, Article 75(3).
14. The Singapore Constitution, Part XII, provides for the use of the Internal Security Act (a colonial hangover) under which the Minister for Home Affairs, at the direction of the President, may issue preventive detention orders against persons who are suspected of acting in a manner that endangers Singapore's security. There is an Advisory Board to review individual cases periodically, and a Board of Inspection to examine detention facilities.
15. In a preliminary report issued on 13 December 2005, the Swiss senator Dick Marty, who was the investigator appointed by the Council of Europe's Committee on Legal Affairs and Human Rights, said his investigation had 'reinforced the credibility of the allegations concerning the transfer and temporary detention of individuals, without any judicial involvement, in European countries'. See also his subsequent report, containing much new information, *Alleged secret detentions and unlawful inter-state transfers of detainees involving Council of Europe member states* (Council of Europe: Parliamentary Assembly Doc. 10957, 12 June 2006), available at <http://assembly.coe.int/Documents/WorkingDocs/doc06/edoc10957.pdf>.
16. *Undisclosed U.S. detention sites overseas: Background and legal issues* (Washington, DC: Congressional Research Service Report for Congress, 12 September 2006).
17. European Parliament, Temporary Committee on the alleged use of European countries by the CIA for the transportation and illegal detention of prisoners, Final Report, 26

January 2007; available at <http://www.europarl.europa.eu/comparl/tempcom/tdip/default_en.htm>.

18. Mark Danner. *Torture and truth: America, Abu Ghraib, and the war on terror* (New York: New York Review of Books, 2004), 33.

19. For accounts of decision-making on detainees, see Jack Goldsmith, *The terror presidency: Law and judgment inside the Bush administration* (New York: W. W. Norton, 2007); and Philippe Sands, *Torture team: Deception, cruelty and the compromise of law* (London: Allen Lane, 2008).

20. See also US Department of Justice, Office of Legal Counsel, Memorandum for William J. Haynes II, General Counsel of the Department of Defense, 'Re military interrogation of alien unlawful combatants held outside the United States', 14 March 2003.

21. Jack L. Goldsmith and Neal Katyal, 'The terrorists' court', *International Herald Tribune* (13 July 2007), 7.

22. ISAF was originally established in Afghanistan in January 2002 on the basis of UN Security Council Resolution 1386 of 20 December 2001, passed unanimously. Subsequent resolutions extended and modified ISAF's mandate, structure, and scope of operations.

23. Military Technical Agreement between the International Security Assistance Force and the Interim Administration of Afghanistan, 4 January 2002, Article III(1). Text in *International Legal Materials*, 41/5 (Washington, DC, September 2002), 1032. Text (plus annexes) also available at <http://www.operations.mod.uk/isafmta.pdf>.

24. 'Memorandum of Understanding between the Ministry of Defense of the Islamic Republic of Afghanistan and the Ministry of Defense of the Kingdom of Denmark concerning the transfer of persons between the Danish Contingent of ISAF and Afghan authorities' of 8 June 2005, and amendment of 1 May 2007. Both documents available at <http://www.ambottawa.um.dk/en/menu/InfoDenmark/Denmark + in + Afghanistan/Detainees>; accessed July 2009.

25. 'Arrangement for the transfer of detainees between the Canadian Forces and the Ministry of Defence of the Islamic Republic of Afghanistan', Kabul, 18 December 2005. Supplemented by an agreement of 3 May 2007. Both documents available at <http://www.afghanistan.gc.ca/canada-afghanistan/documents/index.aspx>; accessed July 2009.

26. 'Memorandum of Understanding between the Ministry of Defense of the Islamic Republic of Afghanistan and the Minister of Defense of the Kingdom of the Netherlands concerning the transfer of persons by Netherlands military forces in Afghanistan to Afghan authorities.' The text of this agreement, concluded in late 2005, and previously available at a different URL, is now available at <http://static.ikregeer.nl/pdf/BLG7493.pdf>; accessed July 2009.

27. 'Memorandum of Understanding between the Government of the United Kingdom of Great Britain and Northern Ireland and the Government of the Islamic Republic of Afghanistan concerning Transfer by the United Kingdom Armed Forces to Afghan Authorities of Persons Detained in Afghanistan', Kabul, 30 September 2006: <http://www.publications.parliament.uk/pa/cm200607/cmselect/cmfaff/44/4412.htm>; accessed May 2009.

28. 'Standard Operating Procedures: Detention of Non ISAF Personnel', SOP 362, 2nd edn., ISAF Headquarters, Kabul, 23 May 2006, para.1.

29. See Amnesty International, 'Afghanistan—detainees transferred to torture: ISAF complicity?', London, November 2007, 20–30.

30. Jelena Pejic, 'Procedural principles and safeguards for internment/administrative detention in armed conflict and other situations of violence', *International Review of the Red Cross*, 87/858 (2005), 375–91.
31. Bruce 'Ossie' Oswald, 'Detention of civilians on military operations: Reasons for and challenges to developing a special law of detention', *Melbourne University Law Review*, 32/2 (2008), 553.
32. United Nations Security Council, S/RES/1624 (2005), adopted at the Security Council summit meeting on the 60th anniversary of the United Nations, 14 September 2005.
33. See e.g. a report of the June 2009 meeting of the Copenhagen Process, available at: <http://www.denmark.dk/en/servicemenu/News/InternationalNews/ProgressMade InInternationalDetaineePolicy.htm>; accessed July 2009.

18

Outsourcing Torture: Extraordinary Rendition and the Necessity for Extraterritorial Protection of Human Rights

David D. Cole

On 26 September 2002, Maher Arar, a Canadian citizen, was on his way home, changing planes at John F. Kennedy Airport on a two-leg flight from Switzerland to Montreal. Delays are not uncommon at Kennedy Airport, but Arar's was extraordinary. He did not make it home for more than a year. Before he could catch his connecting flight, United States officials detained Arar, and eventually locked him up for two weeks. During that time, they interrogated him at length, denied his initial requests for a lawyer, and held him incommunicado for a week. When they finally allowed him to make a phone call, he called his family in Canada, and they arranged for a lawyer in New York to represent him. The lawyer met with Arar as soon as possible, on a Saturday, his tenth day of detention.

US officials responded to Arar having met an attorney by hastily arranging a highly unusual proceeding in his case for the following evening—a Sunday evening. The hearing, at which they told him they might deport him, not to Canada, but to Syria—began at 9 pm and ran for six hours, until 3 am Monday morning. Arar repeatedly claimed that he feared being tortured if sent to Syria (he was born in Syria, so had dual nationality, but had lived in Canada his entire adult life). US officials told Arar that his lawyer had chosen not to appear at the Sunday evening hearing. In fact, the only notice they provided her about the hearing was a voicemail message they left on her office phone that same Sunday evening—when her office was closed. The next morning, Arar's lawyer returned the message by calling immigration officials to inquire about Arar. They told her—falsely—that he was being transferred to a New Jersey jail, and that she would be informed of his whereabouts once he arrived there. In fact, federal officials were at that moment taking Arar to an airport, where he was placed on a federally chartered jet. Only as he got on board did US officials serve Arar with his deportation order—telling him that he was in fact being sent to Syria. The officials never served the notice on Arar's attorney, and never told her where he had been taken.

Why would the United States stop a Canadian citizen who was simply changing planes on his way home, and forcibly redirect him to Syria? The United States is generally thought to have better relations with Canada than with Syria. But Canada does not have a record of arbitrarily detaining and torturing suspects; Syria does. In fact, the United States State Department 2002 report on human rights in Syria stated that Syria used 'torture in detention . . . arbitrary arrest and detention [and] prolonged arbitrary detention'. It cited reports that the Syrians had used all of the following torture tactics: 'administering electrical shocks; pulling out fingernails; forcing objects into the rectum; beating, sometimes while the victim is suspended from the ceiling; hyperextending the spine; and using a chair that bends backwards to asphyxiate the victim or fracture the victim's spine'.[1]

US officials have claimed that they obtained 'diplomatic assurances' from Syria that it would not torture Arar. They have not explained why they considered such assurances reliable, when they do not seem to find anything else Syria tells them credible, and when their own State Department report noted that the Syrian government 'denied that it uses torture'. In any event, the assurances failed, because upon his arrival Syrian security officials immediately took Arar into custody and began to torture him while asking him questions virtually identical to those the US authorities had asked him when he was detained in New York. They beat him with an electric cable, and threatened him with electric shocks and 'the tire', a torture device, while interrogating him for eighteen hours. They ultimately kept him locked up for nearly a year in a cell the size of a grave—three feet by six feet by seven feet.

After about a year, the Syrians released Arar, announcing that they had found no evidence that he had engaged in any wrongdoing. He returned home to Canada—bypassing Kennedy Airport this time. The Canadians undertook a comprehensive investigation of his case, and ultimately released a 1,100-page report fully exonerating Arar, finding that he had engaged in no wrongdoing whatsoever, and was an entirely innocent man. The report also found that Canadian authorities had provided misinformation to the Americans, telling them that Arar was a 'target' of a terrorism investigation when he was not, but that the Canadians had never been told by US authorities that they planned to send him to Syria. Canada's Parliament unanimously issued Arar an official apology, and the Canadian government paid him $10.5 million (Canadian) in damages for its part in his mistreatment.

Meanwhile, the United States has refused to acknowledge any wrongdoing in the case. It still has Arar on a watchlist that bars him from entering the country. When Congress held a hearing on his case in 2007, executive officials rejected a request by members of Congress that Arar be permitted to come to Washington to testify at the hearing. He had to testify by videoconference instead. When Arar filed a lawsuit seeking to establish that what happened to him was illegal, the United States responded by arguing that he had no constitutional rights because he was not an American citizen, and that in any event his legal claims challenging his rendition should be dismissed because the US communications with Canada and Syria regarding his transfer to Syria were secret and could not be disclosed. A district court and a divided three-judge panel of the court of appeals ruled that Arar's claims could not be adjudicated because they touched on sensitive national security and foreign affairs concerns. The full court of appeals agreed to rehear the case, and decision is pending.

Maher Arar was a victim of a tactic developed by the United States in the wake of the terrorist attacks on the World Trade Center and the Pentagon of 11 September 2001. The tactic, known as extraordinary rendition, is a peculiarly twisted adaptation of the corporate practice of 'outsourcing'. Just as corporations in developed countries have exploited the relative ease of global transportation and communication to relocate production to countries with less restrictive laws and lower costs, so the United States in the global war on terror has outsourced interrogation of terror suspects to countries with fewer restrictions on interrogation tactics. Both practices seek to exploit transnational opportunities to evade legal constraints. In both settings, the challenge for law is how to defeat efforts to exploit such transnational opportunism.

Renditions to torture, or extraordinary renditions, are part of what US officials under President Bush coined the 'paradigm of prevention'. On their view, the United States needed to act pre-emptively in the fight against terrorism. The use of coercive force was justified not only to hold proven wrongdoers accountable for their past or ongoing criminal activity, but to prevent feared future attacks.[2] Because no one can predict the future, these tactics were often directed against persons—and countries—based on necessarily speculative predictions about what they might do in the future. Preventive detention, preventive war, and coercive interrogation have all been justified in the name of preventing the next attack. Arar was a victim of this approach. US officials had no evidence of his engaging in wrongdoing—if they had, they could have tried him for those acts, or delivered him to Canada so that it could try him. They only had suspicions, fed by the false Canadian report that he was a target of an investigation. And when US officials could not get the answers they wanted by interrogating Arar themselves, they sent him to Syria to see if the Syrians could get the answers.

Because the entire renditions programme was carried out in secret and remains shrouded in secrecy, it is not known precisely how many others were subject to these practices, but Arar was not alone. On 1 January 2004, Khaled al-Masri, a German national, was abducted by the CIA while on holiday in Macedonia, rendered to Afghanistan, tortured, and detained incommunicado for nearly five months. He was unceremoniously released on an abandoned roadside in Albania when US authorities realized that he had been picked up in a case of mistaken identity.[3] In a 2007 speech to the Council on Foreign Relations, CIA Director Michael Hayden suggested that the number of persons rendered since 11 September 2001 had been in the 'mid-range double figures'.[4] Human Rights Watch has identified fourteen persons who had been rendered to Jordan alone.[5] As of this writing, the Obama administration has not taken a public position on renditions. However, in a disturbing sign, it invoked a 'state secrets' privilege to argue that a lawsuit on behalf of victims of renditions to torture should be dismissed because it involved national security secrets that could not be disclosed. However, even if the Obama administration were to end the practice, it is important to assess its legality, for it may prove tempting to government officials again in the wake of future terrorist attacks, in the United States or elsewhere.

Extraordinary renditions, like the preventive paradigm more generally, coexist uneasily with the rule of law. When a state seeks to take coercive action against an individual, the rule of law generally requires that it do so under rules that apply equally to all, that it act transparently, that it provide the individual with a fair hearing, and that it respect fundamental human rights. Yet in Arar's case, the US government has argued that Arar's rights were not violated because he is a foreign national, and therefore was not entitled to any constitutional rights, invoking an explicit and all-too-common double standard.[6] Renditions are by definition carried out in the darkness of secrecy. In Arar's case, government officials initially held him incommunicado, and then lied to Arar and his lawyer to ensure that he could not invoke the protection of a court. They have subsequently argued that all retrospective relief is also barred by the need to maintain secrets. And the very purpose of an extraordinary rendition is to take someone beyond the protection of the law, so that he can be subjected to interrogation tactics that would be barred in any regime governed by human rights law. Because rendition is by definition a transnational practice that seeks to avoid domestic legal constraints, international human rights may well be the most important response. If the rule of law is to be effective in eliminating this practice, it needs to apply across national borders.

This chapter argues first that extraordinary rendition, or rendition to torture, is illegal under international law, in particular the UN Convention Against Torture and Other Forms of Cruel, Inhuman, and Degrading Punishment or Treatment. The 'territorial' loopholes the Bush administration sought to exploit to justify the practice, most of which depend on the transnational character of the practice, are predicated on misinterpretations of the Torture Convention, an international treaty designed to outlaw torture everywhere and under all circumstances. The Torture Convention expressly bans expelling individuals to countries where they face a risk of torture; *a fortiori*, it must ban transfers that are *designed* to subject an individual to torture. It imposes an absolute prohibition on torture, and expressly extends that prohibition extraterritorially. The Bush administration nonetheless invoked outmoded notions of territorial limits on its legal obligations to avoid accountability under international law. But the international human rights revolution of the past fifty years has increasingly rejected such limiting conceptions of strict territoriality, and has instead adopted the view that human rights norms apply wherever a state exercises effective control over an individual or area with respect to the right in question. Where a state has an individual in its physical custody, it cannot avoid the strictures of international law, and specifically the Torture Convention, by outsourcing the individual.

In addition, I will argue, rendition to torture violates domestic US laws, both constitutional and statutory. The fact that much of the harm occurs outside US borders should not shield government officials from the dictates of their own laws, particularly where the laws expressly contemplate enforcement against conduct that takes place at least in part overseas.

Much of the debate about renditions, and about the related practice of deporting foreign nationals to countries with notorious torture records, centres on the permissibility of 'diplomatic assurances'. Such assurances, used by the United States, the United Kingdom, and several other countries, involve obtaining a promise from a country known for torturing its suspects that it will not torture a particular suspect if that suspect is delivered to it. The practice of relying on diplomatic assurances is questionable under any circumstances: there is little reason to trust the promise of a country that has already tortured repeatedly in violation of its promise to abide by the Torture Convention; and in any event, compliance with assurances seems almost impossible to monitor effectively. But diplomatic assurances are especially illegitimate in the context of extraordinary rendition, where the entire purpose of the transfer is to have the suspect interrogated, and where the entire practice is shrouded in secrecy and extralegal practices that make assessment and enforcement of promises virtually impossible. In this setting, the risks of torture are simply too great to permit the use of diplomatic assurances. If the United States wanted to ensure that Arar not be tortured, it had an option directly available to it—deport him to his home country of Canada, which does not have a record of torturing its suspects.

The arguments in favour of rendition to torture are utilitarian; by helping to elicit information from terrorist suspects, security services may be able to thwart planned terrorist attacks and thereby save innocent lives. It is a watered-down form of the 'ticking time-bomb' argument made in favour of torture. The argument fails for all the reasons that the ticking time-bomb argument fails.[7] One will virtually never know whether the suspect knows where the bomb is, whether the information might be obtained without resort to torture, and whether torture will compel him to speak falsely rather than truthfully. In the rendition setting, moreover, the requirement of imminence that makes the ticking bomb hypothetically powerful is absent; if there is time to ship a suspect off to a third country, the threat cannot be truly imminent. At the end of the day, the ban on torture is and should remain an absolute one; and resort to international transfers to avoid it should not be tolerated. There are many other ways to thwart terrorism than by resorting to torture.

TERRITORIALITY RECONSIDERED: RENDITION AND THE TORTURE CONVENTION

It should not be surprising that rendition to torture violates international law. The prohibition on torture is one of the most well-established norms in international law. It has the status of a universal, non-derogable *jus cogens* norm, meaning that it permits no exceptions. It shares this status with the prohibitions on slavery, genocide, and summary execution. Such prohibitions cannot be evaded by erecting the screen of territoriality. Just as it would violate the prohibition on slavery and genocide to send someone to another country to be made a slave or a genocide victim, so, too, it violates international law to send someone to a third country to be tortured.

The UN Convention Against Torture and Other Cruel, Inhuman, and Degrading Treatment or Punishment (CAT), a treaty ratified by the United States in 1994, prohibits all forms of torture, and also prohibits the transfer of persons to countries where there is a substantial likelihood that they will be tortured. Article 3 provides that no state 'shall expel, return (*refouler*) or extradite a person to another State where there are substantial grounds for believing that he would be in danger of being subjected to torture.'

Article 3 was explicitly engaged by the decision to remove Maher Arar from the United States to Syria, as he was unquestionably 'expelled'. Some have questioned whether Article 3 covers the more typical rendition, in which a state transfers an individual between two other states, without ever bringing the individual into its own state. The United States' Congressional Research Service has opined, for example, that the terms 'expel, return, or extradite' in Article 3 of CAT may not cover a rendition that occurs entirely outside the rendering country's borders. When CIA officials render an individual from Afghanistan to Egypt, for example, the CRS reasons, the transfer may not constitute an expulsion, return, or extradition.[8] The CRS narrowly reads 'expel' to be restricted to expulsions from the acting state's own borders, and not other forms of transfer.

The argument that the Convention does not apply to a state's forcible transfer of an individual that occurs wholly outside the state's borders ultimately rests on the notion that legal restrictions presumptively should not apply extraterritorially. As an historical matter, international law traditionally considered sovereignty and territoriality and jurisdiction to be coextensive. In the modern era, however, as Professor Sarah Cleveland has carefully documented, human rights norms have increasingly been interpreted to apply not only within a state's own borders, but wherever the state exercises effective control over a place or a person.[9] Thus, the Inter-American Commission on Human Rights has stated that the obligations of the American Convention on Human Rights apply wherever a state exercises effective control over an individual, regardless of territorial considerations.[10] It similarly reasoned that the rights articulated in the American Declaration of Rights apply wherever the state has control over an individual, because the rights inhere in human dignity, and therefore it should not matter where the individual is found.[11]

The European Convention on Human Rights has not been interpreted quite so expansively, yet it, too, extends its obligations beyond a state's borders where the state exercises effective control over an area. The United Kingdom's Law Lords, for example, have held that ECHR rights apply in a British prison maintained in Basra, Iraq, because the British Army exercised effective control over the prison.[12] The European Court of Human Rights has stated that the obligations of the European Convention extend wherever a state exercises effective control over an area outside that state's jurisdiction, and has further noted that 'a State may also be held accountable for violation of the Convention rights and freedoms of persons who are in the territory of another State but who are found to be under the former State's authority and control through its agents operating— whether lawfully or unlawfully—in the latter state.'[13]

The Convention Against Torture expressly provides that its obligations extend to 'any territory under the state's jurisdiction',[14] language that the United States points to in asserting that the Convention does not apply to US actions taken outside US borders. The UN's Committee on Torture, however, which is charged with interpreting and monitoring compliance with the Torture Convention, has interpreted this language to extend the treaty's obligations to any *area* under the de facto or *de jure* control of the state, and to any *person* over whom the state exercises de facto or *de jure* control, regardless of territory.[15]

One of the core obligations imposed by the Torture Convention, the one most directly implicated by renditions to torture, is expressly designed to limit torture extraterritorially. It bars states from transferring individuals to other countries where they face a risk of being tortured. As noted above, Article 3 prohibits any effort to 'expel, return, or extradite' an individual to a country where he faces such a risk. Does this cover renditions conducted entirely outside a state's own borders? In keeping with the spirit of the Torture Convention, the term 'expel' should be read broadly to include any forcible transfer of an individual out of the country in which he is residing, regardless of which state is involved in the transfer. Given the absolute nature of the ban on torture, and the sweeping ban on all forms of otherwise legal transfers where there is a risk of torture, such a reading is more consistent with the purpose of the Convention than the Bush administration's reading, which would free states to deliver individuals to torture so long as they effect the transfer without bringing the individual within their borders. It is inconceivable that the framers of the Convention meant to carve out a loophole affirmatively permitting informal transfers to torture while prohibiting all formal transfers. In fact, the drafters added the reference to 'extradition' to the original draft of Article 3 to ensure that it would 'cover all manners by which a person is physically transferred to another state'.[16] Thus, to interpret the CAT prohibition not to apply to informal transfers would violate the intent of the treaty.

The United States Congress appears to have accepted the broader understanding of the Convention. In the Foreign Affairs Reform and Restructuring Act of 1998 (FARRA), enacted to implement Article 3 of the Convention Against Torture, Congress stated that it is against United States policy to 'expel, extradite, or otherwise effect the involuntary return' of a person to a country where he faces a danger of torture, '*regardless of whether the person is physically present in the United States*'.[17]

Even where human rights treaties do not expressly bar transfers to torture, but merely bar torture itself, they have been interpreted to prohibit all transfers to countries where individuals face a risk of torture. Thus, the European Convention on Human Rights prohibits torture, but contains no language barring the removal or transfer of individuals to other countries where they might be tortured. Nonetheless, the European Court of Human Rights has ruled that the Convention's prohibition on torture implies a prohibition on any kind of transfer or forcible removal of an individual to a country where there are substantial grounds to believe that he will be tortured.[18] If a human rights treaty that prohibits torture but is silent on forcible transfers nonetheless implicitly prohibits all transfers to countries posing a risk of torture, surely a Convention that expressly prohibits both torture and transfers should be interpreted just as broadly.

In addition to implicating the Torture Convention's '*non-refoulement*' obligation not to send persons to a risk of torture, extraordinary rendition also implicates the Torture Convention's principal obligation not to torture. When a nation transfers an individual to another country *for the purpose of subjecting him to torture*, its actions are morally indistinguishable from torturing the individual itself. The '*non-refoulement*' obligation is triggered even where a state has no desire to have an individual tortured, but there are nonetheless substantial grounds to believe that the individual would face the *risk* of being subjected to torture if returned. In renditions to torture, the purpose is to obtain information using interrogation methods that amount to torture. The Torture Convention unquestionably and absolutely bars the United States from torturing an individual directly. That same prohibition ought to be triggered where the United States conspires with another country to have an individual subjected to torture—wherever the torture occurs.

Here, too, domestic US law supports this reading of international law. Congress implemented the Torture Convention by making it a crime for US officials to subject individuals to torture *abroad*.[19] If the Torture Convention applied only within the United States' borders, such a criminal law would not have been an appropriate implementation of the Torture Convention.[20]

As this analysis suggests, there are good reasons to interpret the Torture Convention to bar renditions to torture, even when effected wholly outside the state's own borders. That interpretation is consistent with the intent of the treaty's framers to bar torture absolutely, and to extend its obligations extraterritorially through the '*non-refoulement*' obligation. At the same time, the fact that the Bush administration sought to exploit arguments of territoriality to evade responsibility under the Convention cannot be ignored. Other states may well cite the US example in the future. If this interpretation is not firmly and authoritatively rejected, it may require amendment of the treaty to make the ban on renditions explicit. As the United States has shown, even highly implausible loopholes may be exploited by nations that perceive themselves to be facing a crisis of national security.

US LEGAL RESTRICTIONS AND RENDITIONS

The Constitution's Due Process Clause

Rendition to torture, like torture itself, also violates domestic US law, including the Constitution's due process clause. Here, too, as under the Torture Convention, the principal question is whether government officials can avoid the strictures of legal prohibitions by entering into extraterritorial agreements with third countries. Here, too, there are strong arguments that even as a purely domestic law matter, the fact that the torture has been outsourced should not immunize federal officials from liability.

Had US officials, instead of sending Maher Arar to Syria, simply tortured him in an interrogation room at JFK Airport, they would unquestionably have violated his due process rights. The fact that his rights were violated through joint action taking place in two countries does not render US officials' conduct permissible for two reasons: (*a*) the constitutional violation arose in the United States; and (*b*) the Constitution bars US officials from subjecting individuals to torture outside US borders, particularly when the officials wilfully transported Arar overseas to evade constitutional restrictions.

Torture 'shocks the conscience' and conduct that 'shocks the conscience', the Supreme Court has ruled, violates due process. Indeed, the Supreme Court case establishing the 'shocks the conscience' standard for due process violations, *Rochin v. California*,[21] found that stomach pumping for drugs in a hospital violated due process precisely because it was 'too close to the rack and screw'. The use of any physical coercion—or even the threat of physical coercion—to obtain a confession introduced in a criminal case has also been declared to be a violation of due process.[22] Some suggest that it is less clean whether the use of physical coercion in interrogation violates due process where the evidence is *not* used to incriminate the suspect, but the better argument is that any physical coercion for interrogation purposes violates due process regardless of how the state uses the fruits of the interrogation.[23]

The fact that victims of rendition tend to be foreign nationals, not US citizens, does not deprive them of due process protection against such conscience-shocking treatment. In Arar's case, the constitutional violations arose while he was detained in the United States, so the case for applying constitutional protections is especially strong.[24] But even where foreign nationals are abducted and rendered from countries outside the United States, and do not set foot in the United States, substantive due process may bar US officials from delivering a person in federal custody to foreign officials for the purpose of inflicting torture. While the Supreme Court has sometimes declined to extend constitutional protections to foreign nationals outside US borders, in *Boumediene v. Bush*[25] the Supreme Court in 2008 ruled that the constitutional right of habeas corpus extends to foreign nationals held outside the United States at Guantanamo Bay naval base. Favouring pragmatism over formalism, the Court rejected the view that rights necessarily stop at the border, and reasoned that they may extend to foreign nationals outside US borders where it would be neither impracticable nor anomalous to apply them. There is nothing impracticable or anomalous about holding US officials to the prohibition on torture when they conspire with others to subject an individual to such treatment beyond US borders. The prohibition on torture is universal, as reflected in the Torture Convention and customary international law. Accordingly, there is no basis for concern about different standards of acceptable or unacceptable torture in different countries. The concern that federal officials must be able to operate abroad in a legal and political framework very different from that of the United States does not arise with respect to torture, because torture is never legally permitted anywhere.[26]

Domestic Statutory Restrictions on Rendition to Torture

Rendering an individual to a third country to subject him to torture also violates several domestic US statues. Congress, for example, has made it a felony to subject an individual to torture outside the United States, or to conspire to do so.[27] Congress limited the criminal statute to torture inflicted *outside* the United States only because torture inflicted within the United States was already a crime under both federal and state assault, battery, and murder laws.[28] But the expressly extraterritorial reach of the torture statute reflects an understanding that the prohibition on torture does not stop at the border. Where federal officials send an individual to a country where he faces a risk of torture for the purpose of eliciting information, they have conspired to pursue an unlawful objective—torture abroad—and have committed an overt act in furtherance of the conspiracy—the rendition itself.[29] As the Congressional Research Service concluded, 'Clearly, it would violate US criminal law and [Convention Against Torture] obligations for a US official to conspire to commit torture via rendition, regardless of where such renditions would occur.'[30]

In addition, federal officials who are complicit in subjecting an individual to torture abroad may be civilly liable under the Torture Victim Protection Act (TVPA). That act states that '[a]n individual who, under actual or apparent authority, or color of law, of any foreign nation—(1) subjects an individual to torture shall, in a civil action, be liable for damages to that individual'.[31] Here, too, Congress explicitly sought to extend the prohibition on torture extraterritorially, making torture actionable when inflicted under colour of foreign law.

But are federal officials who deliver an individual to another country in order to have him tortured acting 'under color of law of any foreign nation'? The district court in Arar's case ruled that federal officials could be held liable under the TVPA only if they acted at the direction of the Syrian officials; otherwise, it reasoned, the federal officials were acting under federal law, not foreign law.[32] But in a joint enterprise, it is surely possible for federal officials to act under colour of *both* jurisdictions' laws, and therefore to be liable for their part in subjecting an individual to torture under colour of a foreign country's law.

Finally, rendition to torture violates the Foreign Affairs Reform and Restructuring Act of 1998 (FARRA), which provides that:

> It shall be the policy of the United States not to expel, extradite, or otherwise effect the involuntary return of any person to a country in which there are substantial grounds for believing the person would be in danger of being subjected to torture, regardless of whether the person is physically present in the United States.[33]

While FARRA itself does not create a private right of action for individuals to sue in federal court, it is further evidence that Congress understood the prohibition on torture reflected in the Torture Convention to bar US officials from sending an individual to a third country for torture.

In sum, US constitutional and statutory law reflects an understanding that the prohibition on torture may not be evaded simply by transferring suspects to third countries to have them commit the offence. There are no loopholes in the prohibition on torture.

DIPLOMATIC ASSURANCES

Government officials have asserted that the United States obtained assurances from Syria that it would not torture Arar, and that this made his removal lawful. Bush administration officials have claimed that such assurances have generally been obtained where there was a concern about the possibility of torture. Other nations, including the United Kingdom and Italy, have sought diplomatic assurances in order to deport individuals to countries where, absent such assurances, they would face a substantial risk of being tortured. Can diplomatic assurances from countries with a demonstrated record of torture sufficiently reduce the risk of torture to permit removal where it otherwise would not be permitted?

There are at least three reasons for healthy scepticism. First, there is little reason to trust a country that has a record of torture merely because it has promised not to torture in a specific case. Diplomatic assurances are generally obtained only where, absent such assurances, there is a likelihood of torture. But if this is the case, it raises a central question about the reliability of assurances, given that no country admits that it engages in torture. Virtually all nations have signed the CAT, and have thus already committed themselves to honouring an absolute prohibition on torture under all circumstances. Yet many countries nonetheless engage in the practice, as documented by human rights reports and complaints of governmental and civil society organizations. It is those countries that are most likely to pose a substantial risk of torture, and therefore it is those countries from whom diplomatic assurances are likely to be sought. If these countries routinely engage in torture in direct violation of their own explicit treaty promises, what justification is there for believing that they will honour a much less formal bilateral side agreement?

Second, if assurances are to be truly reliable in terms of reducing the risk of torture where it otherwise exists, substantial monitoring and oversight would be essential. Absent extremely intrusive and costly monitoring, it is highly unlikely that any state can be held to its promises—particularly given the practice, noted above, of lying about torture where it is practised. Torture occurs behind closed doors, and it is difficult to know what happens in an interrogation room or prison cell if one is not actually there. States have learned to inflict torture, moreover, in ways that leave no physical marks (consider waterboarding, for example). Thus, short of 24/7 monitoring, it is difficult to know how a promise not to torture could be verified.

Consider the case of the Swedish government's expulsion of two Egyptian asylum-seekers in December 2001 on the strength of diplomatic assurances obtained from the Egyptian authorities. Once in Egypt, the men were detained incommunicado and reportedly tortured.[34] In reviewing this case, the Committee Against Torture rejected the use of diplomatic assurances to guard against such a strong risk of torture, and noted that because of the assurances, the Swedish official in Egypt responsible for monitoring the treatment of the two Egyptians concealed evidence that they had been tortured.[35] For these reasons, the Special Rapporteur of the UN Commission on Human Rights has said that 'post-return monitoring mechanisms do little to mitigate the risk of torture and have been proven ineffective in both safeguarding against torture and as a mechanism of accountability'.[36]

Third, diplomatic assurances are especially problematic in rendition cases. Renditions are typically conducted in secret, without any of the transparency that would be essential to any meaningful and accountable regime of assurances. And where the very purpose of a transfer is to facilitate interrogation, the risk that torture will be used by countries that have a practice of relying on torture for interrogation is simply too great, particularly given the alternatives available to the state. If the purpose is indeed interrogation without torture, it will rarely be necessary to send the individual to the torturing country. The interrogation can be conducted where the individual is, by countries that do not torture. If officials believe that interrogators from a particular country might be better suited to conduct the interrogation, the interrogators can be brought to the suspect, rather than the other way around, so that monitoring of the interrogation can be maintained. In Arar's case, for example, US officials were free to interrogate Arar while he was in the United States, and could have sent him to Canada for further interrogation. If they felt the Syrians had something legitimate and legal to add to the process, they could have brought them to Arar and monitored the interrogation, rather than sending him to Syria and closing their eyes to what followed.

CONCLUSION

Rendition to torture is wrong as a moral matter, illegal as an international and federal legal matter, and likely to be counterproductive as a security matter. The United States' reliance on this tactic has occasioned widespread and justified criticism around the world. The tactic plays into al-Qaeda's hands by providing ideal recruitment propaganda, and makes it more difficult for allies and potential allies to work together with the United States. It should be plain to see that just as torture itself is wrong and illegal under all circumstances, so is transferring a human being to another country to have it engage in the same illegal behaviour—no matter where the transfer begins and ends. The international ban on torture was meant to be absolute, and while that is generally understood to mean that it permits no exceptions, it should also be understood to permit no immunity through exploiting cross-border opportunities. There should be no 'forum shopping' for torture.

The United States' attempt to exploit loopholes based on outmoded conceptions of territoriality to justify its actions runs counter to the spirit of the Torture Convention, its interpretation by the international committee charged with enforcing and monitoring it, and to the growing trend in international human rights law of extending obligations beyond national borders, to areas and individuals over whom the state exercises effective control. The loopholes exploited by the Bush administration should be authoritatively rejected—by courts, scholars, and the Obama administration. That this is even a question shows how far the United States strayed from fundamental principles of the rule of law in the wake of 9/11.

NOTES

Professor, Georgetown University Law Center. As a cooperating attorney with the Center for Constitutional Rights, I represent Maher Arar, whose story is told here, in a lawsuit against US officials alleging that his treatment violated US laws and the Constitution. See *Arar v. Ashcroft*, 414 F.Supp.2d 250 (E.D.N.Y. 2006), aff'd, 532 F.3d 157 (2008), rehearing en banc granted, decision pending.

1. Bureau of Democracy, Human Rights, and Labor, United States State Department, 'Syria: Country Reports on Human Rights Practices, 2001,' 3 Mar. 2001, <http://www.state.gov/g/drl/rls/hrrpt/2001/nea/8298.htm>.
2. For an extensive analysis and critique of the 'paradigm of prevention', see David Cole and Jules Lobel, *Less safe, less free: Why America is losing the war on terror* (New York: New Press, 2007), arguing that the preventive paradigm has caused the United States to compromise some of its most fundamental commitments to the rule of law, and has made the country more vulnerable to terrorist attack over the long run.
3. For a detailed account of Mr. El-Masri's ordeal, see Council of Europe, Parliamentary Assembly, Report, Committee on Legal Affairs and Human Rights, Rapporteur Mr. Dick Marty (Switzerland), 'Alleged secret detentions and unlawful inter-state transfers of detainees involving Council of Europe member states', Doc. 10957, 12 June 2006, 25–32.
4. Remarks of General Michael Hayden to the Council on Foreign Relations, 7 Sep. 2007; <https://www.cia.gov/news-information/speeches-testimony/2007/general-haydens-remarks-at-the-council-on-foreign-relations.html>.
5. Human Rights Watch, Report, 'Double jeopardy: CIA renditions to torture', 7 Apr. 2008; <http://www.hrw.org/en/reports/2008/04/07/double-jeopardy-0>.
6. See generally David Cole, *Enemy aliens: Double standards and constitutional freedoms in the war on terrorism* (revised edn.; New Press: New York, 2005); Neal Katyal, 'Equal protection in the war on terror', *Stanford Law Review*, 59/5 (2007), 1365–94.
7. See David Luban, 'Liberalism, torture, and the ticking bomb', *Virginia Law Review*, 91/6 (2005), 1425–61.

8. Congressional Research Service, 'Renditions: Constraints imposed by laws on torture' (updated 5 Apr. 2006), 13–14.
9. Sarah Cleveland, 'Geography or control? International jurisdiction and constitutional protection for aliens abroad', Manuscript on file with author.
10. *Victor Saldaño v. Argentina, Petition*, ¶ 17, IACHR Report No. 38/99, 11 Mar. 1999, <http://www.cidh.oas.org/annualrep/98eng/Inadmissible/Argentina%20Salda%F1o.htm>.
11. The Commission wrote: 'Given that individual rights inhere simply by virtue of a person's humanity, each American State is obliged to uphold the protected rights of any person *subject to its jurisdiction*. While this most commonly refers to persons within a state's territory, it may, under given circumstances, refer to conduct with an extraterritorial locus where the person concerned is present in the territory of one state, but subject to the *control* of another state—usually through the acts of the latter's agents abroad', *Coard and Others v. the United States ('US military intervention in Grenada')*, IACHR Report No. 109/9, Case No. 10.951, Sec. V, ¶ 37, Sep. 29 1999; <http://www.cidh.oas.org/annualrep/99eng/Merits/UnitedStates10.951.htm>.
12. *R (on the application of Al-Skeini and others) v. Secretary of State for Defence*, [2007] UKHL 26, [2007] All ER (D) 106 (Jun), 13 June 2007.
13. *Issa and Others v. Turkey*, § 69 ECtHR appl. No. 31821/96, Judgment, 71, 16 Nov. 2004.
14. Convention Against Torture and other Cruel, Inhuman or Degrading Treatment or Punishment, 26 June 1987, Arts. 2(1), 16(1).
15. The Committee has stated that the obligations of the CAT extend to 'all <u>areas</u> where the State Party exercises, directly or indirectly, in whole or in part, *de jure* or *de facto* effective control. . . . "[T]erritory" under article 2 must also include situations where a State Party exercises, directly or indirectly, *de facto* or *de jure* control over <u>persons</u> in detention, since, in such circumstances, the State Party is able to carry out the obligations of this Convention' [underlines provided, italics in original]. The Committee Against Torture, *Draft General Comment 2: Implementation of Article 2 by States Parties*, 16; <http://www.ohchr.org/english/bodies/cat/docs/AdvanceVersions/ CAT.C. GC.2.CRP.1.Rev.2.pdf>.
16. Herman Burgers and Hans Danelius, *The United Nations Convention Against Torture: A handbook on the Convention Against Torture and Other Cruel, Inhuman, or Degrading Treatment or Punishment* (Dordrecht: Martinus Nijhof Publishers, 1988), 126. Burgers and Danelius were two of the original drafters of the Torture Convention, and their treatise is the definitive work on the subject.
17. FARRA, para. 2,242 (a), in Omnibus Consolidated and Emergency Supplemental Appropriations Act of 1999, Pub. L. No. 1–5–277 (1998).
18. *Cruz Varas v. Sweden*, 201 Eur. Ct. H.R. (ser. A) (1989); *Vilvarajah and Others v. United Kingdom*, 215 Eur. Ct. H.R. (ser. A) (1991); see Association of the Bar of the City of New York & Center for Human Rights and Global Justice, 'Torture by proxy: International and domestic law applicable to "extraordinary renditions"', New York, 2004, 41–2.
19. 18 U.S.C. § 2340A.
20. The International Covenant on Civil and Political Rights (ICCPR), which the United States ratified in 1992, prohibits torture and cruel, inhuman, and degrading treatment. Like the European Convention on Human Rights, it does not expressly prohibit forcible transfers, but the Human Rights Committee charged with interpreting the ICCPR has interpreted its prohibition on torture and cruel, inhuman, and degrading treatment to include an obligation on states not to 'expose individuals

to the danger of torture or cruel, inhuman, or degrading treatment or punishment upon return to another country by way of their extradition, expulsion, or *refoulement*.' Human Rights Committee, General Comment 20, *Article 7*, 1992, UN Doc. A/47/40; see also Human Rights Committee, General Comment 31, *Nature of the General Legal Obligation on States Parties to the Covenant*, 2004, U.N. Doc. CCPOR/ C/21/Rev.1/Add.13, para. 12 (finding in Article 2 an obligation 'not to extradite, deport, expel or otherwise remove a person from their territory, where there are substantial grounds for believing that there is a real risk of irreparable harm, such as that contemplated by article…7'). Thus, transferring an individual to a country where he faces a risk that he will be tortured violates the ICCPR. The ICCPR is not self-executing, and therefore does not give rise to a private cause of action, but it is nonetheless binding on the United States as a matter of international law. The Geneva Conventions also prohibit renditions to torture in international armed conflicts, but Common Article 3, which the US Supreme Court has ruled governs the conflict with al-Qaeda, a non-state actor, is silent on the subject of transfers or removals. However, Common Article 3 flatly prohibits torture, and cruel or inhuman treatment of detainees, and like the ECHR, could be interpreted to include an implicit ban on transfer of persons where they might be subject to torture or cruel or inhuman treatment.

21. 342 U.S. 165, 172–73 (1952).
22. *Colorado v. Connelly,* 479 U.S. 157, 163 (1986): 'certain interrogation techniques, either in isolation or as applied to the unique characteristics of a particular suspect, are so offensive to a civilized system of justice that they must be condemned' (quoting *Miller v. Fenton,* 474 U.S. 104, 109 (1985)).
23. See *Chavez v. Martinez,* 538 U.S. 760 (2002); Seth Kreimer, ' "Torture lite", "full-bodied torture", and the insulation of legal conscience', *Journal of National Security Law and Policy,* 1/2 (2005), 187–229.
24. See *Correa v. Thornburgh,* 901 F.2d 1166, 1171 n.5 (2d Cir. 1990) (unadmitted foreign national is protected by substantive due process); *Ngo v. INS,* 192 F.3d 390, 396 (3d Cir. 1999) (excludable alien is 'a 'person' for purposes of the Fifth Amendment' who 'is thus entitled to substantive due process') (citing *Wong Wing v. United States,* 163 U.S. 228, 238 (1896)); see also *Sierra v. INS,* 258 F.3d 1213, 1218 n.3 (10th Cir. 2001).
25. 128 S. Ct. 2229 (2008).
26. Convention Against Torture, *Supra,* note 14.
27. 18 U.S.C. § 2340A.
28. See S. Rep. No. 103–7, 59.
29. David Weissbrodt and Amy Bergquist, 'Extraordinary rendition and the torture convention', *Virginia Journal of International Law,* 46/4 (2006), 618–21.
30. Congressional Research Service, Renditions: Constraints Imposed by Laws on Torture (updated 5 April 2006), 12. The CRS Report goes on to state that it is less clear whether criminal sanctions would apply were a person transferred for harsh treatment not rising to the level of torture. Ibid.
31. Pub. L. No. 102–256, 106 Stat 73, 28 U.S.C. §1350, note, §2(a).
32. *Arar v. Ashcroft,* 414 F.Supp.2d 250, 287 (E.D.N.Y. 2006) (appeal pending).
33. FARRA, § 2242(a), in Omnibus Consolidated and Emergency Supplemental Appropriations Act of 1999, Pub. L. No. 1–5–277 (1998).
34. *Agiza v. Sweden,* Communication No. 233/2003; see generally Human Rights Watch, 'Empty promises: Diplomatic assurances no safeguard against torture', April 2004; and

'Still at risk: Diplomatic assurances no safeguard against torture', April 2005; Report of the Special Rapporteur on Torture, Theo van Boven, to the General Assembly, 23 Aug. 2004, para. 37.

35. Committee Against Torture, Communication No. 233/2003, 20 May, 2005, U.N. Doc. CAT/C/34/D/233/2003, 4.24, 8.1, 12.15, 13.4, 13.10.

36. The Secretary General, Report of the Special Rapporteur on torture and other cruel, inhuman or degrading treatment or punishment, 46, submitted to the General Assembly, 30 Aug. 2005, U.N. Doc. A/60/316; see generally Weissbrodt and Bergquist, 'Extraordinary rendition and the torture convention', 621–4.

19

Terrorist Beheadings: Politics and Reciprocity

Alia Brahimi

INTRODUCTION

Our enemies, in the 'war on terror', exhibit a marked preoccupation with what is going on in the West. While Osama bin Laden references a lecture at Chatham House,[1] Ayman al-Zawahiri quotes a character from one of Disraeli's novels[2] and cites English proverbs.[3] Certain events, too, are seized upon as confirmatory evidence of al-Qaeda's strategic narrative. Just as the 2001 anthrax attacks were analysed by bin Laden as America's punishment from Allah,[4] the brutal leader of Al-Qaeda in Iraq, Abu Mus'ab al-Zarqawi, stated that Hurricane Katrina 'occurred because people in Iraq or Afghanistan—maybe a mother who had lost her son or a son whose parents were killed or a woman who was raped— were praying to God and God accepted their prayers'.[5]

It comes as little surprise, then, that the Bush administration's controversial detention policies feature prominently in terrorist narratives. Guantanamo Bay is repeatedly invoked by al-Qaeda to undermine the moral standing of the United States, as the opposing side in the 'war on terror' and as the spearhead of Western civilization. Bin Laden has consistently denounced the Western value system because 'all manners, principles, and values have two scales: one for you and one for everybody else',[6] and Guantanamo Bay is triumphantly pointed to as proof of this: '[W]hat happens in Guantanamo is a historical embarrassment to America and its values, and it screams in your hypocritical faces: what is the value of your signature on any agreement or treaty?'[7] Ayman al-Zawahiri similarly wonders: '[W]here are the international agreements and UN treaties? What about human rights—in fact, how about just even animal rights?!'[8] The effects of such fulminations are not confined to rhetoric, however. Though the beheading of hostages is often analysed in terms of ritualistic sacrifice or Islamic historical precedent, this article suggests that the phenomenon can be understood politic-ally, in terms of terrorists' efforts to link the wretched fate of those they take as 'prisoners' to that of the Muslims held in notorious 'war on terror' facilities

No doubt, it is difficult to speak of al-Qaeda as taking 'prisoners of war' because it is a non-state actor which, despite being afforded a safe haven in north-west Pakistan, does not have exclusive control over a territorial base. Although not a direct equivalent to 'prisoners of war', we will examine the kidnapping and beheading of hostages by al-Qaeda linked groups in Iraq: Abu Mus'ab al-Zarqawi's *Tawhid wa Jihad* group, which was later re-named *Qaidat al-Jihad fi Bilad al-Rafidayn* and is referred to in English as Al-Qaeda in Iraq; the Islamic Army in Iraq (*Al-Jaysh al-Islami fi al-Iraq*); and *Ansar al-Sunna*. Since 2003, it is estimated that 534 foreigners have been taken hostage in Iraq, of which 73 were executed.[9] Many of these hostages are civilians rather than soldiers (mainly contractors working in Iraq), but, significantly, they are represented by their *captors* as 'prisoners of war'. This is usually based on the notion that civilians in Iraq forfeit their non-combatant status by virtue of aiding and abetting the country's occupation. The analysis will begin by exploring terrorist justifications for beheading their hostages in the context of the Islamic *jihad* tradition. It will then consider the political factors influencing the adoption of beheading hostages as a tactic, with a focus on the concept of reciprocal treatment.

PRISONERS OF WAR IN ISLAM

The fate of any prisoners taken in battle was, in classical Islam, left up to the discretion of the caliph, who had the legal option of executing them, enslaving them, conducting a prisoner exchange, releasing them for ransom, or simply setting them free. A tradition dating back to the first Muslim community, however, shirked the option of execution. After the Battle of Badr, the Muslims found themselves in possession of seventy prisoners and, while the famous military commander ibn Khattab exhorted that they be decapitated immediately, the Prophet followed Abu Bakr's advice to ransom them and set them free. Abu Bakr had argued morally that the prisoners were 'our kith and kin', and instrumentally that these seventy souls were potential Muslims who could one day be guided by Allah to Islam. Muhammad al-Shaybani, the eighth-century jurist, thus instructed that 'the prisoner of war should not be killed, but he may be ransomed or set free by grace'.[10] Indeed, at verse 47:4, the Quran commands that 'when ye have thoroughly subdued them, bind a bond firmly [on them]: thereafter [is the time for] either generosity or ransom'.[11]

More radical Quranic commentaries, such as that of Sayyid Qutb, argue that, in fact, 'Allah did not like the Muslims to take prisoners at Badr and then set them free for ransom'. Qutb cites one continuation of the Abu Bakr tradition which states that the next day, Abu Bakr and the Prophet were found with tears in their eyes, as Allah had issued the rebuke contained in verse 8:67: 'it does not behove a Prophet to have captives until he has sufficiently slaughtered in the land'.[12] Qutb argues that when Muslims are outnumbered by the enemy, they are to fight ferociously and, it would seem, execute all captives because, firstly, 'the killing... aims to give strength to the Muslims and weaken their enemies, until the Muslims reached a stage when they could set prisoners free either as a favour or for a ransom'. Secondly, he maintains that such killing demonstrates to Allah that there is no sympathy in the hearts of the Muslims with the unbelievers. Interestingly, Qutb upholds that taking ransom amounts to sinfulness, because it involves material gain—implying, then, that execution is actually the more morally laudable course.[13]

Mawlana Sayyid Abu Ala Mawdudi, whose writings were hugely influential on the intellectual development of Qutb, also notes that prisoners should only be taken after the enemy has been completely crushed, and likewise warns against the 'greed for ransom'. He does allow for the possibility of execution of prisoners in exceptional cases, but he emphasizes that the general law is that a man can be killed only during war, and that prisoners, when taken, should not be put to death. Mawdudi also lays out a series of traditions which enjoin the Muslims to treat their captives humanely, arguing that 'Islamic law does not permit prisoners to be kept without food or clothing, or be subjected to torture', and goes on to suggest that it is legal for prisoners to be enslaved (but well treated), for prisoners to be made *dhimmi*, subjects of the Islamic state, and for prisoners to be set free as an act of grace, which, he maintains, was a common practice of the Prophet. Thus, he concludes, those who take verse 47:4 as directing prisoners to be simply freed or ransomed 'do not know what different aspects the question of the prisoner of war has, and what problems it has been creating in different ages and can create in the future'.[14]

For modernists such as Maulvi Cheragh Ali, however, verse 47:4 means precisely that the treatment of prisoners of war is restricted to 'either free dismissal or ransom'. Indeed, Ali, writing in nineteenth-century India, draws on his knowledge of Arabic to translate 8:67 as ' "it is not for any Prophet that prisoners may be brought to him in order that he may make slaughter in the land", which means, that it is not proper for a Prophet to take prisoners of war in order to slaughter them'.[15] Ali takes great pains to outline the kind treatment of prisoners of war by Muhammad, and to expose the various traditions of the Prophet allegedly executing prisoners of war as either spurious or fictitious.[16]

Indeed, there is plenty of Islamic support for the view that prisoners are at all times to be treated charitably by the Muslims, based on the Quranic verse which states 'and they feed, for the love of Allah, the indigent, the orphan, and the captive' (76:8). Numerous corroboratory sayings are also attributed to the Prophet, including 'I command you to treat captives well'. Perhaps the most famous tradition cited in this regard is that which relates how the prisoners at Badr were given bread, morning and evening, while the captors themselves made do with only dates. Thus, according to Mawdudi, 'no precedent has been found when a prisoner might have been mistreated in [the Prophet and his Companions'] time'.[17] However, while a great many Muslims would argue that, by extension, execution is absolutely unconscionable ('Islam totally prohibits abusing, insulting and reviling any prisoner of war, let alone slaying him slaying him like a sheep'[18]), others cling to the special cases in which prisoners of war were killed in the Prophet's time to establish execution (and, in particular, beheading) as a legal option.

One such ideologue is Yusuf al-Ayyiri, the prolific al-Qaeda theorist killed by Saudi security forces in 2003, to whom beheading represents a genuinely Islamic course of action. In his treatise *A Guide for the Perplexed on the Permissibility of Killing Prisoners*, published on a pro-Chechen web site in 2002 and written in response to the outcry over the execution of Russian prisoners, Ayyiri argues that the Prophet dealt with prisoners in many different ways, including execution, in order to maximize the benefit to Muslims. He considers a variety of interpretations of the Islamic position on prisoners—with the view that amnesty and ransom are the only two options at one end of the spectrum, and the view that all infidels, polytheists, Christians, and Jews are to be executed at the other—and concludes that the Imam, or someone acting on his behalf, can choose between execution, amnesty, ransom, or enslavement.[19] The Imam must make this judgement depending on which option would bring the greatest benefits to Muslims, a formula which will be discussed at greater length later.

This show of legality is not, however, confined to the realm of the ideologists. In videos depicting the beheadings of hostages taken by al-Qaeda-linked groups in Iraq, the executioner, invariably dressed in black, reads a list of the captive's 'crimes', and presents him with the opportunity to offer any last words. One French journalist recounted that, upon kidnap, he was interrogated and then evidence was put before a tribunal, presided over by Sheikh, which decided whether he and his fellow hostages were to be negotiated over.[20] As Kenneth Bigley's killer prepared to decapitate him he stated that he was carrying out 'the sentence of execution against this hostage'.[21] Saudi Arabia, which still uses beheading as a form of capital punishment, maintains that the difference between its policies and that of radical groups is that the condemned in Saudi Arabia have been convicted of crimes—however, radical *jihadi* groups, too, present their slaughtered as convicted criminals.

This implication of criminality may be an appeal to the right of captors to punish prisoners for crimes beyond belligerency, for:

> According to Muslim law, a prisoner *qua* prisoner cannot be killed . . . This does not preclude the trial and punishment of prisoners for crimes beyond rights of belligerency.[22]
>
> [The prisoner] is subject to no punishment for being a public enemy, nor is any revenge wreaked upon him. . . . But a prisoner of war remains answerable for his crimes committed against the captor's army or people before he was captured, and for which he has not been punished by his own authorities.[23]

In this vein, Abu Mus'ab al-Zarqawi, the bloodthirsty leader of Al-Qaeda in Iraq until his death in 2005, insisted that the people he killed were not hostages, but spies, for whom execution was the appropriate sentence.[24] After the beheading of an Egyptian national whose tongue was first cut out, one radical Saudi preacher, Abd al-Rahman ibn Salem Al-Shammari, congratulated Zarqawi by observing that 'a spy has been slain, and this spy looked like an Arab, had an Arab name, and spoke Arabic!'[25]

Beheading itself, as a form of execution, is most commonly justified with the first part of Quranic verse 47:4: 'when ye meet the unbelievers [in fight], smite at their necks; at length, when ye have thoroughly subdued them, bind a bond firmly'. Indeed, this verse is readily cited by non-Muslims seeking to suggest that the savagery exhibited by radical *jihadi* groups in Iraq is integral to the Islamic faith. In an article for the journal *Middle East Quarterly*, Timothy Furnish argues that 'ritual beheading has a long precedent in Islamic history and theology' and concludes that Islam 'is anything but a "religion of peace". It is, rather, a religion of the sword with the blade forever at the throat of the unbeliever.' Furnish refers to the two Quranic verses which mention beheading (47:3 and 8:12), before laying out a series of contexts in which beheading has been utilized in Islamic history. He points out that beheadings still occur in Saudi Arabia today, and upholds that they are sanctioned by Islam. His article also labels as apologists those Imams and historians who denounce such beheadings as contrary to Islam, because 'Islamists justify murder and decapitation with both theological citations and historical precedent'.[26] This reasoning appears problematic, however, when it is considered that the attempt to *justify* an action by appealing to Islamic tradition does not entail that the action is, at once, *justified* by Islamic tradition.

Indeed, a host of prominent Muslims would uphold that it is not. The abduction and beheading of hostages has been, and continues to be, decried as profoundly un-Islamic. For example, Egypt's foremost religious scholar, Sheikh Muhammad Tantawi, argues that 'such beheadings and [the] mutilation of bodies stand against Islam and have nothing to do with *sharia*'.[27] (Indeed, mutilation and desecration of corpses is considered an egregious offence in Islam, as the Prophet was reported to have said, 'I will not mutilate him; if I do, Allah will mutilate me though I be a Prophet.') Dr Jasser Auda, a founding member of the International Union for Muslim Scholars, similarly insisted: 'Islam has nothing to do with these beheadings...beheading is not the way that the Quran, to quote it again as a reference, dealt with prisoners of war.'[28] Essam al-Arian, a senior Muslim Brotherhood leader, described the beheading of Korean hostage Kim Sun-il in June 2004 as an 'action that cannot be representative of Muslim or Arab morals'.[29] Likewise, the spiritual leader of the Shia in Lebanon, Ayatollah Muhammad Hussein Fadlallah, labelled Sun-il's beheading as a 'brutal and barbaric act' which harmed Islam's image around the world.[30] When two French journalists were abducted later in the summer, Fadlallah made clear that it was 'a brutal operation on the human level, a bad one on the Islamic level, and a losing one on the political level'.[31] The Association of Muslim Ulemas in Iraq, too, publicly condemned the beheadings as actions prohibited by the *sharia*.[32] In terms of the Muslim population at large, even Zawahiri recognized, in a letter to Zarqawi, that 'among the things which the feelings of the Muslim populace who love and support you will never find palatable are the scenes of slaughtering the hostages...And we can kill the captives by bullet. That would achieve that which is sought after without exposing ourselves to the questions and answering to doubts. We don't need this.'[33]

To be sure, the beheading strategy pursued by the likes of Zarqawi in Iraq did not help al-Qaeda with its most serious source of vulnerability: the questionability of its authority to lead a *jihad*. In classical writings, the Imam, or caliph, was to decide between beheading, enslaving, ransoming, exchanging, or releasing a prisoner, with beheading permissible 'only in extreme cases of necessity and in the higher interests of the state'.[34] Mawdudi, too, noted that 'if there was a special reason for which the ruler of an Islamic government regarded it as necessary to kill a particular prisoner (or prisoners), he could do so. This is not the general law, but an exception to it, which would be applied only when necessary.'[35] Ibn Taymiyyah argues that 'the *sharia* enjoins fighting the unbelievers but not the killing of those who have been captured', but he acknowledges that execution is an option if the Imam deems it appropriate.[36] At one stage in his *siyar*, Shaybani notes that the Imam can, in fact, execute a prisoner if, upon examining the situation, he decides it is 'advantageous to the Muslims'.[37] The Imam, then, as the lawful and recognized head of the Muslim state, is the party qualified to conduct the difficult balancing act involved in judging the higher interests of the Muslims, just as any consequent execution is to be conducted upon his authority.

Thus, as Ayiri revives the classical position on prisoners of war—arguing that the Imam, or someone acting on his behalf, can choose between killing, amnesty, ransom, or enslaving the prisoner, depending on which option most benefits Muslims—he arrogates the role of Imam to al-Qaeda. However, when scores of religious leaders, from Ayatollah Fadlallah to Sheikh Salman al-Odah, argue that al-Qaeda's policies harm Islam and act against the interests of Muslims,[38] the qualifications of its leaders to direct a *jihad* are simultaneously subjected to intense scrutiny. Just as Mullah Omar's concern, in early 2001, over the actions of those sheltering in Afghanistan led him to pronounce that 'any *fatwa* issued by Osama bin Laden declaring *jihad* against the United States and ordering Muslims to kill Americans is null and void. Osama bin Laden is not entitled to issue *fatwa* as he did not complete the mandatory twelve years of Quranic studies to qualify for the position of *mufti*',[39] so, eight years on, those radicals withdrawing their support from al-Qaeda because of the damage caused to the Muslim world emphasize that 'all of them—bin Laden, Zawahiri, and others—are not religious scholars on whose opinion you can count. They are ordinary persons.'[40] Hence Zawahiri's directive to Zarqawi to end the counter-productive beheading of hostages: 'we don't need this'.

It seems, then, that the decision taken by certain *jihadi*s to pursue beheading as a means of dealing with captives is by no means a purely religious phenomenon. As Michael Doran succinctly put it, 'you can come up with a *sharia* justification for it, but you can come up with a *sharia* justification for a lot of things'.[41] Indeed, the Bush administration uses international legal arguments to justify its denial of Geneva protections at Guantanamo Bay; it does not necessarily follow that the Bush administration's course of action is essential to international law. The beheading of hostages is not, as Furnish would maintain, a ritualistic end in itself. Instead, there are five interrelated political factors informing the adoption of such a tactic.

THE POLITICS OF EXECUTING PRISONERS

In the first place, the fact that the beheadings are frequently filmed and broadcast online indicates that this savagery serves an important media function (Zarqawi himself is believed to have released footage of ninety captured hostages, seventeen of which were executed on camera). In fact, to the mind of one commentator, 'it's absurd to even speak about it in [a legal context]. There are terrorists, extremists, who want to draw attention to themselves at maximum impact by gruesome images and horrific acts.'[42] Loretta Napoleoni points out that, as opposed to the criminal groups who are responsible for the majority of kidnappings in Iraq, 'terror groups use hostages primarily to inflame western public opinion, not to raise money. Hostages are released only if the political demands attached to their freedom are met.'[43] Indeed, 'a non-American is more likely to be targeted if the objective is cash, an American if it is for propaganda or terror purposes. US military hostages are almost guaranteed execution.'[44] It would seem that a narrow focus on the symbolism of the sword in Islam obscures the distinctly political forces in play.

In his treatise entitled *The Management of Savagery*, Abu Bakr Naji recommended:

> A group should be formed whose purpose is to communicate what we want to say to the masses and focus their attention on it... It may even necessitate undertaking a military operation to achieve the objective. For example, we kidnap a hostage and then provoke a large outcry over them and demand that the television reporters and the media networks announce what we want to say in full to the people in exchange for handing over the hostages. The previous is just a hypothetical example and it is possible that what we want to announce is a statement of warning or a statement justifying a very important, critical action, and the like.[45]

If the terrorists' demands are not met, however, hostage-taking has the potential to achieve another important objective—sowing terror. Naji notes that 'the policy of violence must also be followed such that if the demands are not met, the hostages should be liquidated in a terrifying manner, which will send fear into the hearts of the enemy and his supporters'.[46] An article issuing targeting guidance which appeared in al-Qaeda's 'Camp al-Bittar' training publication also observes that one of the purposes for human targets must be 'to spread fear in enemy lines'.[47] Illustrating Naji's logic, Qaidat al-Jihad demanded, in late 2004, that Japan withdraw its soldiers in exchange for the life of Shosei Koda. After Koizumi's refusal, Koda was decapitated while kneeling on an American flag. His severed head was then placed atop the corpse; both were later found on a Baghdad street, wrapped in the bloodied flag.

Certainly, the fate of hostages taken by the most readily brutal groups in Iraq is often dictated by nationality. Georges Malbrunot, the aforementioned French journalist who spent four months in captivity in Iraq, observed that 'on Planet Bin Laden, they look first at your nationality. Had we been British—or from another coalition country—we would have been decapitated within days.'[48] The British former hostage, Norman Kember, was also informed by his captors that his Church group was very fortunate to have been captured by the Sword of Righteousness Brigade and not Zarqawi's *mujahidin*, as Zarqawi would have immediately executed the American and Kember. In fact, Zarqawi had made an attempt to purchase Kember and his colleagues, but his offer had been refused.[49] In this way, the broadcast of beheadings issues a bloody warning to the Western world, while at the same time conveying to Muslims that revenge is being wreaked upon the architects of the 'Crusader' invasion.

In addition to media spectacle, the beheading of hostages is, secondly, designed to force political outcomes. The Qutbist tactic of spreading fear is geared towards inducing the occupation forces to leave Iraq. Thus, Sheikh Yusuf al-Qaradawi, long on the record as opposing beheadings, was quoted as telling a conference in Cairo that 'the abduction and killing of Americans in Iraq is an obligation *so as to cause them to leave Iraq immediately*'.[50] Qaradawi's instrumentalist reasoning, which provoked controversy in the Islamic world, is surely shared by those *jihadis* whose *raison d'etre* it is to drive the US-led coalition from Iraq. And not without some success: after Angelo de la Cruz was abducted and threatened with beheading if Filipino forces did not leave immediately, the government in Manila moved forward its withdrawal date, despite sharp criticism from the Bush administration, and de la Cruz was freed.[51] A RAND report which appeared in the *Chicago Tribune* also noted that 'the surge in kidnappings coincided with intensified US efforts to attract additional support from other countries. But no new nations signed on to send troops to Iraq. Who wanted the grief?'[52] Further, as the cost of ensuring the safety of personnel skyrocketed, many companies active in Iraq's reconstruction quit the country.

A third function of the execution of prisoners is the achievement of political aims within the *jihadi* movement itself. An important biography of Abu Mus'ab al-Zarqawi argues that the execution of Nicholas Berg, the American telecom worker whose beheading began the series of executions of hostages in Iraq, was carried out in order for Zarqawi to establish himself as the unifier of the Sunni extremist movement in Iraq. According to Jean-Paul Brissard, with Berg's beheading, Zarqawi had 'decided to strike a great blow that would convince the different factions to rally behind him'.[53] As such the vicious act was dramatically personalized, as it was released under the title 'Sheikh Abu Mus'ab Zarqawi Slays an American Infidel', and it is believed that Zarqawi himself wielded the knife. Napoleoni suggests, likewise, that Zarqawi's 'entry into the business of kidnapping and beheading hostages was one of many strategies to build his status in Iraq and win the approval of Osama bin Laden'. Napoleoni upholds that Berg was beheaded before the receipt of approval from al-Qaeda, and the act was intended to signal that Zarqawi was planning to continue his *jihad* in Iraq, despite the opposition of many Iraqis, with or without bin Laden's support.[54]

As it turned out, despite the union, six months later, of Zarqawi's group with al-Qaeda, bin Laden and his close lieutenants were not won over by Zarqawi's strategy of savagery. It appears that at least two letters were sent to Zarqawi, urging him to desist from his terror campaign. Zawahiri wrote to him in 2005 recommending that he stop his attacks on the Shias, and warning him that scenes of slaughter were not helpful to al-Qaeda's cause. As mentioned above, beheadings were singled out as unnecessarily bloody and inviting of unwanted 'questions about the usefulness of our actions in the hearts and minds of the general opinion'.[55] A few months later, another bin Laden aide reminded Zarqawi that operations against the enemy in Iraq are only considered successful, in the long run, if they do not contradict al-Qaeda's larger strategic goals. Alienating the people, he insisted, went against all of the fundamentals of politics and leadership.[56] In turn, after Zarqawi's death in June 2006, instances of kidnapping and beheading in Iraq dramatically decreased.

A fourth political function of the execution of prisoners is to induce the enemy to more readily conduct prisoner exchanges. Muhammad Hamidullah explains that as regards Muslim prisoners of war, 'it is the duty of the [Muslim] state to seek their release by giving money from the public treasury. The Quran clearly lays down that a portion of the state income is to be allotted for *freeing the necks*, which is interpreted as aiding the prisoners and slaves to get themselves freed.'[57] Majid Khadduri, too, notes that 'the Imam, in his turn, is under obligation to make every effort to release the Muslim captives by exchange in persons or property.'[58] To that end, the al-Qaeda strategist Abu Mus'ab al-Suri recommends that the kidnapping of Americans and 'Crusaders' is the best instrument for facilitating the duty of rescuing Muslim prisoners.[59] Indeed, a great part of Abu Laith al-Libi's message decrying 'the war of prisons and captivity' is devoted to outlining 'the compulsory nature of rescuing the captives' in Islamic jurisprudence, and stressing that the Prophet conducted exchanges using those captured on the battlefield or 'picked up from a road or a valley or a mountain pass'. He ends the message, in fact, by announcing al-Qaeda's 'readiness to receive any Muslim captive exchanged with any party, by any party'.[60] The savage treatment of Western captives, then, is in some part aimed at facilitating this important Islamic duty. Indeed, the American hostage Eugene Armstrong was murdered in an explicit attempt at leverage: 'the fate of the first infidel was cutting off the head before your eyes and ears. You have a 24-hour opportunity. Abide by our demand in full and release all the Muslim women, otherwise the head of the other [Jack Hensley] will follow this one.'[61]

RECIPROCITY

The lot of 'prisoners' taken by *jihadis* is commonly linked to that of Muslims held in such notorious facilitates as Abu Ghraib and Guantanamo Bay. Thus, a fifth political element of the brutal treatment of prisoners is the notion of reciprocal treatment. Prisoners are brutalized and dehumanized in an effort to equate the status of the Western captive to that of the Muslim captive (in fact, they are often abducted solely for that purpose). Vengeance is exacted against

Westerners for the degradation endured by the Muslims in their custody. The most powerful symbol of this logic is the appearance of many of the condemned hostages in orange jumpsuits—the standard uniform for Muslims interned at Guantanamo Bay—which is used to signal that for Muslim captors, too, the 'gloves are off'. Nicholas Berg, whose graphic beheading spurred a wave of similar executions in Iraq, can be seen, in the horrific video of his death, sitting on the floor with hands tied behind his back, dressed in an orange jumpsuit. In fact, rather significantly, Berg's murder was conducted shortly after the story of detainee abuse at Abu Ghraib had broken.[62]

Given the outrage surrounding the publication of the pictures depicting the dehumanization of Iraqis, and the sense of shame which pervaded the Muslim world, Zarqawi's bloody act was certainly timed so as to represent his faction as the capable and committed guardians of Islamic justice. In the video, Zarqawi makes clear that he had tried to exchange Mr Berg with some of the detainees in Abu Ghraib prison, but his offer was refused. He continues:

> So we tell you that the dignity of the Muslim men and women in Abu Ghraib and others is not redeemed except by blood and souls. You will not receive anything from us but coffins... [of people] slaughtered in this way.... How can a free Muslim sleep well as he sees Islam slaughtered and its dignity bleeding, and the pictures of shame and the news of the devilish scorn of the people of Islam—men and women—in the prison of Abu Ghraib?[63]

Thus, from its very inception, the policy of slaughtering prisoners was explicitly depicted as a response to the barbarism endured by Muslim captives.

As the beheading of foreign hostages in Iraq continued, so did the strategy of linkage with the circumstances of Muslim prisoners. The American Jack Hensley, for example, was decapitated in September 2004 after Zarqawi's group unsuccessfully demanded the release of all female prisoners held in US prisons in Iraq: 'The Muslim blood is not water, and the honour of Muslim women won't go to waste. Bush, eat your heart out, and Blair, may you cry with tears of blood.'[64] Hensley's fellow hostages, the Briton Kenneth Bigley and the American Eugene Armstrong, met a similarly horrific end. After a lull in the execution of Americans in Iraq of more than a year, possibly accounted for by the two al-Qaeda letters condemning Zarqawi, the Islamic Army in Iraq announced that it had beheaded US security consultant Ronald Schulz. Again, the release of Iraqi prisoners had been demanded, and the execution was accounted for with the argument that 'the war criminal Bush continues his arrogance, giving no value to people's lives unless they serve his criminal, aggressive ways'.[65]

Osama bin Laden is confident that 'reciprocal treatment is a part of justice'[66] and that 'retaliation and punishment should be carried out following the principle of reciprocity'.[67] Although it can be assumed from the intercepted letters to Zarqawi that bin Laden did not support his deputy's savagery, it is clear that the *jihadis* who slaughtered their hostages shared his belief that reciprocity applies to the conduct of war (Zarqawi, for example, argues that 'God permits us to do the same thing to [the infidels] in return, with the same means they employ'[68]).

Leaving aside the question of whether US treatment of its detainees in the 'war on terror' in any way invites the decapitation of Western civilians and soldiers as a parallel, it is worth noting that there is little precedent for a 'reciprocity' analysis in the Islamic tradition on the ethics of war. Sohail Hashmi observes that 'strict reciprocity has never been established as a principle of the Islamic ethics of war: wanton disregard for humane treatment of combatants and non-combatants by the enemy does not permit Muslim armies to respond in kind'.[69] Sheikh Wahbeh al-Zuhili, the head of *fiqh* at Damascus University, also contends that the principle of reciprocity was embraced by Islam to establish standards of fairness and impartiality, but 'if the fundamental ethical and moral principles are breached, Muslims should not do the same'.[70]

In his Quranic commentary, even Sayyid Qutb explicitly shuns the argument which brings in the notion of reciprocal punishment to flout Islamic standards of warfare. At one stage he states that 'these principles had to be observed even with those enemies who had persecuted [the Muslims] and inflicted unspeakable atrocities on them'.[71] Later, he reaffirms that 'Islam maintains its own high moral principles and does not recommend resort to the same obscene methods used by its detractors'.[72] In the modern day, and in response to the savage treatment of captives in Iraq, very similar arguments have been made. Sheikh Ahmad Kutty, for example, argues that 'even in the case of retaliation in war time, there are ethics that a Muslim must honour'. He maintains that while fighting and retaliating, Muslims must always act within the permissible limits prescribed by the *sharia*. 'By keeping to the higher moral ground and holding steadfastly to our values and ethics in war time', Kutty concludes, 'Muslims will be blessed by the victory from Allah against our oppressors.'[73] Likewise, in his denunciation of beheadings as sinful violations of the teachings of Islam, the Egyptian scholar Sheikh Abdel Haliq Hasan al-Sharif quotes Saladin's famous explanation for his kind treatment of captured Crusaders: 'They commit these atrocities motivated by their own morals, and we do what our religion dictates.'[74]

Offering a slightly more nuanced approach, Sheikh Abdulmajid Subh maintains that the Iraqis who took part in the beheadings were reacting to the abuse of their brothers at Abu Ghraib, thus placing blame on the initial actions of the Americans. While this particular position is very similar to that put forward by Zarqawi and other extremists, Subh makes clear that neither act is justified, and condemns 'in the name of Islam and its laws that any captive be beheaded or humiliated in any way'.[75] Thus, even the explicit recognition that Muslim prisoners are being abused does not, to the minds of a series of Muslim scholars, permit Muslims to derogate from their own code of conduct.

CONCLUSION

Although the beheading phenomenon is represented, by those who perpetrate it as well as by some Western commentators, as a profoundly Islamic ritual, its adoption as a tactic by *jihadis* in Iraq was an outgrowth of important political factors, including reciprocal treatment. For sure, it is likely that terrorists would kidnap and behead hostages regardless of American detention policy. Nevertheless, it is significant that their bloody (and tenuous) interpretation of the Islamic tradition on prisoners of war is often defended, in the end, with references to the circumstances of Muslim prisoners in, and the standards of, the West. In this way, beheadings can be viewed less as symbolic of the Islamic tradition on warfare and more as representative of an explicit race to the bottom in dealing with prisoners in the war on terror.

NOTES

1. Videotape address, 29 October 2004, reprinted in Bruce Lawrence, *Messages to the world: The statements of Osama Bin Laden* (New York: Verso, 2005), 242.
2. *Knights under the Prophet's banner* (Autobiography, 2001), reprinted in Laura Mansfield, *In his own words: A translation of the writings of Dr. Ayman Al-Zawahiri* (Old Tappan, NJ: TLG Publications, 2006), 183.
3. 'Letter from Ayman al-Zawahiri to Abu Mus'ab al-Zarqawi, 11 October 2005', reprinted in Mansfield, *In his own words*, 270.
4. 'Bin Laden's sole post-September 11 interview aired', *CNN* (5 February 2002).
5. 'Al-Zarqawi: Katrina an answer to prayers', *CNN* (11 September 2005), <http://www.cnn.com/2005/WORLD/meast/09/11/zarqawi.message/>; accessed 8 July 2008. Interestingly, this argument was heard in Christian evangelical circles, too, as preachers such as John Hagee suggested the devastating hurricane was punishment for New Orleans' sinfulness and its hosting of the Gay Pride Parade.
6. Bin Laden, Letter to the Americans, 6 October 2002, in Lawrence, *Messages to the world*, 169.
7. Ibid. 170.
8. Ayman al-Zawahiri, 'Four years after the New York and Washington raids', September 2005, in Raymond Ibrahim (ed.), *The Al Qaeda reader* (New York: Broadway Books, 2007), 178.
9. Pamela Hess, '1,500 Kidnapped in 2007 Says US Intelligence Agency', *Associated Press* (14 October 2008).
10. Majid Khadduri, *The Islamic law of nations: Shaybani's Siyar* (Baltimore, MD: Johns Hopkins University Press, 1966), 91.
11. Unless otherwise stated, quotations of the Quran are taken from Abdullah Yusuf Ali, *The Holy Quran* (Birmingham: IPCI, 1999).
12. Note that this is the most common variation on translations of 8: 67, but it is not Yusuf Ali's. He translated the verse as 'it is not fitting for a Prophet that he should have prisoners of war until he hath thoroughly subdued the land.'
13. Sayyid Qutb, *Fi Dhilal al-Quran* [In the shade of the Quran], vol. 30, trans. and ed. M. A Salahi and A. A. Shamis (London: MWH, 1979), 301.
14. Abu Ala Mawdudi, Sayyid, *Tafhim al-Quran* [Towards understanding the Quran], trans. and ed. Zafar Ishaque Ansari and Abdul Aziz Kamal [online source] <http://www.tafheem.net>, discussion at 47: 4.
15. Cheragh Ali, *A critical exposition of the popular Jihad* (Calcutta: Thacker, Spink and Co., 1885), 85.

16. See ibid. 76–110.
17. Mawdudi, *Tafhim*.
18. Sheikh Abdel Khaliq Hasan al-Sharif, in *fatwa* entitled 'Slaying American civilians in Iraq' (4 July 2004), <http://www.islamonline.net/servlet/Satellite?pagename=Islam Online-English-Ask_Scholar/FatwaE/FatwaE&cid=1119503548466>; accessed 7 June 2008.
19. Yusuf al-Ayyiri, 'A guide for the perplexed on the permissibility of killing prisoners', originally posted at <http://www.qoqaz.com>, reprinted in 'Pro-Chechen Islamist website: Islamic religious interpretation permits killing of prisoners', MEMRI, 27 October 2001, [online publication] <http://www.memri.org/bin/articles.cgi?Page= subjects&Area=jihad&ID=SP43402>; accessed 9 May 2005.
20. Alex Duval Smith, 'If I had been British, I'd be dead', *Observer* (2 January 2005), <http://www.guardian.co.uk/world/2005/jan/02/iraq.france>; accessed 12 May 2008.
21. 'Hostage Bigley murdered in Iraq', *BBC News* (9 October 2004), <http://news.bbc.co.uk/2/hi/uk_news/3728594.stm>; accessed 9 Oct. 2004.
22. Muhammad Hamidullah, *Muslim conduct of state* (Lahore: M. Ashraf, 1945), 206.
23. Ali, *A critical exposition*, 77.
24. See 'Unnamed Arab Islamist speaks to al Hayat about al-Zarqawi's aims in Iraq', *BBC Monitoring Service* (12 September 2004).
25. Quoted in 'The sheikh of the slaughterers: Abu Mus'ab Al-Zarqawi and the Al-Qa'ida connection', MEMRI, 1 July 2005 [online publication] <http://memri.org/bin/articles.cgi?Page=archives&Area=ia&ID=IA23105>; accessed 12 July 2005.
26. Timothy R. Furnish, 'Beheading in the name of Islam', *Middle East Quarterly*, 12/2 (2005) <http://www.meforum.org/article/713>; accessed 12 Aug. 2005.
27. Quoted in 'Saudi Arabia's beheading culture', *CBS News* (25 June 2004) <http://www.cbsnews.com/stories/2004/06/25/world/main626196.shtml>; accessed 12 July 2008.
28. In *fatwa* entitled 'Beheading civilians . . . Islamic?' (25 July 2006) <http://www.islamonline.net/servlet/Satellite?cid=1123996016596&pagename=IslamOnline-English-AAbout_Islam%2FAskAboutIslamE%2FAskAboutIslamE>; accessed 7 June 2008.
29. Hussein Dakroub, 'Lebanon's top Shiite cleric condemns kidnappings, killings of foreigners by Islamic militants', *Associated Press* (23 June 2004).
30. Gary Schaefer, 'World unites in condemnation of beheading of South Korean hostage in Iraq', *Associated Press* (23 June 2004).
31. Sudha Ramachandran, 'Iraq held hostage to terror', *Asia Times* (25 September 2004) <http://www.atimes.com/atimes/Middle_East/FI25Ak01.html>; accessed 1 June 2008.
32. Loretta Napoleoni, *Insurgent Iraq: Al-Zarqawi and the new generation* (London: Constable, 2005), 172.
33. 'Letter from Ayman al-Zawahiri to Abu Mus'ab al-Zarqawi', 273.
34. Hamidullah, *Muslim conduct of state*, 209.
35. Mawdudi, *Tafhim al-Quran*.
36. In *Al-Siyasa Al-Shariyya fi Islah Al-Rai wa Al-Ra'iyya*, reprinted in Rudolph Peters, *Jihad in classical and modern Islam* (Princeton, NJ: Markus Wiener, 1996), 50.
37. Khadduri, *The Islamic law of nations*, 100.
38. For a discussion on consequentialist opposition to al-Qaeda from within the radical Islamic movement see Alia Brahimi, 'Crushed in the shadows: Why al-Qaeda will lose the war of ideas', *Studies in Conflict and Terrorism*, 33: 2 forthcoming February 2010.
39. Arnaud de Borchgrave, 'Osama bin Laden- "null and void"', *United Press International* (14 June 2001).

40. Sayyid Imam al-Sharif in Lawrence Wright, 'The rebellion within', *New Yorker* (2 June 2008) <http://www.newyorker.com/reporting/2008/06/02/080602fa_fact_wright?currentPage=all>; accessed 8 June 2008.

41. In Christy Oglesby, 'Experts: Beheadings pervert legitimate law', *CNN* (21 July 2004) <http://www.cnn.com/2004/WORLD/meast/07/21/beheading.background/>; accessed 21 July 2004.

42. Dr Samer Shehata, quoted in Oglesby, 'Experts'.

43. Napoleoni, *Insurgent Iraq*, 154.

44. Hess, '1,500 Kidnapped in 2007'.

45. Naji, Abu Bakr, *The Management of savagery*, trans. William McCants (2005), <www.ctc.usma.edu/naji.asp, 96>; accessed 12 September 2007.

46. Ibid. 78.

47. Abdul Aziz al-Moqrin, 'The targets inside the cities' [online publication] 29 March 2004 <http://www.intelcenter.com/Qaeda-Targeting-Guidance-v1–0.pdf>; accessed 12 May 2006.

48. Smith, 'If I had been British'.

49. Norman F. Kember, *Hostage in Iraq* (London: Darton Longman & Todd, 2007), 9.

50. Emphasis added. See 'Reactions to Sheikh Al-Qaradhawi's fatwa calling for the abduction and killing of American civilians in Iraq', MEMRI [online publication] 6 October 2004 <http://www.memri.org/bin/articles.cgi?Area=sd&ID=SP79404>; accessed 21 Oct. 2004. Qaradawi later distanced himself from the remarks, but he also offered the aforementioned argument that the supposed 'civilians' in Iraq were actually aiding and abetting the occupation, and thus subject to being killed. Hence, in his own denunciation of beheadings, Dr Jasser Auda made clear that 'even if we agree, hypothetically, to the weak argument that says that those civilians who serve the invading troops are partners in the transgression, these hostages would then be "prisoners of war". And beheading is not the way that the Quran, to quote it again as a reference, dealt with prisoners of war.'

51. 'Philippines' Iraq hostage freed', *BBC News* (20 July 2004) <http://news.bbc.co.uk/2/hi/middle_east/3909127.stm>; accessed 21 July 2008.

52. Brian Michael Jenkins, Meg Williams, and Ed Williams, 'Kidnappings in Iraq strategically effective', *Chicago Tribune* (29 April 2005) <http://www.rand.org/commentary/042905CT.html>; accessed 12 Mar. 2007.

53. Jean-Charles Brisard, *Zarqawi: The new face of al-Qaeda* (Cambridge: Polity, 2005), 131.

54. Napoleoni, *Insurgent Iraq*, 172.

55. 'Letter from Ayman al-Zawahiri to Abu Mus'ab al-Zarqawi', 272.

56. 'Letter from Atiyeh Abd al-Rahman to Abu Mus'ab al-Zarqawi' (11 December 2005) <http:// www.ctc.usma.edu/harmony/CTC-AtiyahLetter.pdf>; accessed 12 Feb. 2008.

57. Hamidullah, *Muslim conduct of state*, 204.

58. Majid Khadduri, *War and peace in the law of Islam* (Baltimore, MD: Johns Hopkins University Press, 1962), 130.

59. Abu Mus'ab al-Suri, 'Musharraf's Pakistan: The problem and the solution..! A necessary obligation' [online publication] October 2004 <http://www.tawhed.ws>; accessed 3 Nov. 2007.

60. al-Libi, Abu Laith, 'Countering the war of imprisonment', [video address] 24 May 2007 <http://switch3.castup.net/cunet/gm.asp?ClipMediaID=877084&ak=null>; accessed 3 June 2007. Foremost among those that al-Libi sought freed was the

London-based preacher Abu Qatada, who was released on bail, in June 2008, after failed attempts to deport him to Jordan.

61. 'American hostage killed by Iraqi captors', *Sky News* (21 September 2004) <http://news. sky.com/skynews/Home/Sky-News-Archive/Article/200828513226898>;   accessed 12 July 2008.

62. The report first detailing the abuse was aired on the CBS programme '60 Minutes' on 28 April 2004; Berg was executed on 7 May 2004.

63. See Dexter Filkins, 'Iraq videotape shows decapitation of an American', *New York Times* (12   May   2004)   <http://www.nytimes.com/2004/05/12/international/middleeast/ 12TAPE.html?ei=5007&en=6f7e5ccbcdf9b417&ex=1399694400&partner=USERLAND &pagewanted=print&position>; accessed 26 June 2008. See also 'Video shows US man beheaded', *BBC News* (11 May 2004) <http://news.bbc.co.uk/2/hi/middle_east/3705409. stm>; accessed 26 June 2008.

64. 'Body of slain American hostage found', *CNN* (22 September 2004) <http://www.cnn. com/2004/WORLD/meast/09/22/iraq.beheading/>; accessed 23 June 2008.

65. 'US hostage killed, Iraq militant group says', *NBC* (8 December 2005) <http://www. msnbc.msn.com/id/10382110/>; accessed 26 June 2008.

66. Audiotape address broadcast on *Al-Jazeera*, 12 November 2002, reprinted in Lawrence, *Messages to the world*, 173.

67. Bin Laden Interview with John Miller, *ABC Television*, May 1998 (text available online) <http://www.pbs.org/wgbh/pages/frontline/shows/binladen/who/interview.html>.

68. Quoted in Brisard, *Zarqawi*, 144.

69. Sohail H. Hashmi, 'Interpreting the Islamic ethics of war and peace', in Sohail H. Hashmi (ed.), *Islamic political ethics: Civil society, pluralism, and conflict* (Princeton, NJ: Princeton University Press, 2002), 212.

70. Sheikh Wahbeh al-Zuhili, 'Islam and international law', *International Review of the Red Cross*, 87/858 (2005), 275.

71. Sayyid Qutb, *Fi Dhilal al-Quran* [In the shade of the Quran] vol. 1, trans. and ed. M. A. Salahi and A. A. Shamis (Leicester: Islamic Foundation, 2001), 272.

72. Ibid. 329.

73. Ahmad Kutty in *fatwa* entitled 'Even in retaliation... ethics must be honoured', 12 May 2004, <http://www.islamonline.net/servlet/Satellite?cid=1119503548456& pagename= IslamOnline-English-Ask_Scholar/FatwaE/FatwaEAskTheScholar>; accessed 7 June 2008.

74. Abdel Haliq Hasan al-Sharif in 'Slaying American civilians in Iraq'.

75. Abdulmajid Subh in 'Slaying American civilians in Iraq'.

20

Conclusion: Prisoners and Detainees in Current and Future Military Operations

Sibylle Scheipers

What does historical experience tell us about the challenges we are facing today? This conclusion focuses on the issue of prisoners and detainees in current operations and in the short- to medium-term future. It takes stock of the most recent experiences with the treatment of detainees and discusses them in the light of the insights provided by the previous chapters. Although the new US administration has announced far-reaching changes in its detention policy, it is still vital to address the current challenges. Perhaps it has even become more important, since the details of the new policy are yet to be developed. The conclusion addresses two questions: does the legal regime relating to prisoners and detainees in armed conflict need a general overhaul? And, should irregular fighters be treated worse in captivity than regular troops?

MORE LAW, NEW LAW, WHAT LAW?

That the prisoner regime is facing challenges in current military and counter-terrorism operations is undisputed; the question is how to tackle this problem. In particular, this question has been discussed in terms of whether changes to the existing legal rules are necessary. A number of policy-makers and commentators have suggested that the Geneva-based legal framework cannot be applied to the 'war on terror'. In their view, the opponent's nature and tactics are simply too new and unprecedented to be covered by the existing legal rules, which were made for an entirely different form of conflict.[1] Many others, including ICRC lawyers, vehemently dispute this position. In doing so, they spell out in detail how the Geneva Conventions and other legal rules should be applied to prisoners and detainees in current military operations.[2] They seem to suggest that the legal framework is far from obsolete, though it may need clarification and interpretation in some areas, such as administrative detention for instance. In his chapter in this volume, John Bellinger takes the middle ground by arguing that the existing legal framework offers very little with respect to the treatment of detainees in current military operations. While he does not argue that the 'new' nature of the conflict renders the law obsolete, he does suggest that the legal framework has to be supplemented with new rules in order to meet the current challenges.

In a similar vein, the scholarly debate has tended to treat the issue of detention in current operations primarily as a legal one. The US prison camp in Guantanamo Bay, Cuba, and other detention sites are frequently referred to as 'legal black holes',[3] indicating that their inmates were denied the legal protections that they should be able to enjoy. This suggests that it is the *absence of the law* that lies at the roots of the problem. Some scholars have analysed the situation by drawing upon Carl Schmitt's concept of the exception. In his *Political Theology* Schmitt attempts to 'rescue' the meaning of state sovereignty by radically reconstructing it *outside* of the remit of the modern state's rule of law structures and its democratic institutions.[4] Instead of being trapped by the constitution and parliamentary accountability, Schmitt argued that the sovereign ruler could only retain their executive power by being able to declare a 'state of exception': 'Although he stands outside of the normally valid legal system, he nevertheless belongs to it, for it is he who must decide whether the constitution needs to be suspended in its entirety.'[5] Scholars such as the Italian philosopher Giorgio Agamben have analysed the Bush administration's detention policy (and its security policy more generally) through the lens of Schmitt's concept of the exception, and have concluded that its emphasis on the latitude of executive power in conjunction with the suspension of legal rules seem to be inspired by a Schmittian sense of authoritarianism.[6]

But is the problem of detention in recent military operations really a result of the absence of the law? Is the metaphor of the 'legal vacuum' correct? On closer inspection, Guantanamo and the general detention policy of the Bush administration do not seem to be characterized by a legal vacuum. On the contrary, as Anthony Lewis writes in his introduction to the so-called *Torture Papers*, a compilation of legal memos and opinions on detention produced during the Bush administration's first term: 'They [the *Torture Papers*] also provide a painful insight into how the skills of the lawyer—skills that have done so much to protect Americans in this most legalized of countries—can be misused in the cause of evil.'[7] In fact, Guantanamo and the Bush administration's detention policy more generally are built on legal opinions and memos. This brings them in line with a number of cases of colonial or intra-state war, some of them discussed in this book, in which detention was regulated within the framework of some kind of emergency rule: while emergency powers traditionally suspend certain legal provisions and protections and shift power to the executive, they are often decided upon by the legislative, enacted as a means of law, and justified by lawyers in a legal vernacular.

So if the absence of the law is not the problem, maybe it is the erroneous and morally corrupt interpretation of the law? Maybe the law has just lost its independence from the realm of policy and from questions of expediency? Maybe it is the case that 'legal opinions became an expression of policy'?[8] To a certain extent, this assessment is correct. As David Cole shows in his chapter, the legal discourse surrounding the practice of 'extraordinary renditions' was based on interpretations of legal treaties, most importantly the Convention against Torture, that violated the treaties' intent.

While the prohibition of torture and of transfers to torture is relatively uncontested and defined in several treaties and conventions, there are other areas in which the law is not as clear-cut, for instance administrative detention or security internment (Adam Roberts in this volume). However, this does not mean that in these areas the proverbial 'legal vacuum' does exist. These areas can be regulated within the existing legal framework. This has happened in previous military operations such as Kosovo.[9] However, due to the fact that the law is in fact under-specified in this area, their successful regulation will partly depend on responsible and prudent *political* decisions. Hence, regarding the question of how to remedy the detention disasters of the Bush administration and how to avoid their repetition in the future, part of the answer will be 'policy, not law'. This approach is backed by recent experience: certainly the US Supreme Court's repeated rulings on the rights of detainees in Guantanamo and elsewhere undermined the Bush administration's detention policy and kept the issue on the political agenda, but ultimately it took a new administration to indicate a change in the policy, even though the details of the new policy are still rather vague. In the same vein, Fleur Johns argues that it was precisely the *lack* of genuinely political decisions that led to the emergence of Guantanamo.[10] Instead of acknowledging the indeterminacy of the law in specific areas and acting upon it in a responsible and prudent way, policy-makers preferred to hide behind pseudo-authoritative legal opinions and memos. In contrast, political responsibility would have implied the acknowledgment of the risks related to the decision and the awareness that it is the decision-maker's entire political integrity that is at stake in such situations. In other words, part of the answer to the question of how to address the current challenges regarding prisoners and detainees is to reconstruct Schmitt in a non-authoritarian way. With Schmitt, that would mean to acknowledge that the partial indeterminacy of the law requires political decisions. Against Schmitt, it also implies that those decisions have to be made in accordance with the broader legal framework; that is, within the remit of the determinate aspects of the law.

Critics of such a view would argue that if the law is partly indeterminate, our task is to fill the gaps with new legal rules. However, two arguments should caution against such an approach: first, 'filling the gaps' would mean that the law would lose part of its flexibility, and therefore its ability to be applied to new situations. Armed conflict has changed and continues to do so, so the challenge lies in avoiding knitting too tight and specific a net of legal rules that only applies to one type of conflict, but not to others. Second, regardless of the amount of legal rules, there will always be a gap between a rule and its application. Some situations may be clear-cut, but others will be less so, and will require a decision on what legal rule to apply. Of course, the law will evolve and it may change over time, but creating a watertight, depoliticized legal regime on prisoners and detention cannot and will not be the objective of this process. Political decisions will inevitably continue to play a role.

But if so much hinges on responsible and prudent political decisions, what should be the normative foundations of these decisions? The next section will outline some basic considerations on the category of irregular fighters, since this group of individuals seems to create most problems in current operations.

IRREGULAR FIGHTERS—'UNLAWFUL COMBATANTS', 'UNPRIVILEGED BELLIGERENTS'?

That irregular fighters should not enjoy the same protections as their regular counterparts seems to be a matter of common sense. The current debate focuses on the question of how they should be treated and what minimum standards and protections should apply to them. However, in order to outline a meaningful normative framework for legal rules and political decisions on the detention of irregulars, it is necessary to question the tacit assumptions on which the current debate is based.

The moral condemnation on irregular fighters is based on two characteristic aspects of their identity and their behaviour: first, they are said to put civilians at risk by hiding among the civilian population and by using civilian infra-structure and resources for their supply and communications. They are more likely to jeopardize the civilian population's well-being either directly by looting etc., or indirectly by exposing them to armed attack by the opponent. Hence, according to the official narrative of international humanitarian law, irregular fighters undermine one of the core principles of the law of armed conflict, namely the distinction between combatants and civilians. This is the rationale behind the legally codified prisoner regime from the 1863 Lieber Code to the 1949 Geneva Conventions, which excludes irregular fighters from the privileges of POW status. Additional Protocol I is the first treaty to lower the threshold for lawful combatancy slightly, but it still retains the possibility of unlawful combatancy.[11] However, as law-makers were aware that excluding a group of individuals from legal privileges can lead to massacres and atrocities, they built a safety measure into the legal framework: minimum standards for humane treatment such as the Martens clause and Common Article 3 of the Geneva Conventions. Nevertheless, the overall legal construction appears to suggest that combatants who do not fulfil certain criteria should be treated worse than those who do.[12]

For this approach to be morally justified we would need to assume that penalizing irregular captives fulfils a deterrent function and indeed enhances the protection of civilians. However, historical experience cautions against this assumption. Repressive measures by regular forces against irregulars often openly envisaged collective punishment actions against the nearest village or settlement because the civilian inhabitants were perceived to help or at least to tolerate the presence and the activities of irregulars. In addition to the purposeful targeting of civilians, civilians often become accidental targets of armed attack or sweep-up operations against irregulars precisely because it is hard to distinguish the former from the latter. In fact, this seems to be the core problem that has beset all arrest and detention operations in campaigns against irregulars. The justification brought forward by the regular side is often that this inadvertent lack of distinction is ultimately caused by the irregulars, but it is at least debatable whether this is a sufficient reason to go ahead with such operations anyway.

The second core argument with respect to the unprivileged status of irregular fighters is that they do not abide by the law of armed conflict themselves—they fail the reciprocity test. In this vein, granting them legal privileges would go above and beyond what common sense conceptions of fairness would require. In this view, the law of armed conflict is essentially a code of conduct on a contractual basis. The reason why soldiers comply with it is enlightened self-interest. If all sides adhere to it, all sides will profit. If one side decides to ignore the legal provisions and employs illegal tactics, the other side is no longer bound by it either. It is undeniable that reciprocity is a strong foundation of the law of armed conflict and that its sustained absence would put the law in jeopardy in the long run. On the other hand, is doing away with legal restriction when the opponent does not abide by them a viable option? As several chapters in this book emphasize, the resort to retaliation in kind has often led to a downward spiral of reprisals and diminishing standards. This observation should at least caution against any straightforward and simple answers to this dilemma.

One final point warrants attention, which relates to a question that is often forgotten in the heat of the battle: what kind of peace is it that we are ultimately trying to achieve? What role will the enemy play in the post-conflict political order? For the Western states involved in current military operations abroad, the answer to this question will rarely be the complete annihilation of the opponent. Again, historical experience tells us that in some cases former rebel leaders or terrorists will play a central role in the post-conflict political order. Even if that is not the case, the minimum requirement in almost all cases is the reintegration of former rebels and insurgents into the local society. A harsh detention regime is likely to have a negative impact on the chances of success of the reintegration process. In cases in which widespread torture is practised over a sustained period of time, as for instance in Algeria, this may damage the fabric of the entire society and make the long-term goal of political stabilization very difficult to achieve.

The question of the impact of detention regimes and the treatment of irregulars more broadly on the post-conflict order is completely absent from the Western legal discourse, but it has played a large role in other legal traditions, first and foremost the Islamic one. While the Western tradition has for a long time treated rebellions and insurgencies as anomalies or 'conceptual opposites' of the kind of warfare envisaged in the international law of armed conflict, the Islamic tradition has a body of rules called *Ahkam al-Bughat* that deal with the treatment of those who rebel against the ruler of the Islamic state. The idea of reconciliation and the return to peace is central to this tradition: '[T]he primary purpose of

Ahkam al-Bughat is the reconciliation of the contending parties and not the punishment or elimination of the dissenters.'[13] To be sure, it is legitimate to fight rebels with military means, but the idea of eventual reconciliation has to be the guiding principle in the fight. Accordingly, prisoners have to be treated with care; most Islamic jurists argue that they must not be executed once captured, and that they have to be released immediately once the rebellion has ended.[14] This approach to rebel captives hinges on two assumptions: first, the rebels may be justified in fighting because they may have a legitimate religious or political grievance (*ta'wil*). Although there is some debate over whether and how the 'correctness' of this grievance needs to be established, the basic idea is that rebellions are not per se unjustified.[15] Second, rebels should be granted greater, though not unrestricted, latitude with respect to their tactics, since they are forced to fight from a position of weakness: 'those who fight "from below" must have room for manoeuvre, since the forces of the establishment typically enjoy overwhelming advantages'.[16]

Just like the 1949 Geneva approach to irregular warfare, the Islamic approach to rebellion is not without problems. Most importantly, the problem of what qualifies as a legitimate grievance cannot be satisfactorily resolved.[17] Moreover, it is questionable whether *Ahkam al-Bughat* is applicable to contemporary resistance movements, since it hinges on the idea that both the rebels and the ruler acknowledge that they have something in common, some higher political or religious aim.[18] Despite these issues, the Islamic tradition can serve as a conceptual contrast to the Geneva regime. It can highlight the Geneva rules' tacit assumptions—their state centrism and their punitive approach to irregular warfare—and thus allow us to question whether they are morally justified and politically prudent.

NOTES

1. See for example John C. Yoo and James C. Ho, 'The status of terrorists', University of California Berkeley, Boalt Working Papers in Public Law, 25 (2003); John Reid, 'Twenty-first century warfare—twentieth century rules', *RUSI Journal*, 151/3 (2006), 14–16.
2. See, among others, Silvia Borelli, 'Casting light on the legal black hole: International law and the detentions abroad in the "war on terror"', *International Review of the Red Cross*, 87/857 (2005), 39–67; Jelena Pejic, 'Procedural principles and safeguards for internment/administrative detention in armed conflict and other situations of violence', *International Review of the Red Cross*, 87/858 (2005), 375–91.
3. See Fleur Johns, 'Guantanamo Bay and the annihilation of the exception', *European Journal of International Law*, 16/4 (2005), 613–35.
4. Carl Schmitt, *Politische Theologie: Vier Kapitel zur Lehre von der Souveränität* (1922; Berlin: Duncker & Humblot, 2004).
5. Ibid. 14.
6. Giorgio Agamben, *State of exception* (Chicago: University of Chicago Press, 2005).

7. Anthony Lewis, 'Introduction', in Karen J. Greenberg and Joshua L. Dratel (eds.), *The torture papers: The road to Abu Ghraib* (Cambridge: Cambridge University Press, 2005), xiii. This is not to say that all lawyers approved of this approach. Dissenting voices, in particular from the US armed forces Judge Advocate Generals' offices, are documented in the volume as well.

8. Philippe Sands, *Torture team: Deception, cruelty and the compromise of the law* (London: Allen Lane, 2008), 275–6.

9. See Pascal Dupont, 'Detention of individuals during peacekeeping operations: Lessons learned from Kosovo', in Geert-Jan Alexander Knoops and Roberta Arnold (eds.), *Practice and policies of modern peace support operations under international law* (Leiden: Transnational Publishers, 2006), 249–59.

10. Johns, 'Guantanamo Bay', 635.

11. See 'Introduction'.

12. See Geoffrey Best, *Law and war since 1945* (Oxford: Clarendon Press, 1994), 333ff.

13. Khaled Abou El Fadl, 'Ahkam al-Bughat: Irregular warfare and the law of rebellion in Islam', in James Turner Johnson and John Kelsay (eds.), *Cross, crescent, and sword: The justification and limitation of war in Western and Islamic tradition* (London: Greenwood, 1990), 153.

14. Ibid. 162.

15. Ibid. 158.

16. John Kelsay, *Arguing the just war in Islam* (Cambridge, MA: Harvard University Press), 193. The 1977 Additional Protocols go some way to acknowledge this aspect, but the reason for their lowering the threshold for lawful combatancy is rarely mentioned in the current debate.

17. El Fadl, 'Ahkam al-Bughat', 158.

18. Kelsay, *Arguing the just war*, 194.

Index